ONE SIGNAL
PUBLISHERS

ATRIA

Spell Freedom

THE UNDERGROUND SCHOOLS THAT
BUILT THE CIVIL RIGHTS MOVEMENT

ELAINE WEISS

ONE SIGNAL
PUBLISHERS

ATRIA

New York Amsterdam/Antwerp London Toronto Sydney New Delhi

ONE SIGNAL
PUBLISHERS

ATRIA

An Imprint of Simon & Schuster, LLC
1230 Avenue of the Americas
New York, NY 10020

Copyright © 2025 by Elaine Weiss

Cover image: Black citizens of Wilcox County, Alabama, voting for the first time, 1966

All rights reserved, including the right to reproduce this book or portions thereof in any form whatsoever. For information, address Atria Books Subsidiary Rights Department, 1230 Avenue of the Americas, New York, NY 10020.

First One Signal Publishers/Atria Books hardcover edition March 2025

ONE SIGNAL PUBLISHERS / ATRIA BOOKS and colophon are trademarks of Simon & Schuster, LLC

For information about special discounts for bulk purchases, please contact Simon & Schuster Special Sales at 1-866-506-1949 or business@simonandschuster.com.

The Simon & Schuster Speakers Bureau can bring authors to your live event. For more information or to book an event, contact the Simon & Schuster Speakers Bureau at 1-866-248-3049 or visit our website at www.simonspeakers.com.

Interior design by Davina Mock-Maniscalco

Manufactured in the United States of America

1   3   5   7   9   10   8   6   4   2

Library of Congress Cataloging-in-Publication Data has been applied for.

ISBN 978-1-6680-0269-8
ISBN 978-1-6680-0271-1 (ebook)

CONTENTS

CONTENTS

I t was a Monday afternoon, May 17, 1954, when the news broke.
Bells clanged from wire service teletype machines in newsrooms around the country, signaling a major bulletin. Evening newspapers stopped the presses to rewrite their front pages. Radio and television announcers interrupted daytime programs to rush on air. The news was stunning: the United States Supreme Court had just ruled that racial segregation of public schools was unconstitutional. In their unanimous decision in the *Brown v. Topeka Board of Education* case, the justices of the high court struck down the legal precedent of "separate but equal" educational facilities, exploding the foundation of state segregation laws.

News of the decision reverberated through the nation, especially jolting the southern states, where political, social, and economic life was built upon Jim Crow segregation policies. Black leaders hailed the decision as "the greatest event since the Emancipation Proclamation," while southern white politicians and editorial writers immediately denounced the ruling as a catastrophe that could destroy "the southern way of life." They labeled the arrival of the decision "Black Monday."

Septima Poinsette Clark would have been teaching in her classroom that afternoon, inside the segregated and overcrowded Archer elementary school on Nassau Street in Charleston. She'd been teaching children in dilapidated Black public schools for almost forty years.

Mrs. Clark was the daughter of a former slave who had been fighting Jim Crow limitations and humiliations all her life. She was a fifty-six-year-old widow, a mother, a veteran teacher, and a community activist with gray streaked through her hair, sensible shoes on her feet, and pointy eyeglasses perched on her nose. Word of the Supreme Court decision thrilled her.

From her position on the executive board of the Charleston branch of the NAACP, she had been keeping close track of the legal proceedings for six years. She had watched the case develop and expand from its roots in a tiny South Carolina town—brought forward by the courage, grit, and tears of Black parents—all the way up to the US Supreme Court.

Yet Mrs. Clark knew that such fundamental change wouldn't come easily. She understood that the societal reformation promised by the *Brown* decision would require more than just a court order. It would require a fight. Her own community must be willing to stand together to demand their rights as American citizens.

As in the Bible stories she loved, news of the ruling came to her like a trumpet sounding in the wilderness, a summons to act, and she was ready to heed that call.

On a sea island off the Charleston coast, Esau Jenkins had finished his morning jitney bus route by the time the news was announced. As usual, he had driven his neighbors—cooks and maids, factory and shipyard workers—from Johns Island over the bridge to their jobs in the city. Along the route, he had completed the morning vocabulary lessons he gave to his bus riders and delivered his usual pep talks, spoken in Gullah from the steering wheel, about democracy and political power.

Mr. Jenkins was a barrel-chested, bighearted, forty-four-year-old businessman, a husband and father of eight children, a church elder, and a community leader. He was a serious man with a hearty laugh, a clipped little brush mustache perched over his lip. His evenings were filled with community, church, and NAACP meetings. Afternoons he devoted to his commercial ventures— the motel, the café, the record store. He believed a Black man, a Black community, needed to be economically self-sufficient, under no white man's thumb. Jenkins was always busy, always planning, always thinking about how to improve conditions on his island.

He was elated to learn of the court's decision. He had been fighting for better schools on Johns Island for years. He knew how very unequal the ramshackle one-room cabins the state provided for rural Black children really were, with cast-off textbooks, cracked blackboards, and few supplies— not even a toilet. But would the district school board—they were all white men—actually integrate the schools, give an equal education to all children? Jenkins was an optimistic, but not a naive, man. He understood how withholding proper education from Black children, limiting job opportunities for Black adults, and trapping them in menial labor were essential tools of white control.

Nothing would change unless the white men in charge were pushed. And they couldn't be pushed until Black people had political power. Until elected officials had to answer to Black voters. But very few people on his island could vote—South Carolina made sure of that: the poll tax, the literacy test, the harassment. It was too hard and too dangerous to try to vote. Most of his neighbors had given up trying, so his island remained neglected and poor.

To Mr. Jenkins's mind, this Supreme Court decision was very good, but it was just one step. To see desegregation, or any other improvements, really happen on his island, his community needed to gain some political muscle. They needed to have a voice on the school board, a say in their local and state government. They needed to vote.

———◆———

Bernice Violanthe Robinson was most likely combing and setting her customers' hair in her Glamour Beauty Box salon on Dewey Street in Charleston that afternoon. The news on the radio would have interrupted the chatter of her clients getting their 'dos, but the women who came to Robinson's shop were accustomed to having a strand of politics braided into their hair.

The news was heartwarming to Mrs. Robinson. She had grown up in Charleston's segregated schools, and upper grades weren't even offered in what were called "Negro schools" then. She had to move to New York City, where she lived with her older sister, to attend high school. In that northern city she learned that Jim Crow didn't rule everywhere: you didn't have to ride in the back of the bus there, you could sit wherever you wanted in the movie theater, could eat in restaurants serving white and Black people alike. When she came of age, she registered and voted in New York elections, and no one gave her any hassle. She hated moving back to Charleston, to the restrictions of the South.

But she had to move back home to take care of her elderly parents. The first thing she did was join the Charleston NAACP, and now she was chair of the membership committee. When her salon customers complained about this or that Jim Crow indignity they had suffered, she recommended confronting injustice by joining the NAACP. She convinced those who were nervous about joining, skittish about being associated with such a "militant" race organization, that they could join secretly by having their membership cards and NAACP mailings sent to her beauty shop. That way the mailman or their boss, their husband or their pastor, need not know.

Robinson encouraged her customers to register to vote, too. She was involved in all the local voter registration drives, though she got frustrated when people said they wouldn't bother registering because voting was "white man's business." They had grown too accustomed to being shut out.

Bernice Robinson cheered the court's decision that day. But as a beautician, she didn't know what she could contribute toward desegregating the schools, beyond talking to her customers about it, convincing them it was important to get involved in promoting change. When she had her clients in a Beauty Box chair, they were her captive audience, and she could be very persuasive.

———◆———

Myles Falls Horton was far from his home in the Cumberland mountains of Tennessee when the court's decision was announced. He was in Washington, DC, to consult with his old friend Senator Estes Kefauver about a political problem. Horton was in a difficult spot.

Some of his fellow white southerners believed he was a traitor to his race; some powerful government officials thought he was disloyal to his country. They were after him—and his school. His persecutors were turning up the heat as the South braced for the Supreme Court's decision on the *Brown* case.

Horton was a white, rural southerner, but he believed that racial segregation was morally and legally wrong, corrosive to the soul of the South, and a liability for the nation. He simply rejected the whole idea of it. His Highlander Folk School had been openly and proudly flouting Tennessee's Jim Crow laws for more than two decades. Highlander wasn't a traditional school, it was a social justice education and training center for adults, and it was the only place in the South where Black and white people could, for a week or two, live and learn together in a fully integrated community. It was a place where they could, as Horton liked to say, "tea and pee" together. He enjoyed being called a "Radical Hillbilly."

The senator was delayed that Monday morning, pushing back their appointment a few hours. Horton took advantage of the fine spring day to read a newspaper, sitting on a bench on the Capitol grounds very near the Supreme Court building. With time to kill, he walked across the street to the white marble building where the words "Equal Justice Under Law" were chiseled into the front pediment. Horton was surprised that the building seemed quiet and eerily deserted. He wandered through the main corridor alone.

Suddenly, the doors to the court chamber flew open and a noisy crowd of people rushed out. Amid the commotion, Horton spotted NAACP lawyer Thurgood Marshall, who'd argued the *Brown* case before the court. Horton pushed his way over to Marshall to ask what was happening. "We won, we won!" Marshall shouted. Chief Justice Earl Warren had just announced the decision in the *Brown* case.

"What are you doing here?" Marshall asked Horton incredulously. The two men had known each other for years. "How did you know to come right now?" There'd been no advance notice of the announcement; even Marshall had relied on a secret tip to alert him. Horton hadn't known, he admitted; it was purely coincidental that he'd wandered into the building. In this strange way, Myles Horton learned of the *Brown* decision before the news was reported to the world.

The decision signaled to Horton that it was time to quicken the pace at Highlander. They had already been holding workshops on school desegregation for more than a year, in hopeful anticipation of a positive ruling. The upcoming summer workshops must now tackle strategies for implementing the court's decree. It was time to bring more Black community leaders to his mountain campus to strategize, sharing tools and techniques to help rally their neighbors for the coming battles over desegregation.

Horton realized that the court's ruling, striking down the legal foundations of racial segregation, would infuriate the southern states, and likely make him, and Highlander, the target of more virulent attacks. Nevertheless, he was determined to make Highlander the place where Black southerners and their white allies could plan and then build a new world together.

CHAPTER ONE

Monteagle Mountain

I n the last week of June 1954, just six weeks after the *Brown* decision was announced, Septima Clark journeyed to a mountaintop. It was a long trip, a bumpy 650 miles from the South Carolina Lowcountry to the Tennessee Cumberland plateau, with a steep, twisty climb up Monteagle Mountain on the final stretch. Mrs. Clark sat in the passenger seat of a sedan driven by a Charleston friend who had told her about this school on the mountain and urged her to enroll. The *Brown* decision had convinced Mrs. Clark this was the right time to take action and go.

The trip itself was risky: two middle-aged Black women making their way alone across three Deep South states, through expanses of Klan country, careful where they could—and could not—stop along the way. The women's clothes were dusty and their hair mussed from the hot wind blowing into the car's open windows, but it was so much better than sitting, or standing, in the back of a long-distance bus.

They were headed to the Highlander Folk School, a racially integrated retreat and training center run by white people, perched above a sundown town, about fifty miles northwest of Chattanooga. The place called itself a school, but it did not sound like any school Mrs. Clark had ever known—there were no formal classes, no tests, no grades. Her friend at the wheel claimed it was the only place in the South where Black and white people could sit down together to talk, really talk, about racial problems. Talk was all fine and good, Mrs. Clark agreed, but she was looking for more than talk. Highlander was offering a workshop on strategies for school desegregation, and she wanted a plan.

Mrs. Clark realized people back home in Charleston might whisper about her coming here, her school principal might get angry, and her family might get upset; it might cause her some grief. But she didn't care. She was willing to take the risk. She was traveling to this faraway Tennessee mountain to prepare herself for the future. For the tomorrow she'd been waiting for, praying for—working for—all her life. Mrs. Septima Poinsette Clark was riding up Monteagle Mountain to arm herself to vanquish Jim Crow.

———◆———

The tires of the car crunched on the gravelly road as the final turn brought the Highlander Folk School compound into view. It wasn't much to look at: a rambling, shingled farmhouse surrounded by a few outbuildings, nestled in a grove of trees, a marshy little lake behind, a few metal chairs scattered on the grass. Young white staffers carried the visitors' valises to the dormitory; two narrow beds took up most of the space in Clark's small room. She hardly had time to rinse the dust off her hands and face before an old iron school bell clanged outside, calling everyone to dinner.

Mrs. Clark stepped into the stream of people—a mélange of skin colors, a medley of regional accents—filing into the dining room. There was a buzz of hellos and quick name exchanges as the two dozen or so visitors found places at the long wooden dining tables. The chatter grew louder as platters, bowls, and pitchers were carried out from the kitchen and the food passed down the table, family-style: white hands to black hands, then black to white, everyone sitting shoulder to shoulder. The forbidden act of eating together seemed shockingly natural and ordinary here.

A chair scraped against the floor as a man stood up at his place. He was of medium height and build, his brown hair neatly clipped and parted to the side, his face pale and rather bland but pleasant. His eyes were bright, framed by laugh crinkles, as he scanned the faces around the room. He welcomed everyone to Highlander, his voice somewhat high-pitched and reedy, laced with the sharp tang of the West Tennessee mountains where he was raised. He introduced himself as Myles Horton.

So this was the man Septima Clark had written to, seeking admission to this workshop, listing her qualifications and community affiliations, and requesting a full scholarship. She had been blunt—she couldn't afford the $48 tuition and board on her schoolteacher's salary without aid. This was the Myles Horton her Charleston friend raved about, so taken with his earnest approach and progressive ideas. This was also the man the Charleston newspapers had run articles about earlier in the spring, calling him a subversive, an agitator, a Communist agent. It seemed the fashion these days to call everyone you didn't agree with a Communist, so Mrs. Clark didn't pay much attention to all that.

Horton launched into his well-practiced welcome patter. He was about to celebrate his forty-ninth birthday and had been operating this social justice training center on Monteagle Mountain for more than two decades. He had launched Highlander in the depths of the Depression in 1932, to help struggling Appalachian communities understand the forces crushing their lives and livelihoods. He understood these mountain people, he had grown up among them, poor schoolteachers' son. He wanted to teach them how to come up with communal solutions, their own ideas of what they needed, and what they wanted to do to improve their lives.

Horton had helped southern miners and lumbermen, farmers and steel workers, organize, cooperatize, and unionize. He taught them how to run a meeting, stand up for their rights, and push for fair treatment. He was there with them in the union halls and on the picket lines; he'd gotten beaten up, shot at, and run out of too many towns to count. Highlander got involved in all the New Deal programs that could throw a lifeline to the region's workers and became an official education facility for the Congress of Industrial Organizations. Union training was the center's bread and butter for years, and hundreds of union workers, both white and Black, had attended Highlander workshops. From the very beginning, Highlander's policy was to reject segregation both in principle and in practice. Didn't make a big deal of it, just put everyone together in the meeting rooms, the dining hall, the bathrooms, and sleeping quarters.

For all this, Horton was despised by the region's mine owners and steel companies, hated by hosts of lumber magnates and factory bosses, cursed by a good many sheriffs and politicians in Tennessee for being a troublemaker. He had already amassed a fat file at FBI headquarters in Washington as well as thick folders in various state office buildings in Nashville; FBI agents were constantly snooping around Monteagle, talking to the neighbors, trying to dig up dirt. Horton was proud of having acquired so many high and mighty enemies, and with the *Brown* decision reverberating, he expected there'd soon be more.

Just in the past year, Horton had decided to steer Highlander into rough new terrain, straight into the thorniest issue the South faced: race relations. He was convinced there could be no progress, no future for the southern states, without tackling the race issue: the segregation and subjugation of its Black citizens by law, by custom, and by violence. The segregated "southern way of life" was evil and immoral, he was certain, but also socially and politically untenable as the nation entered the second half of the twentieth century.

Horton kept his ear close to the ground, stayed in touch with regional activists and progressive groups, and was sure he felt a stirring, like the little tremors before an earthquake. And now there was the healthy shock of the *Brown* decision, and that could shake things up but good. Horton was trying to figure out how Highlander could play a role, help his fellow southerners— Black and white—navigate the powerful shifts he sensed were coming, sooner rather than later, peacefully or not.

Highlander was "a school for problems," as Horton liked to describe the place, where solutions could emerge from the collective experience and wisdom of the participants. Highlander students were encouraged to bring the social and political problems facing their communities to the workshop for discussion by the group, and over the course of a week or two, brainstorming and debate would help develop some practical approaches for the students to take home. Highlander would then support them in executing that plan in their community.

Mrs. Clark leaned forward as he spoke. She tended to put her hand on her chin when she was listening intently. This was just what she wanted to hear. She had brought a bundle of problems with her, the ones her community in Charleston faced but preferred to ignore. To her mind, apathy was the number one problem back home—apathy and passivity—both bitter inheritances from centuries of slavery and repression. But she often got in trouble for saying this aloud. So she was eager to discuss this in the workshop, to brainstorm with the group about possible solutions. There were so few people back home with whom she could share these issues.

One was her NAACP friend Ruby Cornwell, who refused to patronize any shop in Charleston that didn't allow Blacks to try on dresses, shoes, or hats, or wouldn't hire Black clerks. Mrs. Cornwell also wrote frequent letters to the editor about the injustices endured by her community—as did Mrs. Clark—and both insisted that the newspapers use their proper titles, including that "Mrs." designation of respect that white women routinely received but Black women did not. Clark and Cornwell could commiserate about the sorry state of racial relations in their city and the lack of will to change things, something Clark couldn't do with her fellow teachers or her family, who got jittery whenever she got involved in another campaign.

Yet it was really the second part of Horton's description of the goals of the workshop that excited Mrs. Clark most: the expectation that each of them would leave with a blueprint, an action plan. They would promise to actually *do* something to promote desegregation once they got home. This was not just talk.

As Horton wrapped up his introduction, he mentioned that every night singing would be on the agenda—group singing was central to the Highlander experience—tapping the emotional power of melded voices. Myles called up Highlander's cultural director, his wife, Zilphia.

Mrs. Horton strapped on her accordion and played a few warm-up chords while offering her own words of welcome. She was almost six feet tall and dark haired, with deep-set eyes beneath a fringe of bangs on her forehead. Zilphia was a classically trained musician who had defied her family to marry Myles. She first came to Highlander in 1935, when she was twenty-four, to attend a six-week labor organizing workshop, married Myles three months later, and made her life here on the mountain with him and their two children. Her father, a coal mine manager who stood on the opposite side of Highlander on the picket lines, disowned his daughter.

Zilphia had a rich, sweet alto voice and loved the old-time mountain songs and stories, scouring the hollers, cabins, and churches of the region to bring them back to Highlander. She transcribed the melodies into musical notation, tweaked the lyrics, and put them to use. She taught the songs to everyone who came to the school, carried them along with her accordion to the picket lines and soup kitchens to bolster spirits, and shared them with her folk-singer friends who made pilgrimages to Highlander to refresh their repertoires. These troubadours then carried the songs north and west and around the country, singing them at coffeehouses and festivals, swapping them in jams. Zilphia also brought poetry and drama, dance and visual art into the Highlander curriculum, enhancing the search for social justice with beauty and creativity. Everyone loved Zilphia, called her the soul and spirit of Highlander. She was the warm, creative balance to Myles's more analytical approach.

Zilphia passed around the mimeographed and stapled pages of a Highlander songbook so everyone could sing along. She began with some bouncy familiar work tunes; as usual, some of the group jumped right in to join, others more hesitant. Then she switched up the mood to a plaintive gospel melody, making the churchgoing folks feel more at home. Then a sweet spiritual everyone knew.

Zilphia closed this first sing-along session with a song she called a Highlander favorite, a tune Mrs. Clark might recognize as the old church hymn "I'll Be Alright," which had been repurposed by striking women tobacco workers into a rallying song and brought to Highlander in the mid-1940s. The Charleston women workers had changed the "I" in the song to "We" to emphasize their solidarity, and Zilphia and her friend Pete Seeger had modified the melody and the rhythms, written some new lyrics. It would take Clark and the others a few days to learn this new song, now called "We Shall Overcome."

After dinner, Septima climbed the stairs to her room and met her roommate, a chatty writer from New Jersey. They had a friendly conversation, then turned off the lamps. Lying in the narrow bed in her nightgown, Clark tried to grasp the extraordinary situation unfolding in the dark: her roommate was a white woman who seemed totally unfazed by sleeping in the same tiny room with her, a Black woman, a stranger. They shared a bathroom, too. Clark had never encountered anything like this; it would be so shocking at home in Charleston. If her mother were still alive, she would have been horrified, and frightened. Mrs. Clark found it simply astonishing.

———◆———

Myles Horton returned to his desk after dinner, as he had done most nights that spring, trying to repair the damage. His upbeat welcome to the new Highlander cohort and full-throated singing to Zilphia's accordion in the dining room masked his panic. Everything he had worked for, all he had built at Highlander, even the well-being of his family, were suddenly in jeopardy.

Right when the racial reckoning he had advocated was starting to take shape, when the *Brown* decision was promising to crack open southern segregated society. Right when he was trying to position Highlander as the ideal place to develop new strategies for breaking Jim Crow's back and enticing donors to support the work. This was the moment he had worked toward; two decades of his and Zilphia's sweat and sacrifice.

Instead, Highlander was in peril. Horton was having to apologize, or at least explain, why a photo of him—being dragged out of a US Senate hearing—had been splashed on page one of the *New York Times* and reproduced in newspapers all around the South.

He picked up a microphone, placed it close to his mouth, and began dictating letters into a recording machine.

———— ◆ ————

Mrs. Clark sat in the Highlander library that first morning of the workshop, a whitewashed cinder-block structure anchored by a massive stone chimney, enhanced inside by soaring wooden beams, skylights, and bookshelves. In a physical manifestation of Highlander's communal spirit, the library was designed by an architect friend, then staff and workshop students built it themselves from local wood and stones.

Mrs. Clark carried into the library a stylish tote bag, a gift from her friend Elizabeth Waring in New York City. It was the kind of luxury item she would never buy for herself, but it seemed very fitting to carry her notebooks, clippings, and pens into this workshop—dedicated to the great potential of the *Brown* decision—inside a gift from the Warings. Without Judge Waring, there might not have been any such far-reaching court ruling like *Brown*. Without the support of both the judge and Elizabeth, Septima Clark might not have had the nerve to come to Highlander.

Clark listened as her classmates introduced themselves: a professor of economics and dean of men at Morehouse College; another professor from Atlanta University; a liberal-leaning white editor of a Little Rock newspaper; an official of the American Friends Service Committee; an assortment of northern writers and teachers, and community activists from across the South.

When it was Mrs. Clark's turn, she would describe herself in her clear, well-modulated teacher's voice, cultivated over many semesters at the front of classrooms. She always sat erect in her chair, the way she insisted her students do when she called upon them. She was a handsome woman, her skin the color of coffee with a bit of cream, her face smooth and open, accentuated by the high cheekbones of Native American ancestors on her mother's side. Her eyes were soft and expressive, topped by shapely arches of brow

She was a widowed schoolteacher, a church lay leader, sorority sister, and officer in the NAACP, she could tell them in the soft, rounded vowels of her native city. She belonged to a long list of community organizations, boards, and committees—her evenings and weekends were consumed with meetings—but she was probably too modest to mention them all. When the introductions had gone all around, Myles Horton asked the signature first question that opened every Highlander workshop: What do you want to learn during your time here? Mrs. Clark's ambitions were straightforward but not simple: she wanted to learn how to get people in her Charleston Black community, parents and teachers, excited about the prospect of school desegregation, and willing to work for it. She knew there was some strong reluctance, especially among her fellow teachers, who feared desegregation would jeopardize their jobs. She also hoped to learn how to pressure Charleston's all-white school board to implement the Supreme Court's order, as she was sure they'd dig in their heels. More broadly, she wanted to learn new methods to make her community wake up, stand up, seize this historic moment to demand their rights. She saw the *Brown* decision as a great opportunity, and she wanted to learn how to make good use of it.

Clark hadn't known what to expect at Highlander. What living in an intense, secluded little community of strangers—white and Black strangers—might be like. She was surprised by how much she liked it. She found the workshop discussions tremendously stimulating, even if they sometimes bounced off topic. Even these detours were profitable, as her classmates brought such varied experiences and perspectives into the mix. Hearing white people speak so frankly, so passionately, about racism was fascinating.

Myles Horton gleefully provoked debate, questioned, challenged, poked; Mrs. Clark loved that. She rarely raised her voice. She possessed a calm, supremely dignified, demeanor, but she wasn't shy about expressing her opinions either. She always raised her hand and spoke up in meetings, and she didn't let misapprehensions, sloppy thinking, or downright lies slide. People didn't always appreciate her candor and corrective comments—her fellow teachers in Charleston certainly did not—but here at Highlander, that sort of honest disagreement was welcome as they grappled with the ramifications of the *Brown* decision, including the role of Black teachers and clergy.

So often over the years, when she had tried to convince others to stand up with her against Jim Crow injustice, Mrs. Clark had encountered paralyzing apathy and fear among her fellow teachers, her friends, neighbors, pastors, and even within her own family. While she understood the root of their reluctance—a Black person who stood up could very well be shot, or lynched, by their white neighbors—there was also the stickier matter of complacency. Many of her fellow Black citizens, she was convinced, had been beaten down so long they had given up, took their second-class citizenship as immutable, and couldn't see the benefit of risking their lives to put up another losing fight.

Others—and this enraged her—had grown comfortable with the Jim

Crow system, made their own accommodations to it, and even established some base of power within it. They seemed just fine with maintaining the status quo. The Black minister who received gifts from the white merchants in town in exchange for keeping parishioners quiet. The Black school principal who enjoyed status by not rocking the boat of unequal education for his students. She couldn't accept this stance; she viewed it as craven. There were many fronts in the battle against Jim Crow, and different strategies were required to attack each flank.

Clark was heartened to see that people at Highlander didn't just talk and posture, the way they did at many of the NAACP, YWCA, PTA, and other board meetings she attended—they worked. They brainstormed and argued, designed and planned strategies. She joined a project compiling a desegregation handbook for community activists, detailing the nuts and bolts of how to build grassroots support and push for change. Her classmates wrote skits and did role-playing exercises dramatizing the kinds of difficult encounters they might expect to face back at home. They analyzed documentary films that Horton projected on a screen in the library. They learned aspects of federal law and practiced public speaking and communications tools for advocacy.

Beyond the substantive training, Clark enjoyed the informal, spontaneous chats that came so easily at Highlander. They were the sort of friendly yet substantive interactions between Black and white people that were made impossible under the talons of Jim Crow. Mealtime chatter was lively, sometimes boisterous, laughter bouncing off the walls. Private conversations were thoughtful and occasionally candid. Groups gathered on the lawn, reading newspapers and magazines, trading comments, singing.

The food was fresh and plentiful; vegetables grown in the Highlander gardens, eggs from the farm chickens; there was a cow for milk, and some pigs. Like everyone else, Mrs. Clark did stints in the kitchen and dining room, amused to be washing up or setting tables, the kind of work church women like her did all the time. But here she was, doing it alongside Black men—ministers, professors—and all manner of white folks, all of whom were not usually found in kitchens.

They took hikes to Eagle Cliff for picnics, sitting on the rocks, admiring the expansive vista of hills, valleys, and rivers spread out below. Before dinner, the group often stretched out on the grassy banks of the little Highlander lake (more like a pond) to swim and splash together, or stand knee-deep in the shallows to chat. These late-afternoon tableaux at the lake were especially poignant to Clark, who had fought for years to win access to the local beaches for Charleston's Black residents. The city was surrounded by water, but the lovely sand beaches were restricted to whites. The public swimming pools and most of the parks were also totally closed to her.

In the evenings they sat around campfires, danced, and sang together, coming together in a more personal way, united in a realm beyond words. There was square and circle dancing, with lively fiddling and someone calling the figures. It was fun to try: the steps, the swings, the do-si-dos; Black hands holding white. Mrs. Clark used to like to dance way back when, but she never even dreamed of this kind of mixed dancing. It was the sort of thing Black parents warned their children about, frightening them with what could happen if they tried. Perhaps, someday, if the potential of the *Brown* decision could be fulfilled, the next generation would be able to dance together like they did at Highlander.

After dinner, Zilphia Horton led them in medleys ranging from gospel hymns to mountain folk ballads, union fight songs, and even a few show tunes. She had a gift for getting everyone to join in, sometimes accompanying the singing from the piano; other times roaming the room with her accordion. It hadn't taken long for everyone to learn the words to "We Shall Overcome."

The final day of the desegregation workshop was July Fourth, and the Hortons hosted a barbecue at their house celebrating both the holiday and the *Brown* decision. Independence Day had a special meaning this year. Before Septima Clark and the other workshop participants departed, Myles sent them off with a reminder that they had work to do in their communities, and it would not be a simple, one-dimensional task. Beyond the strategies for school desegregation they'd hammered out and their responsibility to promote these ideas in their own towns, there was a broader goal to keep in mind. For desegregation to be successful, there needed to be more democratic representation, more Black citizens on school boards and in public office. And for that to happen, a next step would be required.

"We will have better schools only when all citizens register and vote," Horton insisted. Septima Clark headed home to Charleston, knowing what she had to do.

CHAPTER TWO

Henrietta Street

S eptima Poinsette Clark returned home to Charleston, to the house she shared with her sister Lorene, on the street where they'd grown up. She was energized, fizzing with excitement, ideas pulsing through her mind and a plan of action taking shape. Lorene always got a bit nervous when Septima launched into a new crusade, and this time would be no different.

The house at 17 Henrietta Street was a modest, wood-shingled version of the classic Charleston architectural style known as the "single house," featuring a two-story porch, called a piazza, running along the side, with a small entry door in front. The house was Septima's proudest possession, purchased in 1948 when she returned to Charleston and could finally afford it. Her mother would no longer be at the mercy of white landlords who had so often humiliated the Poinsettes when they couldn't pay the rent on time.

As soon as Septima returned from Highlander, Lorene could sense a new attitude in her sister. She watched Septima at the dining room table, doing her Highlander homework, sketching out her schedule for action. She was drawing a lesson plan to guide her fellow teachers, her students, and their parents into the new—but frightening—promise of integrated schools. She had returned from her week at Highlander with a jolt of confidence and an expanded vision of what was possible. Her time on the far mountain had also made her feel less lonely, as if she were now part of a new team, surrounded by a wider circle of comrades who shared her zeal for breaking down racial barriers.

"I thoroughly enjoyed the week I spent at Highlander," Septima wrote to her friends the Warings, "It was so new, so different, and living and learning there together meant so much to me."

———◆———

Victoria and Peter Poinsette named their second child Septima Earthaline when she came into the world in Charleston in May 1898, just two years after the

Supreme Court's *Plessy* verdict pronounced racial segregation constitutionally legal. Septima wasn't the seventh child—she had no obvious connection to the Latin term for seven—but was named for a maternal aunt in Haiti, where *septima*, in the local dialect, meant "sufficient."

As the family expanded, they moved to a rented house on Henrietta Street, parents and eight children crammed into four rooms and a kitchen with no running water, an outhouse in back. It was an integrated street, as some Charleston neighborhoods were at that time, but Victoria forbade her children to play with the white children on the block. She imposed her own segregation; she did not trust white people.

Victoria Anderson had been born free in Charleston, but after her mother died, she was raised by relatives in Haiti, in an independent Black nation where she did not live under the indignities of Jim Crow and even received a decent education. She never quite adjusted to moving back to the American South when she was eighteen; she could never accept being treated like dirt by whites, and resented it always.

Peter Poinsette was a house slave on the plantation of Joel Poinsett, a South Carolina legislator and diplomat who brought home from his time as ambassador to Mexico a showy red flowering plant, which gained popularity as a Christmas-season decoration bearing his name. Young Peter worked alongside his mother in the big house and was assigned to accompany the master's sons to school, carrying their books while they rode on horseback to and from the schoolhouse. Peter waited outside with the horse, through heat, chill, or rain for hours as the boys received their lessons. He never learned to read or write himself, and for most of his life he used an X to sign his name. During the Civil War, when he was in his teens, Peter served as a slave servant to those same master's sons in the Confederate Army. During the long Union siege and bombardment of Charleston, Peter delivered water and supplies to Confederate troops defending the city, defending his enslavement.

Peter never expressed bitterness about his years of slavery, which he accepted as God's will, and he was proud to bear the name of Poinsette (somehow the extra flourish of a final e was tacked on) as it carried some degree of status in Charleston. Stripped of their own family ties and names while enslaved, freemen like Peter often took the surnames of their owners after emancipation. And in the postbellum South, Black families' social standing in their own communities could still be tied to the wealth and reputations of the families who had once possessed them.

Peter emerged from slavery a gentle and passive man, without a trade or literacy skills, ill-equipped to provide for his large family. Victoria needed to work, and though she was very clever and moderately educated, as a Black woman, her options limited to poorly paid domestic service work. "She was never a servant, and she wasn't going to be one," Septima said of her mother. "She used to boast that she 'never gave a white woman a cup of coffee'—because she felt that would make her a servant." Instead, Victoria took in laundry to wash and iron at home, and the Poinsette house was constantly filled with steaming tubs of clothes. Septima and her sisters slept in the bedroom where their mother heated her heavy irons on the hearth and pressed clothes long into the night. Peter worked at various jobs as a waiter, cook, and janitor.

Church and faith were Victoria's anchors and solace, and she marched Septima and the other children almost a mile down Calhoun Street to Old Bethel Methodist Church every Sunday for services and two classes of Sunday school. Victoria was the undisputed boss of the family, capable and strong, but also difficult: demanding, rigid, temperamental, even volatile. Septima learned to bow her head and hold her tongue to avoid inciting her mother's flashes of anger, to duck the risk of a whipping or slapping.

The attribute that Septima would eventually come to appreciate most in her mother was fearlessness. Victoria always acted unafraid, or at least she never allowed others to see her fear, even when facing down hostile white men or policemen. She refused to cast her eyes down when passing a white person on the street, step into the gutter to allow them to pass, or allow them to invade her home. She was a powerless Black woman demanding to be seen and refusing to acquiesce to an evil social compact. Septima would absorb these lessons in resistance from her mother, combining them with the humility and kindness displayed by her father, putting her inheritance to good use.

From the time she was a little girl, Septima wanted to be a teacher. Teaching was a highly respected profession, with a modest but steady income, a path into the middle class. She played teacher with her siblings and cousins, gaining the affectionate nickname Little Ma. By the time she finished seventh grade in the "Negro" public school and took an exam that allowed her to skip eighth grade, she could qualify for a basic teaching certificate; she was only fourteen years old.

But Victoria would not allow Septima to end her education so early and insisted she attend the distinguished Avery Normal Institute, a private school for Black students run by the American Missionary Association, which had trained Charleston's Black teachers and civic leaders since Reconstruction. How the Poinsettes could possibly pay the $1.50 monthly tuition, Victoria didn't know, but she simply declared that Septima would go to Avery. The Lord would provide. As in some Biblical parable, Victoria's prayer was answered. A young housewife living on Henrietta Street offered to pay Septima to watch her children after school and on evenings, and this arrangement allowed Septima to earn enough to cover Avery's tuition.

Septima considered Avery a paradise: an imposing redbrick building with a cupola on top, a grand, polished wood staircase in the entry, bright classrooms with tidy rows of desks. Best of all, there was a spacious library where she could explore a world of books not possible before. She excelled in her studies, graduated with excellent grades, and passed the state examination for a teaching license. But her teachers believed she was "college material" and visited her parents to convince them to send their daughter to Fisk, the famed Black college in Nashville. Septima realized this was financially impossible for her family. She would have loved to go to college, but she argued against it. Rather than college, she told her parents, she could immediately realize her dream of becoming a teacher, with the added benefit that her salary could contribute to the family income. The only catch was that she couldn't teach in Charleston—Black teachers were not permitted, even in the Black schools.

Septima Poinsette set off on her first teaching assignment in September 1916, soon after her graduation from Avery. She made her way to Johns Island, sitting in a motorboat winding its way through the rivers and marshy creeks separating the Charleston peninsula from the Sea Islands off the city's coast. Her mother had accompanied her to the Tradd Street dock, fussing over her bags, both of them trying not to cry. It wasn't a very long trip, about fifteen miles as the gull flies, but it might as well have been a journey to the moon.

The boat held about a dozen passengers and boxes of freight, making stops along the way as it puttered down the serpentine inlets to the island. The trip normally took about nine or ten hours if the tides were favorable and the boat wasn't stranded on the mud flats. What Septima found when she finally arrived on the island was shocking to her: a place so close to the city, yet isolated, desperately poor, and, to her mind, primitive.

Johns, like most of the Carolina and Georgia Sea Islands stretching in a chain along the Atlantic coastline, was once the home of Indigenous peoples who farmed its fertile soil and fished its waters. Waves of European settlers in the seventeenth and eighteenth centuries drove out the native tribes and began cultivating lucrative crops of indigo, rice, and cotton, importing West African and Caribbean slaves to do the backbreaking work. But the swampy, subtropical islands were also fertile breeding grounds for malaria and yellow fever, prompting white land owners to decamp to Charleston, leaving their Black overseers to manage the plantations. With few white masters living on the islands, the enslaved communities were able to retain many elements of their African cultural traditions.

During the Civil War, the Carolina Sea Islands were the first areas to be captured by Union forces in the siege of Charleston, and the islands' slaves were the first to be freed. During Reconstruction, parcels of the abandoned plantations were distributed to the formerly enslaved residents, allowing for a greater degree of Black landownership on the islands than other areas of the state. But with no land route to the mainland, Johns Island farmers couldn't engage in much trade or commerce, and the island remained an isolated hinterland.

Septima's lodging was in a drafty attic room, lit by a single kerosene lantern hung from bare rafters, in the crowded home of a family willing to take in boarding teachers. Her accommodations were luxurious compared to the rough shacks of most of the island's Black residents, walls papered with newspaper pages, not even an outhouse; they had to relieve themselves in the backyard, fouling the groundwater. Such poor sanitation made infection, disease, child mortality, and premature death facts of life on the island.

She was assigned to teach at Promise Land School on the Bohicket Road, on the western side of the island, a two-room log and mud cabin serving 132 students in grades K–7. By virtue of her graduation from Avery, Septima, still a teenager who had never taught a class before, was made the school's principal, supervising another teacher who handled the younger children. Septima was paid $35 a month, most of which she sent home to help support her family, and she was greatly annoyed to learn that the teacher at the white school across the road earned $85 a month for teaching the only three white children in the vicinity. She would learn that sort of disparity was not unusual.

There were no desks in the classrooms of Promise Land, only rows of backless benches for the students to sit on, and to write they crouched on the floor using the benches as desks. There was no blackboard when she first arrived, and the few textbooks were outdated and worn, cast-offs from the white schools. Children walked miles from their homes to the school—some without shoes—across creeks and deep mud. Attendance was erratic, as children as young as seven were forced to work in the fields, bound by the sharecropping contracts their families had signed with the landowners. The older children were kept in the cotton fields until December and could attend classes only until early spring when planting season began. There was good reason why most Black adults on Johns Island and the other Sea Islands were illiterate. White landowners and officials, who ruled over the majority-Black Sea Islands, wanted to keep it that way.

Septima was appalled by the crude conditions she encountered on the island, but she came to love the people of Johns. As she became more fluent in their Gullah dialect's lilting patois of West African, Caribbean, and Low-country phrases, she grew closer to the islanders. Soon everyone was calling her Miss Seppie. At night she gave reading lessons to the parents of her students and other adults, patiently instructing them by lantern light. Miss Seppie found great satisfaction in bringing the magic of the written word to adults who'd never mastered their letters, and her gentle and affirming teaching style put her hesitant older learners at ease. She was embraced, invited to family parties and neighborhood celebrations. She visited homes to give cooking and sewing lessons, helped make christening gowns and wedding dresses, sat in the church pews and swayed in the ecstatic worship services of the island's praise houses. She became part of the community.

But life for the young teacher was "quite a struggle," she admitted. Teaching so many children on different levels with scant resources was exhausting. Her diet was poor, and she suffered frostbite on her feet from trudging to school in icy mud and standing in the damp chill of the schoolhouse. With no doctor on the island, folk medicine—a mix of herbal knowledge and voodoo—was the usual treatment for all ailments. But the prescription given to Miss Seppie, a hot potato applied to the frostbitten area, made matters worse; she almost lost her toes. Victoria visited her daughter on the island just once, and was horrified by Septima's living and working conditions. But Septima had grown attached to the islanders, if not the island, and was determined to see her assignment through. She taught on the island for two years. It was only the irresistible offer of a teaching position at Avery—which as a private school could hire

Black teachers—that lured Miss Seppie from her shack schoolhouse back to Charleston.

When Septima Poinsette returned to teach at the Avery Institute in the fall of 1918, her family did not know that she had already secretly joined the NAACP. They didn't know that she and a few fellow teachers had dared to enroll in the newly formed Charleston chapter by furtively slipping the dollar bill of their membership dues into the upturned parasol of a local NAACP organizer on the street. "We didn't want anyone to see us putting it in," Septima recalled, "because we knew the trouble it would cause."

The willingness of the NAACP (which was established in 1909 by a co-alition of Black and white progressives) to publicly confront racial injustice made the organization dangerous in the eyes of southern whites. But it was also controversial among many Black people, some of whom feared NAACP activities invited violent reprisals.

To her family's distress, sweet and decorous Septima seemed very willing to court trouble. In her first term at Avery, in fall 1918, the Charleston NAACP launched a campaign to overturn the ban on Black teachers working in the city's "Negro schools." Charleston was the last remaining city in the South to bar Black teachers from its classrooms, exiling them to the impoverished rural districts like Johns Island, and leaving Black city children without role models at the blackboard.

When the all-white school board rejected the local NAACP's request for a policy change, the NAACP took the daring step of carrying their demand directly to the state legislature and bolstered its campaign with a massive peti-tion drive. Septima enthusiastically joined the door-to-door canvassing effort, collecting signatures in support of hiring Black teachers. She even recruited her sixth-grade Avery students to knock on doors with her, giving them an early lesson in political involvement. The petition drive collected signatures from almost two-thirds of Charleston's Black residents, and those signature sheets were dramatically carried through the streets of the state capital in Columbia into the legislative chamber as part of the NAACP's clever maneuvering in the statehouse. The following school year the first Black teachers were hired in Charleston city schools, though they were paid less than half the salary of white teachers.

Septima considered this campaign her initiation into political action, but it also marked her first brush with resistance from her own community. Some of her fellow teachers at Avery disapproved of her involvement, and she claimed her principal did not support the effort. But Septima had witnessed the power of collective action to force change and the ability of the NAACP to take up the fight against injustice. And win. It convinced and emboldened her.

Yet her family's fears of white backlash in response to NAACP victories were tragically borne out that following summer, in 1919. In the economic dislocation and recession following the end of World War I and the acceleration of the Great Migration of southern African Americans to the North, whites found themselves competing with Black people for jobs and housing, heightening tensions. That summer, enraged white mobs rampaged through Black neighborhoods in twenty-six American cities. An estimated 250 Black men, women, and children were shot, lynched, or burned alive in these bloody race riots, which tore through Charleston in May. The fighting reached the edge of Henrietta Street, where the Poinsette family stood on their porch and could hear the mob "bursting down the street, screaming and hollering," as Septima later recalled. Her frightened family retreated into their house, locked the doors, and stayed safe, but several of their neighbors were beaten or shot, two Black Charlestonians were killed, and many more were injured or arrested.

———— ✦ ————

Tensions were also high in the Poinsette household that summer. Septima lived under her parents' roof as a twenty-year-old working woman, but she was still treated as a child. She chafed under her mother's strict rules and judgmental attitudes. The Great War was over, Charleston was a bustling port for returning Navy ships, and women were not only on the cusp of winning the vote, they were also shedding their corsets—and, to Victoria's mind, their morals—in a bid for greater freedom. There was, no doubt, some element of good-daughter rebellion in Septima Poinsette's mind when she fell for a sweet-talking sailor at a USO dance downtown.

Neri Clark was a Navy cook with a sixth-grade education, a "mountain man" from North Carolina, a snazzy dresser almost a decade older than Septima. He swept her off her feet at the dance, but his ship was sailing the next day, so she assumed nothing would come of the encounter. But when Clark sailed into Norfolk four months later, he used his three-day pass to visit Septima in Charleston, and a romance quickly bloomed. Mr. Clark was the kind of man her mother had warned her about. "Somebody must have put some voodoo on you," Victoria Poinsette scolded her daughter, so besotted by a man she hardly knew, a low-class stranger from another state.

Septima was a very attractive young woman, her hair fashionably coifed and tucked behind her ears, her dresses simple but stylish, but she was, as her mother feared, quite naive about men. The stress on Henrietta Street grew unbearable, and at the end of the school year, Septima left Avery to take a job in a fishing village north of Charleston, where she could double her monthly salary, but more importantly, be free of her mother's constant criticisms. Months later, when Neri was back in port again, he hitched a ride to the village where Septima was teaching and, after a few days of courting, asked her to marry him.

She brought her boyfriend to Henrietta Street to obtain her parents' blessing but did not receive it. "You marry him over my dead body," Victoria told her daughter. Septima defied her mother and married Neri Clark in the fishing village where she was boarding; her parents did not attend. Soon after the wedding, Neri sailed off again, and while he was at sea, Septima gave birth to a baby girl, whom she named Victoria to honor, and assuage, her mother. But the midwife hadn't noticed that the baby was born with a serious defect. By the time doctors operated to correct the condition, it was too late; baby Victoria lived just twenty-three days.

Septima was despondent. She was convinced that losing the baby was punishment from God for disobeying her mother. She had violated the Fifth Commandment; it was her sin. Returning to Charleston, she walked down to the Battery, at the tip of the peninsula where the Ashley and Cooper Rivers flow together, stared at the water, and contemplated drowning herself. Her deep religious faith told her that suicide was also a sin, but her pain overwhelmed any qualms. It was only the arrival of her younger brother on his bicycle, dispatched by Victoria, who sensed her daughter was in deep despair, that distracted Septima from her violent intention, snapping her back from the brink.

She walked home to Henrietta Street with her brother, still heartsick, but grateful for being rescued from her own destructive impulses. From that day onward, she would search for the reason why God had spared her that afternoon at the Battery, for the purpose the Lord had in mind for her life.

Neri soon left the Navy and insisted the couple move to Dayton, Ohio, where he had once worked. Septima, expecting again, was willing to move to this strange city, far from her southern roots, thinking of it as a fresh start for them both. The marriage was proving to be rocky; she found Neri was vain, selfish, often mean. She could only hope that the new baby, the prospect of building a family together, would smooth things. Not long after they arrived in Dayton, Septima gave birth to a healthy baby boy, naming him for his father.

Septima was still in the hospital when she learned that her husband held secrets. He was one of those sailors who, quite literally, had a woman in every port. He had already been married and separated (likely not legally divorced) before wedding Septima and was also keeping a mistress in Dayton. When Septima confronted her husband about his betrayal, he told her to leave.

She couldn't face her mother, who had been right about Neri, so she sought refuge with her husband's family in North Carolina, who graciously took her and the baby in. Ten months later, Neri died of kidney failure in Dayton.

It was, in many ways, easier this way. Septima was freed from the shameful status of an abandoned wife and took on the more acceptable role of a grieving widow. Yet she felt she still could not return to Charleston, could not abide the side glances, the whispers, the gossip at church, or on Henrietta Street. She could not stand her mother's I-told-you-so lectures. She would insist upon being called Mrs. Clark for the rest of her life, though her time as a wife had been very short, and she chose never to marry again. Mrs. Clark became a widowed, single, working mother who needed to find a new home, a new job—and a new purpose.

She seriously considered becoming a Methodist missionary, finding meaning in a life devoted to service to God. But how could she leave her baby to go off to some corner of the world, and how could she support little Neri on a missionary's subsistence pay? She must be practical, so she settled for a less exotic career as a teacher, uplifting Black children in the segregated schools of the South. She became an evangelist for learning.

Homesick for the Lowcountry, Miss Seppie, now Mrs. Clark, returned to Promise Land School on Johns Island in the fall of 1927 with toddler Neri, boarding in a cramped and drafty house. The boy soon came down with whooping cough, measles, and other illnesses and was tormented by the ubiquitous swarming mosquitoes. The island still lacked adequate medical care, forcing Mrs. Clark to admit this was not a healthy environment for her son. She made the wrenching decision to leave little Neri with his paternal grandparents in North Carolina.

For the next two decades she would live alone while her son was lovingly raised by her in-laws. The separation caused her "a lot of sorrow," but it was a necessary arrangement; the best for her boy. She sent money for Neri's care; she visited when she could; she cried many nights.

———— ✦ ————

It was during this second teaching stint on Johns Island that Mrs. Clark encountered a fourteen-year-old boy named Esau Jenkins. He came to her classroom and asked her to give him reading and writing lessons, help him go beyond the few grades he had been able to complete in the island schools. He was working full-time by then, helping his father grow cotton on the family's patch of land, using his rudimentary math skills to catch the cotton ginner trying to cheat his father.

Esau was a young man with big ideas: he wanted to convince his dad to switch from cotton, which he realized was a doomed crop (the exhausted soil, the invading boll weevils) to growing and selling vegetables to the greengrocers in Charleston. Esau had a businessman's mind, but he needed better skills, and looked to Mrs. Clark for help. She mentored Esau, and he made good progress, but after three years, she left Johns Island again, lured to Columbia, the state capital, by better pay and the chance to teach at what was considered the premier Black pubic school in South Carolina.

Clark taught in Columbia for eighteen years, from the time she turned thirty until she was almost fifty years old, living in boardinghouses or tiny rented rooms. She spent her summers working in children's camps or caretaking jobs for extra money, while also taking classes to slowly accumulate the credits for her college degrees. It took decades. She earned a bachelor's degree from Benedict College in 1942, then her master's from Atlanta University, where she studied with W. E. B. Du Bois. She actually enjoyed living in Columbia; it was more open and exciting than Charleston, less class-conscious and clannish. Without the burdens of childcare, she joined an array of professional societies, Black women's clubs, charities, and civic groups. She attended interesting lectures, played bridge, had a social life for the first time.

The Second World War brought her sleepless nights: her son was drafted into uniform, and she was terrified he would be killed. She occupied her restless evenings with a specialized type of war work: teaching young, illiterate Black soldiers stationed at Fort Jackson to sign their names and read basic instructions and road signs. She worked under the guidance of an expert in adult literacy education, Lou Wil Gray, who trained Clark in simple but effective teaching methods tailored for grown-ups. (Clark had already worked with Gray during the Depression years, when New Deal programs promoted adult remedial learning, and she could earn extra money teaching night classes.) At Fort Jackson, she taught young men going off to fight for democracy the rudimentary skills their rural segregated society had failed to provide.

Mrs. Clark joined the Columbia chapter of the NAACP soon after arriving in the city, and it was with this group that she would undertake what she called her first "radical act"—working on the campaign to win salary equalization for South Carolina's Black teachers. Black teachers in the state were paid less than half the salaries of their white counterparts with the same educational credentials and classroom duties. The US Supreme Court had already upheld a federal court decision that race-based pay disparities within school systems were unconstitutional, but South Carolina was ignoring the ruling. The NAACP brought a suit to force compliance; Legal Defense Fund attorney Thurgood Marshall came to argue the cases.

Clark tried to rally her fellow Columbia teachers to sign a petition supporting the suit, but she met significant resistance from those unwilling to put their jobs, and possibly themselves, at risk by pressing legal action. Undeterred, she made impassioned pleas at teacher meetings and helped gather key evidence for the case, including affidavits from both white and Black teachers. She also procured the most valuable documents, copies of the paychecks of sympathetic white teachers, proving the stark racial disparities in pay. Federal Judge J. Waties Waring ruled in favor of the NAACP and the Black teachers, and Septima Clark was proud to have played a small part in the victory.

She might have stayed in Columbia, but for her mother's stroke. After a year of commuting to Charleston by bus every weekend to help Lorene care for their mother, Septima moved back to Henrietta Street in 1947, found a job teaching in the city's segregated schools, and managed to buy the house a year later. She joined the boards of local civic organizations, from the YWCA to the Tuberculosis Society. She also joined the Charleston branch of the NAACP and was soon brought onto its executive committee. Her mother and sister watched warily as Septima brought her "militant" ideas back to her hometown.

Lorene had followed Septima into a teaching career, never married, and after the death of their mother in 1952, kept the household going while Septima went out into the world. Septima relied upon Lorene to drive her to meetings and events, as Septima owned a car but had never learned to drive. "I was always too impatient to drive a car," Septima would say. Lorene didn't like to get involved in politics and race matters. She sympathized but didn't get as worked up about such things as her sister. And since Septima had returned from Highlander, she was on a tear.

Septima plunged into her agenda, making telephone calls to set up meetings, crisscrossing the city to visit contacts, arranging to give presentations. Her strategy was based upon her deep knowledge of her hometown, her extensive community connections, and strongly influenced by the new methods she had learned at Highlander.

Within two weeks of coming home in mid-July, Septima reported to Myles Horton that she had already spoken to the Tobacco Workers Union and the International Organization of Longshoremen, the Charleston Voters Clinic—as well as her colleagues on the NAACP Executive Committee and the Interracial Committee of the YWCA—about organizing the city for school desegregation.

Like some revivalist pastor or stumping politician, Clark made open-air speeches on the campus square of South Carolina State College in Orangeburg, extolling the virtues of Highlander and the importance of supporting school desegregation. She didn't ask permission to speak, she didn't clear it with the college administration, she "just stole the chance, a kind of soap box on the corner affair," she proudly reported to Horton. "Every chance I get I'll sell Highlander," she promised him.

She urged her audiences to send delegations to Highlander for inspiration and training, as soon as the next workshop in early August. This would help them prepare for the new school year, the first since the *Brown* decision. She encountered hesitation. To be fair, it was very short notice to ask people to set aside a week and make a long trip to Tennessee in the middle of summer. But Mrs. Clark was never patient with wishy-washy excuses. "They like the ideas, listen attentively, but to me that's not enough," she wrote to Horton. "I want action."

There was one person she was especially eager to recruit to Highlander: her former student on Johns Island and colleague on the Charleston NAACP executive board—Esau Jenkins.

Mrs. Clark caught up with Jenkins in the latter part of July 1954—it wasn't easy, he was a very busy man—and tried to convince him to go to Highlander in August. By then, Jenkins was a forty-four-year-old husband and father, a successful small businessman, and a civic leader on Johns Island. Mrs. Clark was sure he was just the sort of person Highlander was looking for, and that the school could be of real benefit to Jenkins, too. Mrs. Clark knew he was doing great work on the island, but she also knew he needed more help and support.

At first, Jenkins told her he couldn't take off for a week to go to some mountain in Tennessee. This was the height of the summer season for his motel and cafe, and he couldn't afford to be away. He had insurance payments due, bills to pay. But Mrs. Clark would not let her former student off the hook so easily. It won't cost you a nickel, she told him. She would arrange for Highlander to pay his way, and she would even go with him. Jenkins tried many more excuses, but Mrs. Clark summoned her teacherly persuasive skills: Highlander might be able to help you with the bus, Esau, she told him.

Days later, Esau Jenkins and Septima Clark were on their way to Monteagle Mountain.

CHAPTER THREE

Esau's Bus

E sau Jenkins had a reconditioned school bus that he drove from Johns Island over the bridge to Charleston every weekday morning and evening, carrying his neighbors to and from their jobs in the city. But it was more than just a vehicle, it was the engine of his great plan.

Jenkins began driving his bus in the mid-1940s, transporting Johns Island students, including his own children, to Burke Industrial School, the "Negro public high school" in the city. There was still no school beyond seventh grade for Black students on Johns. Educational facilities had barely improved since Miss Seppie was teaching at Promise Land, and a generation later most Black adults remained illiterate and trapped in menial labor.

To break the cycle, Jenkins and his fellow islanders pressed the Charleston County school board for a proper high school for their children. At first, school authorities ignored them, then came up with a bucket of excuses, and finally tried to placate the parents by allowing Black island students to attend Burke—if they could get there.

Jenkins promised to get them there. He bought a used bus and began driving the Black students to Burke, but he didn't think that was a real solution. The Black islanders still needed their own high school; the white students had three. Jenkins and his fellow parents kept pushing, nimbly climbing over every bureaucratic obstacle thrown in their path. By this time South Carolina was trying to fend off the NAACP's legal efforts to desegregate schools by building more "equal" Black facilities, and in 1951 the brand-new Haut Gap High School opened on Johns.

It was a startling victory for a community so accustomed to losing. The success was a testament to Jenkins's vision, skill, and gumption, boosting his standing as a community leader. He wanted the win to be a lesson for his island, proof of the power of organized action. Still, to make any sustained progress, he was certain, Johns Islanders needed to develop political muscle as well.

Esau Jenkins was a proud race man, deeply committed to the welfare and advancement of his people. He was a devout Christian who believed that he was indeed his brother's keeper. He was what today might be called a social entrepreneur: coming up with creative, even risky, solutions to entrenched problems. Doing well by doing good.

He carried himself with a brisk sense of purpose, dressing his stocky frame in the attire of a businessman: white shirt, jacket and tie, short-brimmed fedora. Not the country bumpkin Charleston whites expected a Sea Islander to look like. Jenkins prided himself on being a problem solver, a community mechanic trying to fix the things that needed repair. He had always approached life in that practical way.

When he realized he needed more than his weak fourth-grade education to make a decent living, he went to Miss Seppie for help, and later he enrolled in adult night school in Charleston to earn his equivalency diploma. When the cotton crop petered out, he prodded his father to go into growing and trucking vegetables, saving the family's small farm.

When he noticed most of the greengrocers in the city were Greek immigrants who spoke little English, Esau took lessons in Greek. "Here comes the Colored Greek," the grocers would greet him as he made his rounds. But for Jenkins it was more than just a friendly gesture; by speaking the merchants' language, he could deal with them directly, cutting out the produce middleman's fees. He had discovered it was important to speak the language of those you want to persuade. These days, when he spoke to his people on the islands he spoke in his native Gullah dialect; when he talked to powerful white people in Charleston, he spoke in Lowcountry English, with a strong Gullah accent.

When the truck farming couldn't support his growing family (he had married his wife, Janie, when he was seventeen, and they were raising eight children), he branched into new ventures: a motel, café, fruit shop, record store, the bus service. A Black man, a Black community, needed to be self-sufficient, Jenkins believed, beyond the white man's control. Economic independence—owning your own land, your own business—was an essential brick on the road to freedom. But it was tough for a Black man to get fair credit from the white-owned banks, holding back the island's economic development. Jenkins was hoping to fix that someday with the creation of a citizens' credit union.

There were so many things on the island to fix: Too many island babies died; his Janie had given birth to thirteen babies, and five of them didn't make it past infancy. The island needed a health clinic. It also needed paved roads, a proper sewage system, better schools, electricity lines to every home. Jenkins believed his island's many problems could be solved only by joint effort, much in the way islanders traditionally fished with big skein nets cast into the river, pulled by many hands.

He saw that that too many Black men on the island were being maimed and murdered while their white killers walked free. Too many Black men were being framed for rape or charged with killings they did not commit, and they couldn't afford to post bail or hire a lawyer to plead their case. Jenkins was convinced the Black men of Johns needed to rally to defend themselves. Not with guns, though many of his neighbors stocked guns for protection in their homes, but with the fist of the law.

So in 1948 Jenkins brought together a dozen or so friends to form the Progressive Club, and membership quickly grew. Each member donated twenty-five cents a month to build a legal defense fund for islanders facing Jim Crow injustice. The fund provided money for bail, and Jenkins tapped his NAACP connections to find lawyers to take the cases. It was still hard to receive a fair trial before an all-white jury. In South Carolina, only registered voters could serve on a jury, and there were very few Black voters on Johns Island. Jenkins required every member of the Progressive Club to register and to vote.

The Progressive Club began meeting at Moving Star Hall, the praise house on the north side of the island, the semisacred space where Jenkins had grown up and first felt the power of a collective voice. On Sunday mornings, islanders attended services at their own churches (the Jenkins went to Wesley United Methodist), but on Sunday evenings they gathered at Moving Star Hall to hold the kind of Gullah devotional services that were rooted in African tradition. Filled with song and shouts, rhythmic clapping and feet stomping, these praise services were not led by clergy; anyone could stand up to testify or preach, anyone could begin singing or shouting. Others spontaneously joined the song, melodies and harmonies blending, intricate rhythms driving the music, rocking the room.

Moving Star Hall held the strong voices of an oppressed community. It was the perfect place for Progressive Club meetings, as it provided a great example of the communal traditions of the island. The simple, whitewashed cabin was built in 1917 as the home of the Moving Star Society, the mutual aid group assisting islanders in need: tending to the sick, burying the dead, providing food to the hungry, rent for the indigent, prayers for the distressed. Part prayer circle, part welfare agency, Moving Star took care of its own. That was part of the mission Jenkins envisioned for the Progressive Club as he gradually broadened its portfolio beyond legal defense to citizen action and community empowerment. An essential element of Jenkins's empowerment plan was the ballot box.

Voting was the only way to make white elected officials pay attention to Black citizens, Jenkins insisted. Threaten them at the polls with a solid Black vote; there were twice as many Black adults as white ones on Johns Island. That was democracy! Jenkins knew this would be an empty threat as long as the Black citizens of Johns Island delivered empty ballot boxes, because they did not, or could not, vote.

Jenkins understood there were many reasons Johns Islanders, and their neighbors on James, Wadmalaw, Edisto, and Yonge islands didn't vote. The poll tax. The difficulty in reaching the county registration offices in Charleston, open only a few hours on two days each month, making it impossible for working people. The intimidation of the registrars, who so often demeaned and bullied Black applicants, and who could, on a whim, deny a registration card. The fear that if their landlord or employer learned they had attempted to register to vote, they might get evicted, fired, or worse.

But the most common reason they didn't even try to register was the literacy test. The tests were supposedly mandatory for all voters, but white people were given a pass; only Black citizens were subjected to examinations. The registrars demanded that Black applicants be able to read aloud and interpret whole sections of the archaically phrased state constitution. They had to enunciate the "crimes" that might disqualify them from registering: miscegenation, bigamy, sodomy, larceny, moral turpitude. The test was a major barrier. Jenkins decided to use his bus to ram through that barrier.

Esau had expanded his bus service to meet the needs of his neighbors, who, with the opening of a new bridge, found employment opportunities in the city's factories, mills, docks, and the kitchens of Charleston's elegant homes. From his steering wheel, Jenkins held forth about the goals of the Progressive Club and the importance of voting, but only a few of his passengers were registered. So he began an experiment with his captive audience. He sent away for a copy of the state constitution and voter registration laws. Janie typed up the sections his passengers would need to read and understand for the literacy test. Esau distributed the pages on the bus, a cocooned classroom rolling down the road past white people who, had they known what was going on inside, would be outraged. As it was, they paid no attention.

On the forty-five-minute early morning drive, Jenkins would discuss with his riders the procedures for registering and voting, coaching them on the definitions and pronunciations of the words they would need to know in the constitution. In between stops he would explain elements of the laws for those who couldn't read on their own. Upon arrival in Charleston, those who had to start work early would depart, but those with a later clock-in time stayed on the bus with Jenkins for a class of line-by-line reading and interpreting the required portions of the constitution. Jenkins often conducted another lesson on the evening commute back to the island. As the monthly Charleston County registration days approached, Jenkins intensified the lessons, promising to accompany those who felt ready to take the test on the trip to the registrar's office.

One morning, a passenger on Jenkins's bus approached his driver's seat and declared she wanted to vote. "I don't have much schooling, Esau," Alice Wine told him. "But I would like to be somebody. I'd like to hold up my head with other people. I'd like to be able to vote."

Mrs. Wine was forty years old, with barely a third-grade education, and had recently left the fields to work as a laundress in Charleston. "I cannot read this Constitution because I did not get but just so far in school, and I cannot pronounce these words," she told Jenkins. She couldn't read much at all, she confessed, but she could memorize very well. She knew her Bible by heart, and she knew all the words to the old songs she loved to sing in Moving Star Hall. And she remembered her parents talking about how Black people had once voted, way back when.

"If you are willing to help me," she promised, "I will show you that I would be one that would be willing to vote in every election." Jenkins gave Mrs. Wine extra tutoring on the bus, helping her pronounce the unfamiliar words she would have to recite for the test. "When I get to them hard words, my tongue gets so heavy until I couldn't pronounce the words," she complained to Jenkins. "No," he told her, "the hard words is the things for you to learn."

When Alice felt ready to take the test, Esau escorted her to the registration office in Charleston, but he honestly didn't think she would be able to pass. When it was her turn, Alice aced the test, proudly waving her registration receipt. She had memorized everything, so she hadn't needed to read a word. She joined the Progressive Club and voted in every election.

Her registration card was her prized possession, but Mrs. Wine wanted to continue her lessons to actually learn to read and to write, to become what Jenkins called a "first-class citizen." But Jenkins was no teacher, he didn't know how to teach basic literacy, and the commute on the bus didn't provide enough time or space to even learn the ABCs. His rolling voter-prep bus had managed to place a number of his passengers on the voting rolls, but those were the people who could already read well enough, or those like Alice who had prodigious memorization skills. He wasn't equipped to help all the others who'd have to start from scratch if they were ever to become voters. His bus wasn't enough. He needed something more.

———————◆———————

Mrs. Clark enjoyed a warm welcome when she returned to Highlander with Esau Jenkins at the beginning of August 1954. Highlander didn't feel as exotic or strange to her this time, and in the span of less than a month she had developed a remarkably strong attachment to the place.

This second workshop was larger, drawing Black and white participants from all over the nation. Mr. Jenkins fit right in, though he had never experienced anything like this place or these people. He was rather quiet at first, but his sunny confidence and earnestness drew people in, and his sense of mission made them take him seriously. In his vivid, Gullah-flavored depiction of the challenges his neighbors faced on their island, he captivated his classmates. For most of his listeners in the Highlander library, the Sea Islands were foreign and exotic, but the daily struggles he described would be familiar to any Black person living in the rural South. Recounting his attempts to organize and spur his island to political action, he quickly won admirers.

Esau decided he liked Highlander. He appreciated that his white classmates weren't mean or disparaging, didn't call him boy, didn't wave his concerns away. They listened, were encouraging, made suggestions. Nor did they seem threatened by his goal of Black political empowerment. In Charleston County, when white people noticed that Jenkins was bringing Johns Islanders from his bus to the registration office every month, the registrar began taking two-hour lunch breaks, closing the place down when his people came to enroll. When that didn't work, the white political bosses offered Jenkins a bribe: stop this registration nonsense, and we'll reward you, they had said. "We're not for sale," he had answered. The white people at Highlander at least *seemed* to be different.

And his Black classmates had not once scolded him to be more realistic, be careful, go slow.

Myles Horton sat back and observed Jenkins carefully during the week of the workshop. He was impressed. Horton had come to realize that Highlander was in flux, caught in the transition from labor to civil rights advocacy. He had won a grant from a foundation in Chicago to develop rural community leadership, but the first projects had failed miserably. He had learned some valuable lessons from the mistakes, but it was still an expensive failure. He needed to try again and do better. And Esau Jenkins might be just the man Highlander needed.

------- ♦ -------

Mrs. Clark was able to get better acquainted with Mrs. Horton on this return visit. They chatted while Zilphia typed skit scripts or prepared song sheets for the evening sing-along. Septima was taken by Zilphia's warmth and sincerity, with her "rugged strength and bright beauty," as she called it. There were new songs to learn in the evenings, sprinkled in with the traditional tunes. Esau joined in the singing, just as he always did in church and in Moving Star Hall, and while this style of singing was different from what he was used to, it stirred the spirit all the same. The "Overcome" song went straight to his heart. The "we" in the chorus captured the will and resolve he hoped to convey back to his island.

Every Highlander workshop week ended with what Myles called "finding your way back home" a discussion of how the participants intended to use their Highlander training in their community. When it was his turn, Esau Jenkins said his Johns Islander neighbors needed to attain political power though the vote, and to get his community excited about voting, Jenkins intended to give them someone to vote for: himself. He would run for office, declaring himself a candidate for a seat on the Johns Island district school board. "Not that I think I can win the election," he admitted, since there weren't enough Black voters on the island yet. "But I want to prove to my people that a Black man can run for office and not get killed."

CHAPTER FOUR

The Judge

T he Supreme Court's *Brown* decision, under discussion in the Highlander library, was no abstract legal concept for Mrs. Clark, nor just a distant national news story. She had spent her life in segregated schools, first as a student and later as a teacher, waging her own campaigns against the inequities of her state's cruelly divided education system. But the *Brown* case wasn't just a suit challenging the school segregation practices in Topeka, Kansas. The case known as *Brown v. Board of Education of Topeka* was actually five cases challenging segregated public schools rolled into one. These cases originated in Kansas, Virginia, Delaware, Washington, DC, and Mrs. Clark's home state of South Carolina. Each was pursued through the state and federal courts by NAACP lawyers as part of the organization's concerted legal assault on state-mandated Jim Crow laws.

The South Carolina case that was bundled into Brown was called *Briggs v. Elliott*, and had been initiated in 1947 by a group of Black parents in the town of Summerton, in rural Clarendon County, about seventy-five miles north and east of Charleston. The affair began very modestly, with the parents simply asking for a school bus for their children. As it was, their children had to trudge up to nine miles each way, through dusty or muddy cotton and corn fields and across swollen creeks (a rowboat was sometimes required) to reach their run-down Black schools.

Though the population of Clarendon County (roughly thirty thousand at the time) was 70 percent Black, and Black school-aged children outnumbered white children by three to one, the white students of the county were served by more than thirty shiny buses taking them to well-equipped brick school buildings. Black students had no school buses at all to transport them to the one- or two-room, overcrowded K–12 schools of the segregated system. The buildings were little more than wood shacks lacking electricity, toilets, or running water. Nevertheless, the district school board chairman, a white sawmill owner named

Roscoe Elliott, refused the parents' plea for a bus: "We ain't got no money to buy a bus for your niggah children," Elliott told them flatly.

The Black parents of Summerton, most of them poor tenant farmers or laborers living in dismal dwellings, were intent upon providing better educations for their children than the inferior schooling they had received. Many of the fathers had served their country in World War II, and returned home impatient with the status quo of racism in their hometown life. The mothers had kept their families afloat through sacrifice; they clipped ration books and saved nickels to buy Double Victory war bonds, supporting the war effort abroad and promoting improved racial equality at home. They were ready to stand up for their children, spurred and organized by a local minister and schoolteacher named Joseph Armstrong DeLaine. Rev. DeLaine partnered with the South Carolina state NAACP office to explore suing the Clarendon County school board for bus accommodations.

Thurgood Marshall, the NAACP's chief Legal Defense Fund attorney, came down from New York City to examine the situation and recognized the potential of pursuing the Summerton parents' claims; the NAACP was actively seeking out such test cases. The parents' first suit, seeking equal bus transportation for their children, was thrown out of court on a technicality, but Rev. DeLaine and the parents refused to give up.

South Carolina law mandated its schools be completely segregated, and like other southern states, it relied on the notorious 1896 *Plessy v. Ferguson* ruling of the Supreme Court that codified Jim Crow by declaring that segregation was fine—as long as facilities provided for Black people were "equal." But they were never equal. For every dollar the Clarendon County school district spent to educate a white student, it allocated less than a quarter coin for a Black student. Well then, Marshall told the parents, force the whites to balance the books and pay up to make the schools separate *and* equal. "Equal Everything," Rev. DeLaine declared.

The parents hadn't dared dream of such a demand, but they were emboldened by Marshall's plan, and a petition seeking "educational advantages and facilities equal in all respects to that which is provided for whites" with over a hundred signatures was delivered to the district school board. Everyone understood that putting their name on this petition could be dangerous. The racial power dynamics in Clarendon County had not changed much since the Civil War. Whites were in complete control of political, economic, and daily social life, and woe to any Black man or woman who tried to challenge the situation. The names on the petition were posted in the county courthouse for all to see.

The pressure and punishments began. White landowners and employers, landlords and bankers gave the petition signees a choice: take your name off that school petition or lose your job, your home, your credit, even your mules. Your kids might get hurt. The threats were not subtle. Frightened families asked for their names to be removed from the petition.

But a core group of Summerton's Black parents, led by Rev. DeLaine and supported by the South Carolina and national offices of the NAACP, refused to back down; they escalated the fight. Twenty-one parents agreed to become plaintiffs in a suit against the Clarendon County school board, and Thurgood Marshall agreed to take on the case. The first plaintiffs listed on the suit were Harry Briggs Jr. a thirty-year-old Navy veteran and gas station attendant, and his wife Eliza, a motel maid. So the suit filed by Thurgood Marshall in the United States District Court for the Eastern Division of South Carolina in 1949 bore Harry Briggs's name as lead plaintiff and Clarendon schools superintendent Roscoe Elliott as defendant.

On the day before Christmas 1949, Harry Briggs's boss at the gas station on Summerton's Main Street, where Briggs had worked for fourteen years, gave him a holiday gift of a carton of cigarettes and fired him. Eliza Briggs was let go from her motel job. With five children to support, Harry would eventually be forced to leave the family to find work in Florida, and it would be years before the family was reunited. The other plaintiffs suffered similar retributions: one father lost his job selling and delivering Esso gasoline; a mother not only lost her motel job, but her family was also forced off the land they'd rented for generations, leaving them homeless. Teachers were dismissed; a decorated war veteran was refused financing for his tractor; another farmer couldn't get his cotton ginned at the county's white-owned mills. Very soon, all twenty-one parents who agreed to be plaintiffs in *Briggs v. Elliott* had lost their jobs.

Rev. DeLaine also lost his teaching job in Clarendon County, as did his wife, two sisters, and a niece. And the harassment continued: threats on the reverend's life arrived in the mail, speeding cars tried to force him off the highway, strangers hassled his children, and he feared for their safety. His house was set on fire and burned to the ground while the Summerton fire department watched but did not lift a finger to save it.

"Is this the price that free men must pay in a free country for wanting their children trained as capable and respectable American citizens?" Rev. DeLaine wrote in an angry open letter to the people of Summerton.

Septima Clark jumped into the effort to help DeLaine and the embattled Summerton parents. Her colleague Modjeska Simkins, secretary of the South Carolina NAACP, was spearheading a national fundraising drive to help the unemployed plaintiff families survive. Clark was in close touch with Rev. DeLaine and personally worked to place his older children in safe schools out of state, away from the threats being heaped on the family.

When the *Briggs v. Elliott* case reached the federal district court in Charleston in November 1950, it was assigned to Chief Judge J. Waties Waring, a sixty-nine-year-old jurist who'd sat on the federal bench for seven years. Just days before the trial was to begin, on the morning of the pretrial conference, Waring called the lead plaintiff's attorney Thurgood Marshall to his chambers for a most unusual consultation.

———◆———

Julius Waties Waring was an eighth-generation Charlestonian, the son of a Confederate soldier, scion of a family of slaveholders. He graduated near the top of his class at the College of Charleston, read law under the best tutelage, married a woman from a well-to-do family, hung out his shingle, and built a successful career with little reason to question the society that nurtured him. He did stints as an assistant US attorney and Charleston's city attorney, and in 1942 Waring was nominated by President Franklin Roosevelt for a federal judgeship.

Waties Waring held the enviable security of a lifetime appointment to a high judicial bench, the respect of colleagues, and the adoration of his hometown. His courtroom in the ornate, Second Renaissance Revival–style federal courthouse on Broad Street was just a block or so from his stately home on Meeting Street. But within the polished mahogany grandeur of his chambers, within the tastefully appointed comforts of his home, and within his own heart and mind, Waties Waring had begun to grow uneasy.

Waring's personal and professional transformations occurred around the same time, in the mid-1940s, just as he was settling into his seat in the courthouse. He found that the wide range of cases brought to his courtroom began to open his eyes to aspects of segregated South Carolina law—and Jim Crow injustice—he hadn't paid attention to before. What he had accepted and defended for decades, the routine subjugation and humiliation of Black citizens under the law, began to appear both legally and morally indefensible.

At the same time, Waring exploded his own domestic tranquility. One evening in 1945 he returned home and announced to his wife of thirty-two years that he had fallen in love with another woman and wanted a divorce. He claimed that his marital dissatisfaction was exacerbated by his wife's refusal to share his new race-conscious outlook, but whether or not this rationale explained his motivations, his wife eventually agreed to the divorce. Soon thereafter, Waring married Elizabeth Mills Avery Hoffman, a tall, vivacious, and very opinionated woman he had met playing bridge foursomes.

Charleston society was scandalized: divorce was not even legal in South Carolina at the time (the judge persuaded his stunned wife to move to Florida for ninety days to acquire residency and then file for divorce), and it was certainly not socially acceptable. But what truly angered the judge's family and soon-to-be former friends was that the new Mrs. Waring held extremely liberal, and to their minds, misguided views about race, which she was not shy about sharing. Worst of all: she was a despised Northerner, a Yankee. That was unforgivable. The newlywed Warings were not invited to Charleston dinner parties, or anything else, ever again. But Elizabeth was only part of the reason they were shunned. In his courtroom, Judge Waring had begun to display a new—and, to some observers, alarming—sensitivity to cases involving race.

In February 1944, NAACP attorney Thurgood Marshall, working with the South Carolina NAACP (including Mrs. Clark, who was living in Columbia at the time), had filed suit in federal court challenging the disparity in pay between the state's white and Black teachers. Black teachers not only worked under horrendous conditions in their neglected segregated schools; they were paid about half of the salary of white teachers of similar education and experience. Clark helped gather evidence for the trial, compiling a sheaf of shockingly unequal pay stubs from Black and white teachers.

Even so, Marshall had little expectation of prevailing in the case. He assumed Waring was "just another southern jurist" and that he would have to endure "the usual legal head whipping" in Waring's court before taking the case to the appellate level. "It was the only case I ever tried with my mouth hanging open half the time," Marshall later recalled, because "Judge Waring was so fair." The judge's unexpected fairness forced the school board into a consent decree to equalize teacher pay.

A 1946 criminal case particularly influenced Waring's thinking: the brutal police beating and blinding of a young, Black, decorated war veteran, Sergeant Isaac Woodard, just hours after he was demobilized from the military. Woodard was still wearing his uniform on a bus heading home, displaying a soldierly stature and confidence that annoyed the driver. At the next scheduled stop, the driver alerted the local police chief that he was delivering a troublemaker into the chief's territory. As soon as Woodard stepped off the bus, he was attacked by the police chief, who gouged his eyes out with his blackjack.

The state of South Carolina declined to prosecute the police chief, and only after a loud chorus of complaints (conducted by actor Orson Welles on his nationally broadcast radio show) did the Truman administration bring the police chief to trial in federal court, in Judge Waring's courtroom. Waring was appalled by the trial he presided over: the federal prosecutor did a sloppy, inept job, and the all-white jury acquitted the policeman within minutes. It was a travesty, and it changed Waties Waring. He called it his "baptism of fire" and became convinced that Jim Crow justice was no justice at all.

During the following years, Waring would rule on a series of racial discrimination cases that rocked the underpinnings of white political power in South Carolina. In July 1947 he declared the state Democratic Party's "white" primary illegal, ruling that Black voters could not be prevented from voting in party primaries, which, in states like South Carolina where one party dominated, amounted to the real election. The state legislature tried to defy the ruling by creating the legal fiction that the Democratic Party was simply a private, whites-only club, not a public political entity. Judge Waring struck down that ploy. Then they passed legislation requiring all Black people attempting to enroll in the Democratic Party to sign an oath swearing that they opposed social and educational racial integration. Thurgood Marshall filed suit, and the judge slammed down the oath, too. Waring's rulings infuriated the state's white political establishment but energized the Black community: in the 1948 Democratic primary, the first after the decision, more than thirty thousand Black citizens cast their ballots.

Waring handed down another decision in 1947 finding that the University of South Carolina's law school could not reject a qualified Black applicant on account of race. Waring directed the university to either admit the Black student, close the law school altogether, or provide a new, state-funded law school open to Black students. Desperate to avoid integrating, the university was forced to establish a law school at historically Black South Carolina State. Waring also abolished racial segregation in his courtroom and appointed a Black bailiff to maintain order.

The name Waties Waring soon became an epithet in Charleston. The public pronouncements of his new wife, Elizabeth, blasting the benighted racial attitudes of the city's white establishment, exacerbated the situation. Editorials in the city's main newspaper, the *News and Courier*—whose editor was Waring's nephew—denounced the judge. Petitions called for the judge's impeachment, accusing Waring of advocating "revolution on the part of the Negro against white South Carolina." The KKK burned crosses on the Warings' lawn on Meeting Street. A brick was thrown through the Warings' living room window, landing near the table where they were playing canasta. The state legislature allocated money to buy the couple a one-way ticket out of the state. Charleston representative Mendel Rivers introduced impeachment proceedings against Judge Waring into Congress.

It was around this time, early in 1950, that Septima Clark first met Judge and Elizabeth Waring. Judge Waring was already a hero in the Black community for the surprisingly progressive judicial decisions pouring out of his courtroom. Elizabeth Waring was being vilified, called "the Witch of Meeting Street" by the Charleston newspapers, accused of being a bad influence on her husband. Septima Clark and her colleagues on the board of the Coming Street YWCA, the Negro branch of the Y, decided it might be interesting to invite Mrs. Waring to speak at their annual meeting. The invitation was extended and accepted. Then the uproar began.

The white women of the Charleston Central YWCA administration were livid when they heard about the invitation and insisted that it be quietly rescinded. Mrs. Clark, who was chairwoman of the Coming Street administration committee, refused to disinvite Mrs. Waring. She felt the white women provided no good reason, except their hatred of the judge's wife. Clark was summoned by the Charleston YWCA's white chief executive and presented with a prepared statement to the press claiming the invitation had been sent in error. Clark refused to sign the lie.

The attempt to suppress Elizabeth Waring's talk soon leaked to the press. Now, as Clark described it, the fat was in the fire. Reporters called Henrietta

Street to interview her; letters to the editor filled the pages of the newspapers; rumors of possible violence at the meeting ricocheted around town. Septima was resolute, and mostly calm, even when Judge Waring called to suggest she post strong men at the light switches of the Y meeting room, to guard against the Klan trying to plunge the room into darkness as prelude to an attack. Clark's family was not so calm; they were terrified.

On the night of the annual meeting, Victoria Poinsette sat in the audience watching her daughter, seated on the stage, introduce Elizabeth Waring. Tall imperious, and ferocious, Mrs. Waring launched into a lacerating screed against the "stupidity" and the "selfish and savage white supremacy way of life" of the white Y women who had tried to squelch her talk. She went on to describe white southerners as "sick, confused, and decadent people" who were "full of pride and complacency, morally weak and low."

"White supremacist southerners have done everything to break your spirit," she told her predominantly Black audience, many of whom had never heard a white woman say things like this before. "But your spirits are forged in the furnace of persecution . . . and have risen triumphant."

Elizabeth Waring's speech was truly shocking to her audience. Most especially to Victoria Poinsette, who was convinced that some incensed white person was going to shoot Mrs. Waring, along with Septima, up on the platform. Victoria became, quite literally, paralyzed with fear. She couldn't move her legs; she had to be carried out of the meeting room and driven home to Henrietta Street. Meanwhile, Judge Waring gleefully distributed printed copies of his wife's remarks to the reporters in the room, to make sure they got every word.

That night, the telephone rang so incessantly at Henrietta Street that Septima had to take the receiver off the hook to try to calm her distressed mother. Victoria imagined every nighttime sound as the Klan breaking into the house. In the morning, Elizabeth Waring's verbal assault on southern society had made the headlines, not only in Charleston, but in the national press. The Warings were delighted. Elizabeth was invited to appear on television's *Meet the Press*, where she defended, even amplified, her denunciations.

Septima Clark began to be invited to dine at the Warings' house on Meeting Street.

Shunned by Charleston white society, the Warings began to socialize with the local Black activists they had met in town. They invited their new friends to teas, lunches, and dinners, welcoming them through the front door of their home. When Mrs. Clark began to receive the Warings' invitations, she was both flattered and flustered. She was self-conscious about her appearance, feeling obliged to buy a new dress and have her hair straightened and coifed at the beauty parlor, in preparation for their dinners.

Mrs. Waring invited a friendly reporter and photographer to chronicle these taboo interracial repasts in her dining room. Soon Mrs. Clark appeared in a color photo of a Waring dinner party in the April 29, 1950, issue of *Collier's* magazine, under the headline "The Lonesomest Man in Town." The judge and Mrs. Waring did not look the least bit lonely, surrounded by their Black friends, all smiling and obviously enjoying a spirited conversation. The sympathetic article and provocative photo, mocking every southern racial convention, further enraged white Charleston. To be sure, quite a few Black Charlestonians didn't like it either, and they made that perfectly clear to Mrs. Clark.

After the principal of Clark's school saw her leaving the Warings' house after dinner one Sunday, he paid a visit to her home to warn her that he didn't think "the time was ripe" for such interracial socializing. "That's a dangerous thing to do," he'd said. "How in the world could you do it?"

Clark's friendship with the Warings became the topic of a heated faculty meeting at her school. "They say the reason we want integration is to socialize with them," one teacher yelled at her. And, the colleague continued, pointing an accusing finger, Mrs. Clark was herself proving the white people were right to believe that.

The teacher had hit a nerve. As everyone in the faculty room understood, at the emotional core of white segregationists' arguments for keeping school-children separated was the belief that if Black and white children sat together in classrooms, ate together in lunchrooms, enjoyed the comity of classmates, they would grow too comfortable with one another and view themselves as equals. This would lead directly into friendships and socializing, cascade into inter-racial dating, devolve into intermarriage, and culminate in what segregationists called the "mongrelization" of the white race. The same sophistry was used to argue against adults sitting in proximity on buses or movie theaters or lunch counters. Where Blacks saw desegregation as a matter of equality, dignity, and respect, white segregationists posited it as a matter of pride, power—and sex.

The faculty room erupted in denunciations of Clark's behavior. Mrs. Clark listened and parried with her own interrogation of her colleagues: Do you allow anyone else to decide whom you will marry, what car or dress to buy? No, they answered, annoyed. Well then, Clark calmly replied: "I think I have the right to make my own decisions and select my own friends." This ended the conversation, but not the disapproval of her fellow teachers.

At the same time, Thurgood Marshall and his NAACP Legal Defense team came to view Judge Waring as that rarest of creatures, a fair and even sympathetic southern judge, and tried to steer cases to his court. In 1950, when Marshall brought the *Briggs v. Elliott* case to Waring's court, and the judge surreptitiously called Marshall into his chambers, Waring was certainly aware that the meeting stretched the bounds of judicial protocol—and neutrality. But Judge Waring also surmised that he could neither serve on the federal bench in Charleston nor continue to live peacefully in his native city much longer. He didn't have much to lose.

———◆———

When Judge Waring's chamber door closed behind them, he revealed to Thurgood Marshall the purpose of the secret meeting: "I don't want to hear another separate but equal case," Waring told Marshall. "Bring me a frontal attack on segregation." Marshall was a bit stunned. "We don't think this is the case," Marshall replied, "we don't think this is the time."

Marshall and his colleagues had worked methodically for years to build a legal structure of court victories and case law that could eventually support a powerful NAACP assault on the constitutionality of segregation. Some of his own NAACP colleagues thought he was being too cautious, too slow in his approach. Now here was a federal judge demanding he take a shortcut, upsetting the careful blueprint.

"This is the case and this is the time," Judge Waring insisted.

Waring had been watching recent Supreme Court rulings desegregating graduate schools, and thought he spotted the court's new openness to the idea that racial segregation at all levels of education could no longer be legally justified. The judge had devised a plan: Marshall should withdraw the current *Briggs* suit, then revise and resubmit it. The new pleading would argue not that segregated schools ought to be equal, but that there should be no segregated schools at all. The provision in South Carolina's constitution mandating segregated education violated the Fourteenth Amendment's equal protection clause, and it must be struck down. Similar segregation laws were on the books in seventeen states, so this case could have broad implications. If Marshall provided a more powerful case, Waring would convene a three-judge federal panel to hear it.

"You're going to lose in the three-judge court," Waring explained bluntly to Marshall, knowing that his two federal bench colleagues, who were staunch segregationists, would never agree with the legal premise of the case. It would be a two-to-one ruling, but Waring could write a dissent. "Then you're automatically in the Supreme Court," Waring told Marshall. "That's where you want to be."

Marshall was upset by the judge's insistence that he pivot to such a risky, shoot-for-the-moon strategy but felt he had little choice but to comply. Marshall withdrew the original *Briggs* brief and turned to his legal team to refocus on a larger, more difficult target: segregation itself.

In recasting the *Briggs* suit, the NAACP lawyers supplemented their legal arguments with a new and very controversial element—psychological testing—offering a qualitative assessment of the effect segregated schools have on Black students. Social psychologists Kenneth and Mamie Clark had developed a series of experiments to gauge how being raised in a segregated society warped the self-esteem of Black children. One of their experiments involved dolls—identical except that one had dark skin, one had light—and the Clarks observed how children responded to them. They found that Black children consistently identified with the white dolls and chose them as the "good" dolls, rejecting the dolls of their own skin color as "bad." The damage, subtle but profound, had been done.

On the morning of the trial in May 1951, the parent plaintiffs of Summerton awoke well before dawn, dressed in their Sunday best, and piled into cars and trucks for a caravan into Charleston, intent on witnessing the first day of arguments in the federal courthouse. They stood patiently in a long line with hundreds of other Black people, snaking around the block and spilling into the street, all waiting to get a seat in the courtroom.

Septima Clark wanted to be there to witness this epic legal battle. But she had to be in her classroom. However, her activist friend Ruby Cornwell was first in line at 7 a.m., grabbing a seat in the front row of spectators. In the evening she would report every detail to Mrs. Clark and Mrs. Waring.

The Summerton parents watched Thurgood Marshall and his team present the opening legal arguments against Clarendon County's segregated school system, augmented by expert witnesses and Dr. Kenneth Clark's testimony about the results of his doll tests on their children. The defense lawyer for the

Clarendon school board admitted that the system's Black and white schools were in no way equal but argued that the state was making good-faith efforts to address the imbalance with a new spending plan to upgrade and build better Black school facilities. The trial went on for another grueling day, after which the three judges retired to begin writing their opinions. During the next three weeks, while Judge Waring was writing, his wife fielded a barrage of threatening phone calls to their house, gruff voices warning the couple: "You had better get yourself a bodyguard."

When Waring delivered his written dissent to the court clerk in mid-June, he wrote on the envelope that if he were killed or incapacitated in any way, physically or mentally, before his colleagues finished filing their opinions, his dissent should be made public.

Just as Waring had predicted, the ruling came down, two to one, in favor of the Clarendon school board, with his fellow judges upholding the state laws of segregation. But his dissent, arguing that South Carolina's school segregation laws not only violated the Fourteenth Amendment, but that the *Plessy* doctrine of separate but equal was a sham, made a powerful legal case. "Segregation in education can never produce equality . . . ," Waring wrote. "Segregation is *per se* inequality."

"It is an evil that must be eradicated," Waring went on. "It must go, and must go now."

Thurgood Marshall, defeated but emboldened, carried the *Briggs* case, and Judge Waring's dissent, to the US Supreme Court.

———◆———

Briggs v. Elliott became the first of the five NAACP cases challenging public school segregation to reach the docket of the US Supreme Court. The court decided to bundle them together, with the plaintiff in the Kansas case, Oliver Brown, given lead billing.

The first oral arguments in the *Brown* case were heard at the court in early December 1952. Observing closely, but from a distance, was J. Waties Waring, recently retired from the federal bench. He and Elizabeth had escaped Charleston for New York City after issuing his dissent in the *Briggs* case. In retirement, Judge Waring reviewed drafts of the Marshall team's briefs submitted to the court. Waring's *Briggs* dissent was a pivotal part of Marshall's argument.

After the first hearing, it became clear that the justices were divided in their thinking. Chief Judge Fred Vinson seemed disinclined to topple the *Plessy* precedent. Unable to come to a resolution by the end of the court's term in June 1953, a second round of arguments would be heard in the fall.

But in the fall, Chief Justice Vinson died unexpectedly of a heart attack. President Dwight Eisenhower nominated California governor Earl Warren to the chief justice chair; Warren was viewed as a moderate judicial choice. The case was reargued before the new chief justice in December 1953. For the next six months, the nation waited nervously for a decision.

"I keep my fingers crossed," Mrs. Clark wrote to the Warings in New York. "But I never feel discouraged. I know that each step is a stepping stone in the right direction."

CHAPTER FIVE

Red Roadshow and Black Monday

W hile the nation awaited the Supreme Court decision on *Brown* in March 1954, federal marshals dragged Myles Horton out of a hearing room in New Orleans, writhing and screaming. "They're treating me like a criminal," Horton yelled as the guards put him in a hammerlock, twisted his arms painfully behind his back, pushed him out the door, and threw him onto the hallway's marble floor.

"We know about you," one of the marshals sneered, "and were warned that you would have to be thrown out. You are dangerous, and we know it."

In the hallway, Horton stood up, straightened his eyeglasses, smoothed his wrinkled suit jacket, and assumed the posture of a proud, if shaken, martyr. He had just been ejected from what was called the "Red Roadshow"—the sordid witch-hunting performances of Senator James O. Eastland of Mississippi. Eastland was one of the Senate's most vociferous segregationists, who had recently found a profitable platform mixing his fixations on white supremacy with the jitters of the Red Scare.

Eastland's Internal Security subcommittee of the Senate Judiciary Committee was the poor cousin of the House's more famous Un-American Activities Committee, and the jealous sibling of the Permanent Subcommittee on Investigation of the Senate's Government Operations Committee, chaired by the grandstanding junior senator from Wisconsin, Joseph McCarthy. McCarthy had garnered all the fame, all the headlines, with his ruthless, reckless, and often groundless accusations of Communist infiltration in all branches of government, the military, the press, and the arts. Willfully wrecking lives and careers, McCarthy's name would become the synecdoche for this era of congressionally sanctioned terror known as the Red Scare.

Eastland saw an opportunity to grab some of McCarthy's spotlight by holding his own sensational hearings down south—he was running for reelection in the fall, and it could be helpful. He also wanted to stifle the calls for racial desegregation he heard growing louder. If Eastland could target and malign the southern white leaders of this racial equality coalition, drag them through the mud, and douse them with the red paint of Communist affiliation, he might make them, and their cause, toxic to any true-blooded American.

Senator Eastland staged his down-market version of a McCarthy hearing in New Orleans during three days in mid-March 1954. Horton was served with a subpoena, as were three of his longtime colleagues in the social justice cause in the South. All of them had close ties to the Highlander School.

One of Senator Eastland's targets was Virginia Durr, a Highlander board member and national leader of a campaign to abolish the poll tax. She and her husband, Clifford, had returned to his hometown of Montgomery after their stint in Washington as Roosevelt New Dealers, but their outspoken criticisms of white hegemony in their native region, combined with Clifford's legal defense of Black activists fighting Jim Crow, made the couple very unpopular in Alabama. Eastland's subpoena to Virginia carried an additional barbed hook: her sister was married to Supreme Court justice Hugo Black, who, very soon, would be deciding the *Brown* case and the fate of segregation in the South. It was widely rumored that Justice Black, a fellow southerner, was inclined to weigh in on the side of desegregating the South's schools. If Jim Eastland could insinuate that Hugo Black's own sister-in-law was a Communist agent, a Communist dupe, or at least a sympathetic fellow traveler, the stench could envelop Justice Black and the court's decision as well. Horton and the others decided they would not cooperate with Eastland's sham show trial.

Virginia Durr took the stand, but in protest of what she considered an illegitimate investigation, she remained defiantly mute. Her performance infuriated Eastland, which was very satisfying to her. She went so far as to take out her compact to powder her nose on the stand while the questions were being thrown at her. Eastland's committee also paraded a string of paid informers and well-compensated "expert witnesses" to the stand, who made a lucrative living serving up fabulist tales of Communist conspiracies and cabals.

On the third and final day of the hearing, Horton was called to the stand. As planned, he denied all allegations that he was ever a member of the Communist Party or that Highlander was associated with it, and he refused to answer many questions. He sought to explain the legal and moral basis of his refusal by reading a prepared statement into the record. Senator Eastland was not interested in his reasons and refused to allow Horton to read the statement.

Over the pounding of Eastland's gavel, Horton began to read aloud his statement, a manifesto on conscience and constitutional rights, a righteous rebuttal of Eastland's attempt to brand opposition to segregation as subversive and Communist.

"Take him out. Throw him out," Eastman bellowed. "We are not going to have any self-serving declarations."

The wire service photographers captured Horton being hustled out in the marshals' tight grip, and the photo ran the next day on the front page, above the fold, of the Sunday *New York Times*, accompanied by an article and a follow-up piece later that week. Reports on the hearing, and Horton's forcible ejection, were published around the country, including in Septima Clark's hometown paper, the *Charleston News and Courier*.

At first Horton felt a surge of satisfaction about his performance—he had taken a principled stand, he had not backed down—but his elation quickly evaporated. The extensive newspaper coverage paired the words "Communist" and "Highlander" in print: "Ejected Witness Denies He Is a Red" was the *New York Times'* headline, linking the two in the minds of readers, despite all Horton's passionate denials. That ink would be hard to erase. Eastland had also accomplished his goal of implying that Justice Hugo Black was somehow compromised by his sister-in-law Virginia Durr: "Justice Black Kin Accused of Pro-Red Acts," trumpeted the *Chicago Tribune*.

Eastland also took revenge, holding Horton in contempt of Congress and threatening him with imprisonment. Eastland further insinuated he might begin investigating Highlander's tax-exempt status. This could cripple Highlander. Had Horton been righteous or reckless? When Horton returned home, he had to explain to Zilphia and the children that he would likely be going to jail for a year. The kids enjoyed making a little game of planning how their dad should spend his time behind bars, choosing the books they would send to him, but the strain on Zilphia was obvious.

Horton also realized that the newspaper coverage would lead to awkward phone calls and notes from his board, and more ominously, from his funders: the individuals who sent regular checks and the philanthropic foundations that fueled Highlander's major programs. In the foul McCarthy-era atmosphere of guilt by association, they would be understandably nervous about any connection with an organization tinted with red in the press.

He had to explain; he had to justify his actions at the hearing. He held meetings with Highlander's staff and the Monteagle community, mailed a long letter to all "Friends of Highlander," and made visits to his donors. He went to Washington seeking advice from his old Chattanooga friend, Estes Kefauver, on how to deal with the contempt-of-Congress threat. Kefauver—who'd been Highlander's lawyer before he went into politics—promised to protect Horton from Senator Eastland's wrath. Horton also asked some of his allies, the ones with distinguished positions or recognizable names, to pen statements of support for his stand against Eastland. The most valuable of these came from Eleanor Roosevelt, long a steadfast supporter who mailed a $100 check to Highlander every year: "I want to congratulate you on your statement," she wrote to Horton. "We need courage in these difficult days, and I feel your statement shows just that."

All through the spring, Horton solicited more letters of support, wrote more letters of explanation, dictated personal appeals into the recording machine. "We need all the help we can get to counteract the bad publicity, which is widespread," Horton wrote to a friend. "If something is not done soon, people in the South will be afraid to take a stand against segregation."

———— ◆ ————

Eight weeks after the Eastland hearings, on a Monday in mid-May, Chief Justice Warren stepped to the microphones to announce the decision of the court.

Warren had taken the assignment of drafting the majority opinion himself and had worked hard to bring around those of his colleagues who were inclined to dissent. For the good of the nation, a decision of this magnitude needed to be firm and unanimous, Chief Justice Warren told his colleagues.

"We conclude . . . unanimously . . . that in the field of public education the doctrine of 'separate but equal' has no place," Warren announced. "Segregated educational facilities are inherently unequal."

Warren had inserted the word "unanimously" by hand into his reading copy of the decision, it was not in the official text. "When the word 'unanimously' was spoken," Justice Warren later recalled, "a wave of emotion swept the room;

no words or intentional movement, yet a distinct emotional manifestation that defies description."

Sitting at the lawyers' table, Thurgood Marshall realized that without explicitly citing Judge Waring's dissent in the *Briggs* case, Warren was clearly echoing the wording of that dissent, making it the centerpiece of the court's rationale.

As news of the decision spread, Black leaders and editorialists hailed the decision. The nationally circulated *Chicago Defender* stopped the presses to put out a special edition—"Extra, Extra, Extra: Kill Jim Crow Schools"—and later ran an editorial proclaiming, "Neither the atom bomb nor the hydrogen bomb will ever be as meaningful to our democracy as the unanimous decision of the Supreme Court...."

Veteran educator and civil rights champion Mary McLeod Bethune went on live radio that afternoon: "I rejoice as a pioneer in the field that I have lived to hear with my own ears and see with my own eyes and feel with my own heart this great, inevitable decision.... America may hold her head higher now among the nations."

But on the floor of the US Senate in Washington, James Eastland of Mississippi bellowed, "the South will not abide by nor obey this legislative decision by a political body." Senator Harry Byrd of Virginia called the decision the "most serious blow that has yet been struck against the rights of states."

In Atlanta, Governor Herman Talmadge denounced the ruling, reiterating his vow that "there never will be mixed schools while I am governor." And in the US House, Senator Eastland's Mississippi colleague Representative John Bell Williams labeled the day of the decision "Black Monday."

The Warings' Fifth Avenue apartment was the place New York City's civil rights community celebrated that night. NAACP executives Walter White and Roy Wilkins were there, sipping champagne and offering toasts to the *Brown* decision and Judge Waring's part in shaping it.

Walter White lifted his glass and said that when he'd learned of the decision earlier in the day, "I thought of Waties. I thought of the pounding he took when he wrote the dissenting position in South Carolina . . . and the night they stoned your house." White also saluted the bravery of the Black parents of Clarendon County, who "took a stand even though to take such a stand might have meant death at almost any time. They had the courage to stand up."

In Summerton, Clarendon County, no reporters asked Eliza Briggs for her reaction to the Supreme Court's vindication, but she would remember feeling "really happy and glad that we didn't lose our case." Her husband Harry, who was still trying to find work, was optimistic: "Well, I said, that's it. I guess we'll have freedom from now on."

CHAPTER SIX

Radical Hillbilly

T he idea of Highlander had come to him in a dream, on Christmas night
1931. He was on a yearlong sojourn in Denmark, deep in his searching
period, the restless quest of a young man looking for purpose. Myles Horton
was a son of the Cumberland mountains; his family was poor, but so were all
their neighbors. His parents had instilled the values of church, community, and
education in their sons, and Myles had worked his way through high school and
college, taking up manual labor, earning money as a YWCA youth organizer
and a Presbyterian vacation bible school supervisor. As he traveled through his
native rural Tennessee, he noticed the exploitation of farmers and workers, the
collapse of their hope, the withering of their spirit. He decided he wanted to
do something to help.

In the fall of 1929, when he was twenty-four years old, Horton entered
Union Theological Seminary in New York City to explore the role of religion
in building a more just society. He read widely—everything from the Gospels
to Marx and Lenin, William James and John Dewey—and forged a lifelong
bond with radical Christian theologian Reinhold Niebuhr. But Horton decided
he was not cut out for the ministry, rejecting church structures he viewed as
more invested in perpetuating the status quo than advancing moral living. In
1930 Horton transferred to the University of Chicago and spent a graduate year
studying sociology, but these formal studies did not satisfy his needs either; he
chafed at the orthodoxies and bureaucratic hierarchies of traditional education.
He wanted to devote himself to something else but didn't know what.

Horton was still fascinated by moral and spiritual development and in the
problems of the rural working class, the world in which he'd been raised. He
heard about something called the Danish Folk School movement, so he went
abroad to live in the small towns, the fishing and farming villages, where such
schools were thriving. Local people came together to sing folk songs, read their
own history and poetry, discuss their common economic and social problems,

and cooperate to bring about practical, not pie-in-the-sky, fixes. Horton found the process remarkable: it was church and school, town meeting, folk concert, and labor rally rolled into one. He wanted to implement this model back home, so on that Christmas night he sketched out a vision of what a school like this could look like transplanted to the Appalachian hills.

"I can't sleep, but there are dreams," he wrote in his journal that night. "What you must do is go back, get a simple place, move in and you are there. The situation is there. You start this and let it grow. You know your goal. It will build its own structure and take its own form. You can go to school all your life you'll never figure it out because you are trying to get an answer that can only come from the people in the life situation."

Horton returned to America to refine his folk school concept with advice from knowledgeable education advisers, including innovator John Dewey and settlement house pioneer Jane Addams of Hull House in Chicago. He teamed up with a like-minded southern idealist named Don West, and they found a sympathetic benefactor in Dr. Lilian Johnson, a retired professor who allowed the pair to experiment with their idea on her farm in Monteagle, Tennessee. They had found their place, and they christened it "Highlander Folk School" in honor of the rugged mountain people they hoped to help.

Like a patient fisherman, Myles Horton would let a Highlander workshop discussion spool out into far waters, then expertly reel it back in. He used his bespoke version of the Socratic method to draw out the participants, probe and challenge them, get at the nut of their thinking. His manner was gentle and folksy, but his questions were pointed, and he often injected a contradiction or complication to shake up complacent thinking. His devil's advocate provocations kept things lively, and sometimes it got loud. The goal was always to get people thinking, challenge them, pull them out of their mental ruts, expand their perspective, guide them onto unfamiliar, even uncomfortable, paths.

Horton had developed his unorthodox pedagogy by trial and error through the years, mixing his theoretical readings and life experiences into a kind of potent, mountain moonshine educational brew. He was determined not to dictate answers to those who came to Highlander—he saw himself as no more than a guide in their process of articulating their problems and finding solutions together. The education offered at Highlander was not merely for personal edification, it was education for action.

From the very beginning, Horton put the concept of democratic living and equality of the races into practice by ensuring his students worked and boarded together. When skeptics questioned the wisdom of his integrated campus, Horton would explain with cheeky sincerity: "Highlander is just too poor to be segregated. We can't afford two toilets, two dining rooms, two tables. We're poor and just have to mix everybody up." He was very proud of running the school in complete violation of the state's segregation laws. He enjoyed his role as a "Radical Hillbilly."

By the summer of 1954, Myles and Zilphia had been operating Highlander for more than two decades, through times of economic depression, world war, and labor strife. But as the *Brown* decision forced the nation to confront a racial reckoning whose dimensions were still unknown, the Hortons felt both energized and on edge. Myles had to deal with political and financial repercussions, while Zilphia contended with the emotional consequences.

Every unfamiliar car driving up to the Highlander compound after the Eastland hearings caused a spasm of fear to rip through Zilphia's stomach. Was this a federal marshal coming to arrest Myles for contempt of Congress? Zilphia was used to the threats and harassment Highlander attracted: the FBI snoops, the mine and mill bosses' goons, the Grundy County Crusaders who had marched on the mountain to protect the neighborhood from the "reds" of Highlander. The schoolteachers in Monteagle who called her daughter "Comrade Charis" and told the child to go home to "those n— kids you live with." The panic of having to rush the children to the house of a friendly neighbor when an attack on the compound was threatened. As much as anyone could get used to such things, shrug them off, Zilphia did. But this latest threat to Myles, from a vengeful US senator, unnerved her. Zilphia steadied herself by singing. Every evening she took up her accordion or dulcimer and taught new workshop groups the song that had become Highlander's anthem, "We Shall Overcome."

CHAPTER SEVEN

Prepare

I n the fall of 1954, Charleston's Black schoolchildren carried the flyer home to their parents in their book bags. Men and women visiting the Negro branches of the Y picked up a copy in the lobby. There were stacks of the announcement at many Black churches after Sunday services, on tables at the Black union halls, in the barber shops, beauty parlors, and grocery stores.

"Where do YOU stand on DESEGREGATION?" the flyers asked in bold letters. In the first days of the school year, the Black citizens of Charleston were asked this question by the officers of their local NAACP. It was not a simple question. "Are you getting emotionally and intelligently prepared for the practical application of the Supreme Court Decision of May 17th?"

Yet Black communities across the South were working in a vacuum. While the *Brown* decision had struck down the legal basis of school segregation, the justices put off discussing any specific remedies, time frame, or manner of enforcement until the next term. White southerners welcomed this year of delay as breathing room—an interlude when nothing needed to be done to advance desegregation—but it placed Black students, parents, and teachers in an uncomfortable limbo.

Without a timetable or clear enforcement procedures forthcoming from the court, southern state NAACP leaders had to decide how to move forward. As the school year began, the Charleston branch needed to inform and prepare its community, so it called everyone together for a mass meeting.

One of Mrs. Clark's projects during the summer had been to help arrange this forum, and she would be one of the speakers, presenting what she had learned about organizing for school desegregation at Highlander.

But the flyer lying on the kitchen tables of the Black homes of Charleston also dared say out loud what many were quietly thinking: the *Brown* decision was about more than just integrating schools. It portended the integration of all other aspects of public life.

"How will we accept it when it comes to all restaurants, theaters, golf courses, at the Bus Station, on the City Buses?" the meeting announcement continued. "Desegregation is coming no matter how you personally feel—how prepared are YOU for it?" Truth was, few were prepared. For most Black South Carolinians, desegregation was still a hazy and unsettling dream.

The school mass meeting was just one of Mrs. Clark's recent projects to spur community involvement in desegregation, fulfilling her Highlander promise to organize at home. She was speaking at churches, PTA meetings, and women's groups, writing op-ed articles and reports while keeping up her usual frenetic schedule of civic committees—as well as teaching her seventh graders. "I'm busy as ever, calmly fighting this segregation issue," Clark happily reported to the Warings in New York.

While Mrs. Clark was drumming up support for desegregating Charleston's schools, the white citizens of Indianola, Mississippi, were meeting to respond to the threat of Black children entering their own children's classrooms. About a hundred of the area's most influential planters, bankers, lawyers, and government officials met in the Indianola town hall in mid-July to form the first White Citizens' Council to defend segregation and the "southern way of life." The idea spread very quickly to other towns and other states.

———◆———

The South Carolina NAACP wanted to celebrate Judge Waring's contributions to the *Brown* decision and racial progress with a tribute banquet in November 1954. The Warings had sworn they would not return to Charleston until segregation was ended, but they agreed to attend this event. Mrs. Clark was helping plan every detail of the banquet, from the plates and silverware to the menu and flowers.

When the Warings arrived at the Charleston train station, they were greeted by several hundred cheering Black citizens. The aggrieved response of white Charlestonians toward Judge Waring's return was captured in a ditty published in the newspaper: "Seems like some coloreds acting smarty / Is giving him a nigger party." The gymnasium of the Buist elementary school was packed with more than three hundred local, state, and national civil rights activists eager to show their appreciation to "Our Judge." Mrs. Clark sat at a head table, clapping vigorously for every encomium tendered to the judge, feeling a swell of pride as he accepted an engraved bronze plaque of thanks. The Warings were deeply moved by the tribute: "Elizabeth and I were overjoyed at the love and affection shown by our people."

The following day, the Warings stepped into Septima Clark's living room for a celebratory luncheon with a few "freedom loving friends," as Clark described the occasion. The visit meant a great deal to Septima. Lorene could only hope the neighbors didn't notice. After that visit, as they had previously vowed, the Warings would never set foot in Charleston again.

————— ✦ —————

On election day, November 2, 1954, just days before attending the Warings' banquet, Esau Jenkins was on the ballot for the district school board election. Making good on his promise, he had begun his campaign as soon as he had returned from Highlander in August, rallying his family, friends, and Progressive Club members to collect the one hundred signatures necessary to qualify for a spot on the ballot. He began knocking on doors, rousing his bus passengers, church congregants, PTA members, and Moving Star Hall neighbors to register, with the exciting chance to vote for one of their own for the first time. There were three white men also running for the school board seat, and Jenkins knew he didn't have a chance, but winning wasn't the point.

On election day, one Johns islander emerged from the polling place astonished: "Man, Esau Jenkins' name on that voting machine," he told his buddies. "You better go on down there and vote." And they did: of the 200 Black Johns Island citizens registered to vote in 1954, 192 voted for Jenkins. But there were still 450 registered white voters on Johns, so Jenkins placed third, ahead of one of the white candidates. A very respectable showing, but he would need more Black voters if he ever hoped to win that seat.

After the Waring banquet, Esau Jenkins welcomed Zilphia Horton into his home on Johns Island, which raised eyebrows. What was a white woman doing sleeping in Esau and Janie's house? This was unheard of on Johns Island, where few mainlanders, Black or white, ever ventured to the island. Esau had been to the Hortons' house, and he thought they should visit his. He was not ashamed of his humble home, or his impoverished island. If they were serious about trying to help him and his community, they should see it for themselves. The Hortons accepted the invitation, not only as an act of courtesy but one of due diligence: they needed to decide if Jenkins and his island were suitable prospects for a new Highlander project, a grant-funded experiment to train rural community leaders; ultimately, Myles couldn't get away, but Zilphia was glad to make the scouting expedition.

Esau smoothed some of those elevated brows when he brought Zilphia to church with him on Sunday morning. He drove her, with Janie and the children, to Wesley Methodist in his bus, picking up parishioners along the way. Zilphia met with students in the Sunday school, joined the congregation for services in the chapel, and spoke to the Ladies' Auxiliary. When Esau and the pastor invited Zilphia to sing at the service, she won over any skeptics in the pews with her soulful renditions of hymns and spirituals.

Zilphia spent two days and nights with the Jenkins, forging a sympathetic bond with Janie. Esau and Janie were a team, just like she and Myles, working together for a better world while trying to sustain a marriage and raise a family. Janie supported Esau in all his community work, managed the various business ventures, and tended to their house, garden, and children. She was the family anchor. The Jenkins were determined to put every one of their children through high school and college; two of the older girls were already graduated and working as teachers, two sons were serving in the military, and the rest, including a toddler, were still at home.

All the while, Zilphia was observing Esau, taking stock of how he kept his finger on the pulse of his community, how he worked with his neighbors, and how they responded to him. She was impressed with his energy, his passion, his sense of mission, and believed Johns Island could be a promising place for developing local Black leadership.

Zilphia returned to Charleston, staying the night with Septima on Henrietta Street before heading back to Monteagle. A few weeks later, Septima and Esau smoothed the way for Myles to visit and meet with a variety of island residents—teachers, farmers, fishermen, and clergymen—on front porches, at a meeting of Jenkins's Progressive Club in Moving Star Hall, and at small gatherings in the Jenkins' living room.

Clark and Jenkins served as Horton's interpreters and guides into the closed, and understandably wary, island society. White men rarely, if ever, came to the island with benevolent intent, so a white fellow from Tennessee snooping around would naturally arouse alarm. Only Johns Islanders' trust in Jenkins and their affection for their former teacher, Miss Seppie, allowed Horton entry into the Sea Island world. Even then, it would take time for them to warm to him. Horton required some translation assistance, too, as he had a hard time understanding the Gullah phrases and strong accents he encountered.

Mrs. Clark also arranged for Horton to speak to the Charleston County Black teachers association about desegregation and political action, emphasizing the importance of increasing Black voter registration. These were Septima's teacher colleagues, from the city and the islands, many of them either politically apathetic or truly frightened. They feared for their jobs, as they enjoyed no tenure protections and could be summarily dismissed for "agitation." Clark hoped Horton's persuasive presentation could allay the teachers' fears. But the principal of the school where the meeting was held was soon fired for allowing the group—discussing such explosive topics—to convene in his school.

This visit was only the first of many trips the Hortons would make to the island in the next months, sometimes bringing their children. Staying with the Jenkins helped Myles acclimate and immerse himself in the island's culture, it gave him a passport for acceptance. He went fishing with the island men, cut cabbages in the fields, helped load trucks, dandled children on his knee, sat in church and Moving Star Hall, all the while talking to the islanders about their lives and troubles. Myles needed to understand this place, earn the trust of the islanders, learn what they needed and wanted, get a better handle on how Highlander could help. He couldn't just parachute in and prescribe solutions. The answers had to emerge from the people, and he could barely understand what they were saying. It would be a slow, often frustrating, but essential acclimation process.

Esau would tell Myles, over and over again, exactly what his island needed: a school for teaching adults reading and learning how to vote. A school that would prepare them to become proud citizens who wanted better things. That was the basic thing—not the only thing—but the key to everything else.

CHAPTER EIGHT

Deliberate Speed

T hrough late 1954 and early 1955, the nation was waiting for the other shoe to drop. Waiting for the Supreme Court to tell the American people just how the *Brown* decision should be implemented by the states and school districts. The justices, having made their legal philosophy clear in their initial opinion the previous May, were purposefully vague on the practical aspects of the remedy, kicking the issue down the road into the spring 1955 docket. The waiting only intensified tensions, with both opponents and supporters of racial segregation staking out their ground, even if it wasn't clear how the court might alter the contours of the terrain.

During those months, Thurgood Marshall and the other NAACP attorneys presented additional arguments to the court, and there was hope in the civil rights community that the justices would issue a decisive desegregation mandate, including an immediate start and strict implementation deadlines. A firm stance would signal that the court was serious about protecting Black citizens' constitutional rights and was not going to tolerate delay or obstruction in obeying the law.

Attorneys for the school board defendants in the *Brown* case, joined by the attorney generals of other southern states, argued that they should be allowed to go about desegregating as they saw fit, at their own pace. They insisted the court should impose no specific directives, no date for beginning, no deadline for completing the process, little oversight. To disrupt treasured southern traditions and social patterns too quickly would be traumatic—for white people.

The court itself was unsure of how to proceed. The five cases bundled into *Brown* were based in four different states and the District of Columbia, each dealing with different local circumstances. The justices doubted they could design a one-size-fits-all solution. And given the vitriolic reaction to the *Brown* decree in the South so far, they were nervous about inflaming the situation further. The justices were also feeling pressure from President Eisenhower, who never supported the *Brown* decision, and who, facing reelection, didn't want anything to further rile white southerners' anger.

Septima Clark and Esau Jenkins just couldn't stand still and wait for the Supreme Court to quit dallying—they had too much real desegregation work to do. In the early months of 1955, Septima continued to use her positions on Charleston's segregated civic and charity boards—the YWCA, Community Chest, Tuberculosis Society—to press from within for change. Maintaining separate white and Black boards and facilities was not only insulting, she argued, but a waste of organizational energy and resources. But she found few allies willing to join her in a revolt.

Mrs. Clark was also working part-time for Highlander, conducting research on Johns Island for a handbook on rural leadership. She set up more opportunities for the Hortons and Highlander staff to come to the islands, working directly with Mr. Jenkins on raising political awareness by arranging conferences and workshops, panel discussions, and kitchen table conversations. Gradually, more islanders began to show interest, especially the younger generation, who had obtained a high school education, perhaps attended college, or had come home from military service in Korea restless for change. Farmers and fishermen, ministers and maids started turning out for meetings about leadership and voting. In the process, they also discussed health care, housing, jobs, and education. Zilphia brought her instruments and songs, Myles brought his folksy, probing questions, and the islanders grew a bit more comfortable with the Hortons from Tennessee.

Septima also worked as a Highlander scout, identifying islanders with the potential to be trained as neighborhood leaders and convincing them to attend a summer workshop at Highlander. Myles had already come to the realization that Clark and Jenkins were Highlander's best hope for recruiting more Lowcountry Black people to Monteagle: not the professors, clergy, and elite Black professionals who were already drawn to Highlander, but the ordinary Black folks who were, he was certain, going to have to fight for desegregation and voter rights on the ground.

In one month, Septima made ten trips to Johns Island, gathering information for the handbook, interviewing fourteen prospective community leaders, and drumming up Highlander recruits at Sunday church services. Mrs. Clark was in frequent contact, by phone or letter, with the Highlander staff in Tennessee, and she enjoyed the sense of team spirit and belonging she had forged with them. So when Myles asked if she would consider running several of the workshops at Highlander the following summer, she was more than pleased to accept. It would mean being away from Charleston for several months, and she wouldn't be able to teach summer school as she usually did to supplement her income, but Highlander promised to match her $500 pay, plus cover her expenses. She would also have to cajole Lorene into lending her old Chevrolet to drive the island recruits to Monteagle, but she would work that out.

In the meantime, Jenkins was busy perfecting his new voter registration system, an outgrowth of his run for school board. He had spurred many islanders to vote for him, and now he wanted to capture that momentum, encouraging each voter to recruit two more Black islanders willing to register. He was running a contest in his new Citizens' Club—an expanded version of the Progressive Club, focused on voting and political action—with prizes for those who brought in the most new registrants. After new recruits were prepared to take the literacy test, usually by memorizing the passages, Esau would drive about twelve of them to the registrar's office each month. Escorting small groups to register would avoid raising suspicions among whites, and the cumulative effect could be powerful. He planned to run again for school board. He already had fifty new voters on the books since the new year.

On the last day of May 1955, as Septima Clark was finishing her classroom teaching and finalizing plans for the summer workshops she was to direct at Highlander, Chief Justice Earl Warren announced the Supreme Court's follow-up to its *Brown* decision, the implementation decree that came to be called *Brown* II.

The court affirmed its judgment that school segregation was unconstitutional and called for a "prompt and reasonable start to full compliance." But it set no date or even time frame for beginning the process, no deadline for achieving desegregation, no benchmarks for progress. Instead it returned the five *Brown* cases to the lower federal district courts from which they had come—the same courts that had denied the Black petitioners and had upheld school segregation—leaving it to them to determine whether school districts were desegregating "with all deliberate speed." The oxymoronic phrase, a version of "make haste slowly," captured the ambivalence of the high court as the nine justices searched for compromise among themselves and within a fractured nation.

The *Brown* II edict was a profound disappointment to Thurgood Marshall, the NAACP, and the broader civil rights community. It was a gift to segregationists, who now felt emboldened to stonewall, or even openly resist desegregating their schools, with little or no consequence. When asked by reporters for his interpretation of what "all deliberate speed" meant, Marshall replied: "SLOW."

Trying hard to present a positive face to the press, Marshall took comfort in the idea that the original *Brown* decision still stood: School segregation was unconstitutional. The court hadn't backed down on the fundamentals. But *Brown* II slammed on the brakes, making broad school desegregation much harder to accomplish. The NAACP would have to fight each individual recalcitrant school district. Parents would have to sign petitions demanding desegregation in their children's schools, exposing themselves to great danger and enduring protracted trials. It would be very costly to pursue all these cases— in time, money, and, possibly, lives. But the NAACP pledged to do it.

That night, Septima commiserated over the phone with her friends the Warings in New York City. Like so many others, she was upset by the court's lack of urgency, and its lack of decisiveness, accommodating the complaints of white segregationists at the expense of the rights and welfare of Black children.

Judge Waring was also disappointed by the court's hedging in *Brown* II. In his *Briggs* dissent he had written "segregation must go, and it must go now," but the Supreme Court, which had accepted his constitutional reasoning, now spurned his urgent remedy. A year ago, he had honestly thought that after some kicking and screaming the southern states would reluctantly obey the *Brown* ruling and that any state that refused would be punished. But *Brown* II made it seem like the court had capitulated to the tantrums and threats of Jim Crow's apologists.

The judge understood the ramifications of the court's hesitance: how much more difficult the road ahead would be for achieving school desegregation. He was also cognizant of the human toll. All those brave Black people who had stuck out their necks as plaintiffs in the landmark civil rights cases decided in his courtroom would continue to suffer.

Many of the *Briggs* suit parents, having lost their livelihoods and homes, were forced to move out of state, their families scattered. George Elmore, the grocery store businessman in Columbia who had brought his case challenging the South Carolina Democratic white primary to Judge Waring's court, was punished with not only Klan harassment but financial ruin. Elmore was denied credit by local banks, suppliers cut off deliveries to his store, and he was bankrupted. His wife suffered a nervous breakdown from the stress and had to be institutionalized, his children sent north to live with relatives. A few years later, he died, a penniless and broken man.

Mrs. Clark was comforted by the phone conversation with Judge Waring, who reassured her that no matter the inadequacies of *Brown* II, the original ruling still stood as the law. Yes, school integration might take longer to achieve, but it was up to the people to make it happen. The court's enforcement failure might finally awaken Black citizens who'd been complacent before.

"It's always good to talk to you," Clark wrote to the Warings the next day. "It peps us up and seems to allay doubts and fears." She carried the Warings' message of encouragement and commitment to her colleagues: "All day at school, and with other groups, I flashed your words," she reported.

"Now that the Supreme Court has opened a door for you," she had repeated to her community that day, echoing the judge's admonition, "it's up to you to work harder than ever, and walk through that opened door."

CHAPTER NINE

The Woman from Montgomery

T he woman seemed so anxious, Mrs. Clark noticed on the first day of the workshop in the summer of 1955. The slight, fortysomething woman who had come to Highlander by bus from Alabama would hardly say a word. She was mum in the workshop, reticent even in the dining room. She was certainly attentive, taking detailed notes on the discussions, writing on lined notebook paper, her head bent down. She listened, but she wouldn't participate. Clark, leading her first school desegregation workshop at Highlander, was trying to figure out how to reach this woman, how to draw her out, put her at ease.

Septima knew that the woman was a leader in the NAACP in Montgomery, secretary of the chapter, director of the youth council, and was recommended for a scholarship by a white Highlander board member, Virginia Durr. She seemed quite intelligent and well-spoken—when she did speak—but she was timorous. Behind her rimless glasses her eyes were bright and inquisitive, but there was also a look of quiet despair.

Mrs. Rosa McCauley Parks was indeed nervous about being at Highlander. Her husband, Raymond, though he was also a committed civil rights activist, wasn't altogether pleased about her going to this strange place in the Tennessee mountains. She couldn't tell her boss at the Montgomery Fair department store, where she worked as a seamstress, why she was taking two weeks off without pay. She was fearful of people back home learning she had come here; the harassment of her family might increase.

But Virginia Durr, who recommended her, and Edgar Daniel (E. D.) Nixon, longtime Brotherhood of Sleeping Car Porters organizer and NAACP leader in Montgomery, had encouraged her to go, believing she would benefit from the open and optimistic atmosphere of Highlander. They knew she was depressed by the intractable racial problems in her city, exhausted by the years she'd devoted to the cause of racial justice with little to show for her efforts.

Mrs. Parks had come to know Virginia Durr by sewing for her family. The Durrs were having a hard time in Montgomery, owing to their involvement in civil rights work and Clifford's legal defense cases for Black clients. They were ostracized by Montgomery's white society, and Clifford's law practice was struggling. Virginia's family regularly sent hand-me-down clothes to the Durrs' three daughters, and Virginia hired Mrs. Parks, whom she knew through Montgomery civil rights circles, to alter the dresses for her children. In the privacy of the Durrs' home, while Parks was sewing, the two women had long talks about racial issues in the city, sharing their frustration with the lack of progress. When Myles Horton told Durr he had a scholarship available for a desegregation strategy workshop, she suggested Mrs. Parks.

Rosa Parks had been deeply involved in the Montgomery NAACP chapter for more than a decade. She had been strenuously resisting Jim Crow oppression all her life. She demonstrated this in small acts of defiance: she refused to drink from designated "colored" water fountains; would not abide by the demeaning ritual of paying her bus fare in front, then having to reenter through the back door. Sometimes, on a crowded bus, she even balked at having to move to the back seats, protesting just long enough to make the point.

She and her husband were intensely involved in voter registration drives, anti-lynching campaigns, desegregation initiatives. Raymond Parks had been fighting racial injustice issues since the Scottsboro Boys case, the Alabama teenagers wrongfully convicted of rape in 1931; he worked for years to free them. Raymond was a barber, and his barber's chair was an organizing platform. The Parks' apartment in the Cleveland Court public housing was the place for civil rights meetings any night of the week. Mrs. Parks taught her NAACP Youth Council teenagers to assert themselves, too. She cheered them when they demanded to borrow books from the segregated downtown public library, urged them to write letters to their legislators. She took them to the Freedom Train—the US government's touring patriotic education exhibit—when it rolled into Montgomery in 1948. She insisted that they be able to view the cornerstone documents of American democracy alongside, not separate from, white children, and she led them in.

Forming a dynamic partnership with E. D. Nixon, Mrs. Parks deftly handled the administration of the Montgomery NAACP chapter, helping expand its activities and take a more aggressive role in the community. Parks also traveled through the city and around the state documenting incidents of brutality and injustice against Black people, collecting testimony in an effort to seek legal redress. But there was rarely any justice.

The pervasive discrimination, humiliation, and violence endured by her neighbors, especially the sexual violence suffered by Black women, enraged her. The failure of the justice system to protect Black citizens embittered her. The resigned acceptance of all this by her community, so demoralized by years of oppression, frustrated her. Beneath her shy and demure demeanor, Mrs. Parks was seething.

By the time she arrived at Highlander in late July 1955, she described herself as "rather tense and maybe somewhat bitter over the struggle that we were in." She was so nervous about making the trip to Highlander that she asked Virginia Durr to accompany her on the bus on the first leg of the journey, as far as Atlanta. "Just getting on the bus, I found myself going farther and farther away from surroundings that I was used to, and seeing less and less of black people," she remembered. She hadn't realized Highlander was run by white people until she arrived.

Everyone at Highlander was welcoming, but Parks still didn't feel comfortable talking about racial matters around white people. Clark was the only Black person on the Highlander staff, and the forty-eight people attending the workshop were evenly mixed between Black and white participants. "I was somewhat withdrawn and didn't have very much to say," Parks recalled. A lifetime of confronting hostile whites had left deep scars. Clark understood this. Highlander was a new and somewhat bewildering experience for Black southerners. She had felt that disorientation herself the year before, on her first night at Highlander, sleeping in the same room with a white woman.

Earlier in the summer, Clark had learned an important lesson from Myles Horton about this process of adjustment, when the first group of her recruits from Johns Island arrived at Highlander. She had secured scholarships for them, while Esau Jenkins's Citizens Club had held a fundraising tea to pay for their other expenses. Septima had convinced her sister Lorene to loan her Chevrolet, they packed six people in, and Jenkins drove them all to Monteagle. Clark and Jenkins tried to prepare the islanders for what Highlander would be like, but most of them had never traveled farther than Charleston, and a few had never left the islands. It was hard for them to imagine what living together with white people would be like. Like all prudent Black travelers in the Jim Crow South, they brought food for the car trip; stopping on the road was dangerous. They had packed a great deal of food, enough chicken and fixings to feed themselves for several days, because they could not believe that they could, or should, eat with whites at the Highlander tables. The idea was too far-fetched.

The islanders refused to come to the dining room, insisting on eating their chicken in their dormitory rooms. This distressed Clark—the whole point of the Highlander experience was to live in an integrated community. Horton was unperturbed: when they run out of chicken, when they get hungry, he said with a puff on his pipe, they'll come down to eat. It took several days, but they finally did come down to join the others at mealtimes. It still wasn't easy for them. At home they might be beaten or even killed for daring to sit with whites at a table. The fear was a tough thing to shake. Mrs. Clark learned not to push too hard; everyone had to acclimate to this strange new world at their own speed.

Septima made time to sit and talk with Rosa privately, quietly, gently; one Black woman to another. She could empathize with the frustration and isolation Rosa felt as a NAACP soldier; she could commiserate about the loneliness and harassment she faced. She tried to assure Rosa that it was safe at Highlander, that the whites here could be trusted, they wouldn't report her to authorities in Montgomery. Rosa's tense muscles gradually began to relax.

After several days, Mrs. Parks began to enjoy her adventure in integrated communal life and appreciate the sly role reversals. She took special pleasure waking up in the morning to "the smell of bacon frying and coffee brewing" in the Highlander kitchen, "and knowing that white folks were doing the preparing instead of me."

She formed a special bond with Septima but also developed a level of admiration and comfort with Myles Horton that surprised her. The way he and Zilphia were able to make Highlander's integrated community seem totally natural—exposing the customs of segregation as all the more absurd—amazed her. "Myles Horton just washed away and melted a lot of my hostility and prejudice and feeling of bitterness toward white people," she would recall, "because he had such a wonderful sense of humor." Parks especially enjoyed hearing Myles's description of how he answered the frequent incredulous question posed to him: How do you manage to get Black and white people to willingly eat together? "First, the food is prepared," was Horton's standard reply. "Second, it's put on the table. Third, we ring the bell."

"I found myself laughing," Parks recalled, "when I hadn't been able to laugh in a long time."

The ten-day workshop was intense, packed with facts, statistics, strategies, and firsthand reports from the front lines of the emerging desegregation battlegrounds in the South. The group grappled with both philosophical and practical aspects of implementing desegregation: the distinction between desegregation and integration. How to educate and organize parents and the broader community. How to present demands to local school boards; what approaches to take, what language to use. Should the desegregation process be immediate or gradual? Mrs. Parks distilled the discussions on the pages of her notepad:

"Gradualism would ease the shock of white minds. Psychological effect," she wrote. "Disadvantage—give opposition more time to build greater resistance. Prolong the change."

Mrs. Parks had rejoiced when the *Brown* decision was first announced the year before; it allowed for a moment of hope. But with *Brown* II leaving desegregation plans up to local districts, school desegregation was, at least as far as Parks could see, hopeless in Montgomery. If anything, things had gotten more difficult for Parks and the NAACP in the year following *Brown*. Obscene phone calls to her home increased; local NAACP leaders suspected their mail was being opened.

Just a few weeks before she was scheduled to leave for Tennessee, one of Mrs. Parks's NAACP Youth Council members, fifteen-year-old Claudette Colvin, had refused to give up her seat on a Montgomery city bus. "I paid my dime, I don't have to move," the feisty teenager yelled as three burly policemen dragged her off the bus, handcuffed and arrested her, and threatened to molest her in the patrol car.

Montgomery's Black activists were both enraged and excited by the arrest: this might be the legal case they had been waiting for to challenge the legality of the city's bus segregation. The NAACP began raising money for Colvin's defense fund, with the checks addressed to the Parks' apartment. But there were questions about whether Claudette was the right defendant: she was so young, a bit impulsive. Could she withstand the scrutiny, pressure, and abuse she would likely face? In the end, the NAACP backed away from her as a suitable defendant. Colvin, a slightly built teenager, was ultimately convicted of assaulting the three brawny policemen who had manhandled her. Mrs. Parks was still upset about the whole thing.

Clark continued to try to soothe Parks and gently prod her to talk about her work in Montgomery. By the second week of the workshop, Rosa was more relaxed, more social, but still reticent. She was by nature a shy woman, not very talkative. Eventually, in the intimacy of the women's dorm room, she was coaxed to join the chatter and divulge small details of her life and work. Over the course of her ten days on the mountain, Rosa began to realize that she was drawing optimism and gaining strength from her Highlander colleagues. Their creativity, their resolve, their bravery—even their ability to laugh—was so impressive to her. She greatly admired Septima Clark's calm and unflappable demeanor, her gentleness combined with an iron will to force change.

The white people at Highlander were kind, interested, and treated her in a way she never thought possible: as an equal. "I was forty-two years old, and it was one of the few times in my life up to that point when I did not feel any hostility from white people," Parks would remember. "I felt that I could express myself honestly without any repercussions or antagonistic attitudes from other people."

At the conclusion of the workshop, Myles asked his "finding your way back home" question, and Rosa mustered the courage to be frank: she promised to continue her work with the young people of the NAACP Youth Council, bolstering their efforts to confront injustice. But she did not think anything meaningful could be accomplished in Montgomery. No mass movement was possible in "the cradle of the Confederacy," Rosa said, because the Black community "wouldn't stick together."

Rosa found it hard to leave Highlander. It had been a respite, but more than that, an education: "For the first time in my adult life I saw that this could be a unified society, that there was such a thing as people of all races and backgrounds meeting and having workshops and living together in peace and harmony." Rosa was still nervous about traveling back to Montgomery alone, so Septima accompanied her, in the back of the bus, to Atlanta, and then saw her safely onto a connecting bus to Montgomery.

Mrs. Parks carried home in her bag the notebook in which she had written a phrase from the Highlander discussions that struck her as especially meaningful: "Desegregation proves itself by being put in action."

CHAPTER TEN

We Shall

T his is a thing that I have longed to do through the ages and now the opportunity has come," Septima Clark wrote to the Warings while she was leading another Highlander integration workshop in late August 1955. "It is making me very happy." Not to say it wasn't a challenge for her. Directing the workshops was physically and intellectually demanding. "We all worked like Trojans, morning noon and night, putting out a revised Guide to Action pamphlet and one on the Mechanics of Integration," she reported to the Warings. "We argued late into the night over issues."

Jumping into the distinctive Highlander culture and adjusting her teaching style to the workshop mode took some doing, too. Bouncing back and forth from Charleston to Monteagle Mountain, making the 650-mile trip six times in two months, was wearing. But she loved it.

After she escorted Mrs. Parks to Atlanta, Mrs. Clark continued on to Charleston, was home for just a few days, then boarded a bus back to Monteagle, a seventeen-hour overnight trip. She didn't mind. She shared a little bedroom in the Highlander main house with a rotating cast of white women roommates, and she enjoyed getting to know them. The cool mountain nights were refreshing, so different from summer nights in the Lowcountry. She found Highlander to be a joyous place: living together, the work, the ideas, the connections with many different kinds of people. Knowing she was helping nurture a new cohort of activists was richly rewarding.

Esau Jenkins drove Lorene's car, packed with Johns and Wadmalaw Island recruits, on three round trips to Monteagle that summer. He had become a Highlander regular. Between what he had learned in the Highlander workshop the previous summer, the winter and spring follow-up meetings and conferences on Johns Island, and the mentoring he received from Horton and Clark, Jenkins was maturing both as a community leader and a political activist. He no longer insisted on dominating every meeting, giving such long-winded speeches that the audience tended to leave before he had made his point. He was learning to delegate, allowing others to have a voice and express opinions. And he was allowing some new island leaders to emerge, no longer feeling quite so threatened by them. The Warings were so impressed by what they had heard about Jenkins's work from Clark that they sponsored a scholarship in his honor for a Sea Islander to attend Highlander.

"My ideas of community leadership have changed in many ways since my stay at Highlander last year," Jenkins confided to Horton. "I found that giving others something to do in help making better citizens in a community is very important. My old ways of doing was slow."

———— ♦ ————

Mrs. Clark had also convinced another of her Charleston NAACP colleagues, Bernice Violanthe Robinson, to venture to Highlander that summer of 1955, making the trip in the Chevrolet. Robinson grew up in Charleston, and was actually a cousin of Clark's—their mothers were sisters—but relations between the sisters weren't warm, so Bernice and Septima hadn't known each other growing up. It wasn't until both women returned to Charleston in the late 1940s, after living away from the city for many years, and both became active in the NAACP, that they grew more familiar.

Robinson was almost a generation younger than Clark—she was just past forty when she came to Highlander, and she was impressive: smart, witty, and vivacious. She turned heads with her beauty and style, wearing dresses that flattered her figure, and always the latest hairdo. Bernice Robinson was a beautician, a business owner, an optimistic woman, but also mad as hell about having to live under Jim Crow.

She was the ninth child in her family, and while money was always scarce, her parents taught their children to aim high and develop a skill. She went through the highest grades available to Black students in Charleston's public schools but moved north to New York City to complete high school, living with a sister in Harlem. New York was a revelation to sixteen-year-old Bernice: a place where Black people were not required to sit in the back of the bus or subway car, not herded into the "buzzard's roost" balcony of the movie theater, not made to enter a building through a separate entrance or use a designated toilet. She relished attending concerts at Carnegie Hall and the Apollo Theater. Robinson set her sights on a professional singing career, but her sister took ill, and they were both forced to return to Charleston.

Robinson married, gave birth to a daughter, and was divorced within the next few years, returning to New York to begin a new life with her daughter in the freedom of the North. There, she registered and voted for the first time, and no one gave her any hassle. She worked in a garment factory by day and took cosmetology classes at night, opening a beauty parlor in Harlem with a friend.

Soon after the Second World War, her parents' health declined, and she needed to return home to care for them. Very reluctantly, Bernice and her daughter came back to Charleston in 1947—the same year Septima returned to care for her ailing mother—and she felt the racial constrictions in her hometown even more keenly than before. She got into a verbal fight with a white man on a city bus who insisted she move to the back. It was hard to adjust after she had seen what life could be like.

The first thing she did upon her return was to join the Charleston NAACP, where she met her cousin Seppie and served on the executive board with Esau Jenkins, rising quickly to become branch secretary and membership chair. She opened her own beauty parlor and bought her supplies from Black-owned businesses, giving her a measure of independence from the white-controlled economy. Her shop became an unofficial NAACP recruitment outpost, a safe place where women could read the organization's literature and discuss serious issues.

Robinson became deeply involved in the NAACP's voter registration campaign in 1948, following Judge Waring's ruling that opened the South Carolina Democratic primary to Black voters. In the busy weeks before elections, she would often leave women under the dryer in her shop to escort others to the registration office. "If you get too hot under there," she would call out to her stranded customers as she rushed out the door, "just cut her off and come out!"

Bernice was just the kind of person her cousin believed would benefit from the Highlander experience, and Septima gently twisted her arm to agree. It meant closing the beauty shop for two weeks and losing income, but Bernice eventually gave in. She liked Highlander immediately. The integrated living didn't faze her at all; she was more surprised by the mixing of classes, the abandonment of all trappings of social status. She didn't even realize she was rooming with a millionaire white woman—she knew her only by her first name.

Another thing Robinson loved about Highlander was the singing. She had once aspired to a singing career, but now she sang only in church. The nightly group singing, in harmony with white people, was special. She knew some of the songs, but there were many new ones that Zilphia had gathered, and they were fun to learn. Bernice was familiar with the original hymn melody of "We Shall Overcome" but this version, the "we" in the chorus, the sense of unity and strength it evoked, it just grabbed the soul.

Toward the end of that August 1955 workshop, Myles asked his "finding your way back home" question, exploring what the participants intended to do when they returned to their communities. Bernice said she wanted to organize new citizen groups around Charleston to help push for school desegregation. When it was Esau Jenkins's turn, he announced his new goal: last year it was registering more voters to get him elected to the school board—and he intended to run again in the next election—but now he had a more ambitious plan. "I need a school . . . to teach my people," he told his classmates in the Highlander library. He needed a night school where adults could learn to read and write so they could register to vote, and learn why they should vote; so they could become politically aware, become better citizens.

Jenkins told them the story of his school bus voter-prep project, and of his passenger Alice Wine earning her registration by memorization but wanting more, desiring to learn to read and write. For his islanders to aspire to become first-class citizens, to participate fully in the community, to stand tall as modern men and women, they needed to become literate.

His bus wasn't enough. "I need somebody to help me. Tell me how I can get a school going," he pleaded. His story captivated everyone sitting in the library, and the entire conversation pivoted to a discussion of how to help Jenkins. Septima watched Esau with pride and a bit of astonishment. The Gullah boy from the cotton and cabbage patches of Johns Island had the entire workshop, some of them people with advanced degrees and fancy titles, entranced by the simple power of his vision.

Horton nodded sympathetically, but he had been caught off guard. He wasn't quite ready to commit to a major program on Johns Island; he was still in the process of evaluating the situation. But Jenkins's passion was irresistible and his persuasive skills, a plea spoken from the heart, undeniable. Every eye was on Horton, watching how he would respond.

"Let me see if I can find some money for you to set up a school," Bernice

Robinson remembered Horton saying. "You try to find a place, and we'll see where we go from there." The workshop just about burst into cheers. As soon as he returned to Johns Island, Jenkins began hunting for a home for his school.

———◆———

Zilphia Horton was her exuberant self at Highlander that summer, though she and Myles were still feeling the aftershocks of the Eastman investigation. The immediate danger of Myles being imprisoned for contempt of Congress had eased somewhat; no G-man had come up the mountain with handcuffs. But there were other repercussions to worry about: the lingering danger of Eastman tampering with Highlander's IRS tax exemption, and the anxiety expressed by Highlander's own funders, the foundations and donors who had gotten nervous about Eastman's accusations, as overblown as they might be.

Highlander survived on grants, and now that it had switched its efforts from labor education to civil rights training, it lost the cushion of union funding. Horton had to attract new sponsors. Convincing foundations to pledge money to Black civil rights causes was a difficult sell, and those foundations willing to take a chance needed reassurance that they were not affiliating with a red-tinged outfit. The Marshall Field Foundation, established in 1940 by the grandson of a Chicago department store magnate and dedicated to progressive causes and experimental approaches to solving American societal problems, had been alarmed at first by the Eastman allegations but now seemed satisfied with the results of its own inquiry into Highlander's character.

Another of Highlander's funders, the Emil Schwarzhaupt Foundation, created by a German immigrant who had made a fortune in liquor distilling, was dedicated to the development of American citizenship. This foundation was sponsoring the community leadership development project on Johns Island and had proven to be a staunch friend, standing by Highlander through the recent unpleasantness. The irony that Highlander's organizing and training work, considered communistic in the South, was supported by the wealth of some of America's great northern captains of capitalism, was not lost on Horton.

All through the summer, Horton kept a close eye on the intensifying resistance to the *Brown* desegregation ruling. It was as if *Brown* II had not only stymied progress but also opened the floodgates to a wave of southern state fury and defiance. While Septima was conducting integration workshops at

Highlander in July, South Carolina's civic and business leaders gathered at the Roosevelt Hotel in Columbia to form the Committee of 52, a group devoted to resisting any and all integration efforts.

The conference was organized by the editor of the *Charleston News and Courier*, Thomas Waring (Judge Waring's estranged nephew), bringing together a prominent roster of lawyers, bankers, elected officials, company executives, and wealthy planters. Beyond their shared appreciation of white supremacy, the committee maintained that the Supreme Court and federal government had no legal right to force school integration upon the states, and it was the state's duty to resist this imposition. This stance was the foundation for what would soon grow into southern "massive resistance."

In statehouses across the South, legislatures were busy reinforcing the structures of segregation. Some, like Virginia, South Carolina, and Georgia, created official agencies to stonewall school desegregation efforts. Some states or districts would soon pass statutes abolishing public schools to avoid integrating them, providing white parents with tuition vouchers to create state-financed but private "white academies." Most school districts simply ignored any demands to desegregate.

In response to the legal petitions filed by Black parents seeking to integrate their districts' schools, White Citizens' Councils mushroomed across the southern states. They enrolled tens of thousands of doctors, lawyers, bankers, civic leaders, and elected officials, all dedicated to meting out punishment to anyone who dared to try to implement the *Brown* ruling.

During the summer of '55, Black parents in the small farming town of Elloree, about seventy-five miles northwest of Charleston, joined a NAACP petition drive to integrate the school district. The names of the petitioners were immediately printed in the local papers and the white town fathers unleashed a coordinated plan of retaliation against them. They were fired from their jobs, evicted from their homes, banks called in mortgages on their farms, suppliers denied them seed and fertilizer. Black merchants were refused deliveries to their stores, causing shortages of bread, milk and other staples. A pharmacy refused a Black mother the special formula she needed for her hemophiliac baby. The regional distributors of Coca-Cola and Sunbeam bread agreed to cut off supplies to Black merchants, and a general white boycott of all Black businesses and service providers who had signed the desegregation petition was put in place.

To coordinate this effort, the first White Citizens' Councils in South Carolina were born that summer in Elloree and the county seat of Orangeburg, about twenty-five miles away. The members of the Orangeburg councils were described as "elite, church-going, club and business-minded folk." Just a week after the Elloree parents' petition was filed, more than eight hundred white residents joined the town's new Citizens' Council. These councils came to be called the "uptown Ku Klux Klan."

This was now the playbook for White Citizens' Councils responding to desegregation efforts: the coordinated economic intimidation of the Black community in what came to be called "The Squeeze." The South Carolina state NAACP launched a relief effort: fundraising for destitute families, paying rent, delivering food and clothing, arranging for seed and fertilizer supplies. But the Black people of Elloree were hurting. Facing ruin, quite a few of the petition signees removed their names and were forced to renounce the NAACP desegregation campaign.

Orangeburg was the seat of higher education for Black people in the state, the home of Claflin Normal College and South Carolina A&M, and when student leaders on those campuses learned of the plight of the community in Elloree, they decided to help. They demanded their college administration stop doing business with White Citizens' Council members—most of the businessmen in town—who were responsible for the economic suffering. When the colleges, run by white, state-appointed boards of trustees, refused the students' demands, the students called for a hunger strike in the dining halls and demonstrations on campus. They urged students to stop buying Coca-Cola, Sunbeam Bread, and other brands that had caved to the Citizens' Council boycott of Black merchants.

The state NAACP joined the student effort, rallying the community and distributing a list of local businesses owned by members of the Orangeburg and Elloree White Citizens' Councils, calling for a counterboycott of those stores and facilities. In the next few months, white business owners began to feel the pinch of losing Black clientele. A few Citizens' Council members saw their own boycotted businesses collapse, while others tried to woo Black customers back. Soon enough, distributors for the national brands like Coca-Cola quietly resumed deliveries to Black-owned businesses.

Few of the petitioners who had lost their jobs were rehired, even if they acquiesced and removed their names from the desegregation petition. Some had to move away. The desegregation petition was completely ignored by the county school district. The state A&M student leader was eventually expelled from the college, days before his graduation, by the college's nervous Black president. Mrs. Clark was appalled by the college president's lack of a "spine" while she cheered the student leader and his classmates' brave resistance stance. The young people were the future, she believed, the only hope for progress.

When Septima Clark returned home to Charleston from Monteagle in the first days of September 1955, another murder shook the nation. A fourteen-year-old Black boy named Emmett Till, who lived in Chicago, was visiting his relatives in Mississippi during summer vacation. Unaccustomed to southern Jim Crow rules, he didn't avert his eyes when approaching whites, he didn't hesitate to speak to them, and he carried himself with a boyish bravado. He entered a shop to buy some candy, bantered with the white woman behind the counter, and his confidence somehow offended her. She told her husband the teenager had flirted with her, whistled at her. Days later, the enraged husband and a friend dragged Till from his uncle's house, took him to an isolated spot, and beat, mutilated, and shot the boy in the head, then threw him into the Tallahatchie River with a fifty-pound metal fan tied to his neck by barbed wire, sinking the body to the river bottom. Till's bereaved mother insisted that the truth of her son's lynching be known, not hushed up. His battered body was displayed in an open casket at his funeral, forty thousand people filed by to view it, and photos of his brutally ravaged face were published nationwide in *Jet* magazine and the *Chicago Defender* newspaper.

Emmett Till was every Black mother's son; every Black boy in the South knew it could have been him at the bottom of that river. There was northern condemnation of the brutal murder of the child, and even some sympathetic southern reaction. In Black homes there were bitter tears for a boy they had never met, but whose fate they understood too well. At home in Montgomery, Rosa Parks broke down and cried when she saw the photos of Till printed in the press, and she could not shake the anger and despair the images evoked. The murder pained Septima, and she could only pray that the boy's death would not be in vain, but she was disappointed that Charleston's Black ministers and organizational leaders were not protesting the lynching more vigorously from their pulpits and podiums. She brought up Till's murder at every meeting she attended.

When Till's killers were brought to trial a few weeks later and acquitted by an all-white jury after less than an hour of deliberation (the decision would have been quicker, but the jury took time to enjoy bottles of Coca-Cola), a new spasm of grief gripped Black neighborhoods, and extensive media coverage forced the nation to stare at Jim Crow injustice up close.

———— ✦ ————

As Mrs. Clark returned to work for the fall school semester, the mood in Charleston was uneasy. The murder of Emmett Till put everyone on edge, and the white backlash to *Brown*-mandated school desegregation was growing uglier.

South Carolina governor George Bell Timmerman Jr., a staunch segregationist, ordered the state law enforcement agency to investigate how the NAACP was conducting its desegregation petition drives and, more broadly, the operations of the NAACP itself. It was only the first of the state's maneuvers to destroy what it considered the engine responsible for all this desegregation frenzy. Barely two months after the founding of the first White Citizens' Council in Elloree, the number of local councils in South Carolina had ballooned to thirty-eight, with more forming every week. There were already hundreds in operation all over the South. The councils were distributing a pamphlet called "The Ugly Truth about the NAACP," contending the organization was an un-American, Communist-tinged agitator, intent on destroying the southern way of life.

Mrs. Clark's fellow South Carolina NAACP activists became targets: Rev. Joseph DeLaine, leader of the Summerton parents whose petition had initiated the *Briggs* case, was hounded in ever more violent ways. His home in Summerton had already been burned down, and in early October 1955 his new church in Lake City was firebombed and destroyed. Two days later he received a death threat: " . . . rather than let you spread your dirty filthy poison any longer, we have made plans to move you if it takes dynamite to do so."

Within days, Klan night riders attacked his home. DeLaine defended his family by returning the gunfire, chasing the attackers away, but it was DeLaine who was charged with assault, a warrant for his arrest issued. Knowing he would surely be lynched if he was arrested, the minister escaped to New York.

An FBI investigation determined that even with such clear evidence of premeditated racial violence, there was no civil rights violation involved. Those who threatened and attacked DeLaine were never charged, but the minister would remain in exile, fighting extradition to South Carolina and the false charges lodged against him, for the rest of his life.

Esau Jenkins was also being punished for his activism. Two of his adult daughters, both teachers on the islands, were fired from their school jobs in retaliation for their father's voter registration efforts, his NAACP board position, and probably also for his school board campaign. Jenkins appealed to both Horton and Clark for assistance in finding new employment for his daughters. Jenkins insisted he would not give in to the intimidation: he was continuing his voting work, searching for a site for the literacy school, and he intended to run for school board trustee again.

All this intimidation was deeply upsetting to Septima. "I still feel that I want to be militant but calm," she confessed to the Warings. "These are really critical times," she told them in a November 15, 1955, letter. "Negroes are in a rather precarious position and it is hard to tell where the next turn will be." She was trying to maintain her optimism during a dispiriting season: "I still have faith that through all this a beautiful something will emerge."

Two weeks after Mrs. Clark wrote these words, Mrs. Rosa Parks, on her way home from work at the Montgomery Fair department store, boarded a Cleveland Avenue City Line bus at Court Square. After a few stops, when the bus got crowded and the bus driver ordered her to give up her seat to a white man, she refused.

CHAPTER ELEVEN

Rosa's Bus

I could not have faced myself or my people if I had moved." Mrs. Parks would explain. "I had been pushed as far as I could stand to be pushed." Her defiance that night was also spurred by her experience at Highlander, just four months before. Highlander, she maintained, had stiffened her spine and expanded her vision of what was possible.

Parks was charged with disorderly conduct and violating the city's bus segregation codes and placed in the city jail. Virginia and Clifford Durr, along with E. D. Nixon, rushed to bail her out. Returning home, Parks agreed to allow the NAACP to use her arrest as a legal test case challenging segregation on Montgomery's bus system. She was the perfect plaintiff—a dignified, articulate matron—the NAACP needed to pursue a case.

Just hours after Rosa Parks's arrest, the Montgomery Women's Political Council activated its own plan. Led by Alabama State College professor Jo Ann Robinson, the Council worked in secret through the night printing thirty-five thousand flyers announcing a one-day boycott of all city buses on Monday, December 5, the day of Mrs. Parks's trial.

Local Black ministers met in the basement of Dexter Avenue Baptist, where twenty-six-year-old Reverend Martin Luther King Jr. had taken up his first pulpit just the year before. The clergymen agreed to support the Women's Political Council's plan for a bus boycott, urging their parishioners to refrain from riding on the buses as a display of unity.

On Monday morning, after a short trial, Parks was found guilty of violating segregation laws and fined $10, with an additional $4 in court fees. Her young lawyer, Fred Gray, just a year out of law school, would appeal her conviction.

Outside, the boycott began, and city buses ran empty. Black passengers stayed home, hitchhiked rides in private cars, or walked miles to their jobs and schools. Rosa Parks was amazed: her community was sticking together in a way she had never thought possible.

"Rosa? Rosa?" Septima asked incredulously when she heard the news of Parks's audacity on the bus. "She was so shy when she came to Highlander, but she got enough courage to do that!"

Myles was visiting Septima in Charleston when they learned of their former student's act of defiance. They knew of her devotion to civil rights causes, but they were still astounded. "Rosa was the quietest participant in the workshop," Horton recalled. "If you judge by the conventional standards, she would have been the least promising, probably [to do something so bold]."

Virginia Durr, who had arranged for Parks's Highlander visit and was there to tearfully embrace Rosa when she was released from jail, was not so surprised. "When she came back [from Highlander] she was so happy and felt so liberated," Durr told Horton. "And then as time went on she said the discrimination got worse and worse to bear AFTER having, for the first time in her life, been free of it at Highlander. . . . I'm sure that had a lot to do with her daring to risk arrest. . . . You should certainly take pride in what you did for her."

"Had you seen Rosa Parks ('the Montgomery spark plug') when she came to Highlander last summer," Septima related to the Warings, "you would understand just how much GUTS she got while being there."

For the next 381 days, the Black men, women, and children of Montgomery did not ride on the city buses. Black-owned taxis and church vans took over the bus routes while a complex schedule of car pools took people where they needed to go. Rosa Parks helped the Women's Political Council with the complicated logistics of the car pools, working as a dispatcher. But mostly the Black citizens of Montgomery "walked for freedom" through heat, rain, chill, and dark, wearing out the soles of their shoes. They kept up their spirits and stamina at biweekly rallies at a rotating circuit of churches, brought to their tired feet by the singing of hymns and spirituals, and the soaring rhetoric of young Rev. King.

But there was great suffering, too, beyond fatigue and footsoreness. The white backlash was swift and fierce. Incensed white employers fired their Black workers participating in the boycott; Rosa Parks lost her seamstress job at Montgomery Fair department store, and her husband lost his work as a barber.

Soon the fury of white Montgomerians burst into violence: About seven weeks into the boycott, in late January 1956, while Rev. King was speaking at a mass meeting, his home was bombed; fortunately his wife and infant child were not injured. The next night, E. D. Nixon's house was also bombed. When these outrages failed to sap the will of the boycotters, the city convened a grand jury to indict almost one hundred of the protest organizers, including Mrs. Parks, Rev. Ralph Abernathy, Rev. King, and E. D. Nixon, on charges of conspiracy. Photographs of Mrs. Parks being fingerprinted holding her arrest number in front of her chest were reproduced across the country.

The boycott captured the public imagination in a way no other racial protest had before. National and international media sent reporters to Montgomery, providing a year of great human interest copy and riveting photos. Donations of money, food, cars, trucks—and shoes—poured in from around the country. Rosa Parks was dispatched on fundraising trips to cities across the nation, telling the story of the boycott before huge audiences. The woman who had been so reluctant to speak in the Highlander library willed herself to step up to podiums to deliver a message of hope, defiance, and—most surprising to her—solidarity.

On Monteagle Mountain, Myles Horton wasn't shy about claiming Rosa Parks as a distinguished Highlander alumna. What he saw unfolding in Montgomery was the Highlander philosophy come to life: a workshop student carrying her experience home and putting it to work in her community, inspiring others to act, spurring a collective, grassroots push for change.

Just as the bus boycott was galvanizing the Black community in Montgomery, it fueled white outrage in the South. The boycott signaled an assault on the entire architecture of Jim Crow, and revealed a willingness to defy white power. In response, White Citizens' Council chapters sprouted all over the South: in 1956, Mississippi could claim one hundred thousand council members in 235 chapters around the state; South Carolina claimed forty thousand members. Klan membership, which had been in decline, was also booming as klaverns worked in concert with Citizens' Councils to do the dirty work of suppressing civil rights activity. The FBI counted 127 pro-segregation organizations born since the *Brown* decision announcement of May 1954, and FBI director J. Edgar Hoover described "racial tension rising almost daily" with the "south in a state of explosive resentment."

Three weeks into the Montgomery boycott, some of the South's most prominent elected officials convened at the Peabody Hotel in Memphis to forge an alliance against desegregation. Mississippi senator James Eastland huddled with his congressional peers Strom Thurmond of South Carolina and Herman Talmadge of Georgia, as well as governors, congressmen, and officials from twelve southern states.

At the hotel conclave, the men formed the Federation of Constitutional Government to coordinate legal and political efforts to thwart desegregation across the South, at both the state and federal level. They would work together to develop a comprehensive attack on integration, using existing law or inventing new ones to suit their needs. Using their executive and legislative powers, their prominence and connections, they determined to build a legal arsenal to protect the sacred southern institution of segregation.

The southern lawmakers and law enforcers of the federation plotted a coordinated, multipronged assault on the NAACP, which they considered the evil fountainhead of Black fulmination. Senator Thurmond of South Carolina left the Memphis meeting to begin drafting a congressional declaration of war against the federal government. Senator Eastland left the meeting to bring the federation's campaign to the public, traveling all through the South like a segregationist rock star on tour. Barely a month after the launch of the Montgomery boycott, Eastland fired up four thousand South Carolina White Citizens' Council devotees in Columbia. A few weeks later the senator roused twelve thousand Alabama Citizens' Council members in Montgomery, slamming the boycott and the Improvement Association and railing against the NAACP as a Communist front intent upon destroying the South.

Georgia attorney general Eugene Cook returned to Atlanta after the Memphis meeting to collaborate with his fellow southern state attorneys general on a broad legal attack on the NAACP. He was aided by a couple of professional anti-Communists who made a lucrative business of providing dubious research information and highly unreliable expert witnesses to McCarthy-era investigations and publications. In early 1956 these consultants urged southern authorities to "do something" about Rosa Parks and to pay attention to the Highlander Folk School, where Parks had "trained" for the boycott. The for-hire scaremongers suggested to Attorney General Cook that he examine Highlander as the "origin of many of your problems." Cook took their advice.

While the lawmakers and elected officials involved in the Federation for Constitutional Government and the White Citizens' Councils—men who had sworn oaths to preserve and protect the US Constitution—plotted against the federal government, Esau Jenkins received the news that his twenty-one-year-old son had made the ultimate sacrifice for his country.

Herbert Jenkins had hoped to make a career in the military, but he was killed in a training accident while serving in Germany. Esau and Janie had to bury another one of their children, their son's coffin draped in the American flag. Mrs. Clark rushed to the Jenkins' home on Johns Island to comfort the bereaved family and attend the funeral. Septima was deeply moved to find that although Esau was heartbroken, he was able to find meaning, and even hope, in his son's death:

"Now I have more to fight for on Johns Island," Esau told Septima, "since my son gave his life for Americans to be free."

CHAPTER TWELVE

Been in the Storm

S ustained by his faith, Esau Jenkins was confident of his life's purpose. "Long years ago, I ask myself a question: Am I my brother's keeper," he liked to explain. "And the answer that I got was—you are. I decided to do anything I can to help people in order to help myself."

In the first months of 1956, Septima watched her friend convert the pain of losing his son into even deeper commitment to assist his fellow islanders. He scoured the island to find new prospective voters while he scouted for a home for the literacy school that he believed could nurture a whole new crop of Black, first-class, voting citizens.

———◆———

In the late winter of 1956, ninety-five years after the start of the Civil War, 101 members of Congress, representing the states of the former Confederacy, launched an assault upon the federal government. The "Declaration of Constitutional Principals" signed by the southern salons was read aloud in both the House and Senate chambers and entered into the Congressional Record. Drafted by Senator Strom Thurmond, it came to be known as the Southern Manifesto.

"We regard the decisions of the Supreme Court in the school cases as a clear abuse of judicial power," the manifesto declared. "It is destroying the amicable relations between the white and Negro races that have been created through 90 years of patient effort by the good people of both races," the declaration contended in a rosy depiction of Jim Crow codes. "It has planted hatred and suspicion where there has been heretofore friendship and understanding."

The manifesto claimed the South was the victim of an evil plot: "Outside mediators are threatening immediate and revolutionary changes in our public schools systems," it warned. "We commend the motives of those States which have declared the intention to resist forced integration by any lawful means."

With that closing battle cry, the manifesto resurrected a theme of the antebellum South's fight to maintain slavery as a state's right and legitimize state defiance of federal law, concepts that had provided the framework for secession.

The manifesto laid the groundwork for a revived confederation of southern states rejecting desegregation by affirming state sovereignty, making defiance of the law socially and legally acceptable in the South. Within weeks, Alabama, Georgia, Mississippi, South Carolina, Tennessee, and Virginia passed resolutions "invalidating" the Supreme Court's *Brown* mandate; they would be joined by Arkansas, Florida, and Louisiana. When Mississippi unanimously adopted its resolution, legislators cheered and sang "Dixie."

In Virginia, manifesto proponent Senator Harry Byrd called for the southern states to counter desegregation with a campaign of "massive resistance." That massive resistance took solid shape in southern statehouses. Besides the sovereignty resolutions and new laws protecting school segregation, southern legislatures took aim at what they considered the source of racial agitation: the NAACP. In the next two years, state capitals would promulgate more than 230 laws and regulations aiming to cripple the civil rights group.

One of the first legislatures to target the NAACP was South Carolina. Even before the Southern Manifesto was read in Congress, representatives in Columbia readied a bill prohibiting state, county, school district, and municipal employees from membership in the NAACP; membership was grounds for dismissal. The goal was to crush civil rights advocacy and to intimidate teachers like Septima Clark.

Teachers were the core of the Black community and the backbone of the NAACP in the South, so this was a double-barreled assault upon civil rights efforts. The law posed a painful dilemma for Black teachers: forced to choose between their profession and their convictions, their livelihoods and their fight for equality. But it was never a question for Septima Clark.

Septima was already in hot water in Charleston, and she knew people around town were gossiping about her. The Charleston newspapers had printed articles about the PTA conference she had organized in December 1955, featuring Myles Horton as keynote speaker and Zilphia as song leader and facilitator. The news reports hinted at the Communist allegations against Highlander and described Myles as a "champion of integration." The distribution of Highlander's "Guide to Community Action for Public School

Integration," which Septima helped write, was further evidence of the meeting's nefarious intent.

"I just saw your name in the paper," a Black school principal told her with a mix of pity and disdain. "Fools rush in where angels fear to tread." Mrs. Clark remained calm. She learned that another Black principal was spreading rumors on Johns Island that she was an "agitator for integration."

"I just resolved in my mind to wear whatever criticism came along simply as a loose garment," Clark later explained. "I wasn't going to let it gall—or bind me, either."

By the early months of 1956, Clark's ties to the Warings and now Highlander were in full public view, and she could feel the chilly glares from her colleagues. After those newspaper articles appeared, the teachers in her school made her the topic of their morning coffee gatherings, buzzing about the perils of her outspoken stance. Her fellow teachers were already jittery: in those few places where school districts had undertaken some degree of desegregation, Black teachers' jobs had been eliminated. The *Brown* mandate provided no protection for Black teachers deliberately squeezed out by the melding of faculties; school boards used their power to prevent Black teachers from instructing white students. States were also altering teacher tenure rules, making the dismissal of Black teachers all the easier. In the next decade, a hundred thousand Black teachers and principals would be forced from their classrooms, and in 1956 desegregation was already proving to be a disaster for Black educators.

The new South Carolina law required civil servants to sign a sworn oath stating whether they were or were not a member of the NAACP. Since the same legislation made it unlawful to employ a NAACP member, the consequences of an affirmative answer were obvious. "I just read of the proposed firing of all you good NAACP people," Myles Horton wrote to Clark. "All of us here are concerned about the welfare of you and our other friends."

Mrs. Clark tried to rally her fellow Black teachers to stand together in protest. "I had the feeling that if all of them would say: 'We are members of the NAACP' that the legislature would not have said, 'All of you will lose your job' because it would mean thousands of children on the street with no school. But I couldn't get them to see that."

She mailed letters to the seven hundred Black teachers in Charleston

County who were NAACP members, asking them to join her in protesting the "unjust law" to South Carolina officials. Only forty-two responded that they intended to admit their membership; of these, only twenty-six agreed to join her in confronting the superintendent of schools in his office. On the day of the appointment, only eleven teachers showed up, and as the hour of the meeting approached, seven of them bowed out. Only Mrs. Clark and four other teachers met with the education chief. The superintendent dismissed the complaints of the tiny delegation and hustled them out of his office.

Septima realized she had pushed her colleagues too far, asked them to do something they were not prepared to do: "I don't know why I felt that the black teachers would stand up for their rights. But they wouldn't. Most of them were afraid and became hostile." She would look back at this episode as "one of the great failures of my life," a failure both as a teacher and an organizer. She had not readied her colleagues to be bold, not given them reason enough to fight. It was a lesson she would not forget.

———— ◆ ————

The 1956 South Carolina legislative term was dubbed the "segregation session" for the blitz of massive resistance laws put into effect. Working in conjunction with the White Citizens' Councils, legislators (many of whom were council members themselves) moved to make public school attendance optional, opening the door for the creation of "white academies," and withhold state funding from any school or district that did attempt to desegregate. To bolster its offensive against the NAACP, the legislature made any state or county administrator who knowingly employed a NAACP member subject to a $100 personal fine for each infraction.

Lawmakers also targeted the intrepid local lawyers who represented plaintiffs in NAACP-supported class-action suits challenging segregation and other rights abuses. These revised "barratry" rules imposed severe malpractice penalties, including disbarment, upon attorneys pursuing "vexatious" litigation against the state. The goal was to prevent South Carolina attorneys from cooperating with NAACP Legal Defense teams in groundbreaking cases.

Other southern states joined the assault: Some branded the NAACP a "subversive" entity, outlawing it altogether and criminalizing membership. Some states demanded that state NAACP offices turn over their membership and donor lists, exposing members and supporters to enormous danger. Texas

Rangers assisted in raiding the state's NAACP offices, seizing its papers, and shutting it down. Some states imposed outrageous fines or retroactive taxes, amounting to hundreds of thousands of dollars, crippling state NAACP's operations for years. The organization fought back with lawsuits, and almost all these anti-NAACP statutes were ruled illegal, but the time, cost, and effort involved took its toll. Between 1955 and 1957, NAACP membership in the southern states plummeted by almost half, and in the South, some 246 NAACP branches disappeared between 1955 and 1958.

Trapped by this devilish state maneuver, most teachers who did belong to the NAACP simply denied it; a few refused to answer the membership question. Many more resigned from the NAACP to protect themselves and their jobs. Septima Clark, first vice president of the Charleston NAACP chapter, made it known she would not be intimidated or silenced, and she would not renounce her NAACP affiliation. She was willing to face the consequences. She vowed to meet her state's massive resistance with her own moral resistance. When her contract renewal form containing the NAACP question arrived in her mailbox, she returned it with a proud declaration that yes, she was a member of the NAACP.

In Elloree, the South Carolina town punished for demanding its schools desegregate and still suffering from the damage of White Citizens' Council reprisals, Black teachers did what Mrs. Clark had hoped her colleagues in Charleston would do: eighteen teachers resigned their school positions rather than renounce their NAACP membership, and three refused to answer the question about their affiliation. They were all fired. But they were also ready to march into court.

Septima was also fired, or more precisely, her teaching contract was not renewed. "I anticipated this long ago," she told the Warings. "I can take it on the chin. No shock; no surprise." The moment she received her letter of dismissal, she wrote to the Board of Education demanding a hearing. Then she called the president of her Charleston NAACP branch, who alerted the state NAACP president, and both men met with Clark that night in her living room to strategize. Mrs. Clark was determined to sue the school board and hoped the NAACP would take on her case to challenge the law and win her reinstatement. She was ready to fight.

A storm broke over Henrietta Street; Clark's family was both frightened and infuriated by her actions. "Now for my household—not any of them agree with me," she reported to the Warings. "In most cases they feel I'm right, but too outspoken or too hasty."

"Why didn't you resign?" her brother Peter Poinsette scolded her. "You knew since January that they were getting after you." She wanted to make the school authorities fire her, she explained to him, to enable her to press a suit, to allow her to fight back. Peter wasn't a fighter, she understood; like many of her relatives, he never joined the NAACP. "They didn't feel as I did, that they could fight for freedom or for justice. They just didn't have that feeling."

Her sister Lorene took it the hardest. "I can't help being nervous," she told Septima. "I just feel so sick. I just feel like a bowl of jelly." Lorene was also a teacher, and there were threats that even the relatives of NAACP members would be blacklisted. She could not afford to lose her job, especially with Septima now out of work. The telephone rang incessantly at the sisters' Henrietta Street home as word of Septima's dismissal spread, and Lorene complained that she felt as if she had butterflies in her stomach each time she picked up the phone.

"You just let me answer the phone and tell the people I'm a member [of the NAACP] and I've been dismissed," Septima counseled her. "I don't mind at all." But she did mind: she was hurt by the lack of support from her family and colleagues, the feeling of isolation from her community. "My family are fighting me," she confided to Elizabeth Waring. Clark felt alone in her home city, with no allies or friends. People in Charleston were calling her a radical, a communist. People were afraid of her.

When Clark's Alpha Kappa Alpha sorority celebrated her service as chapter president with a testimonial dinner shortly after her school dismissal, her sisters placed a crown on her head, but with few exceptions, refused to pose for photographs with her. "They were sore afraid because they could not be seen with a NAACP rep," she told the Warings. "They dared not take a risk." Clark was deeply pained by this incident; the bitter memory lingered for many years. "My mother had died by the time I was dismissed," Clark explained ruefully. "But I know she would have said: I told you so."

While Septima Clark was confronting the pernicious power of her state's massive resistance, Esau Jenkins's Citizens' Club was enrolling new voters every month, and the club meetings had excited Johns Islanders' interest in political matters. An unexpectedly large contingent attended the local Democratic Party organizational meeting, and this was enough to spook Charleston political officials, who were unaccustomed to having to consider Black voting power. In response, during South Carolina's prolific "segregation session" in the spring of 1956, a minor bill was slipped in, sponsored by the Charleston County delegates, changing the rules of how school board trustees in District 9, encompassing Johns and Wadmalaw islands, were to be chosen. No longer would the trustees be elected by popular vote; henceforth, they would be appointed.

With this one precision strike, the legislature eliminated Jenkins's candidacy, and with it, the prime incentive for his neighbors to register to vote, since they could no longer vote for one of their own. It was a malicious move, and also something of a compliment: his island voters had already managed to strike fear into the white politicians. Jenkins was angry but did not want his islanders to become discouraged or complacent, to give up on voting. Building his people's political strength was too valuable. There would be other candidates to vote for, he would see to that, and his community could find other causes to rally around.

CHAPTER THIRTEEN

Champions of Democracy

E arly one morning in April 1956, Zilphia was alone in the office making copies of song sheets and play scripts on the mimeograph machine. She reached for a Mason jar of what she thought was water, or perhaps she thought it was moonshine, which she sometimes liked to tipple. She sipped it. It wasn't water or moonshine. It was the odorless, colorless chemical fluid carbon tetrachloride, used as typewriter cleaner in the office. She spat it out, rinsed her mouth, and thought she was fine. But enough had seeped down her throat to begin scorching her body from the inside. Myles was away, so Zilphia tried to hide her vomiting. Finally a staff member called a doctor who treated her at home for several days, then sent her to the nearest hospital in Sewanee. As her condition worsened, Myles rushed home. She required more advanced care and was transported to Vanderbilt University hospital in Nashville, her kidneys failing from the poison. Myles brought the children to say goodbye, and within days, with Myles by her bedside, Zilphia died.

Myles was devastated, but he had to be strong for his two young children. He buried his wife in the Summerfield cemetery, adjacent to the Highlander compound, on the mountain she loved. He busied himself with work. His friend and fellow organizer Saul Alinsky called him to Chicago to work on a project, and Horton was grateful for the distraction.

Just a few weeks after Zilphia's death, Myles was in New York City with Rosa Parks to raise money for Highlander in a series of house parties and where she was to appear at a rally for the movement in Madison Square Garden. Rosa seemed tired and nervous. She and Raymond were still without work, they were in dire financial straits, and she'd had to request guards around her apartment building as the threats to her family intensified. The obscene phone calls to their home gave her mother spells of anxiety. Raymond was beginning to drink too much. The stress was causing Rosa to suffer ulcers and insomnia. Virginia Durr was concerned about the Parks' deteriorating living conditions and began to deliver food to the apartment and raise money for rent, appealing to Myles Horton for help. Myles offered Rosa a job on the Highlander staff, but she declined. He eventually arranged for Highlander to provide Rosa with a small stipend of $50 a month to keep the family going.

During her time in New York, Horton arranged for Mrs. Parks to have a private tea with Eleanor Roosevelt at her East Side town house. He took special pleasure introducing "the first lady of the land to the first lady of the South." Mrs. Roosevelt had been a supporter of Highlander since its beginnings. She could be counted on for an annual contribution, a statement of support, and she lent her name to the list of prominent Highlander advisers. The $100 checks she mailed to Highlander from the White House, or in more recent years from her private home, were used by her many enemies as evidence of her radical, and suspiciously red, sympathies. Her FBI file duly noted her support.

Mrs. Roosevelt warmly welcomed Mrs. Parks into her living room, asking many questions about her experience at Highlander and the situation in Montgomery. "Have you been called a Communist yet, Mrs. Parks?" Mrs. Roosevelt gently inquired.

"Yes," Mrs. Parks replied, slightly startled.

"I suppose Myles told you when you were at Highlander that you'd be called a Communist," Mrs. Roosevelt continued. Mrs. Parks said no, Myles hadn't warned her, prompting Mrs. Roosevelt to scold him for not doing so. "If I'd known what she was going to do, I would have told her," he pleaded. "But when she was at Highlander she said she wasn't going to do anything . . . she came from the cradle of the Confederacy . . . If I'd known she was going to start the civil rights movement, I would have told her."

Mrs. Parks also came to his defense: "Yes, he told me later on, after I got arrested," she explained. Horton had rushed to Montgomery to support Parks and the bus strike. "I went down, and I talked to her," Horton added, "because I knew she was going to get it."

Mrs. Roosevelt wrote a sympathetic—and prescient—report of the tea with Mrs. Parks in her syndicated "My Day" column:

> A few days ago I met Mrs. Rosa Parks, who started the nonviolent protest in Montgomery, Alabama, against segregation on buses. She is a very

quiet, gentle person and it is difficult to imagine how she ever could take such a positive and independent stand.

I suppose we must realize that these things do not happen all of a sudden. They grow out of feelings that have been developing over many years. Human beings reach a point when they say: "This is as far as I can go," and from then on it may be passive resistance, but it will be resistance.

That is what seems to have happened in Montgomery, and perhaps it will happen all over our country wherever we have citizens who do not enjoy complete equality. It may be that this attitude will save us from war and bloodshed and teach those of us who have to learn that there is a point beyond which human beings will not continue to bear injustice.

Mrs. Parks traveled from New York to Washington to speak at a leadership conference of the National Council of Negro Women, founded by Mary McLeod Bethune, who had recently died. Septima Clark also attended the event and witnessed how brave, but also how uneasy, Rosa was in her new public role. In her remarks, she gave full credit to her time at Highlander the previous summer for opening her eyes to the possibilities of an integrated society, which spurred her to take action. But Clark took notice of how often Parks swallowed nervously as she spoke and appreciated how difficult this public speaking was for the shy seamstress.

Clark brought Parks to her hotel room to rest between sessions, and there the two women could speak more candidly. Septima was concerned by her friend's anxious state and also annoyed by the way she was being treated by the NAACP and the Montgomery Improvement Association. They celebrated her, but didn't take care of her. Parks faced press interviews alone, and the naturally reticent woman was sometimes reduced to tears by aggressive questioning. The organizations using Parks as a spokeswoman needed to provide her with "a guide and some sort of counselor as she travels," Clark insisted. She feared the strain was becoming too much for Rosa.

———◆———

Clark was facing her own strains. Her outspoken views, her uncompromising civil rights work, Highlander, the NAACP, the Warings: they were all part of her "downfall," as she called it, in Charleston. But they were also the wellspring of a new beginning. When Mrs. Clark told Myles Horton of her dismissal from her teaching job, he was both consoling and calculating. "Oh, I'm so happy," she remembered him saying, as he encouraged her to join the Highlander staff as director of workshops. It was a flattering offer, but she wasn't sure she should accept.

She was fifty-eight years old and had been teaching for more than forty years; she was at the stage when many teachers contemplated retirement. But in addition to losing her job, she had also been stripped of her state pension. She didn't have the luxury of retiring; she needed to find new work. She already had some teaching offers. A few seemed attractive, but she feared they would not allow her the freedom to continue as an outspoken advocate for civil rights. She turned them down. The Warings urged her to come north, and they would help her find a good teaching job in New York City. She could earn much more and live unencumbered by Jim Crow restrictions. She demurred. "I really don't want to leave the south unless I am forced to do so," she told them. "I want to stay here and fight this thing out. Like the slaves, I feel that trouble won't last always."

But she wasn't sure that Highlander—though certainly in the South—was the right place for her. With Zilphia gone, the warmth and welcome she had enjoyed, the joyous spirit of the singing, would no longer be part of life on the mountain. Septima's affection for Zilphia had been more personal and spontaneous than her relation with Myles, which centered on respect and shared convictions rather than an emotional bond. She had qualms about the cold and snowy mountain winters; she wasn't used to that sort of weather. She'd be leaving her sister, moving farther away from her son and grandchildren in North Carolina. And she wondered how comfortable she would be as the only Black staff member at Highlander, the only Black resident of Grundy County.

When she arrived in June to teach at the summer workshops, Clark told Horton she couldn't give him an answer right away, but she would decide by fall. He was willing to wait. For the next three months, in her little bedroom at Highlander, Clark couldn't sleep, racked with worries and indecision. She prayed for divine guidance and tried to discern her path forward.

The workshop topics had evolved since the previous summer. Rosa Parks had returned to Highlander in late winter to help revamp the program to reflect the rapid changes taking place on the ground. The Montgomery boycott demonstrated that southern Black communities were ready to expand their vision beyond school desegregation to other aspects of Jim Crow life and were willing to employ radical new tactics to achieve their goals. The new workshop agenda included strategies for desegregating transportation, housing, and parks as well as schools; creating campaigns for registration and voting; and exploring the role of passive resistance and other forms of peaceful protest.

This was new, and for Clark, exciting territory—a profound shift from court cases to direct community action. But it hewed closely to the way Myles Horton had predicted desegregation efforts might progress. Back in 1954, when Clark had brought Esau Jenkins to Highlander for his first workshop, Horton had told them: "Once you get a lot of people marching and a lot of people in step, you quit taking steps and you run. . . . Within a year's time, within two years' time, we are going to start moving faster." The pace was quickening now. Another community bus boycott was in progress in Tallahassee, Florida.

Mrs. Clark's own fight against her state's NAACP ban and her subsequent firing was going nowhere, however. She sent three registered letters requesting a hearing with the school board but received no response. She appealed for help from the National Education Association, but they sat on their hands. The state and national NAACP were concentrating efforts on the Elloree teachers' expulsion, claiming it provided a stronger case. Her local Charleston branch had promised to meet with the school superintendent to register a protest of her firing, but they'd done nothing. Her sorority did not feel secure enough in the sentiments of its members to lodge a complaint on her behalf. Her church brethren kept silent.

Though she felt thwarted in her own legal pursuit of justice, her work for Highlander was revealing novel and promising approaches to demanding equal rights. She recruited a variety of southern community activists to Highlander that summer to share their techniques, triumphs, and travails. Then she celebrated these pioneering advocates in a publication she titled "Champions of Democracy." The brochure, published and widely distributed by Highlander, was more than just a chronicle of the experiments in resistance discussed at the summer workshops. It was a moving, even poetic, tribute to courageous Black activists and brave communities willing to stand up for their rights.

Clark highlighted the spirit and fortitude of the ongoing Montgomery bus boycott and the valor of Rosa Parks, who returned to Highlander that summer to provide inspiration and report on the remarkable mobilization of her community. She also featured the defiant teachers of Elloree, whom Clark invited to Highlander to discuss their dismissal and legal battle—a topic close to her heart—while also paying tribute to the Black citizens and students of Orangeburg who organized so effectively to withstand the White Citizens' Council "squeeze." And she extolled Esau Jenkins and his burgeoning voter registration campaign on Johns Island. Richly illustrated with evocative photographs, the booklet was Clark's homage to civic heroism.

In an unusually raw, personal, and revealing introduction to "Champions," Clark described herself:

I'm a Negro. / Born black in a white man's land. / My name is Septima Clark. I am a teacher. /

I have spent nearly all my adult life teaching citizenship to children who really aren't citizens. /

I can no longer aid in their education because I joined in the movement to help them claim their citizenship. / I was refused employment for asking for something that rightfully belongs to them.

If "Champions of Democracy" was Septima Clark's proclamation of rage and resolve, it was also something of a birth announcement, heralding the arrival of a southern, people-powered struggle for civil rights that was emerging before her eyes.

One morning late that summer at Highlander, after months of anxious, sleepless nights, Septima "felt a kind of free feeling in my mind." She finally felt sure she'd made the right decision: sacrificing her job on principle, moving on to a new mission. She accepted Myles's offer to become Highlander's director of integration workshops and agreed to move to Monteagle Mountain, with the proviso that she could make frequent trips back home to Charleston. She didn't want to abandon her sister, her community work there, or the new literacy project Esau was hoping to launch on Johns Island. And Horton agreed it was important that she not give the impression that she had been run out of town or was ashamed to return. She was still a proud and active citizen of Charleston, though, like the Warings, she was forced to live in exile.

———◆———

In the fall of 1956, as flashes of resistance were flaring up across the map of the southern states, Mrs. Clark hit the road like a traveling saleswoman, bringing the "Highlander idea" of promoting local leadership to southern towns where the Black community seemed receptive to mobilizing. She spoke at Black churches and colleges campuses, community groups and civic organizations in North Carolina, Florida, Georgia, Alabama, and Mississippi, recruiting potential leaders for the upcoming workshops. Clark was able to reach into these Black communities in ways Horton could not, which made her an effective and valuable emissary for the school. She found it especially gratifying when her visit helped spark the creation of a new citizens' committee or voting initiative. The people were ready to rise, she sensed, they just needed some encouragement. Still forced to sit in the back, she traveled mostly by bus, lugging cases filled with Highlander materials, including "Champions of Democracy."

Clark supplemented her recruiting trips with northern fundraising excursions for Highlander. Dispatching the eloquent and passionate Mrs. Clark to speak about the school's projects conveyed a tone of authenticity to Highlander's interracial efforts. Clark kept the Warings abreast of all her Highlander travels and regularly mailed clippings from local newspapers to them, accompanied by long letters addressed to "My dear, dear friends." Elizabeth mailed back interesting articles and provocative essays on the evils of segregation by the liberal, white southern writer Lillian Smith, which Clark then included in the package of reading materials she assembled for her workshop participants.

Whenever she was anywhere near New York City, Clark always took time to visit the Warings at their apartment. She still looked to them for support and guidance and, to a certain extent, affirmation. She confided in them, expressing feelings and fears she found difficult to share with others; perhaps the physical and social distance between them made it easier. The Warings relied on her as a trusted source of news from the southern battlefronts and occasionally mailed to her small amounts of money, to cover the cost of long-distance telephone calls she made to them. "I can't bring myself to call collect," she admitted to them. "It wounds my pride."

In exile, the judge had taken on the role of an elder statesman in civil rights matters, sought after by the media for expert legal commentary on the latest events. Waring could be found on podiums and panels, on radio airwaves and television screens. Lately he had conducted a televised conversation with the intriguing young man who'd emerged as the leader of the Montgomery bus boycott, Rev. Dr. Martin Luther King Jr. Septima had already told the Warings how impressed she was with the earnest and eloquent Baptist minister: "The Rev. King in Alabama made a wonderful speech on TV," she wrote to them. "It was deep and sincere and showed a new Negro emerging. No fear and a great determination to stand up for the rights."

That same fall, Clark's own rights were on trial in the federal courthouse in Charleston. She sat in the courtroom where Judge Waring had once presided, listening to arguments in the lawsuit brought by the Elloree teachers challenging the South Carolina NAACP membership ban. NAACP Legal Defense lawyer Jack Greenberg made the case to a three-judge panel that the state's ban violated the teachers' constitutional rights of freedom of association. Clark listened intently to the proceedings and thought attorney Greenberg made a "masterful" presentation. But she would soon be disappointed: The judges refused to make any decision about the constitutionality of the NAACP membership ban, just kicked the case back to the state courts, knowing it had no chance of success there.

The NAACP appealed to the Supreme Court, but before the case could be heard, the South Carolina legislature cleverly repealed the original law, replacing it with a seemingly more benign requirement that state and municipal employees list all their organizational affiliations, without specific mention of the NAACP. The Elloree teachers' legal case dissolved and was not revived. The Elloree teachers received no relief, and many of them were forced to leave the state to find new teaching jobs. Some never did find new careers and lived in poverty. Mrs. Clark's case against her own dismissal was never developed by the NAACP. For South Carolina state employees, especially teachers, the revised law made no difference: if they revealed their membership in the NAACP, they were fired. Septima was disgusted and struggled to maintain her equilibrium.

"I can't lose my temper or have any hate in my heart," she insisted to Elizabeth Waring. "It's the price I agreed to pay for holding the line for freedom."

CHAPTER FOURTEEN

The Grocery Store

S eptima and Esau went schoolhouse shopping in the fall of 1956; they were finally ready to begin building the literacy school. They had been preparing for more than two years: a period of exploration, evaluation, trust building— and argument. There were, at times, strong disagreements and divergent goals: Horton wanted to nurture local leaders on the Sea Islands; Jenkins wanted to train voters; Clark wanted to build literate citizens. They settled on a plan that combined all three: an adult literacy school to replace Jenkins's bus-based lessons, but one that would expand into instruction for voter registration, citizenship skills, and civic engagement. Horton had secured funding from the Schwarzhaupt Foundation and approval from the Highlander board to pursue the program. Now they just had to find a place, a pedagogy, and a teacher. None of these was going to be easy.

Clark relished the challenge, eager to channel her recent frustrations into a frenzy of activity. She had always managed to crowd out any doubts or sorrows sitting heavy in her mind or heart by keeping busy. For decades she had been occupied by her teaching, family obligations, church and civic volunteer work; now she had Highlander. The intense travel schedule was certainly exhausting for her—a new place, new people, new bed almost every night for weeks at a time—yet she drew energy from her role as Highlander's evangelist and regained hope by launching the literacy school.

Jenkins had struck out in his first attempts to find a location—rebuffed by a Black pastor concerned that his wife might lose her teaching job if authorities learned of the church's involvement in a voter registration scheme and also by a Black school principal who feared for his own job if the white superintendent found out—so Clark joined him in another search through Johns Island. Again, nothing seemed suitable or available, and they eventually decided the school would need its own space, a place not beholden to a fretful landlord.

Jenkins heard that the district school board was selling one of the old, tumble-down "Negro schools" on the island. He asked to buy it, but the board turned him down, selling it to a white man instead. Within a week, the new white owner offered to flip the school building to Jenkins—at a 50 percent markup—$1,500 cash. It was robbery, but Jenkins felt he had little choice. He asked Clark and Horton if Highlander could help by providing a loan, and Horton agreed to put up the funds with an interest-free loan. With Highlander's financing, Jenkins's Progressive Club was able to purchase the old Mount Zion schoolhouse.

The members of the Progressive Club went to work rehabbing the building: installing electricity and running water, fixing the roof and walls, patching, plastering, painting. They fashioned the front part of the building into a cooperative grocery store, installing a stove and a counter, lining the walls with shelves. Jenkins had long wanted to create a food co-op for the island, allowing people to sell the vegetables from their gardens, eggs and chickens from their farms, and shrimp from their fishing nets to their neighbors. This was the kind of Black self-sufficiency he had advocated for years. In addition to local farm products, the store would stock basic canned goods, cigarettes, soda, and candy, and the revenue could be used to pay back the Highlander loan quickly.

The grocery store was also a useful front, a clever stage set camouflaging the building's true purpose. In the back two rooms, hidden from view, were the classrooms where the literacy classes would be held. "We planned the grocery story to fool white people," Mrs. Clark explained. "We didn't want them to know that we had a school back there."

When Clark's father was an enslaved boy in South Carolina, it was illegal to teach slaves to read or write, as literacy could give those in bondage a measure of awareness and agency, put ideas in their heads. More than a century later, Clark knew that teaching reading, with the goal of training the descendants of the slaves to vote and enter civic life, was still a dangerous enterprise. "We didn't have any windows back there, so white people couldn't peep in," Clark explained. "That's the way we planned it."

What was to be taught in those back rooms, how it should be taught, and by whom were still not fully formulated. In long, animated discussions, Clark and Horton agreed on certain fundamentals: the need for a flexible classroom structure, a welcoming atmosphere, and a creative, nontraditional, teacher. But these two experienced, strong-willed educators came to loggerheads over other essentials.

Clark envisioned basic literacy proficiency as the foundation of the classes: the students learning to read and write letters and numbers, decoding words, signing their names. All very practical. In her mind, the goal was to enable adults to gain competence and, more importantly, confidence. Only then could they stand up as secure and active members of their community, become voters, and claim their rights. Hers was a methodical, holistic approach to building "first-class citizens."

Horton advocated a more targeted plan, emphasizing voter preparation and political awareness; he thought dwelling on functional literacy beyond the registration requirements was not an efficient use of time. Clark thought Horton's concept was shortsighted; he thought hers was too unfocused. Yet both came to realize that it was the Johns Islanders themselves who would ultimately shape the school.

The key to success was to find the right teacher. Clark and Horton agreed that it could not be a white person, who might intimidate the islanders, nor should it be a professional teacher, who would enter the classroom with a set way of doing things. They needed to find someone sympathetic, adventurous, and flexible. The teacher should be committed to civil rights advocacy, comfortable with the islanders and their Gullah language, and willing to work with Highlander. Septima thought she knew the ideal person, and for once, Myles, with no hesitation, agreed.

———◆———

"I never been no teacher, and I'm not going to be a teacher," Bernice Robinson protested when Clark and Horton asked her to teach the literacy class on Johns Island. She wasn't qualified, she insisted. She had only a high school education. She had never stood in front of a classroom before; she didn't know how to teach. "I told you up there at Highlander that I would help you all in any way that I could," she pleaded, but she was beautician, not a teacher.

"That's exactly why you're going to do this," Horton urged. "You know how to listen, and you respect the adults who want to vote." The Highlander emissaries were relentless. "They just laid the law down to me," Robinson recalled. "We don't want a certified teacher because they are accustomed to working by a straitlaced curriculum," they told her, "and wouldn't be able to bend, to give." The island school needed someone "who would not be considered highfalutin," as Septima put it. "Would not act condescending to adults."

"We need a community worker to do it who cares for the people, who understands the people, who can communicate with the people," Clark and Horton maintained. "Someone who has been to Highlander and knows Highlander's philosophy.

"So there's nobody to do it but you," they insisted. "Either you do it, or we don't have the school." The guilt trip was so effective, Robinson felt she had little choice. Highlander, and her own cousin Seppie, were calling her to serve, in a special way, in the struggle. Though she didn't feel qualified or prepared, she gave in, just as Septima knew she would.

Robinson's experience as a beautician outweighed her lack of teaching expertise. Beyond skill with scissors and combs, a beautician needs to be a good listener, lending a sympathetic ear to her clients' personal stories confided from the chair. At her Beauty Box salon, Robinson had created a safe, supportive space for women to talk and vent; she would need to provide a similar haven for the Johns Island class. Beauticians like Robinson enjoyed the trust and respect of their communities, and as an independent businesswoman with a loyal Black clientele, Robinson would not be subject to economic reprisals from white employers or patrons. She also had the kind of bubbly personality, sense of humor, and can-do attitude needed to steer around the inevitable bumps in the road. As an unconventional choice for an unusual project, Robinson was ideal.

Still, "people on the island didn't want to trust Black people coming from the city," as Clark well knew. Islanders felt, with justification, that Black Charlestonians viewed them with disdain, thought them to be backward and crude, made fun of them. But Robinson was no stranger to the island; she had helped Jenkins in NAACP activities there, she had participated in the Highlander workshops and conferences with the islanders. Clark and Jenkins eased Robinson's entry by introducing her around the island, demonstrating that she had their blessing and support. With Jenkins's imprimatur, Robinson was able to speak at the islands' churches, recruiting students for the class. Alert to the sensitivities of her prospective students, being careful not to embarrass or scare them away, Robinson never asked directly whether anyone in the audience was illiterate, she simply asked if they had any "friends" who might benefit from learning to read. Robinson's gentle, oblique approach allowed self-conscious adults to admit that they themselves could use such help and quietly sign up for the class.

Among the very first to enroll was Alice Wine. This class was the fulfillment of Esau Jenkins's promise to her, and she was going to grasp it with both of her strong, sinewy hands.

As the Christmas season approached and final preparations were being made for the Johns Island school, momentous news arrived from Montgomery: there was to be no more segregated boarding and seating on city buses, and the boycott was over. The boycott had been wildly successful in drawing attention to the desegregation fight and bringing the bus company to the brink of bankruptcy, but it was not the boycott itself that won the opening of Montgomery's buses.

It was a lawsuit initiated by twenty-six-year-old Montgomery attorney Fred Gray, aided by NAACP's Thurgood Marshall, challenging Montgomery statutes requiring bus segregation, that forced the city to relent. The suit, brought on behalf of four Black women—including teenager Claudette Colvin—who had been mistreated on the city buses, in violation of their Fourteenth Amendment rights, was decided by the US Supreme Court, citing the *Brown* precedent in the ruling. (Rosa Parks's appeal of her conviction was still pending and was not part of this suit.) Federal marshals delivered the court's desegregation order to Montgomery officials on December 20, 1956, and hours later, in an emotional mass meeting, the Montgomery Improvement Association voted to end its 382-day boycott.

Early the next morning, Dr. King and Rev. Abernathy boarded a city bus, taking front-row seats, a moment recorded for posterity by many camera flash-bulbs. Later that day, a photographer for *Look* magazine coaxed Rosa Parks to pose in the white section of a city bus, creating an image that immortalized her pivotal role. Across the city, Black Montgomerians wept in the streets in an outpouring of relief, exhaustion, and thanksgiving. The mobilization and solidarity of the city's Black community would prove to be the most powerful legacy of the protest, a touchstone for what was to come.

Within days of Dr. King's triumphant bus ride, the door of his house was shattered by a shotgun blast. Snipers fired into the windows of the city's newly integrated buses, wounding several passengers. But the prospect of forcing integration on city transit had taken hold. In Birmingham, Rev. Fred Shuttlesworth announced his plan to lead a "freedom ride" of Black riders occupying the front seats of his city's buses on the day after Christmas. On Christmas night, fifteen sticks of dynamite exploded in Shuttlesworth's parsonage, destroying the house, plunging him into the basement, miraculously unharmed. The next day, a shaken but defiant Rev. Shuttlesworth led his followers onto the buses, where they were arrested.

CHAPTER FIFTEEN

Pencils

O n New Year's Eve 1956, Johns Islanders sang, shouted, stomped, and prayed till "day-clean"—the Gullah term for dawn—at the annual New Year's Watch celebration in Moving Star Hall. The event commemorated their ancestors' historic nighttime vigil, welcoming the first day of 1863, when President Lincoln's Emancipation Proclamation took effect, setting them free. Almost a hundred years later, with many promises of that freedom still unfulfilled, a new sense of hope and possibility was stirring on the island. Just before Christmas, news traveled to the island that Blacks in Montgomery had joined together to defeat Jim Crow. On New Year's Day, Esau Jenkins would open the Progressive Club cooperative grocery store. And later in that first week of 1957, in the hidden back rooms behind the shelves, the Johns Island literacy school would open its secret door.

Bernice Robinson was nervous on that first Monday evening in January as she rode in her brother's car over the bridge from Charleston to Johns Island. It was already dark when they arrived at the Progressive Club cooperative grocery store on River Road, and she had no idea what she was going to do or say once she stepped inside.

Robinson walked past the counter, behind the grocery shelves, to the back classroom. The room was freshly painted, fitted with a rudimentary blackboard, and furnished with adult-size tables and chairs. This was something both Clark and Horton had insisted upon: the classroom must be equipped with furniture meant for grown-ups. They knew that the problem with so many adult remedial reading classes was that they were demeaning. Grown men and women were treated like children: considered "slow" just because they'd never had opportunity to learn to read or write, forced to sit in chairs uncomfortably small. Big men twisted into kiddy-size seats were teased as "daddy-long-legs" and often grew so embarrassed and irritated that they dropped out of the class. These literacy classes would be different.

Still, Robinson didn't know exactly how she was supposed to make this class different, better, or more successful. Septima and Myles had given her no curriculum, offered little specific guidance; she had no lesson plan. The only materials she carried into the classroom that night were a voter registration application, a couple of reading primers lent to her by her sisters-in-law, who were elementary schoolteachers, and a printed poster of the UN Declaration of Human Rights, which Myles had mailed to her from Monteagle. She tacked the declaration onto the classroom wall.

Fourteen Johns Islanders, ten women and four men, were signed up for the class. The class would meet for two hours, twice a week, for two months, with homework in between the lessons. The timing of the semester, during the dead of winter, was intentional. This was what the islanders called the "laying by" season, when outdoor agricultural work was suspended. It was the short gap in the year when farm and fishing laborers, normally working from sunup to sundown, had the time and energy to attend evening classes. The class would have to close once the planting season began again in late February and workers were called back into the fields.

Robinson knew that enrolling in this class wasn't an easy decision. It was hard for adults to admit, in such a public way, that they were illiterate. They had managed to get by for years in most aspects of island life; Gullah was a spoken language, not a written one. They had been able to hide their reading and writing deficiency, compensating for it with memorization. Or they faked it, carrying a pen or pencil in their pocket, a conspicuous display of an instrument they didn't know how to use for writing. Very often they were forced to rely on others—their children, coworkers, ministers, landlords, or bosses—to read documents to them, to figure routine sums. They knew they were often being cheated, misled, bamboozled. If, as Esau promised, this class could help them read and write and figure—and vote, just like the white people did—then it was worth trying.

The men and women filed into the back room quietly, shyly, and found a seat. Most kept their hats and coats on; a damp winter chill seeped in through the walls. Bernice stood before them, her eyes sweeping across their eager faces. They looked at her with anticipation. She smiled, trying hard to tamp down her nerves, not sure how to begin.

"They say I'm your teacher," she said softly. "But I'm not going to be the teacher." There were probably some confused looks. "We're going to learn together."

"You're going to teach me some things, and maybe there are a few things I might be able to teach you," she continued, "but I don't consider myself a teacher. I'm here to learn with you. We'll learn things together."

Her words, hesitant and honest, released the tension in the room. "I think that sorta settled the folks down, put them at ease," she would later recall. By flipping the power dynamic of the typical classroom, Robinson forged an immediate rapport with her students, turning the class into a conversation among adults. "It got them to open up, be willing to learn. That set the stage for everything." Robinson would remember that moment for the rest of her life.

She started out with an exercise from a reading primer she had brought with her but quickly found it totally inappropriate: too juvenile, almost insulting. These were adults, they had a lifetime of experience, learning to read from Dick and Jane was not what they needed. She discarded the texts and asked the class: "What do *you* want to learn?"

They responded with a burst of requests; they had very definite ideas about what they wanted to learn. First, they wanted to be able to write their names, not just the X they had always used as their signatures. Next, they wanted to master reading the words in the South Carolina constitution required to register to vote. They would also like to read a newspaper so they could understand what was going on in the world. They wanted to be able to read their Bibles, not just recite passages from memory. They wanted to know how to fill out a mail-order form so they could buy things from the Sears catalog (shopping trips to Charleston were rarely possible) and learn how to complete a money order for those purchases, as they didn't have bank accounts. In addition, they would like to be able to read and write letters to their family who lived far away.

Robinson took careful notes, recording everything on the class's wish list. That list would form the framework for her lessons and creative teaching methods. She called each student to her desk and asked them to read a short paragraph and sign their names. Many whispered to her, "I can't write" or "I can't read that well." Twelve of the fourteen students could not read or write at all and would have to start from scratch; the others could read a little, but very poorly. But they wanted to learn.

That same week in early January, as the first classes opened on Johns Island, sixty ministers from ten southern states gathered in Atlanta at the invitation of Rev. Dr. Martin Luther King Jr. for what he called the Negro Leaders Conference on Transportation and Nonviolent Integration. The purpose of the meeting was to spread the "Montgomery idea" of nonviolent desegregation protest to other cities, through the auspices of the Black church.

The ministers formed an umbrella organization to coordinate the activities of local church-based civil rights groups around the South and chose Dr. King president of their new organization, which would eventually adopt the name Southern Christian Leadership Conference.

The distinguished men of the cloth who formed the Southern Christian Leadership Conference in Atlanta had no knowledge of the little literacy class beginning on Johns Island, and the illiterate rural laborers sitting in the back room of the grocery store knew nothing of the urban pastors forming a new association dedicated to their liberation.

———————◆———————

In the grocery store they sat, backs hunched over the long wooden tables, elbows akimbo, fingers clenched, eyes fixed on their task. The potbelly stove hissed and sputtered, but the loudest sound in the room was the sharp crack of pencils snapping to pieces. Pencils were splintering all around the room, broken by strong fingers unaccustomed to holding a skinny stick of wood stuffed with graphite.

Those fingers were used to gripping plows and hammers, shovels and fishing nets, wringing laundry and picking crops. Now these fingers, hardened by labor and knotted by age, were trying to pilot a pencil over a sheet of paper laid atop a slice of cardboard, tracing the curves that spelled out the letters of their names.

But the new students were trying too hard, gripping too tightly, bearing down too heavily. Too eager, too anxious, the pencils just snapped under the stress. One after another, their pencils broke, and they mumbled in frustration. Mrs. Robinson told them not to worry, gave them another pencil from the box, and they tried again.

These were the first lessons. The students were practicing a method suggested by Mrs. Clark called kinesthetic writing, one she'd learned when she was teaching illiterate soldiers during World War II. Under Clark's long-distance guidance, Robinson constructed pieces of cardboard with each student's name written in bold cursive letters. They traced the lines of their names with their finger, over and over, building a muscle memory of their signatures. Then they progressed to tracing those signatures with pencils on paper overlaid on the cardboard template. Just holding the pencils was a challenge, so Robinson went around the room, correcting grips, offering encouragement and new pencils. Broken pencils would not deter them. These were the instruments that promised to change their lives, and they were determined to master them.

Although the novice teacher Robinson consulted regularly with the veteran Clark, she used her own creativity to design lessons. Instead of rote drills, she asked her students to tell her a story about their lives, what they did in the fields and in their homes, the tasks of their days, which she transcribed onto paper. Working from their own stories in their own words, the students learned to recognize written words in a context that made sense to them, speeding their reading progress. Robinson led them in sounding out, and learning the meanings of, the words of the South Carolina constitution they would need to know for voter registration. The words they stumbled over were added to the spelling and vocabulary study lists.

Once a student could handle simple writing, Robinson brought in catalogs and had them practice filling out mail-order forms, including doing simple arithmetic. To give the students math practice, she used newspaper grocery ads: If two pounds of beans cost forty-nine cents, how much will four pounds cost? For the men, she used examples they could relate to: How many gallons of gas does it take for a trip from the island to Charleston, how much will it cost to fill the tank of your truck for that trip? How many feet of lumber to build a fence?

Teaching in this one-room schoolhouse, Robinson had to deal with students of different ages working at different levels and at different paces. As the semester progressed, the class grew, almost tripling in size, as the students boasted to their neighbors about all they were learning in school. In addition, many of the women in the class brought their young daughters along with them, not comfortable leaving the girls home alone during the evening hours. More chairs were needed. Robinson, a talented seamstress herself, kept the teenagers busy by teaching them sewing and crocheting, skills they could use to make extra money for the family. She supplemented these craft lessons for the girls with assignments in public speaking, making the back of the grocery store a three-ring circus of learning. Esau often came in to lend a hand.

It was exhausting but joyful work for Robinson, who volunteered her time for the project. Highlander reimbursed her only $50 a month for her travel and material expenses. She paid out of her own pocket the caretaker who watched her mother on the evenings she was teaching. She spent her days and weekends working extra hours in her beauty shop and catching up on the sewing and dressmaking assignments she took to supplement her income. Her nights were filled with creating lesson plans, assembling teaching materials, correcting homework.

"I have never before in my life seen such anxious people," Robinson reported to Clark in the early weeks of the class. "They really want to learn and are so proud of the little gains they have made so far. When I get to the club each night, half of them are already there and have their homework ready for me to see."

One moment in the semester was particularly touching to Robinson. She wrote the names of all the students on the blackboard and asked one woman if she could find her name up on the board. "Yes, ma'am, I sure can," the woman replied, walking to the front of the classroom, taking the ruler from Robinson's hand, and pointing to a spot on the blackboard: "That's my name there, Annie. A-N-N-I-E. And that's my other name down there Vastine, V-A-S-T-I-N-E."

Robinson felt a surge of goose bumps come over her. "It was very emotional. It really meant something to me," she recalled, "to see that woman recognize her name. She could not read or write when she came in that class. And she was sixty-five years old."

One of the most enthusiastic students was Esau's mentee, Alice Wine, who had become a devoted member of the Progressive Club and began working as a cashier at the cooperative grocery store. Robinson noticed that Wine, who was coming along nicely in her reading, still had to count on her fingers to make change for customers. Robinson began tutoring her on simple math skills, using toothpicks and match sticks as counters, until Wine could add and subtract in her head, without relying on the sticks or her fingers.

Robinson supplemented the literacy instruction with nuts-and-bolts information about voting requirements and discussions of citizen rights. By the final weeks of the semester, as Robinson conducted the class, thirty or forty young men and boys could be found gathering in the front room of the grocery store, listening in.

Mrs. Clark couldn't get to Johns Island to observe the class until the very last session, in late February. Robinson asked her to lead the class, to see how the master teacher would handle the instruction. Clark took some of the more difficult words in the South Carolina constitution, broke them into syllables, and made the students practice pronouncing them. Robinson was pleased to realize that she had been employing the same method.

"In two months' time, surprising to say," Clark reported, "there were some who were ready to register." Everyone in the class was urged to attend Citizens' Club meetings and apply what they had learned by getting involved in civic affairs on the island.

Horton also traveled to Johns Island to observe the class and came away amazed: "I wish you could have seen the expressions on the faces of the people learning to read and write and spell," he reported back to the Schwarzhaupt Foundation. "I am not easily impressed because I've seen so many educational ventures flop, but I was impressed to hear the people there talking about integrating the schools and voting while Bernice corrected homework."

Robinson had succeeded in taking the class beyond simple reading and writing, motivating her students to become involved citizens. Demand was strong for another semester, so Clark, Jenkins, and Robinson began planning for next winter's session of what the students were calling "citizenship school."

CHAPTER SIXTEEN

Anniversary

S eptima Clark felt a thrill the moment she boarded the train headed to Washington. All fifteen cars of the train were packed, with several more trains following, all filled with Black men, women, and children dressed for church, heading to the nation's capital on May 17, 1957—the third anniversary of the original *Brown* decision—to attend a Prayer Pilgrimage for Freedom.

Organized by A. Philip Randolph, president of the Brotherhood of Sleeping Car Porters, and cosponsored by the NAACP and the newly formed Southern Christian Leadership Conference, the pilgrimage was to be both a spiritual and political event, a display of unity, faith, resolve—and impatience. The demonstration was a public demand that the US government enforce the desegregation mandate of the Supreme Court, which was being subverted by massive southern resistance. It challenged Congress, where a civil rights bill was languishing, and the White House, which was reluctant to advance any strong civil rights agenda, to live up to America's oft-professed democratic ideals. At the heart of this challenge was a call for strengthened voting rights.

Mrs. Clark marched with the other protesters in a long line toward the marble steps of the Lincoln Memorial. By noon, almost thirty thousand people—mostly Black people, together with several thousand whites—who had traveled from thirty states, were standing with her. It was when she spotted fellow Charlestonians in the crowd, who had chartered an entire train car to make the trip to Washington, that Mrs. Clark began to cry. The sight of people from her own home community, many of whom had resisted her "radical" activism for so long, triggered a rush of emotion.

For three hours the assembled pilgrims listened to a mix of sermons, speeches, and hymns. They shouted "amen" and "hallelujah" and waved handkerchiefs above their heads as a parade of fiery ministers and movement dignitaries offered exhortations from the podium, and a new breed of activist entertainers—Harry Belafonte, Ruby Dee, Sammy Davis Jr., and Sidney

Poitier—lent Hollywood dazzle to the event. The great gospel singer Mahalia Jackson raised her voice in song and hymns. The last speaker was Rev. Dr. King, making his debut speech before such a large audience.

"Give us the ballot," King proclaimed, "and we will no longer have to worry the federal government about our basic rights.

"Give us the ballot, and we will fill our legislative halls with men of goodwill, and send to the sacred halls of Congress men who will not sign a 'Southern Manifesto' because of their devotion to the manifesto of justice."

This was Mrs. Clark's first time hearing Rev. King speak in person, and she was deeply impressed not only with his oratory skills and moral clarity, but his boldness. "King made it clear that this is a demonstration for justice," she reported to the Warings. "King did not ask for anything shorter than the ballot," she wrote to them, "and he promised that this administration will see the hand of the Negro not turning back ever, but shedding blood, imprisoned, and dieing [*sic*] for first class citizenship."

Clark felt a deep spiritual connection to King's plea. "Give Us the Ballot" could very well serve as the rallying cry of the class struggling with their pencils in the little citizenship school on Johns Island, working so hard to become voters. He was speaking for them.

"The ovation he received was tremendous," Clark told the Warings, adding proudly: "He [is] coming to us for our twenty-fifth anniversary" at Highlander.

————— ◆ —————

In the spring of 1957, Myles Horton found himself in the profoundly awkward situation of planning a grand celebration of Highlander's twenty-fifth anniversary while simultaneously fighting to save his school.

It was a lonelier fight for Myles this time, without Zilphia by his side. She had been gone less than a year when he was stunned by a letter arriving from Washington. The Internal Revenue Service, very likely at the urging of Senator Eastland of Mississippi, was revoking Highlander's tax-exempt status as an educational facility. This would destroy his ability to raise funds from foundations, the school's main source of income.

Once again Horton was forced to reach out to sympathetic members of Congress, and to his influential allies, for intervention and supportive public statements. He begged the foundations funding Highlander's work for patience, putting their grants on ice. He also pleaded with Highlander's alumni and friends to dig deep into their own pockets to keep the school going while the IRS ruling was under appeal.

Highlander's wrestle with the IRS unfolded within a broader, concerted governmental assault on civil rights activities. The year before, in 1956, FBI director J. Edgar Hoover had established a special counterintelligence program in his agency, COINTELPRO, to investigate and disrupt what it considered subversive activity, with an emphasis on monitoring civil rights activists. The southern states continued to build fortifications to protect segregation with an expanding array of official bodies. There were legislative investigatory committees—nicknamed "little HUACs"—modeled after Congress's House Un-American Activities Committee—as well as state-sponsored surveillance and intelligence entities, dubbed "little FBIs."

These authorized, taxpayer-funded outfits were endowed with vaguely virtuous names: Mississippi, Arkansas, and Louisiana called theirs "State Sovereignty Commissions"; Alabama had its "Legislative Commission to Preserve the Peace"; Georgia relied upon its "Education Commission." Governors ran these agencies, appointing segregationist lawmakers, elected officials, and law enforcement officers to serve as directors, equipping the offices with professional staffs, broad mandates, and generous budgets. The various southern state units forged communications links and cooperative ties, sharing information and swapping strategies. They also collaborated with their state's White Citizens' Councils, attorneys general, state police, and FBI offices.

The FBI had kept its eye on the Prayer Pilgrimage in Washington in May 1957, sharing information with southern state segregation agencies. Now, later in the summer of that year, the focus moved to Monteagle Mountain.

Highlander was well known at FBI headquarters. The agency had kept track of the school's activities since the 1930s, filed all its publications (including Mrs. Clark's "Champion's of Democracy" brochure), and carefully cross-referenced the names of everyone associated with the school. For a time, Horton was featured on the FBI Knoxville office's Key Figures list and Security Index file, based on unsubstantiated and later disproven allegations.

The agency also fielded dozens of inquiries and complaints every year about the place, responding with a polite "no comment." The FBI had surveilled and investigated the school numerous times over the years, but never found any credible evidence it was advocating communist ideals or subversive action. The agency's policy was to never confirm or deny any of the many rumors circulating about Highlander, and never to reveal that the agency had found no basis for concern. This allowed the rumors to circulate and amplify unchecked.

In late August, just as the anniversary celebrations on the mountain were about to begin, the assistant director of the FBI Louis Nichols wrote a memo to associate director Clyde Tolson that a confidential source in Tennessee had called with information that the Highlander Folk School was "becoming more active."

"They are having a conference to celebrate the 25th anniversary of the school," the informant reported, and attending would be leaders of the bus boycotts in Montgomery and Tallahassee, including Martin Luther King Jr. "From all [the informant] could learn," Nichols wrote to Tolson, "the Highlander Folk School was becoming a center for teaching civil disobedience."

"You are instructed," FBI Director Hoover wrote to the Knoxville field office, "to be alert to information that the HFS might be engaged in such activities."

While struggling to maintain his balance, Horton was determined to celebrate Highlander's quarter of a century of advocating for justice. At this moment, especially, he needed to project an air of optimism and resilience in the face of adversity. This was no time to lie low, play it safe, or shrink away. Standing at the threshold of a new era of struggle, Highlander was looking to the future, helping forge that future, and he wanted the world to know. The anniversary festivities would take the form of a party and homecoming, wrapped around a Labor Day weekend symposium with the theme "The South Thinking Ahead—The Human Aspects of the Integration Struggle."

Hundreds of invitations were mailed, and a press release announcing the event made its way into the pages of the New York Times. It didn't take an informant to glean this information. The invitation list included Highlander's faithful friends, a wide assortment of academics, clergy, and progressive activists, plus the school's alumni roster. Rosa Parks was coming, as were her Montgomery Improvement Association colleagues Rev. Abernathy and Rev. Dr. King. King would deliver the keynote address on the last day of the symposium. Mrs. Clark arranged for some of the community leaders engaged in creative desegregation projects around the South to bring their stories to the symposium, providing the "human aspect" of the theme. Horton was excited. Highlander was, once again, on the cutting edge.

Septima and Neri Clark, 1919.
Septima P. Clark Papers, Avery
Research Center for African
American History and Culture,
College of Charleston, Charleston, SC

Esau Jenkins
Esau Jenkins Papers, Avery Research Center

Zilphia and Myles Horton.
Highlander Collection, Wisconsin
Historical Society

Judge J. Waties and Elizabeth Waring.
Library of Congress

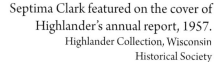

25th ANNUAL REPORT Oct. 1, '56 - Sept. 30, '57

Mrs. Septima Clark, Director of Education, Highlander

PUBLISHED BY HIGHLANDER FOLK SCHOOL • MONTEAGLE, TENNESSEE

Septima Clark featured on the cover of
Highlander's annual report, 1957.
Highlander Collection, Wisconsin
Historical Society

Septima Clark and
Rosa Parks relaxing
at Highlander.
Photo by Ida Berman. With
permission of Karen Berman.
In the Highlander Collection,
Wisconsin Historical Society

LEFT: Bernice Robinson teaching citizenship class on Johns Island, South Carolina. Photo by Ida Berman. With permission of Karen Berman

Johns Island citizenship class student at blackboard. Photo by Ida Berman. With permission of Karen Berman. In the Highlander Collection, Wisconsin Historical Society

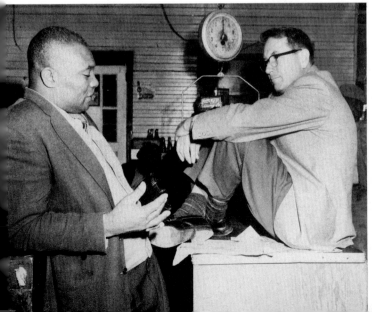

Esau Jenkins and Myles Horton in the Progressive Club grocery store, Johns Island.
Avery Research Center

Septima Clark and Bernice Robinson teaching citizenship class. Photo by Ida Berman. With permission of Karen Berman

Wadmalaw Island citizenship school teacher Ethel Grimball with student. Photo by Ida Berman. With permission of Karen Berman. In the Highlander Collection, Wisconsin Historical Society

Alice Wine, citizenship school student and cashier at the Progressive Club grocery store, Johns Island. Esau Jenkins Papers, Avery Research Center

Rev. Dr. Martin Luther King Jr. with Pete Seeger, Rosa Parks, Rev. Ralph Abernathy, and Myles Horton's daughter, Charis, at Highlander's twenty-fifth anniversary celebration, September 1957. Highlander Education and Research Center archives

Broadside attacking Highlander published by the Georgia Commission on Education, the state's segregation protection agency, fall 1957. Highlander Collection, Wisconsin Historical Society

Myles Horton and Eleanor
Roosevelt at Highlander,
June 1958.
Nashville Banner Photograph
Collection, Nashville Public Library,
Special Collections

Myles Horton watches a
Grundy County sheriff
padlock Highlander's
main building,
September 1958.
Highlander Collection,
Wisconsin Historical Society

Guy Carawan leading singing at mass meeting supporting Nashville lunch
counter sit-in students—John Lewis on far right—Fisk University, April 1960.
Nashville Banner Photograph Collection, Nashville Public Library Special Collections

Dorothy Cotton, Annell Ponder, and Septima Clark of the SCLC's Citizen Education Program in Mississippi, 1963.
Septima P. Clark Papers, Avery Research Center

BELOW: Billboards attacking MLK and Highlander were erected along southern highways, and on the route of the Selma-to-Montgomery march in 1965. Library of Congress

Esau Jenkins with his "Love is Progress" bus.
Esau Jenkins Papers, Avery Research Center

LEFT AND BELOW: Dorothy Cotton teaching citizenship class, Alabama, 196
Photo by Bob Fitch. Courtesy Bob Fitch Photography Archive, Stanford University Libra

LEFT: Septima Clark guiding the hand of a citizenship class student, Alabama, 1966.
Photo by Bob Fitch. Courtesy Bob Fitch Photography Archive, Stanford University Libraries

Septima Poinsette Clark, 1973.
Septima P. Clark Papers,
Avery Research Center

Still, it was hard to plan for a celebration of Highlander without Zilphia, who had breathed life into the place, endowed it with her strength and spirit. Her absence left not only an emotional void but a practical problem: Who would lead the communal singing for the celebration? There could be no Highlander event without singing. Horton telephoned his friend Pete Seeger in New York City.

Seeger always felt a political and philosophical connection to Highlander, reinforced by his professional admiration and personal affection for Zilphia. At this point he shared another kind of connection with Myles: Seeger had also been dragged before a red-baiting congressional panel—the House Un-American Activities Committee—and for his refusal to answer questions concerning Communist connections was indicted for contempt of Congress. He was facing a trial and prison sentence; he had already been blacklisted by radio and television networks, and many performance venues refused to give him a stage. What Zilphia had feared for Myles was happening to Seeger.

Nonetheless, Pete Seeger slung his banjo on his back and made his way to Monteagle Mountain.

———— ✦ ————

Traffic was heavy on the lane leading to the Highlander campus that late August weekend as nearly two hundred guests from twenty-one states arrived for the anniversary festivities. Everything went surprisingly smoothly. The speakers were provocative, the community activists' testimonies inspiring, the discussions lively, the fellowship warm. Pete Seeger served as a roving troubadour, serenading with his banjo. In the evenings, in memory of Zilphia, he led spirited singing, including his version of "We Shall Overcome."

And in what Horton believed to be a stroke of luck, there was a commercial photographer in attendance, a stranger to Highlander who just happened to be passing by. The fellow seemed earnest; he had come from Atlanta on vacation with his wife, said he had always been interested in Highlander. Horton gave him permission to photograph the celebration, thinking Highlander might even buy some of the photos for publicity material. The fellow, Edwin Friend, wandered the grounds, snapping pictures and filming the social aspects of the weekend: people eating together at the long tables, sitting together in the library, swimming in the lake, singing and square dancing in the evenings. All the usual things everyone did at Highlander.

Friend kept busy all weekend. He was aloof and didn't talk much. Mrs. Friend looked distinctly uncomfortable. There was just one thing that seemed strange to Horton, but he was too busy to think much about it. Whenever Friend focused his camera on a group standing or sitting together, especially one including Horton, he would pause and fiddle with his camera until a Black fellow, whom no one recognized, could scoot into the frame and become part of the portrait. This happened again and again. The Black fellow was Abner Berry from New York, and he was also a stranger to Highlander. Horton noticed that Berry and Friend spent a lot of time whispering together, but that seemed natural, since both were outsiders at the Highlander family reunion. Still, Friend including Berry in so many photos began to annoy Horton.

On the final day of the conference, Dr. King arrived with his colleague Rev. Abernathy to attend the morning session and deliver the keynote address. Mrs. Clark was thrilled to finally meet the young man whose progress she had been avidly following, whose words soared, but more importantly, who seemed able to spur people to action. She had been corresponding with him but had not yet met him. King sat in the front row of wooden chairs, alongside Rosa Parks, who also spoke that morning, and Horton joined them there.

Spotting Ed Friend hovering nearby with his camera, Horton asked him to take a picture of the front-row special guests. Friend obliged but took a long time fussing with his camera, as if stalling. He delayed clicking the shutter until Abner Berry shot in from the side and plunked himself down on the floor at Horton's feet, inserting himself awkwardly into the tableau. Horton was angry: "I'm not paying for that picture," he yelled at Friend.

King rose to give his talk, "A Look to the Future," appearing relaxed and informal in his shirtsleeves. King paid tribute to Highlander's "dauntless courage and fearless determination," praising the school for giving "the South some of its most responsible leaders in this great period of transition."

King charted the historical progress toward race equality: "We have broken loose from the Egypt of slavery. We have moved through the wilderness of 'separate but equal,' and now we stand on the border of the promised land of integration." But he also warned of the obstacles ahead, which must be met with nonviolent resolve. "And so let us go out and work with renewed vigor. . . . We must not slow up. Let us keep moving." When King returned to his seat, he joined in a robust closing sing-along led by Pete Seeger. The mood in the Highlander library was buoyant, determined, optimistic.

Ed Friend was positioned outside the library to record King's exit from the library, capturing a sweet, candid moment of King sharing some humorous banter with Seeger, Parks, Abernathy, and Horton's teenage daughter, Charis. Then King hopped into a car for a drive to Kentucky for his next engagement. Relaxing in the back seat, the reverend began humming the tune of one of the songs Seeger had led that morning, one he'd never heard before.

"We Shall Overcome," King remarked, "there's something about that song that haunts you."

CHAPTER SEVENTEEN

Communist Training School

E d Friend rushed back to Atlanta to deliver the film for his movie and photographs to the offices of the Georgia Commission on Education, the state segregation protection agency that had sent him on the undercover mission to Highlander.

The Education Commission was Georgia's "little FBI" agency, reporting directly to Governor Marvin Griffin, who was making a name for himself as a loud crusader against desegregation. The Education Commission operated from what were described as "lavish" offices inside a state building, equipped with a professional staff, five secretaries, and a substantial budget to pursue its mission of protecting Georgia's racial structures. It had the funds to hire consultants, researchers, investigators—and spies.

Edwin Friend was not a random photographer on vacation just passing through Monteagle on Labor Day weekend. He was a state employee with camera skills who moonlighted as the official photographer for Governor Griffin. Friend would soon apply his talents as official photographer for the Georgia Ku Klux Klan.

The Education Commission worked hand in hand with Georgia's White Citizens' Council organization and forged strong connections with many of its counterpart southern state investigative units. They shared intelligence and informers, relied on the same set of for-profit consultants and paid witnesses who sold dubious information about the Communist connections of "race agitators." Highlander figured prominently in these reports, especially since the instigator of the Montgomery Bus Boycott, Rosa Parks, made no secret of her affiliation and affection for the school. When the Education Commission learned that both Parks and Rev. King would be attending Highlander's twenty-fifth-anniversary event in late August, it presented the perfect opportunity to gather some incriminating evidence against the school and its guests. With the approval of Attorney General Cooke and Governor Griffin, the commission dispatched Ed Friend to infiltrate the anniversary events.

Friend trained his lens on the brazen mixing of the races at Highlander, especially the dancing, eating, and swimming together, which he found shocking and disgusting. His wife was so upset by the interracial goings-on that she hid in the couple's hotel room down the mountain for most of the weekend. Friend also got lucky when he discovered the other stranger attending the Highlander festivities, Abner Berry. Friend learned what no one else at Highlander knew: Berry wasn't just a freelance writer whose wife was attending the conference, he was a columnist for the Communist Party's *Daily Worker* newspaper. He was a bona fide Commie. He was Black. And he was at Highlander. It was perfect.

So Friend made sure to place Berry in lots of the photos, positioning him close to Horton and Parks and other southern rights advocates in residence for the weekend. Berry would later say he didn't realize Friend was using him in this way, but just his passive presence in the photos tainted the race movement leaders with a nice splash of red. When King arrived at the conference on the last day, Friend instructed Berry to crash into the photo shoot.

Friend turned over his photographic treasures to the commission at a propitious moment. Barely two days after the finale of the Highlander anniversary celebration, on September 4, 1957, nine Black teenagers attempted to enter Central High School in Little Rock but were turned away by an angry white mob and the rifles of the Arkansas National Guard. Unlike other southern cities, the Little Rock school district had a plan to slowly and hesitantly begin integrating its high schools. But on the first day of school, the students, soon to be known as the Little Rock Nine, were subjected to ugly abuse and denied entry by the state militia.

Governor Orval Faubus claimed he ordered the guard to block the Black students for their own safety, but Faubus—once considered a moderate on race issues—was facing reelection and had discovered the political potency of massive resistance. Supported by his ambitious and rabidly racist attorney general, Bruce Bennett, Faubus dug in his heels. The nine children waited, supported by their parents and local NAACP leader Daisy Bates, who became their protector and spokeswoman as the NAACP filed suit on their behalf. Finally, a federal judge ordered Faubus to admit the Nine to Central, but when they entered, white protesters surrounded the school and the youngsters had to be evacuated.

The mayor of Little Rock appealed to President Dwight Eisenhower for help. Even Eisenhower, so reluctant to take any lead in civil rights affairs, saw the danger of Faubus's open and armed defiance of federal law. Invoking the Insurrection Act of 1807, Eisenhower signed an executive order dispatching a thousand US Army troops of the 101st Airborne Division to Little Rock. He also federalized the Arkansas National Guard, removing the ten thousand guardsmen from Governor Faubus's control. By the end of September, the Little Rock Nine were finally able to enter Central High, protected from vengeful white mobs by the bayonets of US Army paratroopers. Once inside, however, the students were not protected and endured a year of torment from their classmates.

But for Governor Faubus and the southern segregationists, the game had changed. Arkansas's "military occupation" by Washington enraged and emboldened southern governors, launching a new level of massive resistance. "The second Reconstruction of the South is now underway," Governor Griffin warned.

The southern siege mentality was exacerbated by another document President Eisenhower had signed earlier in September: the Civil Rights Act of 1957, the first federal civil rights legislation since Reconstruction. Though the bill was delayed by 120 hours of Senate debate (including a record-setting, twenty-four-hour filibuster rant by Senator Strom Thurmond) and watered down to appease Dixiecrat holdouts, it was finally muscled through the Senate by majority leader Lyndon Johnson.

The act that emerged was a disappointment to civil rights advocates—more loophole than law—but, they convinced themselves, better than nothing. It did establish a civil rights division within the Justice Department and a six-member US Civil Rights Commission to investigate rights abuses. But while the act empowered federal officials to prosecute voting rights violators, this enforcement provision was crippled by an amendment granting a local jury trial, rather than a trial before a panel of federal judges. Everyone understood that there was no way an all-white southern jury would ever convict anyone for obstructing Black voters. Nevertheless, the act was denounced by southern officials as federal infringement on states' rights.

State segregation agencies redoubled their efforts to convince the American public that civil rights proponents were not aggrieved citizens—they were puppets of the Kremlin. This push for "Negro civil rights" was not a home-grown concept, born of American ideals, it was a Communist-controlled plot to destroy the nation. Now the Georgia Education Commission could offer photographic proof.

During September 1957, while the Little Rock crisis was unfolding and the Civil Rights Act was taking effect, the staff of the Georgia Education Commission pored over Friend's photographs, identifying and annotating them. In the first days of October, the staff presented Friend's findings to the highest echelons of state government, including Governor Griffin and Attorney General Cook, as well as officials from Georgia's neighboring states.

The commission had already shared many of the photographs with law enforcement agencies and mailed copies of Friend's film to FBI headquarters and to the national office of the White Citizens' Councils in Jackson, Mississippi. The pictorial exposé was about to go public.

"Highlander Folk School: Communist Training School, Monteagle, Tennessee," screamed the banner headline of the report the commission issued in mid-October, a flashy, four-page broadsheet featuring Friend's photographs accompanied by sensationalist captions and commentaries.

"During Labor Day weekend 1957, there assembled at Highlander the leaders of every major race incident in the South since the Supreme Court decision," the publication declared. "They met at this workshop and discussed methods and tactics of precipitating racial strife and disturbance," the commission's "exposé" continued. "The meeting of such a large group of specialists in inter-racial strife under the auspices of a Communist Training School is the typical method whereby leadership training and tactics are furnished to the agitators." And they were all apparently under the cunning direction of the photo-bombing Abner Berry: "His presence at a meeting such as this seminar insures the Communist Party against deviations from the Party principles," the commission explained in a burst of nonsensical invention.

Supposed evidence of Highlander's communist identity was provided by a recycling of the never-proven and often repudiated allegations against the school made at the Eastland hearings and other red-baiting forums. The "Communist Front Records" of those present at the Labor Day symposium, or even tangentially associated with Highlander, were chronicled in long columns of type. (Support of Henry A. Wallace's 1948 presidential campaign was included as a Communist-aligned affiliation.) It was a tangled and tenuous web, woven with malice, but the publication was an official state document.

In accompanying photo captions, Myles Horton was described as "long regarded as a useful aid to the Communist apparatus." Pete Seeger, pictured singing with his banjo in the Highlander library, was "typical of the entertainer who gives his time and talent to the support of the Communist apparatus."

While even the willfully reckless Georgia Commission couldn't directly pin a Communist label on Parks and King, it did its best to describe their desegregation efforts in sinister terms: "Rosa Parks was one of the original leaders of the Montgomery bus boycott," the publication explained. "This agitation has resulted in strife and violence in the Alabama capital and continues to maintain tension and disquiet." In another photo, Mrs. Parks was described as participating in "group training" at the Highlander workshops, "under the watchful eye" of Communist commander Abner Berry, who could be spotted cowering in a corner of the photo.

The commission paid special attention to the young and charismatic minister from Montgomery, whose face had already appeared on the cover of *Time* magazine earlier in the year, heralded for his leadership of the bus boycott. "The activities of Rev. Martin Luther King represent the ultimate in 'civil disobedience,'" said the commission, attempting to connect King to some nefarious Communist plot: "It is doubtful that Rev. King could have carried on such a program without outside leadership and financing."

"The development, precipitation, and financing of this inflammatory project called for behind the scenes planning and direction," the broadsheet alleged, "beyond the ability or capacity of local people." To her astonishment, Mrs. Clark was given her own star turn in the commission's spotlight. She was listed among Highlander's staff and its board of directors, identified in a photograph showing her leading a panel discussion on integration. "Pictured here are leaders of five recent scenes of racial disturbance and violence," the caption read. "Septima Clark, presently director of Highlander's integration workshops, was associated with the South Carolina-NAACP school teachers incident."

Highlander's flagrant disregard for the rules of southern racial segregation—supposed proof of its Communist-directed quest to erode the nation's moral core—was captured in Friend's photos of mixed dining, square dancing, and swimming. All these scenes, especially those showing Black men and white women close together, were given a salacious spin: "Both the Day and Night Life at Highlander Folk School Labor Day Weekend Seminar were integrated in all respects."

A centerfold pictorial spread featured the photo Friend snapped in the Highlander library showing King, Parks, Horton, and white editor Aubrey Williams sitting in a row, with Abner Berry squatting, head down, at Horton's feet. "These 'four horsemen' of racial agitation have brought tension, disturbance, strife and violence," the caption asserts, "in their advancement of the Communist doctrine of 'racial nationalism.'"

The Georgia Education Commission printed, at taxpayer expense, an initial run of one hundred thousand copies of the publication, mailing it to news outlets, lawmakers, public officials, and segregation and white supremacist associations across the South. It was reproduced or excerpted in pro-segregation newspapers; it made headlines in the nation's mainstream press. Response was so great that soon the commission went back to press for another hundred thousand copies, and the mailing list expanded to Congress, state and federal officials, local civic leaders, and ministers throughout the nation.

The Louisiana Joint Legislative Committee asked for three thousand copies to distribute in its state; the Association of Citizens' Councils of Mississippi requested five thousand, promising, "We will put them in good hands." Barely two months after the brochure's debut, the Georgia Commission decided to print another three hundred thousand copies, mailing them to every post office box in Georgia. The commission boasted that over a million copies of the publication were disseminated in less than a year. Soon Friend's photos, converted into new formats, would take on a life of their own.

———— ◆ ————

When the publication was released, Horton issued a statement to the press denying any Communist role in Highlander's administration or programs, insisting that the school rejected "totalitarian philosophy" on either the left or right side of the political spectrum, whether the Communist Party or the White Citizens' Councils. Both were "morally bankrupt," he insisted, with nothing to offer the South in confronting its racial problems. In subsequent letters and interviews, he railed against Governor Griffin's spying ploy in the service of white supremacy and denounced the unsubstantiated accusations made in the commission's publication. He suggested that the commission probably "planted" Abner Berry at the Highlander event and hinted he might even sue Governor Griffin for defamation.

In the privacy of his office, with his tape recorder microphone in hand, Horton was bitter as he dictated defensive diatribes to lawmakers and Highlander friends and affiliates. "The sharks, seeing that Highlander has been crippled by the Internal Revenue Service revokation [*sic*] of our income tax status, have moved in for the kill," he said in a letter to NAACP president Roy Wilkins. "Although Highlander has weathered many storms in the past, the present one is the most difficult because it is calculated to frighten off our support. But we can always grow and eat turnips," Horton insisted. "Even if they succeed in forcing us to curtail our program . . . Highlander will still be around."

It was not only Highlander he was trying to protect, though that was his primary concern, but the emerging civil rights movement itself. The commission's malicious propaganda gave official permission to every segregationist bigot, who could now justify opposition to civil rights not as a racist stance, but as a patriotic stand against the Communist menace. Horton realized the report's accusations could undermine popular support for the campaigns needed to force change. Even more insidiously, it could chill the determination of Black southerners themselves to wage the tough fight ahead, and undermine their trust in the leaders who were coming to the fore. The Georgia Commission's confection was, Horton had to admit, diabolically clever.

There was some backlash to the publication, with the *Atlanta Constitution*'s moderately liberal editor Ralph McGill blasting Governor Griffin's "gestapo tactics." Quite a few white clergymen complained about receiving the brochure in the mail: "I resent getting a copy of your filthy smear sheet," a Catholic cleric in Pennsylvania wrote to the Georgia Commission, calling it "the most despicable thing I have ever seen."

But the commission could easily ignore these complaints and focus on the congratulatory notes it was receiving, applauding its detective prowess. The FBI was deluged with inquiries from lawmakers and concerned citizens, anxious to know why the agency wasn't investigating and shutting down the Commie-infested, insurrectionist Highlander. Director Hoover shot an impatient memo to the Knoxville bureau staff, reminding them he had instructed them to immediately forward to headquarters any evidence of Highlander engaging in subversive activities or civil disobedience training. The Knoxville office found none.

The Highlander trustees were worried. Although the IRS found no legal basis for rescinding the school's tax exemption and its tax status would soon be restored, the wide circulation of the Georgia Commission report posed a new and broader threat. Horton asked a few of Highlander's most illustrious supporters, including Eleanor Roosevelt, Nobel Prize winner Ralph Bunche, and theologian Reinhold Niebuhr, to publicly defend the school. In a statement distributed to the press, the school's allies denounced the "irresponsible demagoguery" of the Georgia governor and his commission, calling the attack upon the "respected leaders, both white and Negro" who attended the Labor Day Seminar "morally indefensible" and the contents of the published broadside "slanderous material." Their protestations may have soothed some of Highlander's northern supporters, but it did little to quell the uproar in the South. The damage was done. Like the spores of a noxious weed, the commission's words and pictures could not be contained.

Rosa Parks's prominent appearance in the commission's smear sheet only added to her woes. When she had left Highlander after the anniversary celebration, she did not return to Montgomery. She and her family had decided—or rather, were forced—to move away from their home city. Life had become too hard and dangerous: both Rosa and Raymond had been blacklisted from employment, reduced to accepting charity, subjected to incessant hate calls and death threats. Her decision to defy Jim Crow had taken an enormous physical, emotional, and financial toll on them all. Rosa, her mother, and Raymond left Montgomery to join Rosa's brother in Detroit, boarding the train north, reluctantly joining the Great Migration.

Septima Clark was more indignant than frightened by the whole incident. She couldn't deny that her pictorial presence in the commission's faux exposé— with the allegation that she was some sort of provocateur in the employ of a Communist-front organization—was everything her family had ever feared for her. But she wasn't going to allow the furor to deter her from her work. She spent much of the fall on the road, defending Highlander at national conferences, soothing the school's donors and friends, collecting small checks at house parties. She, like the rest of the Highlander staff, was not being paid a salary while the IRS financial crisis lingered. She steadfastly continued her role as a roving movement godmother, visiting the frontline communities engaged in Jim Crow resistance, bringing encouragement, comfort, and support.

Mrs. Clark traveled to Little Rock, met with the nine students and their parents, and invited them all to Highlander for a Thanksgiving weekend of rest and renewal, which they happily accepted. She had already hosted the Black high school students of Clinton, Tennessee, where early desegregation efforts had turned violent. She worked with families in Nashville, where a school had been bombed on the first day of the term, a brazen effort to disrupt integration efforts. She reached out to parents in two towns in western North Carolina attempting to enroll their children in formerly white schools, and she consulted with Black families in the town of Soddy, near Chattanooga, to prepare a school integration petition. "I have been really heartened by the way the rank-and-file people are showing a desire to want to plunge into the mainstream and become first-class citizens," she wrote to the Warings from her travels.

A doctor in Sewanee had told her to take it easy, but she paid him little mind. Sometime in the past year, it's not clear exactly when, she had suffered a mild heart attack at Highlander. She had to stay in the hospital for four days but took some pleasure in knowing that, thanks to the intervention of Myles Horton and Highlander's Sewanee friends, she was the first Black person ever admitted to the town's hospital. She had unintentionally, and temporarily, integrated another white institution.

In the weeks following the publication of the Georgia Commission newspaper, Mrs. Clark didn't worry about herself, fearing for neither her health, safety, or reputation. But she was concerned about what Highlander's public notoriety might mean for the second term of the citizenship school on Johns Island, scheduled to open in early December.

CHAPTER EIGHTEEN

A Dangerous Place

If the Johns Islanders enrolled in the second citizenship school class in the winter of 1958 were aware of Highlander's travails, they weren't bothered by it. Esau Jenkins had told them Highlander was alright, and they trusted him. Esau had even joined the Highlander Executive Council, and he was no Communist. They knew Miss Seppie and Bernice Robinson were genuinely dedicated to helping them. Some of their neighbors had spent a week at Highlander, returning with tales of a magical place where white and Black people ate at the same tables and danced together. Whatever a bunch of white folks in Georgia were saying about Highlander was of no matter. The Johns Islanders were concentrating on learning their letters and getting their voter registration cards.

The citizenship class was even larger this time, with most of last year's students, like Alice Wine, returning for additional training. Robinson enlisted the more advanced students to help the beginners, making the learning a more communal experience, the classmates invested in one another's success. The semester would run for three months, not just two, allowing for more instruction and practice. This entailed more of a time commitment for Robinson, but she was so enthralled by the whole project that she welcomed it: "I became so involved with those people," she admitted, "that nothing else really mattered." She hardly had to do any recruitment to fill the class, as the enthusiasm of the first session's alumni sparked great interest in the community.

During the summer, she and Septima had helped Esau renew the registrations of the voters on the island, as required by South Carolina law. The reregistration process was another government tactic to make voting more cumbersome. That hard-won registration certificate could be lost by simply not remembering, or even realizing, that it must be renewed every ten years. Jenkins was not going to allow that to happen. Door to door, pew to pew, in the cooperative grocery store, in the Citizens' and Progressive Clubs, and in the fishing grounds and cabbage fields, Jenkins made sure Johns Island's Black citizens renewed their vows to vote. When he discovered that white registrars were purposefully making the procedure more difficult for Black applicants, he set up coaching squads and monthly refresher courses. And Robinson's winter citizenship class would nurture a new crop of eager voters.

While the second citizenship class was under way, another voting initiative began. Dr. King and the nascent Southern Christian Leadership Conference (SCLC) launched a Crusade for Citizenship, an ambitious campaign to "double the Negro vote" in the southern states in time for the 1960 presidential election. On February 12, Abraham Lincoln's birthday, King and other ministers announced the crusade from church pulpits in twenty-one southern cities.

"Let us make our intentions crystal clear," Rev. King declared, placing Black citizens' fight for the ballot in the context of other American suffrage struggles, including women's seven-decade fight for the vote. "We want freedom now. We want the right to vote now. We do not want freedom fed to us in teaspoons over another 150 years."

Veteran civil rights organizer Ella Baker was recruited to run the crusade, in which SCLC would serve as a clearinghouse for the voter registration work of existing local organizations and also get churches involved. The synergy could propel community excitement and build political strength. But in the first of many intramovement turf battles, the SCLC crusade encountered considerable resistance from other civil rights groups, especially the NAACP, which feared the initiative would compete with its own registration drives. Ella Baker brought her formidable skills and experience—she had been an NAACP staff organizer for years—to the SCLC's first major campaign, but it was a tough assignment.

The SCLC Crusade and the Highlander citizenship schools were pursuing the same goal but approaching from different directions: one organizing from the top, the other stimulating from the grass roots. The crusade was harvesting eligible Black voters; the citizenship class was growing new ones.

Clark and Robinson had spent the months since the close of the first citizenship class refining and expanding the class curriculum. Septima gathered materials from local government offices and civic organizations like the League of Women Voters (which was, at least in the South, still segregated) about the operations and meeting schedules of public agencies, school boards, and election boards in the area. She took the bureaucratic language and translated it into simple English for the students to digest.

Citizenship school students learned how their local government worked, which departments and elected officials to contact for assistance, how to write a letter of complaint. Bernice led classroom discussions on how becoming a voter could make those elected officials take notice and take action to improve life on the island. She laced the lessons with stories from Black history and current events, with stirring accounts of those risking their lives and livelihoods to confront Jim Crow across the South.

Still, it was the basic instruction in reading and writing that instilled a sense of confidence and pride in the adult students. Pencils still snapped, papers still ripped under the overly intense pressure of a sharp lead point, fingers struggled to curl themselves into the proper grip, but the simple act of signing their names in cursive, by laboriously tracing Robinson's cardboard stencils, was life-altering. "Perhaps the greatest single thing it accomplishes," Clark observed, "is the enabling of a man to raise his head a little higher. Knowing how to sign their names, many of those men and women told me after they had learned, made them *feel* different."

By the end of the winter '58 session, more than sixty students from both the first and second classes had passed the registration literacy tests on the first try. "When students got their registration certificates they would be at school ahead of me," Robinson recounted, "and as soon as I walked in the door, they were waving them in my face, 'I got it! I got it!' And their enthusiasm bubbled on out into the community, to people they knew," who could read and write well enough, but had never registered before. The excitement was contagious.

By the end of 1958, over six hundred Black Johns Islanders were on the voting rolls, tripling the number from just three years before.

"Everybody wanted to know: What's happening? Why are the Johns Island people getting registered so fast," Robinson recalled. Scouts from the neigh boring islands came exploring; their communities wanted the same sort of opportunity that Johns Islanders were enjoying.

Hearing of this interest, in early 1958 Myles joined Septima and Esau in several exploratory trips to the other Sea Islands, gauging the potential for expanding the citizenship schools as well as for developing other Highlander training projects. Horton came away convinced that there was a hunger for the kind of political awareness and participation that Esau had stimulated on Johns. Jenkins, always thinking ahead, was already experimenting with this concept. He was drafting plans for a regional expansion of his Johns Island Citizens' Club and envisioning the next steps in citizenship training—advanced classes in political education. Septima spent much of that spring surveying interest on the other islands, getting acquainted with local leaders and clergy, and identifying the islanders who would benefit from training at Highlander. "Women on the Islands are speaking out," Clark reported to the Warings with pleasure. "They were always in the background. Not now."

Several women on Wadmalaw Island, which sits next to Johns—the curves of the two islands matching like congruent puzzle pieces—were especially keen to begin a citizenship school there and sent representatives to a Highlander workshop. Before long, women emissaries from Edisto Island also reached out to Clark, and a beautician in North Charleston contacted Robinson offering to host a citizenship school in her beauty shop. Word was spreading.

———— ✦ ————

The poison seeping from the Georgia Commission's brochure was also spreading. Horton and the staff could handle the hate mail and threatening phone calls that poured in after the "Communist Training School" pamphlet was published, but they were alarmed when Highlander suddenly lost its insurance coverage in May 1958, endangering its ability to operate.

Horton was probably correct in suspecting that the Grundy County White Citizens' Council and its "Kluxer associates" were behind the punishment. The school's insurance agency cited the "Communist School" publication as a reason underwriters were nervous about Highlander's exposure to Klan arson and other violence. Horton turned to Highlander supporters again, gathering almost $30,000 in pledges to cover any possible damage to the school's property. This self-insuring work-around, coupled with an emergency policy from Lloyd's of London, would have to see Highlander through.

Harder to restore was the more amorphous damage to Highlander's reputation. Horton leaned hard on the school's high-profile friends, imploring them to help. Eleanor Roosevelt had already lent her name to the public defense of the school, but in the spring of 1958 she also promised to support Highlander in person. She would come to Monteagle, which she had never done before.

While Horton and Highlander's supporters, as well as most Black Americans, regarded Eleanor Roosevelt as a heroine, she was roundly despised by many white southerners. Mrs. Roosevelt's outspoken advocacy for workers, unions, and Black people during her White House years (defying the expectation that

First Ladies were supposed to just smile and cut ribbons) infuriated much of the white southern establishment. Her subsequent public career, as an advocate for the United Nations and human rights, and her denunciation of McCarthyism won her new enemies.

Southerners could still recall the bizarre conspiracy theory that had circulated in their towns in the early 1940s: rumors that Black maids and cooks had formed secret "Eleanor Clubs" inspired by their beloved First Lady. The rumors held that the Black women had pledged to rip off their aprons and quit their white households in unison, plunging southern domestic life into chaos. "Whites in the kitchen by Christmas" was the supposed motto of the club conspirators. In another version of the plot, the subversive servants were going to insist upon eating in the family dining room with their white employers in a terrifying demand for social equality. The FBI investigated and found no evidence of any Eleanor Clubs.

Given this history, it was no surprise that Mrs. Roosevelt's planned trip to Highlander also caught the attention of the Ku Klux Klan. The FBI's Knoxville office reported a Klan plot against Mrs. Roosevelt and Highlander: "A confidential informant of the Knoxville Office, who has furnished reliable information in the past, advised that at a meeting of U.S. Klans, Knights of the Ku Klux Klan, the scheduled talk by Mrs. Roosevelt was discussed. It was mentioned that Klansmen plan to go to Monteagle and stop the talk 'even if they had to blow the place up.'"

The FBI took the matter seriously, instructing the Memphis FBI office to notify state officials to be on alert for the contemplated Klan action. Local law enforcement could not be counted upon to provide protection: "Same informant advised it was also mentioned that [the local sheriff] had been contacted regarding this matter and advised the Klan he will not interfere with them if they come in and break up the meeting."

There were reports that the Klan had put a $25,000 bounty on Mrs. Roosevelt's head, a reward to any Klan members who could successfully kidnap the former First Lady. The FBI warned Mrs. Roosevelt that it could not guarantee her safety and advised her not to make the trip to Monteagle. Mrs. Roosevelt rejected the FBI's advice. She had made a commitment to attend the Highlander event and intended to keep her promise.

Mrs. Roosevelt flew into Chattanooga and was picked up at the airport by Horton for the fifty-mile drive to Monteagle. Mrs. Clark greeted Roosevelt when she arrived at Highlander and escorted her into a workshop on voting restrictions and citizenship.

"I was interested to find myself in a large integrated group of about 60 people representing many different groups," Roosevelt recounted in her *My Day* newspaper column, "discussing honestly the difficulties put in the way of voting registration, particularly for the Negro, in the South." Mrs. Clark led the workshop, and the graphic details of voter suppression and harassment that were described shocked Mrs. Roosevelt.

Roosevelt ate lunch on the lawn with the Highlander staff and guests, and after the meal she stood on the porch of the old farmhouse to give an informal talk to the three hundred people arrayed in chairs and blankets on the grass. "You are doing pioneer work here," she told the friendly crowd. "I know of no other school just like this one. It is very important at this time that this demonstration of democracy be made," she said, referring to the easy but intentional integration she witnessed on the grounds.

"This is my first visit to Highlander, but I am very happy that I was able to come here today and see for myself, because I think you are doing here something which at the present time needs very badly to done in our United States. You are demonstrating that it is possible for people to come together as people, not as either white people or Negro people or any other race—just people. And that is very important."

Mrs. Roosevelt did not mention the FBI's warnings of Klan violence aimed at her and the school, but in her account of the visit in her *My Day* column, she raised some of the allegations made against Highlander: "This school, because it does hold integrated meetings . . . has often been accused of being Communist," she wrote. "I saw no evidence that suggested Communist influence, but I thought these were courageous people attempting to show that we could do here at home what we are trying to do in the world, namely, to live together in peace regardless of race or creed."

Mrs. Roosevelt's visit provided a festive moment and a needed morale boost for Horton and the beleaguered Highlander staff. For others, Eleanor Roosevelt's presence just confirmed their suspicions that Highlander was a dangerous place. Highlander aspired to be a dangerous place. Its mission, from the beginning, was to be a source of democratic disruption, a threat to a complacent society that tolerated race and class inequalities. In the early years, it was dangerous to craven capitalists who abused their workers. Now it was proudly dangerous to the structure of southern white supremacist society.

"There is a great ferment in the South," Septima happily reported to the Warings that summer. "I've never seen Negroes standing up for their rights as now."

Voting campaigns—either directed from the top, like the SCLC's Crusade, or stimulated from the bottom, like Highlander's citizenship schools—were still the bedrock of civil rights activities. The vote was still the key. Yet pressing change by the ballot was a slow process that could take years to show results in improving everyday life for most southern Black Americans. There was increasing popular demand for more direct actions, an appetite for an expanded menu of integration targets and protest possibilities.

Clark could see these new approaches reflected in the Highlander workshops she directed. "I see mobilization and unification among Negroes in the deep South from the reports that were given," she told the Warings. More local bus boycotts were being launched, along with other types of consumer "selective buying" campaigns to punish stores and businesses that discriminated against Blacks or cooperated with White Citizens' Council "squeezes." There were more confrontational demands to desegregate not only schools and buses, but also public facilities, parks, and beaches. Students were defying violent mobs to desegregate white schools. Mrs. Clark made it her business to find and bring the local leaders of these projects to Highlander, where they could find guidance and support.

"The leaders in Little Rock, Tallahassee, Tuskegee, Montgomery, Clinton and Nashville have determination and courage to go on," she told the Warings. "They are still working in the face of danger."

In the fall of 1958, a Vanderbilt Divinity School doctoral student brought a group of Nashville college students to Highlander to explore new ways of confronting racial injustice. For more than a year, Rev. James Lawson had been holding informal weekly seminars on the philosophy and practice of nonviolence, employing passive resistance as moral and political instruments. The seminar began with just a handful of Black students from American Baptist Theological School, Fisk University, Meharry Medical College, and Tennessee State meeting in a Nashville church basement. They read and discussed Jesus and Scripture, Mahatma Gandhi, and Henry David Thoreau as moral guides to facing evil with civil disobedience. They practiced the difficult mental and physical techniques of meeting violence with love.

Rev. Lawson had spent a year in federal prison for resisting the draft during the Korean War, then worked as a Methodist missionary in India, taking time to study Gandhi's nonviolent methods before returning to graduate school. Lawson had already become a friend and adviser to Rev. King, the two young ministers shaping and deepening each other's understanding of nonviolence in long conversations. King had urged Lawson to move to the South (where Lawson had never lived before) to help spread nonviolent philosophy in the volatile region where radical change was most needed. Lawson transferred to Vanderbilt's theology school and almost immediately began teaching his seminar.

As the seminar grew and sharpened its political edge, Lawson thought his students could benefit from an intense dose of Highlander-style intellectual debate and integrated living, so he arranged for a weekend visit. On the bus headed up Monteagle Mountain with Lawson were aspiring Baptist ministers John Lewis, Bernard Lafayette, and James Bevel. A new generation of freedom workers arrived at Highlander.

John Lewis was then a nineteen-year-old seminary student from the tiny farming community of Troy, Alabama. He had discovered his vocation as a boy, baptizing and preaching to his family's flock of chickens. Encouraged to "read everything" by his favorite teacher, Lewis was angered when he was refused a library card at the whites-only county library. He drew up a protest petition, demanding equal borrowing rights for Black residents, and while the petition was ignored, it marked Lewis's first foray into political protest. The murder of Emmett Till, a boy his own age, had a deep effect on Lewis, and the Montgomery Bus Boycott, unfolding just fifty miles away from his home, became a pivotal moment in his development. He followed the daily news reports and listened to Dr. King's powerful sermons on the radio.

As a college student, Lewis was drawn to Lawson's melding of spiritual and political activism, putting the social gospel into action to defy Jim Crow. On that weekend at Highlander, Lewis discovered the promise of a fully integrated world. Just like Rosa Parks, when Lewis took his seat in the Highlander dining room, it marked the first time he had ever eaten a meal at the same table with white people, done the dishes with them, much less slept in the same room with them. It was a revelatory experience he would never forget.

Myles Horton also made a deep impression on the young seminarian. Horton's disarming manner, laced with his probing questions and down-home humor, captured Lewis's imagination. Lewis and his classmates had never encountered a white man with Horton's deep philosophical grounding, practical knowledge, and decades-long commitment to social justice. Horton challenged the Nashville students, brought them out of their comfort zones, poked holes in their assumptions, rattled them. His aim was to strengthen their resolve.

Yet the single person who most impressed young John Lewis that weekend at Highlander was Septima Clark. "What I loved about Clark was her down-to-earth, no-nonsense approach," Lewis remembered. "And the fact that the people she aimed at were the same ones Gandhi went after, the same ones I identified with, having grown up poor and barefoot and black."

Mrs. Clark helped reinforce Lewis's own belief that the "lifeblood" of the social justice movement in the South was not going to be the educated elites, the "schooled, sophisticated, savvy upper-crust" of the Black community. The movement was going to be powered by "the tens of thousands of faceless, name-less, anonymous men, women and children"—like his own parents, like the boy he had been—"who were going to rise like an irresistible army as this movement for civil rights took shape."

"I left Highlander on fire."

CHAPTER NINETEEN

Our America

A rkansas attorney general Bruce Bennett was on a mission. He was intent on convincing the public that the Little Rock school desegregation crisis—still making headlines in fall 1958, more than a year after it began—had been instigated by subversive elements, not by citizens asserting their rights under the law. Bennett had failed to convince the Supreme Court to accept Arkansas's plan to delay the desegregation of Little Rock's schools, and in response to the court's ruling in September, Bennett worked with Governor Faubus to close Central High, along with all the city's public high schools, rather than integrate them.

In mid-December 1958 Bennett opened televised hearings on the alleged Communist conspiracy spurring the racial unrest. He employed the same cast of professional anti-Communist witnesses who had sold their services to other such hearings, and for the benefit of his television audience, Bennett added a visual element to his presentation. Ed Friend's moving pictures and photographs of Highlander were broadcast and entered into evidence as proof of Highlander's ties to Communism and malicious involvement in racial strife.

In late January 1959 Bennett also made a generous offer to Arkansas's neighbor, Tennessee. Calling Highlander a "public nuisance" to the region, Bennett promised: "I would gladly come to Tennessee if invited, to lend whatever help I could to close Highlander."

The Tennessee General Assembly gladly accepted Attorney General Bennett's offer of assistance in ridding the state of the Highlander Folk School. Just days after Bennett made his proposal, a resolution authorizing a special legislative investigation was introduced, and by mid-February 1959 a five-member committee was named to probe the school's involvement in subversive activities. Tennessee Bureau of Criminal Identification agents were dispatched to gather evidence and witnesses.

The *Nashville Tennessean* lambasted the investigation as a "witch hunt" to "harass and intimidate the institution because of its candid advocacy of integration." But other Tennessee papers, including the segregation champions *Nashville Banner* and *Chattanooga News–Free Press*, were more supportive of the probe, which promised to alert Americans "to the sordid story of this festering sore atop the mountains in the heart of Tennessee."

———— ✦ ————

While Horton prepared to do battle with the Tennessee legislature in early winter 1959, Highlander's citizenship school program entered its third year, expanding to four locations with over a hundred people enrolled. On Johns Island, the new cohort of students walked the sandy River Road to the Progressive Club co-op grocery store. On Wadmalaw Island, nearly thirty men and women crowded into a tiny shack. On Edisto Island, farther down the coast, more than three dozen new students met in a church meeting hall. And in North Charleston, a dozen women walked the neighborhood's muddy streets to a beauty parlor for their literacy lessons.

The new teachers presiding over these classrooms had already attended workshops in Monteagle, becoming familiar with Highlander's ethos and methods. They had also received instructional advice from Mrs. Clark and Mrs. Robinson on how to conduct these unconventional classes. A new, expanded edition of *My Reading Book* was the basic text, but each teacher was encouraged to tweak the lessons to meet the local conditions and requests of their students.

The new crop of teachers were, like Robinson, volunteers; Highlander paid them $50 a month for their expenses, but nothing for the many hours they devoted to planning and teaching their lessons. These teachers emerged from their communities and were familiar and trusted neighbors, so the self-conscious adult learners did not feel intimidated. This became the model for expanding the cadre of teachers.

Ethel Jenkins Grimball was the only trained teacher among them. The twenty-six-year-old daughter of Esau and Janie Jenkins, Grimball graduated from college with an education degree. But she was denied a teaching position by the Charleston County school board, a crude act of retribution for her father's political activism. Unable to teach in her home county, she found work as a seamstress at the Citadel military academy in Charleston and continued taking graduate education courses. When the opportunity arose to apply her skills to her father's citizenship school project, she eagerly raised her hand. The duty of community service her parents had drilled into their children spurred Mrs. Grimball to volunteer as the Wadmalaw Island class teacher. By day the young wife and mother mended uniforms at the institution founded to protect white Charlestonians from slave revolts; by night she prepared the descendants of slaves to reclaim their citizenship.

An hour's drive south of Wadmalaw, on Edisto Island, a social worker and minister's wife, Alleen Brewer, was eager to form an adult citizenship school, as few of her fellow Black citizens voted. Many couldn't pass the literacy test, but others were simply scared to vote; Brewer wanted to break down both of those barriers. She attended a Highlander workshop in fall 1958 and approached Mrs. Clark about starting a class on the island.

In North Charleston, Mary Lee Davis was a beautician friend of Bernice Robinson, also active in the NAACP, who was frustrated by the way her Black neighborhood was ignored and neglected. The streets remained a muddy mess of dirt paths, garbage left uncollected. She believed that if her neighbors could vote in sufficient numbers, elected officials might respond to them. Robinson brought her to Highlander, and Davis returned home determined to start a citizenship school. She arranged a neighborhood meeting to promote the idea, recruited students, and donated her shop as the meeting place.

Robinson taught that class as well as the one on Johns Island, bouncing between the islands and mainland every night of the week during the 1959 winter semester. She would soon officially join the Highlander staff as field supervisor of the rapidly expanding citizenship project. What had begun as a one-off experiment was now a multisite enterprise, its popularity spread by word of mouth and the passionate proselytizing of Robinson, Clark, and Jenkins.

Horton also recognized the potential of the citizenship school concept to grow beyond the islands, and not insignificantly, to provide Highlander with new and needed foundation support. He was able to convince the Marshall Field Foundation to provide funding for the program's expansion in the South. With this financial backing, Clark and Robinson added another dimension to Highlander's work: recruiting, training, and supporting community volunteers willing to lead the citizenship classes. At Monteagle and in the field, Clark and Robinson became the teachers' teachers.

All that winter, Septima circulated around the islands, roving from class to class, encouraging the teachers, instructing the students, and ironing out problems. She spent hours helping a Wadmalaw island man learn to hold his pencil and took pleasure in witnessing small triumphs: "As they discover the magic secret of writing their names," she observed, "suddenly in their eyes you see a glorious gleam."

The students of the islands citizenship schools opened their *My Reading Booklet* to practice big words and learn about their place in "Our America." They flipped the pages of the booklet, created for them by Mrs. Clark, to a hand-drawn map of the United States with an inset focused on the Sea Islands.

"This is a map of the United States of America," the students learned to read aloud, slowly sounding out the words. "It is the home of a great American Nation. We are a part of that great nation. We are all Americans. Our home is on islands in the Atlantic on the southeast coast of South Carolina. We love this great land."

———— ◆ ————

The Tennessee joint legislative investigation committee began its work on February 21, 1959, in a secret session. The lawmakers and staff conferred with Arkansas's Bennett, Mississippi senator Eastland, and the Georgia Commission on Education to share the findings of their previous probes of Highlander. Ed Friend's film and photos of Highlander were also previewed for the committee. The public hearings then opened in Tracy City, the Grundy County seat, where some of Highlander's Monteagle neighbors testified about the school's reputation in the community. Some of the local witnesses admitted that they had never set foot on the grounds of Highlander, or had little contact with the school. But they still had strong opinions about the place, mostly based on rumors and wild speculation.

Some Monteagle citizens swore that Highlander was un-American because they had never seen the American flag flying over the campus. Other neighbors testified they had seen Black and white students swimming together naked in the Highlander pond, and were sure the school was promoting illicit and lascivious behavior. Several other witnesses were convinced that Highlander "was operated out of Moscow." One claimed that years ago he had seen Zilphia Horton dressed like a Russian peasant woman, singing Russian songs, and he suspected the Horton children, Thorsten and Charis, had "Russian names."

A few of Highlander's local supporters were allowed to testify at the hearings, including two University of the South at Sewanee professors. These white faculty members, along with another dozen of their like-minded colleagues, had already written a letter to the governor protesting the state's harassment of Highlander. The professors' stance was not popular on the Sewanee campus: students circulated petitions denouncing them; alumni of the all-white, all-male college were outraged; fellow faculty members kept their distance. The professors knew they were risking their careers by defending Highlander. Nevertheless, they took the stand.

The committee interrogators took special care in grilling May Justus, who served on the Highlander executive board as secretary-treasurer. Justus and her partner, Vera McCampbell, a teacher in the local schools, served as a bridge between the school and its neighbors and helped guide Highlander's outreach efforts on the mountain. Justus wasn't given a chance to testify about these initiatives: the daycare and nursery school Highlander operated for the Monteagle community; the medical and dental clinics it provided; the canning kitchen and food distribution programs it ran; even the burial assistance it offered to neighbors. The legislative committee was not interested in that.

Vera McCampbell had recently been punished for her association with Highlander: a newspaper photo of her attending Highlander's luncheon for Eleanor Roosevelt was seized upon by the local chapter of the American Legion as proof she was a subversive, unfit to teach children. The legion pressured the school board to discipline McCampbell, and the board gave her an ultimatum: never step foot on the grounds of Highlander again, or lose your job. She refused to renounce her ties to Highlander. She was fired after thirty-four years of teaching in the school district.

Before two hundred spectators seated in the gymnasium of the Grundy high school, Justus was questioned for more than an hour about her work for Highlander, including legal and financial details the committee found suspicious. She was not a trained accountant, she admitted, but parried the committee's insinuations with sardonic wit, annoying her interrogators. Turning from finances to juicier topics, committee lawyers unfolded the Georgia Commission on Education's publication and, pointing to Ed Friend's photo of a Black man and white woman dancing together, asked Justus whether she approved of such interracial intimacy. "I see nothing immoral about it," she replied. "It's a square dance."

"Don't you know it's against the law for whites and blacks to marry in Tennessee," the committee lawyer pressed her. "Yes, sir, but I didn't know that a square dance was part of a marriage ceremony," she retorted. The attorney dismissed her from the stand.

The committee was a bit frustrated by its witnesses' failure to provide any real specifics to nail Highlander as subversive or communist. It was all vague, and at times ridiculous, hearsay. Still, the committee had managed to uncover two technical violations they could pin on Highlander: the school's charter had not been properly filed in Grundy County in 1932, and financial ownership of the Horton home on the Highlander campus was unclear. These became the lynchpin of the government's case against Highlander, the only evidence it could muster.

———— ♦ ————

While Horton and Highlander were being pummeled in Tennessee in late February, the students of the four Lowcountry citizenship school classes received their diplomas in a festive closing ceremony on Edisto Island. Clark, Robinson, and Jenkins joined the class teachers in awarding perfect attendance certificates to more than half the students, a testament to their grit and dedication. Some of the graduates had already passed the literacy tests and held their voter registration cards; the rest would earn them soon. Monthly follow-up classes would continue through the year.

The Edisto Island graduates took a pledge of "each man, get a man" to convince a neighbor or friend to register to vote. They formed the Edisto Voters Association, meeting each month to discuss civic matters and recruit more voters. Mrs. Clark was pleased that women took executive positions in the Voters Association. On Wadmalaw Island, the class formed a Concerned Citizens Club, which also met monthly to explore strategies for improving the island. And the students in North Charleston formed a committee and drafted a petition to demand paved streets and better city services in their neighborhood. The graduates were beginning to think of themselves as first-class, engaged citizens who had a right to express their opinions and concerns to those in power. They had practiced writing letters to their school boards, to their congressman, even to the president of the United States. Becoming a voter gave them a voice in affairs that had always seemed distant and inscrutable; in the realm of the white man's world and beyond their reach. Not anymore.

———— ♦ ————

A few days after the citizenship school graduation, on March 5, 1959, the final set of legislative hearings moved to Nashville. This promised to be a rip-roaring show, featuring appearances by Horton, Arkansas attorney general Bennett, and the Georgia Commission's spy-photographer Friend. Hundreds of spectators filled the city's War Memorial Auditorium, just a block from the Tennessee statehouse. Reporters from around the region packed the press table.

In his statements to the press, Horton tried to project supreme confidence in Highlander's eventual vindication, despite the obvious intent of the committee to ignore all facts that might contradict their predetermined judgments. He adopted a tweedy professorial demeanor in the hearing room, wearing jacket and tie, peering at documents through half-rim eyeglasses. He complied with all demands for records, submitting the school's financial accounts going back to 1932. He touted his willingness to be transparent, inviting the committee members to a luncheon and tour of the campus. They refused, but several committeemen did briefly visit the Highlander library, searching for subversive materials. "There's some hot stuff here," one eager legislator was heard to say. "Aw, it's nothing you can't find in almost any library," his colleague admitted with disappointment.

Horton was called to the witness stand and questioned for nearly five hours, forced to defend himself against the same set of allegations and innuendos he had already faced in previous government inquiries. These accusations had also been investigated and dismissed several times by the FBI, though the Bureau refused to acknowledge its exculpatory findings, and headquarters kept close tabs on the hearings in a news clipping file. As if trapped in a surreal echo chamber, the mere fact that such allegations had once been uttered, even if never substantiated, became the basis for repeating them as fact, citing them as official information. Attorney General Bennett sat with the five Tennessee committee members and their legal counsel, whispering questions and suggestions into their ears.

No, he was not, and had never been, a Communist, Horton repeated in response to sharp questioning. No, Highlander did not teach communism and hatred for America, it helped Americans practice democracy. Had Highlander operated in violation of Tennessee segregation laws "before the 1954 'Black Monday' decision of the Supreme Court?" one committeeman asked. "Yes, sir," Horton replied proudly, Highlander preached and practiced integration.

The committee counsel pounced on this, thrusting in front of Horton's face Ed Friend's photo of the Black man and white woman dancing. In the photo the dancing couple have their arms raised, their hands outstretched behind each other's necks. Is this the kind of integration Highlander advocates? the committee's counsel taunted.

"It's just a folk dance step," Horton insisted. "They're not embracing, they're clapping." Horton stood up, approaching the committee lawyer. "It goes like this." To the lawyer's embarrassment and the audience's amusement, Horton displayed the dance step, encircling the lawyer's neck with his arms, clapping his hands behind the fellow's neck. News photographers gleefully snapped the scene of Horton dancing with his inquisitor, and the image appeared in the press the next morning.

Friend narrated his silent film and stills of Highlander's interracial activities when he was called to testify. The committee steered the photographer where they wanted him to go with leading questions: Was the Highlander anniversary weekend a subversive meeting? he was asked. "It was subversive, sir, to the way that I have been taught to live in America," he replied earnestly. "I have been taught by Southern tradition to keep the races separate. It is the primary motive of this group to tear down the forces that were trying to keep the races separate in the South."

"Was it your observation that they were trying to bring about a condition of chaos and turmoil and strife and stress among people?" one legislator asked. "Among the races, sir, between the races," Friend answered.

"Is it true or not that that is the breeding ground for Communists, under those conditions?" the legislator suggested. "That is my understanding of it, sir," Friend agreed.

Arkansas Attorney General Bennett gave his testimony standing at a large blackboard. He drew a sprawling diagram in chalk with Highlander and Horton at the center, surrounded by a constellation of people and organizations Bennett identified as "known Communists or fellow travelers." Among those in the Highlander orbit were singer Pete Seeger and editor Aubrey Williams, Tuskegee Institute dean and Highlander trustee Charles Gomillion, and, a recent addition, Martin Luther King Jr. Bennett then drew emphatic chalk lines, arrows, and circles, connecting each of them to Horton and his school. The attorney general presented this illustration as proof that Horton and Highlander were at the heart of a "communist-directed southern conspiracy" to spark racial strife and "destruction of these United States as we know them." When he concluded his testimony, Bennett shook hands with the Tennessee legislators, offering words of encouragement: "Run 'em out, boys, run 'em out," he urged. "That's the main thing."

Just one day after the close of the hearings, the Tennessee special investigatory committee began writing its report to the legislature and again took Bennett's advice. It concluded that it had found "considerable circumstantial evidence" that Highlander was, using the attorney general's phrase, "a meeting place for known Communists and fellow travelers" and that it was not a "school in the normal sense of the word." The legislature passed a resolution directing the district attorney general for Grundy County to file suit for revocation of Highlander's charter.

———————◆———————

Six hundred miles away, Thomas Waring, editor of the *Charleston News and Courier*, was paying close attention to the proceedings in Tennessee. Waring's interest was piqued by a specific finding of the legislative investigation: that Highlander was operating an extension school for Black students based on the Sea Islands near Charleston.

Waring traveled to Monteagle to talk with town residents and interviewed Horton for several hours. Horton welcomed the editor, was cordial and open; he had nothing to hide. The result was a series of front-page articles—the paper touted them as exposés—with accompanying editorials, all written in a journalistic tone but with a sharply negative slant.

Waring dug up nothing new or revelatory in his reporting. In the absence of any solid evidence of communist tendencies at Highlander, his newspaper resorted to running a photo of Eleanor Roosevelt's visit to the campus as proof of its dangerous leftist ties. "Because Horton does not wear a beard and carry a fizzing bomb," Waring wrote in the series' concluding editorial, "some people do not recognize him as a revolutionary" trying to "upset basic and established conditions."

Likening Horton and his associates to "termites boring through the underpinnings of the Republic," Waring warned his readers that Highlander wasn't just Tennessee's problem, it was Charleston's too. Especially since Highlander was covertly working in their backyard, on the islands, training poor Black people to become agitators.

Waring sent a reporter to Johns Island to get the scoop. Bernice Robinson noticed a white man snooping around the Progressive Club building, but she refused to talk to him. The reporter found Esau Jenkins emerging from an evening church meeting.

Described as "a soft spoken, mild mannered Negro leader of Johns Island" who was also an "honor member of the NAACP," Jenkins confirmed that

Highlander had been sponsoring citizenship classes on the islands for the past several years. "We only want to make them better citizens," Jenkins insisted. "We want them to understand how to vote intelligently."

"We do not know exactly what is taught in these classes," Waring wrote in a subsequent editorial headlined "Highlander School's Influence Felt Among Charleston County Negroes."

"We do know where Esau Jenkins received his training." It was from the "interracial" Highlander Folk School in Tennessee, found by the recent legislative investigation to be a meeting place for communists and their associates, Waring explained. He warned of the dangers of teaching Black people to vote, as they might practice "bloc voting." Flexing their voting power for their own interests could only bring about racial discord, Waring contended.

Septima Clark and Bernice Robinson were identified as local Charleston women in charge of the classes on the islands, and the Progressive Club was identified as the meeting place of the Johns Island class. "Strangely, not a single white person," the reporter wrote, "including the county school superintendent or even officials of the Island's Citizens Councils, had any direct knowledge the Negro adult classes were being held." Now they did.

Mrs. Clark was, naturally, concerned. What the legal threats to Highlander meant for her job, she didn't know. What the publicity meant for the citizenship schools was more important. While the faraway hearings in Tennessee hadn't made much of an impression on the citizenship students on the islands and North Charleston, unfolding just as the semester came to an end, Clark was worried that the News and Courier articles might be destructive. Such public exposure in the white press might frighten the students and teachers who had taken the risk of participating. It might cause suspicion among their family and neighbors, even place them in danger of violence by angry whites.

Mrs. Clark rushed over to Johns, Wadmalaw, and Edisto to gauge how their students on the islands were reacting to this sudden notoriety. She found one islander on the porch of a store reading the newspaper article aloud to a group of men surrounding him. How did he feel about the article, Clark asked him. "Oh, anytime that white people think that we are getting something done, they're going to be against us," he told her matter-of-factly. "We're going ahead with our school and do this thing." Clark found the same attitude on the other islands. She was relieved. And proud. "I found that the black people weren't afraid anymore."

CHAPTER TWENTY

We Are Not Afraid

B ernice Robinson thought she saw a beam of light slicing through the dark. Then it disappeared. She was sitting on the Highlander lawn, outside the old farmhouse, enjoying the evening breeze on a Friday night at the end of July 1959. Esau Jenkins was sitting under a tree nearby, gabbing with some fellows. Septima Clark was in the dining room, showing a documentary film to the fifty or so participants in that week's workshop on community leadership.

In the four months since the legislature had assigned the local district attorney to figure out a way to revoke Highlander's charter he'd made no moves, so the school resolutely carried on with its work. If anything, the work had increased and intensified. More people were enrolling in the workshops, more places were interested in creating a citizenship school, more communities seemed eager to organize to demand their rights. They came to Highlander to learn how to get started. Successful strategies were analyzed and shared. Pitfalls were mapped. Highlander became the switchboard for connecting experienced and aspiring activists across the South.

Among this week's workshop participants were graduates and teachers of the recent Lowcountry citizenship schools and leaders of the Montgomery Improvement Association, who brought a dozen high school and college students to Highlander for training. Young people were emerging as a dynamic new element in the integration fight; they understood it was a struggle for their future.

Clark recognized the Black youth's potential power and made special efforts to bring them to Highlander. She guided them in absorbing the experience and wisdom of their elders in the struggle but also encouraged their questioning and impatience. She welcomed the youthful energy they added to the mix of workshop discussions.

Clark could hear the sweet, high voices of the young students from Montgomery in this workshop's nightly singing sessions. Music filled the air at Highlander again this summer, as Horton brought the young folk singer Guy Carawan to take Zilphia's place as song leader. Carawan was a thirty-two-year-old singer scraping together a living on the folk music circuit, with several well-received albums to his credit. He had been raised in California, but his parents were southerners—his mother a "Charleston blueblood," as he liked to say—so he felt some kinship to the region. He was a friend of Pete Seeger, Woody Guthrie, and folklorist Alan Lomax and a member of the "People's Song" movement, dedicated to using folk music to awaken audiences to the themes of social justice. He had visited Highlander a few years before, working with Zilphia Horton to make "We Shall Overcome" easier to sing. Now he was back teaching the song to hundreds of new Highlander students.

Horton was away in Europe, attending an international adult education conference. He welcomed the respite after the strain of the hearings. He was gratified that Highlander's friends had rallied to support the school: individual donations had soared, and foundations hadn't blinked. He was convinced there was no legal basis for revoking the school's charter and felt perfectly comfortable leaving the country with Mrs. Clark in charge while he was away.

From the lawn, Robinson again saw lights flash and move, like headlights of a car approaching, then cutting off. She couldn't figure it out.

Inside the main house, in a space adjacent to the dining room where the film was playing, a little girl was twirling, practicing the dance steps she was going to perform when the movie ended. Her grandmother had promised she could. Six-year-old Yvonne Clark was Septima's granddaughter. The girl's mother had died suddenly the year before, leaving Septima's son an overwhelmed widower with three young children. For the next several years, Yvonne would live at Highlander with Septima during the summers, returning to Lorene in Charleston when the school term began. Septima cherished her new mothering role, one she had been denied earlier in her life, and Yvonne had quickly become an adored member of the Highlander family. Septima's granddaughter couldn't even sit on a stool at the Monteagle drugstore's soda fountain to lick her ice cream cone—the store's owner had demanded they leave—but Septima could use the insult to explain to Yvonne that her grandma was working to change those cruel rules.

Yvonne's dance practice was interrupted by a set of loud knocks on the back door. The little girl pulled the door open. A line of big men in uniforms pushed past her. From inside the darkened dining room, Mrs. Clark could see figures moving in the hallway. She left the projector running to see what the commotion was about. "Where is Septima Clark?" barked District Attorney General Albert Sloan. "Where will I find Septima Clark?"

"Here I am," she answered calmly. "I'm Septima Clark."

Sloan beckoned to another man who was holding a piece of paper in his hand. "This is a search warrant," the man announced.

"A search warrant?" Clark repeated incredulously. "What are you going to search for?"

"For liquor," he replied.

"Well, go right ahead," she responded dismissively. "There's no whiskey in this house. You won't even find cooking sherry in our kitchen." How ridiculous. The only beverages served at dinner had been juice, milk, coffee, and iced tea.

In March of that year, Albert "Ab" Sloan had eagerly accepted the legislature's assignment to pursue legal action against Highlander, with the goal of revoking the school's charter. Such a high-profile case could be good for his career. "If they're violating any law up there," Sloan boasted to the press, "I'll push it to the limit." But the legislative investigation committee hadn't given him much to work with. The allegations of subversion and communist activities were too vague and unsupported, producing nothing but squiggles on a blackboard and squishy testimony on the stand. He needed something concrete to pin on Highlander. He kept the place under surveillance, but with the summer wearing on and pressure building to do something, Sloan was getting itchy. Then he got lucky: a tip. You might find booze at Highlander. That would be illegal in dry Grundy County.

Though he knew the tip was flimsy, Sloan convinced a friendly judge to sign a search warrant. He assembled a squad of about twenty state troopers and sheriff's deputies to stage a nighttime raid on Highlander. He also invited a photographer from the *Chattanooga Free Press* to come along to document and publicize the armed incursion.

Sloan directed the deputies to search the school for any trace of liquor. The squad ransacked the staff offices and bedrooms, confiscating money, including Mrs. Clark's wallet. They emptied the bureau drawers and suitcases of the workshop students in the dormitories, tore up their seminar notes, combed through the kitchen and library. They found nothing.

While their colleagues were rampaging through the buildings, two policemen stormed into the dining room, where the movie was still playing, yelling: "Cut the damn thing off!" But only Mrs. Clark knew how to operate the projector. A policeman yanked the projector's electrical plug from the wall, and the film reel sputtered to a stop. The policemen ordered everyone to sit still and quiet, kept the lights in the dining room turned off. Some began to quietly pray.

Not long after the search began, the sheriff took hold of Mrs. Clark's arm, announcing she was under arrest. "But have you found any liquor?" she asked him.

"Never you mind," he snapped. "The General [Sloan] said so. Come on. You'll have to go with us."

As he led her toward the door, Septima pulled back, swiveled, and called over her shoulder: "Look after Yvonne!" The little girl was crying, screaming. "What are they doing to my grandmommie?" she wailed. Bernice gathered Yvonne in her arms to comfort her. "I'll be back in the morning to open up the workshop," Septima assured everyone as she was hustled out the door, her arm wrenched behind her back by a trooper.

A young white man participating in the workshop approached the policeman hauling Clark out of the building. "Aren't you going to allow this woman to talk with her lawyer?" he demanded. The officer glared at him. "You're under arrest too," he shouted. A second white man, questioning Mrs. Clark's arrest, piqued the ire of a different officer, and he was also arrested. Then Guy Carawan entered the scene, protesting Mrs. Clark's detainment. The earnest Californian had never seen anything like this brand of rough southern justice. "You're also under arrest," the police announced, grabbing him.

Mrs. Clark and the three white men were shoved into a patrol car with the windows shut. They waited for almost three hours while the search of the grounds continued. Carawan was upset and loudly complaining: "What are my rights? Don't I have any rights?" he shouted. As a white man, he wasn't used to such callous mistreatment. Clark worried Carawan's griping would provoke the lawmen to violence. Southern Black people had learned long ago, for their own survival, that it was best to quietly obey when in the sights of a sheriff's gun. She urged Carawan to pipe down.

Meanwhile, up at the school no liquor had been found.

Irritated, Sloan ordered his troops to expand the search beyond the bounds of the warrant, to look in Horton's private home. The lawmen threatened to break down the door with an ax if not given a key. They stormed through the house, and in the cellar they found an old, spiderwebbed wooden keg Horton had brought home as a souvenir from Europe. They poured out the bit of liquid inside, decided it smelled like aging moonshine (it was moldy water). They also found a tiny amount of rum and gin upstairs that belonged to a houseguest. (Personal consumption of liquor was always legal, even in a dry county.) The little dregs of alcohol weren't much, but they'd have to suffice. Ab Sloan would make them suffice.

In the dining room, the workshop participants still sat silently in the dark. Fourteen-year-old Mary Ethel Dozier of Montgomery couldn't see a thing. She knew her sister was also in the room, but she couldn't tell where. All she could spot was an occasional glint of light bouncing off the polished wood billy clubs of the policemen standing watch over the room, or a reflection from the butts of their guns in their holsters.

Still in junior high school, Dozier—who changed her name to Jamila Jones—was already a veteran of the struggle. She and her sister had both been members of Rosa Parks's NAACP youth group and active participants in the bus boycott, walking to school for the full year of the protest. Jamila, who loved to sing, had formed a trio with some school friends, singing gospel hymns and "freedom songs" at Sunday fundraising teas for the boycott. Her pastor, Montgomery Improvement Association leader, Rev. Solomon Seay, brought the Dozier sisters, along with others in the organization's junior co-hort, to Highlander to "prepare us for different things we would face," Jamila explained, as their community pressed for integrated facilities and voting rights. She especially enjoyed the nightly singing with Guy Carawan, where she was learning new freedom songs for her trio's repertoire.

In the darkness, Rev. Seay heard a low whistle. Someone in the room, one of the workshop people, was whistling the first notes of a tune. A voice joined the whistle, singing the tune. Another voice joined in, and so did Jamila. The singing spread around the room, the lyrics becoming clear: "We Shall Overcome, We Shall Overcome . . ."

It was the Highlander theme song Carawan had taught them that week. They sang all the verses through, their voices growing louder, bolder. Jamila could hear her sister's out-of-tune voice somewhere in the dark room, and at least knew she was safe. The troopers guarding them circled nervously, clutching their clubs.

After several rounds of the song, Jamila spontaneously sang out a new verse, with words she made up on the spot: "We are not afraid . . . We are not afraid . . . We are not afraid, tonight . . . " A robust chorus joined her, repeating the new verse over and over.

A trooper moved toward Jamila, his hand on his club, shining his flashlight in her face. "Do you have to sing so loud?" he demanded. She could see he was flustered and shaking; the singing had unnerved him. "Would you not sing so loud!?" He was almost pleading.

The teenager from Montgomery couldn't quite believe it. The white man standing over her, with his gun, his billy club, his uniform of official power, was quaking at the sound of Black people singing a song. "It was at that time that I really understood the power of our music," she would remember later. "I understood just how powerful our songs were." The group just sang louder. Outside, sitting in the police car, Mrs. Clark and her companions could hear them singing.

It was after midnight when Ab Sloan called off the search, with the little dregs of booze found in Horton's private residence all he had to show for the venture. He would also have to be creative in coming up with grounds for arresting Clark and the others. She was placed into a separate patrol car for the ride to the justice of the peace in Tracy City, taken on a circuitous route to shake off any possible followers.

"That night I should have been afraid, because they carried me around the mountain and then put me into another car," Clark recalled. "Then they went around another mountain." She was a Black woman alone and at the mercy of agitated white policemen, on a dark mountain road. She honestly didn't know if she would live to see the daylight. "I didn't feel too good riding with them, because I do know that those young mountain boys had beaten others to death, and I had a feeling that that might happen to me."

Standing before the justice of the peace, who had also signed the dubious search warrant, Clark was charged with possessing more than a quart of whiskey. "That's ridiculous," she snapped. The charging document concocted by Sloan also claimed that police had seen Myles Horton walking around the grounds of Highlander drinking from a bottle of liquor. "You saw no such thing," Clark retorted, "he's away in Europe." This small fact didn't seem to matter. Carawan and the two other men were booked on charges of interfering with officers, resisting arrest, and public drunkenness. Everyone at Highlander knew Clark was a lifelong teetotaler and Carawan wouldn't drink anything but milk and orange juice, protecting his throat for singing. The charges were farcical, but the situation was serious.

The four Highlander prisoners were taken to the county jail in Altamont, booked, and fingerprinted. While she was being fingerprinted, District Attorney General Sloan taunted Mrs. Clark: "Septima Clark, did you get a good taste of that liquor?"

"Why don't you test my blood and see if there's any liquor in my veins," she shot back. Sloan ignored her challenge.

Bail was set high—$500 for Mrs. Clark, $250 for each of the men. Clark asked to use a telephone to speak with a lawyer, but her request was denied. She persisted, she knew her rights, and she was finally able to call Highlander.

Clark was put into a jail cell by herself. On the floor above her was a cell filled with men, and whenever they used the toilet the waste dropped down into her space. She sat upright on the hard cot. Carawan and the other young Highlander men were held in the white section of the jail. They were frightened for themselves and worried whether Mrs. Clark was safe.

Then they heard her voice. Singing. Singing sweetly through the bars, an old Sea Island slave spiritual, "Michael Row the Boat Ashore." She sang the version of the song she had learned from Harry Belafonte that summer at a Highlander youth camp workshop.

"Sister help to trim the sails—Hallelujah," they heard her sing, and the song comforted them.

"Jordan river is chilly and cold, Hallelujah . . . Chills the body, but not the soul, Hallelujah."

Septima Clark continued singing in her cell, and she refused to be afraid.

CHAPTER TWENTY-ONE

Padlock

L ater that night, May Justus and Vera McCampbell's telephone rang. They reached under their mattress and pulled out their stash of emergency cash. They dashed to their car, drove to the Altamont jail, paid the $500 bond for their friend Septima's release, and took her back to Highlander. The sheriff refused to allow the women to bail out Carawan and the other men, insisting they needed to stay in jail at least eight hours to "sober up"—part of the ruse to justify their arrest.

In the morning, just as she had promised, Mrs. Clark led the final session of the community leadership workshop, as if nothing had happened the night before. But news of what happened would soon be splashed across the front pages of local and national newspapers, including Clark's hometown paper in Charleston. Wire service dispatches, including photos of Clark during the raid, announced her arrest for possession of whiskey.

Attorney General Sloan crowed about his winning strategy to the press: "The legislative committee gave me information mostly on integration and communism," Sloan told reporters, "and I wasn't satisfied I could be successful at that." The allegations concerning irregularities with Highlander's charter also fell short. He instead latched onto the possibility of finding illegal booze. "I thought maybe this was the best shot and I think now I'll be successful."

On August 6, Mrs. Clark maintained her stoic demeanor throughout the raucous proceedings of her preliminary hearing. Dressed in a dark shirtwaist dress, stylish white hat, and button earrings, Clark remained poised while enduring the three-hour jousting match between District Attorney General Sloan and her defense attorney, Nashville lawyer Cecil Branstetter. On the witness stand, she was unflappable, even as she was subjected to Sloan's surly and condescending questioning. Branstetter jumped to his feet to object to Sloan's crude attempts to intimidate Mrs. Clark, later telling reporters: "I have never before seen a witness so abused as the Attorney-General has abused our witness—perhaps because she is colored."

"I wasn't going to let them scare me to death. I just would not let them," Clark later explained in her memoir. "But it wasn't an easy thing, because when you'd go home you would keep thinking of what they could do, and what they might do. . . ." What she feared most was the blow to her reputation: as a Methodist woman who permitted only a touch of rum in the eggnog at Christmas time. As a trusted—and respectable—leader in the Black community.

The court ordered Clark to appear before the Grundy County grand jury when it convened in early November; Carawan and the two other Highlander men were similarly ordered to stand before the grand jury for their alleged crimes. At the close of these hearings, on August 12, Ab Sloan quickly made his next move: petitioning the court to padlock Highlander immediately, on the grounds that it was a "public nuisance."

Sloan's highly inventive petition maintained that Highlander engaged in the sale and consumption of intoxicating beverages and was the site of "boisterous, noisy, rowdy, and drunken" gatherings. "The place has a reputation of being one where people drink and engage in immoral, lewd, and unchaste practices," Sloan claimed. One striking omission from Sloan's litany of Highlander's supposed wrongdoing was any mention of communist or subversive activity; those spurious allegations had evaporated.

"The charges are preposterous," Mrs. Clark announced to the press. "The real complaint is that Highlander has always been an integrated school, and in recent years has based its program on full citizenship and integration." Tennessee's sinister ambush also had broader implications.

"The threat to silence the voice of Highlander is a threat to the existence of every organization in the nation," Clark warned, "and a threat to the basic freedom of thought and expression of every American."

Septima Clark was not going to be silenced. With Horton still in Europe, she became the public voice of Highlander. She announced that there would be no interruption in Highlander's programs, no pause in its training work while the school braced for its "padlock hearing" in mid-September 1959. Most importantly, the late summer "Citizenship School Idea" workshop, promoting the concept to community leaders and training a large new cohort of prospective teachers from several states, would go on as planned. She, and Highlander, would not be intimidated or distracted.

Clark's friends wrote to console her. "Of course your own fine character and your long life of integrity and purity and nobility is the finest answer to such low charges," Virginia Durr assured her. Dr. King issued a statement calling Mrs. Clark a woman of "integrity, honesty, and courage." A Charleston NAACP colleague urged her to remember "that you are playing a role in which future historians will pick up their pens and list you among the great women of the 20th century."

On the eve of the padlock hearing, Eleanor Roosevelt dedicated her *My Day* column to the Highlander raid and court proceedings, emphasizing the national, and international, repercussions of Tennessee's assault on the school: "The eyes not alone of the American people will be focused on this part of our country. All over the world as well, people will be watching to see what our promise of justice really means in the U.S.A."

———— ✦ ————

The padlock hearing opened on September 14 in a "near carnival atmosphere" inside the Grundy County courthouse. During three days of legal sparring before a circuit court judge, District Attorney Sloan introduced a procession of local residents testifying to Highlander's moral outrages. Witnesses claimed they had seen drunken bacchanals on the campus and spied racially mixed, nude couples having sex inside the school's residential cabins, in the library, on the grass, and in the woods. Highlander was, one witness contended, nothing more than an "integrated whorehouse."

"Integrated Sex Parties Cited" was the headline Septima's sister Lorene, and everyone at Old Bethel Church, and her sorority sisters, could read in the *Charleston News Courier's* coverage of the Highlander case.

Highlander's defense attorney, Cecil Branstetter, managed to discredit many of the lurid fictions presented by the prosecution's witnesses and convinced the judge that Sloan's search warrant was invalid, making the alcoholic evidence from the raid inadmissible. Sloan was reduced to leaning hard on the allegation that Highlander had, years before, broken the law by selling beer on its premises. It was true that Highlander had, during its years working with labor organizers, kept an icebox of sodas and beers in the common room. Thirsty drinkers could pitch in a coin to help restock the supply, but payment was voluntary. Drinking beer was legal, even in dry Grundy County, but selling it without a license was not. When abstemious Mrs. Clark joined the staff in 1956, she objected to beer, or any alcohol, on the premises, and insisted Horton stop the practice, which he did. So there had not been any beer at Highlander for at least three years. Nonetheless, Sloan, desperate for a legal hook, insisted Highlander posed a risk to public safety and must be shuttered while the case wended its way through the legal system.

Judge Chester C. Chattin was not persuaded by Sloan's portrayal of Highlander as a sinkhole of vice, but he did agree that sometime in the past Highlander had broken the law by selling beer without a license. Based upon this finding, which was only a misdemeanor subject to a fine under Tennessee law, the judge ordered Highlander's main building, where the supposed beer sales had taken place, temporarily padlocked until a trial on the charter revocation was held in November. The school could continue operating in the campus's other buildings.

On a Saturday morning in the last week of September, the Grundy County sheriff arrived on the Highlander campus to snap padlocks onto the doors of the old farmhouse. Myles Horton stood behind the sheriff and watched, hands in his pockets.

"You can padlock a building. But you can't padlock an idea," Horton insisted as Clark and the staff continued to conduct workshops in other buildings on the campus. "Highlander is an idea. You can't kill it, and you can't close it in."

———◆———

Albert Sloan was trying his best to kill Highlander, accomplishing the mission the legislature had entrusted to him. He looked forward to the jury trial set for the first week of November. Just days before the trial was to begin, Sloan supplemented his case with what he considered a sturdy new charge: by operating an integrated educational facility, Highlander was violating a 1901 Tennessee statute making it "unlawful for white and colored persons to attend the same school." There was a complicating factor to this new strategy—the *Brown* decision of the US Supreme Court, declaring school segregation unconstitutional—but Sloan was prepared to argue that *Brown* applied only to public schools, not privately run schools like Highlander.

Sloan had previously denied that race had anything to do with his prosecution of Highlander; it was all about protecting Tennesseans from the immoral, subversive culture of the place. As the trial approached, he was changing his tack, pivoting to what everyone knew was the crux of the matter, in a sense being more honest. Horton and his defense team welcomed this, since they wanted to tackle Tennessee's segregation laws head-on.

In the weeks between the September padlocking and the early November trial, Septima Clark embarked on a northern tour to raise awareness of Highlander's plight and solicit funds for the legal battle. Lugging two large leather cases filled with descriptive materials and reels of audiotape recordings of the padlock hearing, Clark offered a dramatic account of the raid and her courthouse inquisition to sympathetic house parties of liberals in New York and other states. When Mrs. Clark returned to Monteagle, she was forced to live in temporary quarters, as her own bedroom on the second floor of Highlander's main building was made inaccessible by the padlock. Shortly before the Highlander trial began in November, Clark was indicted by the Grundy County grand jury for illegal possession of liquor; Guy Carawan and the other Highlander staffers were charged with public drunkenness and resisting arrest. Months later, the state's fabricated case against Septima was quietly withdrawn and charges against the others dropped.

During this tense time in the fall of 1959, Ella Baker came to Highlander to confer with Septima Clark. The SCLC Crusade for Citizenship was a failure, Baker admitted, and much of the reason was that the campaign could not reach grassroots Black voters and was not equipped to help those who could not pass the literacy tests. Baker had been watching the development of Clark's citizenship schools, intrigued by their focus on basic education to prepare the masses of potential Black voters—those ignored by conventional registration campaigns—to participate in civic affairs. She was also impressed with how Clark and Robinson were tapping the energy and skills of Black women as community leaders and citizenship teachers, giving them an entrée into the movement. Baker and Clark forged a close working bond, and Baker left Highlander convinced that literacy education should be incorporated into the SCLC's voter registration efforts, but she had a tough time getting the ministers of the SCLC to take the idea seriously.

———◆———

The Highlander trial opened on November 4, 1959, and the spectacle reminded some observers of another trial, conducted in the same judicial district of Tennessee, almost thirty-five years before. In that trial, the state prosecuted science teacher John Scopes for teaching Darwin's theory of evolution in his classroom, in defiance of state law. The parallels were tantalizing. The trial of Highlander would, as one journalist put it, "determine whether or not the active practice and teaching of equality and brotherhood is 'legal' in the heart of America in 1959."

This jury trial was to determine if Highlander had violated its charter and should be shut down. Sloan presented ample evidence of Highlander's violation of state segregation laws, including a deposition by Georgia Education Commission's spy photographer Ed Friend. Rev. Dr. Martin Luther King Jr's. name was mentioned several times in the prosecution's depiction of Highlander as a promoter of racial integration and agitation.

The prosecution hammered hardest on the accusations that Horton personally profited from the operation of Highlander, bedazzling the jury with tales of elaborate, wholly invented, schemes of financial chicanery allegedly perpetrated by Horton. On the stand to defend himself, Horton's voice broke, and he came close to crying. His, and Zilphia's, life work and sacrifice were being maliciously misconstrued, and the jury was eating it up. The judge instructed the jury to consider only this one charge—whether Horton was guilty of running Highlander for personal gain—and he would rule from the bench on the other charges, including selling beer and the violation of segregation laws.

The jury took just forty-nine minutes to return with a guilty verdict on Horton. The judge declared Highlander also guilty of illegal beer sales and breaking state segregation laws. Allowing both sides time to file additional motions, the judge ordered the padlocks on the school removed until he made his final ruling on Highlander's fate early in the new year.

In mid-February 1960, Judge C. C. Chattin announced that based upon the guilty verdicts of the trial—that Horton had operated Highlander for his own benefit, the school had once sold beer, and it practiced racial integration—Highlander must forfeit its charter and all its property. He appointed a receiver to liquidate the school's holdings as soon as all appeals were exhausted.

"Wind up your affairs," the judge told Horton.

———————◆———————

By this time in February, Septima, Bernice, and Esau were busy running the fourth season of the citizenship schools, which had expanded to new sites. The court ruling in Tennessee was certainly a blow, but Mrs. Clark remained optimistic: Horton vowed to appeal the school's closing to the Supreme Court, and she was sure Highlander would eventually be vindicated. The string of appeals to lower courts would also buy more time, allowing her programs to continue.

Highlander was already thriving in places far from the Monteagle campus: in the citizenship schools, in the extension programs, like Jenkins's political education seminars, and in the activist work of its alumni around the South. As Mrs. Clark watched the citizenship schools propagate into new communities, with requests for even more schools pouring in, she saw proof of Horton's concept of Highlander as not simply a site with buildings, but as a portable, teachable vision of equality and democracy. Tennessee couldn't kill the idea.

CHAPTER TWENTY-TWO

Sit at the Welcome Table

S eptima Clark arrived at the citizenship schools in a turquoise Studebaker, with Guy Carawan at the wheel. There were six classes in session in the Lowcountry during the early winter of 1960, and she wanted to make regular visits to them all, in addition to her usual rounds of community and church meetings. She needed to cover a lot of ground but couldn't drive, so Myles arranged for Carawan to be her driver.

Besides driving, Carawan also conducted "singing schools" for Highlander during these winter months, providing weekly music sessions for each of the citizenship school classes. He had studied ethnomusicology at grad school, so he welcomed the chance to spend time exploring the Sea Islands' culture and folkways, with an opportunity to collect Indigenous music and stories. He lodged in Esau Jenkins's cinder-block motel, near the bridge linking Charleston and Johns Island, while chauffeuring Mrs. Clark.

Septima had to convince Guy that it was prudent for her to sit in the back seat of the car, not in front with him, as the sight of Black and white passengers riding so close together on rural roads would attract unwanted attention. Mrs. Clark was all for breaking Jim Crow boundaries, but she knew to pick her battles. Even though she sat in the back of the Studebaker, they were still frequently pulled over by police, who found it just too strange for a gray-haired Black woman to be chauffeured around by a longish-haired young white guy.

Carawan realized he had a lot to learn about living in the South; Clark and Jenkins became his mentors. Jenkins introduced him around, took him to church services and to Moving Star Hall, where Carawan was fascinated by the singing, shouting, and rhythms he heard there. Septima became what Carawan called his "substitute mother": guiding him, scolding him, schooling him on how to comport himself in this foreign terrain. His folk-hippy garb was not proper attire for attending church services, she admonished him, as poor Black churchgoers proudly wore their best clothes on Sunday, and he must show them respect. Carawan dutifully bought a jacket and tie.

In the back of the Studebaker were Carawan's guitar and banjo, the tools of his trade. Bernice Robinson, whose dream had been to train for a professional singing career, had brought singing into her classes from the very beginning, to relax and cheer her students, but also to express concepts through song. She taught her students new "freedom" words to standard hymns like "Soldiers of the Cross," linking their learning efforts to a larger cause.

Carawan brought the classes' musical interludes to a new level. Melding the Highlander song tradition with the islands' own musical heritage, the singing sessions gave the adult students a joyous sense of unity and common purpose. He asked the students to bring their favorite traditional songs to class, then he carried them to the other classrooms, spreading the folk songs of one island to another. Clark even fashioned vocabulary and spelling lessons from the song lyrics Carawan wrote on the blackboard or distributed on mimeographed sheets. Carawan taught "We Shall Overcome" to every class. "The singing school idea is working wonders," Clark reported back to the Highlander office. "Last night we had some shouting," as the citizenship students got into the spirit.

The original citizenship school at the Progressive Club grocery store on Johns Island was still going strong, taught by new local teachers, while Robinson supervised all the other schools in the Lowcountry as a part-time Highlander employee. When the residents on the southern part of Johns wanted their own school, an additional class was established in the Promised Land section, where Clark had once been a teacher. Ethel Jenkins Grimball was teaching again on Wadmalaw, Alleen Brewer on Edisto, and the North Charleston citizenship school opened again in Mary Davis's beauty parlor.

During the 1960 winter season, a brand-new citizenship school opened on tiny and remote Daufuskie Island, which could be reached only three times a week by a mailboat from the mainland. Daufuskie's population of 140 people was almost entirely Black (there were only eight white residents at this time), so with enough qualified voters it would be possible to pressure elected representatives to provide government help for the neglected island. Clark convinced the Daufuskie community to support a citizenship school as the first step toward that goal. She identified a local leader and a candidate teacher, brought them to Highlander for training, and now Daufuskie had a citizenship school and some sense of hope.

Earlier in 1959, as Charleston County prepared for municipal elections, Robinson and Jenkins had worked together to harness the political momentum generated by the various citizenship classes in the region. Jenkins helped organize registration rallies to build excitement and created an umbrella group—the Citizens' Committee of Charleston County—to coordinate the efforts of Black citizen clubs in the area. Jenkins was, naturally, elected president of this regional organization, which soon opened a storefront office in the city, with a voter registration resource center inside.

Robinson put her citizenship school teaching skills to work in an ingenious approach to the municipal elections. She recruited Charleston women, all Highlander alumnae, to form coaching squads in their wards to help their neighbors register and vote. Robinson trained the coaches, and in a mini-version of the citizenship classes, the coaches taught prospective voters about state election laws they would have to know, how to read the required sections of the state constitution, and how to read an election ballot. The coaches formed car pools to get their students to the registrar's office and stood outside the office door to lend support. Robinson's project helped attain astonishing results: in the ten-day registration period before the election, almost seven hundred Black citizens in Charleston County successfully registered to vote.

The numbers of Black voters still did not reach proportions that could overturn the entrenched white political establishment in elections, but Jenkins began seeing evidence that Charleston politicians were being forced to reckon with the emerging Black vote. A white magistrate judge on Johns Island was running for reelection and came to Jenkins for help. The judge had a reputation for treating Black defendants harshly in his courtroom, but the island's white voters thought he was occasionally too lenient. He was facing an opponent and feared he would lose. The judge noticed that Black registration on Johns had risen sharply in the past few years, thanks to Jenkins's efforts, and realized that if he could win some of those votes, he could edge out his opponent. "What can y'all do?" the judge asked Jenkins.

Jenkins sat behind his desk, savoring the plea of the white judge, and sketched out a deal: if the judge would promise to treat Black people more fairly, not belittle them, or convict them without evidence—just treated them like human beings—Jenkins told the judge, "we will vote for you." This was the sort of political quid pro quo Jenkins knew his people needed. Jenkins informed Johns Island voters of the judge's pledge of fairness if he were re-elected, and the Black voters carried the judge to a slim victory. The judge began treating Black islanders respectfully and fairly in his courtroom. The important lesson, Jenkins stressed, was that Black votes mattered and could produce real change.

———◆———

At the end of December, while the citizenship classes took a short holiday break, Jenkins brought Guy Carawan to Moving Star Hall for the Christmas and New Year Watch Night services. The young musician was mesmerized by the singing, stomping, and clapping. He was deeply moved by the intensity of the spiritual expressions he witnessed in the praise house. From midnight till "day-clean" prayers and testimony, sermons and song rose up from the men and women in the hall, each taking a spontaneous turn.

"This service was the most moving and democratic form of worship I had ever encountered," Carawan marveled. He was told he was the first white man invited to attend the Watch Night service at the hall, and the experience changed his life. Being there also helped him understand the deep roots of faith and pride the islanders brought to their participation in the citizenship schools. Their songs expressed their history of pain and resilience but also fortified them for the hard work of learning to become full citizens in spite of the obstacles and dangers. He decided he wanted to help them preserve this important song tradition.

Carawan sought out the talented singers he heard at Moving Star Hall to learn some of their old songs and stories, passed down only by oral tradition. He got to know Alice Wine, who was a regular at Moving Star Hall, as well as a clerk at the Progressive Club grocery where Carawan led weekly class singing sessions. One day Wine heard Carawan strumming his guitar and singing the spiritual, "Keep Your Hand on the Gospel Plow, Hold On."

"We have a different echo for that," she told Carawan as she offered her version of the song. "Keep your eyes on the prize, hold out," was the chorus she sang, in the way it was sung on Johns Island. Carawan thought Wine's lyrics made the song more powerful, more relevant to the struggle for rights and freedom the islanders were joining. He adopted her version—though he retained "hold on" instead of her "hold out"—and began to sing it in the citizenship schools.

This was the moment Rev. Lawson's Nashville college students had been training for. All the text study and philosophical debate, the role-playing and discipline exercises led to this snowy Saturday morning in mid-February 1960, when their commitment would be put to the test.

They hadn't expected to try so soon; their plans hadn't quite gelled yet. But when those four Black freshmen at North Carolina Agricultural and Technical State College sat themselves down at the Woolworth's lunch counter in Greensboro, asked for a hot dog and cup of coffee, and didn't move when the waitress refused, a fire was lit. There had been other, isolated lunch counter protests in several cities over the years, but they had soon sputtered out. Not this one. In the two weeks since the Greensboro Four had staged their "sit-in" at the counter, hundreds more Black students had joined them, with new sit-in demonstrations erupting in southern cities almost daily: Durham, Charlotte, Tallahassee, Columbia, Baton Rouge. Now it was Nashville's turn. "Greensboro was the message," John Lewis would recall. "If Greensboro can do it, we can do it."

John Lewis prayed before he led his group of students from First Baptist Church to the Woolworth's on Fifth Avenue in Nashville's downtown shopping district. He was just a sophomore, a week shy of his twentieth birthday, but already a leader of Nashville's student movement. Lewis joined over a hundred other students walking silently, two abreast, toward the shopping district, intent upon occupying the lunch counter stools at three busy five-and-dime stores that allowed Black customers to spend their money but would not allow them to sit and drink a cup of coffee. They were dressed in their churchgoing clothes, formal and dignified, with books and Bibles tucked under their arms.

Lewis and a subset of his group entered the Woolworth's, made their purchases—to prove they were paying customers—then took seats at the counter. Seeing them, a white waitress startled: "Oh my God, here's the niggers." Lewis asked if he and his friends could be served but was told, "We don't serve niggers here." The students remained seated, reading or doing homework for the rest of the afternoon. There were a few taunts from a group of young white men ("Niggers, Go Home!"), but the students did not respond; otherwise it was calm. At six o'clock in the evening they all quietly stood and walked out of the Woolworth's. The other groups walked out of the other stores. The first day of the Nashville sit-ins had been dignified and peaceful. Lewis and his comrades were ecstatic: they'd made their point. They hadn't succeeded in being served, but they would be back.

They were back five days later, almost two hundred students walking downtown, dividing into groups, assigned to different stores, taking shifts on the stools. A few days later, the number of student protesters swelled to 340, then 400, and the violence began.

White mobs began to punch and kick the seated students, spat at them, pushed lit cigarettes against their backs, poured mustard and ketchup on their hair, pulled them off the stools, and beat them. The Black students climbed back onto the stools. The police arrived and just watched, not intervening to stop the attacks. Soon the police announced that the students were under arrest for loitering and disorderly conduct, while the white men who had beaten them were allowed to go free.

As Lewis and the other Nashville students were hustled out of the store to the paddy wagons on the street, they sang the song of hope and resilience many of them had learned at Highlander, "We Shall Overcome."

They continued singing in the city jail, while hundreds more students rushed to take their places on the lunch counter stools. The arrested students refused release on bail—"Jail, No Bail" was another form of moral resistance— and when they were found guilty of disorderly conduct, they refused to pay the fines. They were sentenced to a month in the county workhouse.

Sitting behind bars in Nashville were many future leaders of the civil rights movement: Lewis, his roommate Bernard Lafayette, and classmate James Bevel; Fisk students Diane Nash and Marion Barry. The protests spread to the lunchrooms at the Nashville bus terminals. More students were arrested.

News photos and television footage of the students being beaten and hauled off to jail brought nationwide condemnation. Worried about the bad publicity, the mayor of Nashville ordered the students released from jail. But clearly the southern movement had taken a new and unpredictable turn: mass direct-action protest led by fearless young people wielding new tactics. There was no one leader, no overarching coordination, just young people unwilling to accept injustice any longer. In the following weeks, the student sit-in movement exploded across the South: an estimated fifty thousand young people participated in protests in fifty-five cities in thirteen states, with sympathetic demonstrators picketing store chains in northern cities. A new generation had entered the struggle.

Some older civil rights leaders were alarmed by the students' confrontational approach. Thurgood Marshall told the Nashville students they were making a mistake by not pursuing a lawsuit against the stores instead of sitting in. But Dr. Martin Luther King Jr. applauded the courage, commitment, and nonviolent discipline of the students, writing letters of encouragement to them and speaking at a mass meeting in Durham. He hoped the students might add a new, vibrant dimension to the SCLC as its "youth wing." But it was the SCLC's executive secretary, Ella Baker, who most fully recognized the potential power of the students. She consulted with her friend Septima Clark, who was also thrilled by the students' brave initiative, and they worked together to find a way to unite and nurture these young people.

The sit-ins had burst across the South during the final weeks of the 1960 citizenship schools term, sending a jolt of excitement into the classrooms, providing plenty of grist for discussion. The closing exercises were especially lively this year, bringing together all the students from the different sites to meet one another, receive their graduation diplomas, and celebrate the voter registration certificates they had attained, or would get soon. On Edisto Island alone, there were already five times the number of Black voters registered as there had been before the citizenship school program began there only two years before. The upcoming presidential elections in the fall provided an exciting goal, a reason for wanting to vote.

At the graduation, Carawan led a sing-along concert of traditional songs from around the islands, some fitted with new "freedom" verses they had learned to read in class. The students' voices joined together in the finale, singing the Highlander anthem of "We Shall Overcome" within days of when the jailed Nashville students had been singing the same song of solidarity behind bars.

Carawan packed his guitar and banjo into the Studebaker and turned west toward Monteagle to resume his post as Highlander's music director. Robinson returned, at least briefly, to her beauty parlor in Charleston. Jenkins stayed in the islands to gear up for the fall elections. Clark headed to Highlander to prepare for the spring and summer workshops. The programs would proceed, as she'd planned them, while Highlander appealed its charter revocation and closure to the Tennessee Supreme Court. The padlocks on the main house had been removed during this appeal interim, and hundreds of people were already enrolled in the workshops, a gratifying rebuke to the state's closure plans. As she headed back to Monteagle, Clark realized there would need to be some urgent additions and alterations to the workshops. The students' direct-action campaign demanded, and deserved, immediate attention.

Clark, like Rosa Parks and Ella Baker, had always believed that the young generation—with their idealism, impatience, and fearlessness—were the future of the struggle. Suddenly, in this early spring of 1960, the future she had imagined had arrived. Even while the sit-ins continued to spread in March, Clark and Baker were hastily formulating plans to bring together southern student leaders to meet and strategize at Highlander in the first days of April.

Horton was all for it. He saw the enormous boost the student protests could provide to a civil rights movement still struggling to gain momentum. The sit-ins marked "a new phase of democratic action in America," he believed. What the students were doing was the living model of the Highlander idea: a grassroots, locally grown, and organically spread moral protest against inequality and demand for justice.

Horton was invited to a community mass meeting in Nashville and came away impressed with the students' organizational savvy and determination, but he recognized that the students didn't really know where they were headed or how to get there. They hadn't had time to think; they were too busy doing. That's where Highlander could help. Clark and Baker tapped their network of connections throughout the South to identify the student leaders of the major protests and arrange for them to come to Highlander on the first weekend of April. Carawan, who was at Highlander with Clark during these hectic few weeks of planning, described the process as "asking on the grapevine—'Who's really making things happen in your town?'"

This was just what Tennessee and the other southern states feared: widespread, homegrown rebellion against Jim Crow by educated young Black people. The southern governors had believed that by killing Highlander, crippling the NAACP, and harassing civil rights leaders, they could smother the fight for freedom. This was proof they could not.

———————◆———————

On April 1, 1960, more than seventy students, representing seventeen colleges in seven states, arrived at Highlander, stretching the limits of the dorm space. The students didn't mind sleeping on the floor, if they slept at all. The Nashville student leaders were there alongside leaders from Greensboro, Knoxville, Memphis, and other cities in North and South Carolina and Georgia. The atmosphere was celebratory but serious, as the students, so consumed by the drama and demands of their own protests, began to recognize the size of the campaign they had created. This was their first opportunity to meet their far-flung sit-in peers and digest the life-changing experiences of the past two months. Many students couldn't attend the gathering because they were still in jail.

Clark, Baker, and Horton led workshop discussions on philosophy, strategy, and tactics, drawing out the students' motivations and encouraging them to articulate their goals, even their fears. The students wrestled with concepts that would define, and even bedevil, their movement for years to come: Should nonviolence be used as a guiding philosophy or just a useful tactic? Were they willing to accept the painful consequences of civil disobedience? Should they accept bail or stay in jail? How should the student movement relate to the Black communities in their cities and to the legacy civil rights organizations? And what should the role of white allies be in a Black struggle for freedom?

Horton was not going to allow the students to simply bask in the glow of their protests and spout airy aphorisms about justice and morality. That's not how Highlander's brand of education for action worked. He pushed, provoked, and challenged them to clarify their thinking, forcing the young people to define and defend their actions. He didn't lecture or dictate, he just asked questions, as he did in every Highlander workshop, even if the questions were discomforting.

"Horton loved to play devil's advocate," Nashville student leader Bernard Lafayette recalled. "He was arguing the whole question of why do black and whites have to be together. He'd ask: Why do you have to be with white people? Why can't white people eat with whomever they like?

"I had never heard a white man say these things to my face, and he was supposed to be a friend. I got madder and madder. Of course, he was trying to force us to be very clear about what we wanted. He was always pushing you further. I knew what he was doing, but it made me furious," Lafayette later admitted. "You think you have come to some conclusion about something, and there he is, pushing out the walls. That's what a good teacher does."

Horton purposefully made the students feel unbalanced and uncomfortable to strengthen them for the long and tough fight ahead. He did not provide answers, but he did offer sincere encouragement and some important advice:

the students should organize themselves and maintain their independence from other established civil rights groups who might want to harness their energy but co-opt their plans. "He told us never to let [another organization] capture our spirit," John Lewis remembered, "never allow ourselves to become the slaves of any of the old organizations. And he told us not to ever lose hope, but to keep on going." Lewis would recall Horton's words as wise, even prophetic.

Among the students participating in the discussions at Highlander that weekend was a young white woman from Pomona College in California, an exchange student studying at Fisk, who had joined the sit-in protests in Nashville. Candie Anderson had been arrested and jailed, separated from her comrades into a segregated white cell. Lonely and scared, she was comforted by the spirited singing of the Black students, who belted out everything from spirituals to rock-and-roll hits to calypso tunes through the bars. The music had helped get her through her first stint in jail, made her feel part of the struggle. Now, singing helped her and the Nashville students bond with those from other cities during this intense weekend at Highlander.

Guy Carawan sat with the students in the big discussion circles, listening to the debates about strategy and goals. "If we were sitting too long, or all talked out, or if someone just got the impulse, we'd sing," Guy recalled. "I might jump in with a song I had learned, like 'Eyes on the Prize,' 'We Shall Not be Moved' or 'I'm Gonna Sit at the Welcome Table.'" He taught the students the melodies and words, encouraged them to make up lyrics of their own, transform these old songs into "freedom songs." "Welcome Table" was especially good for lunch counter sit-ins.

For many of the students who had never been to Highlander before, this was their introduction to Guy's rendition of "We Shall Overcome."

"It was a perfect song," Candie Anderson thought. "It pulled us together with such power, it had such quiet strength."

———◆———

The students returned to Nashville and the other sit-in cities in the first week of April 1960 to continue their protests. Baker agreed with Horton that the students needed to form their own organization, establish their own agenda. At Monteagle they had formed committees and made the first steps toward an organizational structure. Baker convinced the SCLC to sponsor a follow-up conference of student leaders at Shaw University in Raleigh in mid-April.

In the meantime, the Black community in Nashville bolstered its support for the student sit-ins with a boycott of downtown stores, where Black customers spent an estimated $50 to $60 million a year. Easter was usually a busy shopping time, but this year, women in the city's Black churches spread the "No Fashions for Easter" idea, so the white-owned stores were hurting. The pinch brought a feeble proposal from downtown store owners to experiment with a separate-but-equal type of solution, dividing the lunch counters into white and Black sections for diners. The students rejected the idea as insulting and continued their protests.

Almost three hundred students converged on the Shaw campus for the Easter weekend conference, where they hammered out a blueprint for a new organization, which they called the Student Nonviolent Coordinating Committee. The students continued the heated policy debates they had begun at Highlander two weeks before. Rev. King spoke to them, offering praise for their work. But he received only a tepid response to his invitation for the students to assemble under the SCLC umbrella, to become a young, direct-action division of the SCLC. This was exactly what Horton and Baker had warned them about.

Baker herself offered the students an inspiring but sobering charge in her talk to them, which she titled "More Than Hamburgers." The lunch counter sit-ins were fine and noble, but that was the easy part. Battering down the hardened racial barriers in education, in the voting booth, and in the economy would be much harder and more important. Their work had just begun.

Baker asked Carawan to bring his guitar and songs to the conference in Raleigh, where he introduced the students to his playlist of traditional songs refashioned as freedom songs. He brought Alice Wine's Johns Island version of the song some of the students might have heard their grandparents sing— "Hands on the Gospel Plow"—refreshed as "Keep Your Eyes on the Prize." The song resonated with these young people who were trying to forge their own path in the struggle.

Morehouse College student Julian Bond was, at first, wary of the lanky white troubadour. "When I saw Guy take the stage at the Raleigh conference, my first thought was—'surfer,'" Bond admitted. "With longish blond hair and a fringed jacket, he looked like someone off a California beach." But when he sang, "you could tell he lived the songs, he felt the songs."

It was the first time Bond, and many of the others gathered in Raleigh, heard "We Shall Overcome." "Guy led the audience in singing it," Bond recalled, "and at the conference's end several hundred young people had both learned and adopted 'We Shall Overcome' as their song—as the modern movement's song, just as 'Lift Every Voice and Sing' had been the anthem of earlier generations."

The morning after the Nashville students returned from the Raleigh conference, they awoke to the news that the home of their lead defense attorney, Z. Alexander Looby, had been bombed, dynamite thrown by a passing car. The assassination attempt failed, Looby and his wife managed to escape injury, but the force of the blast destroyed their home and blew out almost 150 windows in the Black hospital a block away.

By noon, more than three thousand students, faculty, and Nashville citizens were marching, three and four abreast, through central Nashville to confront the mayor at city hall. They marched silently, creating a hushed moral rebuke to vigilante violence as their procession snaked through the city. When they reached the steps of city hall, Carawan was there to lead them in "We Shall Overcome." The refrain echoed in the square: "We are not alone . . . We are not afraid."

Mayor Ben West, considered a pragmatic moderate on racial matters, met a delegation of the marchers on the steps. Fisk student Diane Nash, the students' spokesperson, took a step toward the mayor and asked a forthright question: Would he use the prestige of his office to appeal to his citizens to stop racial discrimination and violence? The mayor, facing thousands of angry Black citizens, answered: "I appeal to all citizens to end discrimination, to have no bigotry, no bias, no hatred."

Nash skillfully pushed him further: "Do you mean that to include lunch counters?" she asked. "Do you recommend that the lunch counters be desegregated?"

"Yes" said Mayor West. The crowd erupted in cheers. The mayor immediately tried to qualify his answer—it was up to the store managers, of course, he added—but the cheers drowned out his caveat. "Integrate Counters—Mayor," read the headline in the *Nashville Tennessean* the next morning.

A few weeks later, Nashville became the first southern city to desegregate its lunch counters. The fight was not over, as some store owners refused to comply. The sit-ins, and arrests, would resume in the fall and expand to the city's other segregated spaces.

"Highlander Set Stage for Sit-Ins," the *Charleston News-Courier* reported to its readers with alarm. Myles and Septima could not have been prouder.

CHAPTER TWENTY-THREE

Wade in the Water

By mid-1960, the South was entering what Myles Horton called "movement times." That was his term for the evolutionary stage of political foment when "leadership multiplies very rapidly, because there's something explosive going on."

"People see that other people, not so different from themselves, do things that they thought could never be done," Horton explained. "They're emboldened and challenged by that to step into the water. And once they get in the water, it's as if they'd never not been there."

The thousands of students who had joined the lunch counter sit-ins in the spring of 1960 had plunged into the water. Wading in after them were thousands more Black adults in more than a hundred cities and towns where the protests jolted the segregated status quo. Formerly complacent or frightened communities rallied to support the young people and were, in turn, roused to consider mounting their own acts of resistance. Even in places far from the sit-in sites, people inspired by the courage of the students were beginning to take first steps to reclaim their rights. More than ever before, there was a need to develop local leadership in these communities, to both sustain momentum and deepen commitment. Demand for citizenship schools was surging.

While Highlander's lawyers battled to overturn the death sentence imposed by the Tennessee court, the school remained open and the staff resolutely pushed ahead, actually increasing its programming and expanding the citizenship school program. In whatever time it had left on Monteagle Mountain, Highlander was determined to continue coaxing more people into the water.

"The young people in the sit-in movement have shown that there are many doors now open in the South," Clark wrote to Highlander supporters in the early summer of 1960. "These doors stand open, waiting to be fully used in many communities. What to do and how to do it are the decisions now facing people all over the south."

The student protests had energized the movement, propelled it forward, but also knocked it off-balance. Horton and Clark rushed to devise a series of workshops exploring the "startling and revealing implications" of the student initiatives. Hundreds of people climbed the mountain in the summer of 1960 to ponder the philosophical, strategic, and tactical challenges facing the evolving movement, examining the "new alliances" that could be forged to strengthen the coalition, and the "new agenda" to be pursued. Expanding on the conversations begun with the college protesters in the spring, Horton and Clark again tackled the sensitive topic of what role Black adults should have in a youth-oriented campaign. And what place sympathetic whites—students and adults—might take in a Black freedom movement.

Clark brought movement veterans Rosa Parks, Ella Baker, and Rev. Fred Shuttlesworth to Monteagle, together with about seventy-five old-guard elders and young student leaders to grapple with the thorny issue of white participation. Horton assumed his usual devil's advocate role, but he recognized the imperative for Black leadership to take command of this fight for freedom on every level, without interference (or possibly usurpation) by white allies. Myles knew he himself might be counted among those well-meaning, but perhaps unconsciously domineering, white friends, and he was forced to examine his own place in the emerging movement, too. The discussions were frank, sometimes raw, but productive, yet the issue would roil the movement for years to come.

———————◆———————

The poor sharecroppers of Fayette and Haywood counties in the southwest corner of Tennessee were ready for action. Mrs. Clark made her first visit to them in mid-June 1960, having heard that they were organizing to vote. Few Black citizens had voted in either county since the end of Reconstruction. The last time anyone in Haywood County had dared to even try to register, in 1940, he had been lynched.

These counties were in cotton country, east of Memphis, just above the Mississippi line. Black people accounted for more than three-quarters of the population, but most still lived in a feudal system as sharecroppers or farmhands on the big white-owned plantations. They lived in deep poverty—Fayette was the third-poorest county in the nation at the time—with little education, no land or homes of their own, and no voice in the government that ruled over them. Mrs. Clark was thrilled to learn that there was a move to change that—they wanted to vote.

The immediate impetus came from a recent local trial, in which a seventy-year-old man was wrongfully convicted of murder by an all-white jury. Only registered voters were eligible for jury duty, but there were virtually no Black people on the Fayette County registration rolls, so Black defendants were doomed. The situation infuriated a small group of local Black men, war veterans who had served their country but were denied participation in American democracy. They formed Civic and Welfare Leagues in both Fayette and Haywood counties, with the immediate goal of organizing their neighbors to register to vote. John McFerren, a thirty-four-year-old Navy veteran and gas station owner, led the Fayette group, knocking on doors to convince his neighbors that the local justice system would always be rigged against them unless they were able to provide a jury of peers for Black defendants. Unless they registered to vote.

Tennessee no longer required literacy tests, but there were still plenty of ways to make registration and voting difficult. When McFerren led a contingent of registered Black citizens to vote in the county's Democratic Party primary in summer 1959, they were turned away, told it was a "white primary." The US Supreme Court had ruled racially restricted party primaries unconstitutional years before—Judge Waring had abolished them in South Carolina more than a decade ago—but enforcement in Tennessee was lax, and county political leaders were counting on the stymied Black voters to meekly go home.

McFerren and his Civic and Welfare League colleagues did not go home. They filed a complaint with the Department of Justice, traveling to Washington, DC, to personally present their case to the head of the department's recently established civil rights division. After an investigation of Fayette County registration practices, the Justice Department filed a federal lawsuit—the first under the 1957 Civil Rights Act—challenging the Fayette Democrats' exclusionary policies. In April 1960, in the midst of the student sit-in protests, a federal judge ruled the party's racial exclusions illegal. Fayette officials denounced the decision as federal interference in states' rights. Their real fear was that if Black people continued to register, they would soon outnumber white voters and would be able to decide elections.

In retaliation, the names of those who had registered were placed on a secret blacklist distributed by the local White Citizens' Council. A vicious version of "the squeeze" was applied. Those on the list, and their families, were suddenly dismissed from their jobs, denied credit, or even the ability to shop in local stores, forcing them to travel fifty miles to Memphis for food. Farmers lost their crop insurance and seed supplies. Insurance policies were canceled, and bank loans were called due. Gasoline distributors, buckling to pressure from the Citizens' Council, stopped delivering fuel to McFerren's station, then pulled out his gas storage tanks.

White doctors refused to treat Black patients, and pharmacies would not fill prescriptions. When McFerren's wife went into labor that summer and needed medical assistance, she had to be taken to Memphis to deliver her baby. Viola McFerren was frightened, wary of her husband's involvement in this dangerous business. Many nights he protected their home against night riders, patrolling outside with a shotgun. Despite her fears, Viola helped run the Civic and Welfare League from her kitchen table.

John McFerren did not suffer in silence, nor did he relent in his voter registration efforts. The Fayette and Haywood Civic Leagues publicized their members' plight in press releases and a newsletter, winning the attention of sympathetic groups and the northern press. The NAACP called for a nationwide boycott of the major oil companies complying with the White Citizens' Council ban on supplying gasoline to McFerren and other Black-owned stations in the county. Nervous about the bad publicity, the companies eventually ordered deliveries to resume.

With the 1960 elections just months away, the Civic and Welfare Leagues in both counties mounted intense registration efforts, and Black residents turned out to demonstrate their determination to vote. Their white neighbors were just as determined to stop them. When Mrs. Clark arrived in Fayette and Haywood in midsummer, she saw hundreds of Black people in registration lines snaking around the county seat courthouses, standing for hours in the withering heat. The one registrar on duty purposefully worked slowly to increase the wait time. White neighbors went up onto the courthouse roof to throw red pepper, hot coffee, and paint onto the heads of the Black citizens waiting below.

Mrs. Clark was appalled by the spiteful mistreatment she witnessed but impressed by the dogged resolve of the Black registrants. She wanted to help. The most pressing need was to relieve the suffering caused by the coordinated campaign of economic retribution. Churches and civil rights groups were stepping in to provide food, clothing, fuel, and medicine to the beleaguered Black residents. Clark offered nourishment for their minds and spirits. She arranged for a contingent of Fayette and Haywood activists to attend Highlander workshops on voting, community leadership, and political action later in the summer. The workshops helped the Tennesseans broaden their horizons and build their organizing skills. The chilling reports of harassment they recounted in the Highlander discussion circles were carried home by their workshop mates, creating a wider network of awareness and assistance.

To support the courageous people in western Tennessee, Clark began planning for citizenship classes in Fayette and Haywood. The classes could help those who—while managing to register—were still essentially illiterate and unable to function in the modern world. Most who had agreed to take the bold step to register still did not understand what citizenship meant or how to use it. They had little concept of their people's history beyond their family lore, a limited grasp of their own legal rights or how government worked, and negligible contact with the freedom movement swirling around them.

The citizenship program, which for four years had been, as Horton called it, "island hopping" through the Lowcountry, was now mushrooming on the mainland. Clark and Robinson were handling pleas to establish new schools not only in west Tennessee, but also in several places in Alabama and Georgia. Robinson was invited to the Savannah region by local NAACP leader Hosea Williams, who was launching an ambitious voter registration drive.

A thirty-four-year-old research chemist and World War II veteran, Williams became active in the NAACP after being severely beaten by a white mob when he drank from a "whites only" water fountain in the city. He soon became famous around town for his daily lunch-hour soapbox speeches, railing against Savannah's segregation policies in a downtown park. Williams was energetic, creative, and charismatic but found his attempts to register new voters hampered by the apathy and illiteracy he encountered. He had heard about the citizenship schools on the Sea Islands and called for help from Highlander. Beginning in 1959, Robinson made a series of trips to the city and surrounding county, presenting the citizenship school concept at mass meetings organized by Williams.

In spring 1960, Williams seized the momentum of the student sit-ins to mobilize the Black community in Savannah, organizing a boycott of stores that denied Black people equal treatment and job opportunities. As in Nashville, Savannah's Black families refused to buy their traditional Easter finery and kept their purses shut. Within a month, local merchants were reporting over a million dollars in lost sales. Residents maintained the boycott for another fifteen months.

"We have two great allies in our fight for equal rights," Williams told the Black community at a mass meeting. "These are our money and our vote."

To coordinate the area's campaigns, Williams established the Chatham County Crusade for Voters and also a broader coalition, the Southeastern Georgia Crusade for Voters, and asked Bernice Robinson and Highlander to bring citizenship education to the region. Robinson visited several more times to get acquainted with the community, analyze its needs, and meet with Williams and other local activists. She brought potential teachers to Highlander for training, and Bernice and Septima drew up blueprints for three citizenship classes to open in December.

At the same time, Mrs. Clark was preparing the ground for planting citizenship schools in Huntsville, Alabama. When Clark arrived by bus in Huntsville, she had the name of only one woman, someone she had been told was interested in the movement, written on a piece of paper. Clark found the woman, a Mrs. Harris, as well as her adult daughters, and convinced them to go to Highlander for leadership training. Clark escorted them to Monteagle, then returned with them to Huntsville, embedding herself in the community. For two weeks she walked around town, introducing herself, speaking at churches, luncheons, and parlor meetings. Through the summer, Mrs. Harris and her daughters brought carloads of Huntsville people to Monteagle for workshops. Now plans for five citizenship classes in Huntsville and environs were shaping up to begin in early fall.

———◆———

Clark's efforts to cultivate the Huntsville community paid off. This sort of slow, deliberate, relationship-building approach to recruitment was her forte, but it was expensive in both time and energy. Horton began to question the investment. He thought it was a luxury that Highlander, in its weakened condition, could no longer afford. He didn't seem to understand, Clark fretted. When she was establishing the first classes on Johns Island, she was already known and trusted and had islander Jenkins by her side. In Huntsville, Savannah, and the other new sites, "all the people are strangers to me. They have to learn to trust me," she tried to explain to Myles. "They have to learn to believe in me and not the adverse publicity that they read or hear about me and Highlander."

Clark and Horton clashed again when she began compiling a revised curriculum for the new citizenship schools opening in different states. Septima and Bernice sent away for the voting requirements and constitutions of these states, tailoring the student workbooks and teacher resources to meet the differing state situations. Horton balked at the extra time and work involved and questioned Clark's methods. They began arguing about the approach, screaming at each other in the Highlander office.

"We just had to shout it out," Mrs. Clark explained. The most shocking aspect to her was not their disagreement, but that she had the temerity to raise her voice in anger to a white man. She had never done that before. She took it as a sign of her personal and political maturation, the growth of her confidence and comfort in an integrated world. She was able to consider herself Horton's colleague and equal. He was just a white man with whom a Black woman could forcefully—and loudly—disagree.

In the end, Horton bowed to Clark's classroom expertise in writing the new curricula. But the truth was, Myles was losing interest in the citizenship school project. He was an explorer, not an administrator. He felt that Highlander was at its best innovating and pioneering, creating new approaches to social justice and democratic living, not operating programs. The citizenship school experiment had proven to be a great success, demonstrated that it could be adapted and transplanted, and was in demand in many new places. Success was the problem: the program was getting too big and too expensive for Highlander to handle. Funders were balking at extending their grant support, unsure whether Highlander would even exist in another year. Yet citizenship training was too valuable to the movement to risk losing the program if Highlander was forced to close.

So Highlander changed its relationship to the citizenship schools. It would no longer "run" them, selecting the teachers, operating the schools, and underwriting expenses. Instead, other organizations could sponsor literacy and citizenship classes in their own area, sending prospective teachers for training by Clark and Robinson at Highlander, and use the curricula and methods they had developed. The new plan relieved some of the financial pressure on Highlander, streamlined the staff responsibilities, and allowed rapid expansion of the program. The realignment placed a heavy additional burden on Septima as she and Bernice raced to redesign the teacher training process and materials. But the two women were more than willing to shoulder the extra work to protect and grow the program.

———————◆———————

As the 1960 presidential elections loomed, Ella Baker had given up on SCLC's Crusade for Citizenship and resigned from the organization, frustrated by her inability to work with Dr. King and his fellow ministers. Baker eagerly signed on to help organize the students of SNCC as their adviser.

Baker and Clark shared a different vision from the SCLC's for building an army of voters. The women saw eye to eye on many things concerning the movement, including its shortcomings. Both valued the wisdom and power of grassroots organizing—the rural, the poor, and the unlettered—overlooked by traditional campaigns. Both were distrustful of top-down leadership and wary of charismatic leaders—like Dr. King—preferring a more participatory approach to decision-making. And both women viewed education as the key to unlock Black political and social potential.

"I have a deep and abiding interest in the work you have done, and are doing," Ella had written to wrote to Septima in spring of 1960, in response to Clark's invitation to join a Highlander education committee to design future citizenship school projects. "I don't think I ever told you," she confided to Septima, "but several years ago, when I first read the thrilling account of your experiences in promoting citizenship schools in the Sea Islands of South Carolina, I yearned for the opportunity to meet you.

"Little did I dream, at that time, that we would have an occasion to work together here in our beloved Southland. So you see, I have long since been committed to the idea of 'teaming-up' with you." Baker made several trips to Monteagle that summer of 1960, to participate in workshops and consult with Clark. She would continue to use Highlander as a place for SNCC leaders to retreat, reflect, and argue about major decisions.

In the Highlander library that summer, Ella Baker joined with Rosa Parks and Septima Clark to sing freedom songs. Parks greatly admired Baker and Clark; they were her models of dedicated movement women. She marveled at how Clark, especially, could be so brave in the face of constant danger. "I thought, 'If I could only catch some of her spirit,'" Parks later explained.

"I wanted to have the courage to accomplish the kinds of things that she had been doing for years." Ella carried Septima's citizen education concepts into SNCC as she helped shape that new organization, and the three women singing together in the library would continue to informally work together, and support one another, as the freedom movement evolved.

CHAPTER TWENTY-FOUR

Tent City

A merica's greatest undeveloped potential is not the splitting of the atom, but the Negro vote," Dr. King declared from the stage of a Kentucky voters' rally as the fall 1960 elections neared.

But even the minister had to finally admit that the SCLC Crusade for Voters had done little to develop that potential. The crusade could show only meager southern registration gains and had not managed to build a solid infrastructure to sustain political activity. With the collapse of his signature voting project, Rev. King was more open to considering a new approach. Finally acting upon Ella Baker's suggestions—after she had left the SCLC in frustration—King asked Myles Horton to design a voter education program for the SCLC. They would discuss it after the election.

———◆———

The 1960 election was viewed as a stress test of Black voting strength. The Black electorate in the North had grown large enough to command the attention of the national political parties. News images of white violence against Black students brought the bloody side of massive resistance into American living rooms, raising civil rights as an issue in the presidential campaign. Both Republicans and Democrats included civil rights planks in their campaign platforms, but neither Richard Nixon nor John F. Kennedy had distinguished records on the issue. Black support was split, and all the polls predicted a close race. Rev. King remained neutral while he tried to push both candidates to take stronger stands.

The student sit-ins resumed with the return of students to campus, keeping civil rights protests in the public eye during the fall election season. In places where the combination of sit-ins and economic boycotts by the Black community had succeeded in forcing store owners to integrate their lunch counters, new targets were selected. In cities like Nashville and Atlanta, the focus moved to other establishments: sit-ins expanded to stand-ins at movie theaters, lie-ins and sleep-ins in segregated hotel lobbies, and kneel-ins in segregated churches. Wade-ins and swim-ins at beaches and public pools would soon follow.

John Lewis and the Nashville Student Movement also added voter registration activities to their to-do list. In preparation for the fall elections, students (many of whom, like Lewis, were still under twenty-one and not yet eligible to vote) canvassed door-to-door and distributed literature in Black neighborhoods, sporting lapel buttons reading: WE SAT-IN FOR YOU/NOW STAND UP FOR US. Lewis was pleased to report that the drive netted almost four hundred new Black registrants.

Jenkins and the Citizens' Committee of Charleston County were also gearing up for the elections, marshaling the enthusiasm of Lowcountry citizenship school graduates to get out the vote. Esau was in constant motion, making the rounds of churches and citizen clubs, giving voting pep talks as energetically as any candidate on the stump.

The "second step" political education classes Jenkins had been conducting for the past couple of years gave new voters practice in reading ballots and using voting machines, but also provided instruction on evaluating candidates and studying the issues. One aspect of political readiness Jenkins hammered home to his neophyte voters was the danger of sweet-talking politicians who might try to buy their vote with promises, blandishments, chicken dinners, or outright bribes. Jenkins warned them of the kind of "politician who decides to be good overnight, and only for one night," and taught them to study candidates' records and demand that office-seekers explain and justify their platforms.

Jenkins and his Citizens' Committee colleagues also developed a sophisticated get-out-the-vote system to ensure that those who were registered actually cast their ballot on election day. They kept a record of the registration certificate numbers of members of the local voters' leagues, as well as those who had graduated from the citizenship schools, and arranged car pools to the polls for those who needed transport. On election day, they kept track of who had voted and sent scouting parties to remind those who hadn't yet cast a ballot. Many citizenship school alumni also worked as poll watchers, keeping an eye out for any shenanigans, while others served as support buddies for those nervous about voting for the first time.

The election offered a vivid illustration of the political activity the citizenship schools had stimulated in their host communities. The various voters' leagues established by citizenship teachers and alumni held clinics to teach voters how to navigate the election ballot (in South Carolina there were three slates of presidential electors, with sixty names listed) and offered practice in pulling voting machine levers. The graduates of the North Charleston class, mostly domestic workers, mounted their own neighborhood registration campaign, going door-to-door, coaxing nearly a hundred of their neighbors to register for the first time. Spreading election excitement as they knocked on doors, the women also convinced another twenty-five residents to sign up for the next session of the literacy and citizenship class, meeting again in Mary Davis's beauty parlor.

With the election season building to a climax in October, Mrs. Clark took time to educate herself on the presidential candidates. She diligently watched the presidential debates, but also sought the advice of her friends the Warings, whose political judgment she respected. They convinced her that Kennedy was the better candidate for anyone who cared about civil rights. She committed herself to voting for Kennedy with a sense of hope for the future but could only feel helpless when it came to South Carolinians' options for their US senator: rabid segregationist Strom Thurmond was running for reelection unopposed. There was no choice.

As the candidates made their final pitches to the electorate, Clark worked feverishly to create new Black voters. She was consumed with launching the first Huntsville citizenship class and prepping for the opening of an additional fourteen classes, including five new ones in Savannah. She juggled all this logistical work while figuring out how to scale up the teacher training process. She was developing a weeklong training program for citizenship teachers sent to Highlander by sponsoring organizations, as well as running a full slate of fall residential workshops at Monteagle.

Clark was sixty-two years old, far from home and family, working day and night, driven by a sense of mission. She couldn't afford to allow her thoughts to dwell upon the precarious state of affairs at Highlander, the uncertain prospects for her citizenship project, or her own insecure employment, should Highlander not survive. She just didn't have time to worry.

Just two weeks before election day, an October surprise rocked the presidential race. Dr. King was arrested for participating in a demonstration at a downtown Atlanta department store and sentenced to four months of hard labor in a Georgia maximum security prison. The outrageous sentence sparked a national uproar and posed a test for the presidential candidates. Nixon tried to duck; Kennedy made a shrewder move: he called Coretta King, pledging to help. Robert Kennedy, the candidate's brother, called the Georgia judge who'd sent King to prison and convinced the judge to release King on bail. Dr. King publicly thanked Senator Kennedy for his help; King's father announced he was switching his vote from Nixon to Kennedy and would urge his friends and parishioners to do the same.

John Kennedy won the popular election by a narrow margin, but captured 70 percent of the national Black vote, including a large surge of support by Black voters in the southern states. The swing of Black voters to Kennedy made a difference, helping propel him into the White House, and Black leaders looked forward to having a grateful chief executive in the Oval Office.

For Esau Jenkins, the election results just proved what he had been preaching to his neighbors for years: Black votes mattered. Using the vote strategically could swing outcomes, and white politicians could be forced to pay attention. He was pleased that Charleston County went for Kennedy, but he was thrilled by the election results reported from his Sea Islands: nearly 100 percent of registered Black voters on Johns, Edisto, and Wadmalaw islands turned out to vote. Johns Island Black registrants had jumped from barely one hundred in 1955 to more than seven hundred by 1960, and more Black island citizens than white cast ballots in the national election for the first time in history. After just two seasons of citizenship school classes and the political activity spurred by the voters' leagues formed by class alumni, Black voters on Edisto cast more votes than whites, and Wadmalaw Island's Black turnout came close to equaling the white vote.

The most stunning results of all came out of Fayette and Haywood counties in west Tennessee. Despite constant intimidation and economic harassment, more than twelve hundred determined Black citizens, venturing to the polls for the first time in their lives, voted out the Democratic political establishment. They elected Republicans to office for the first time since Reconstruction. They even split their vote, supporting Republicans at the local level but pulling the lever for Democrat Estes Kefauver in his bid for a US Senate seat. Kefauver had publicly defended their right to register, denouncing the reprisals of the White Citizens' Council. The Black voters of Fayette and Haywood rewarded the candidate who stood with them, and Kefauver won. This was the power of the vote, and they were learning how to use it.

———— ◆ ————

Negotiations between Myles Horton and Dr. King's representative began just after the election, in late November 1960. Horton visited SCLC offices in Atlanta, then King's envoy James Wood came to Monteagle, spending hours talking to Horton and Clark, reviewing the citizenship school records and results. What impressed Wood was not simply the numbers of formerly illiterate citizens who had been transformed into active voters by the schools, but the emergence of neighborhood leaders from the program. Wood came away convinced that SCLC should partner with Highlander to incorporate citizenship education and leadership training into its agenda.

Horton made a counterproposal that was a bit startling. Instead of simply participating in Highlander's existing program, the SCLC should take over the entire citizenship school project, using the Monteagle campus for teacher training, employing Highlander's methods. It was a sensible solution: the citizenship schools could be secured and adopted into a good home, while the SCLC could inherit a proven educational program to revive its voter registration and widen its leadership development efforts. To sweeten the deal, Horton offered to share with SCLC the Field Foundation funds supporting the project and bundle in the expert services of Mrs. Clark.

Wood carried Horton's proposal back to Dr. King and the SCLC, but the ministerial leadership balked at Horton's suggestion that the organization assume responsibility for the entire citizenship school project. The SCLC was still a small operation, with only a few paid staffers working from a tiny Atlanta office; it wasn't ready to swallow such an expansive new project. Horton and the SCLC worked out a temporary compromise: SCLC would encourage its church affiliates to establish literacy and citizenship classes in their towns, build community support and raise funds for the venture, and send prospective teachers for training at Monteagle.

The SCLC announced this new educational partnership with Highlander in early 1961. But messy negotiations would drag on for months, as the terms of the arrangement kept changing, the financial details grew more complicated, and trust and goodwill frayed. For Septima Clark, the next six months would be one of the most distressing periods of her life.

—————— ♦ ——————

The evictions began before Christmas. After the harvest, after the white plantation owners had squeezed the last ounce of work from the Black tenant farmers, just as the freezing weather set in. The Black men and women of Fayette and Haywood counties who had dared to register and vote in the November elections were thrown out of the sharecropper shacks they called home, fired from the farms where they'd worked for decades. Parents, children, babies, and old folks shivered in the cold, their possessions strewn on the ground, nowhere to go.

The Welfare Leagues of both counties rushed to provide basic shelter. A Black landowner allowed the dispossessed to camp on his property. A white merchant anonymously (for his own safety) donated large Army surplus canvas tents. Whole families crammed into the sixteen-by-fourteen-foot tents, sleeping on the cardboard-covered tent floor, hauling water from a distant well, no electricity, no sanitary facilities, traipsing through mud up to the knee. Night riders shot bullets into the tents of sleeping families. Still under the White Citizens' Council's economic squeeze, the tent dwellers weren't able to obtain food, fuel, or supplies. Senator-elect Estes Kefauver called on the Red Cross and the Department of Agriculture to provide aid to the eviction victims, but his plea was rejected. The mayor of Somerville, Fayette County, called the tent city "a publicity stunt."

"They say if you register, you going to have a hard time," a fifty-eight-year-old woman living in her family's cold, damp tent told a visitor on Christmas night of 1960. "Well, I had a hard time before I registered. The reason I registered, because I want to be a citizen. I registered so that my children could get their freedom."

The compound was christened Freedom Village, but it was more commonly called Tent City. Eventually nearly four hundred Black families in the two counties would be evicted for registering and voting, despite legal efforts by the Department of Justice to halt the reprisals. The original Tent City soon expanded to a second location, with hundreds of adults and children living in primitive conditions in the encampments. John McFerren and other local organizers appealed for help, making a fundraising tour of northern cities. Labor unions and churches held clothing and food drives, with Teamster

Union truck drivers delivering supplies from New York in a caravan of "Freedom Trailers."

Mrs. Clark paid close attention to the plight of the Black voters of Fayette and Haywood counties, mindful of the price they were paying. They had lost everything, what little they had owned, yet gained a sense of fierce pride, forged a defiant community. They had aspired to become first-class citizens, grabbed the vote with their own hands, and now were forced to subsist in the mud. But not one of them withdrew their names from the registration rolls.

In Clark's eyes, they weren't martyrs but role models, new champions of democracy. She was immensely proud of them but also felt some responsibility for their dire situation. She had helped train some of the counties' Black leaders in organizing and voter education techniques at Highlander; she was developing citizenship schools to open there in the near future. In the face of this latest act of white vengeance, Clark helped organize relief efforts for the people of Tent City.

The potential of the Black vote was great, as Dr. King proclaimed, and Mrs. Clark believed. But the cost of the vote could be very dear.

CHAPTER TWENTY-FIVE

Literacy to Liberation

M rs. Clark was climbing a flight of stairs in the Charleston library when she felt the pain. She had to stop, sit down. She couldn't take another step. It was late January 1961, and she had been running hard since the start of the new year. She was probably just tired. She had a lot on her mind. She had barely taken time to celebrate Christmas with her family and buy toys for her grandchildren before returning to Highlander for an intense stretch of work. Soon after New Year's Day, she and Bernice brought more than fifty beauticians from Alabama and Tennessee to Monteagle for a workshop on participating in the movement. Bernice wanted to instill in her fellow beauticians the idea that they could take a leadership role in the struggle for social justice.

Civic service was a responsibility of their profession, the beauticians gathered at Highlander were told, and they could meet this obligation by using their shops as voter education and registration centers. The women discussed the dynamics of the movement, forged a sense of unity singing freedom songs, and decided on a first project: helping establish a health center for the homeless of Fayette County. The beauticians set an ambitious goal of raising $1,500 for the health facility, asking members of their professional association to set up donation boxes in their shops for customer contributions, and to themselves donate the cost of "one hairdo" to the cause.

Mrs. Clark then boarded a bus to Montgomery, where she met with the Montgomery Improvement Association (MIA) to plan for citizenship schools in the city, the first SCLC affiliate to participate in the new training arrangement. Clark urged the MIA to send a large delegation for teacher training at Highlander, and Ralph Abernathy's wife, Juanita, herself an experienced teacher, was among the first volunteers. Within a few months, the MIA teachers would be running five classes, enrolling 235 students, and by the summer of 1961, attendance would swell to 435 students.

Professional teachers were now welcomed to the ranks of citizenship school instructors, a change from the original Highlander emphasis on avoiding career teachers who might not be flexible enough in the classroom. So many Black teachers had lost their jobs, as the result of the closing of Black schools, and the southern states' assault on NAACP members; now they were eager to contribute their skills to the movement. The first cohorts of teaching recruits arriving at Highlander in the spring of 1961 included not only retired teachers but farmers and carpenters, ministers and salesmen, barbers and morticians, domestic workers and dressmakers. No matter their background, prospective citizenship teachers were required to be able to read aloud well, write legibly on a blackboard, and be willing to accompany their students to community meetings and voter registration offices.

In weeklong workshops and weekend refresher sessions, the instructors and supervisors learned the nuts and bolts of running a citizenship school, from finding a meeting place and recruiting students to ordering classroom supplies. They were introduced to the successful methods honed in the Sea Island classes, including signature tracing and using stories, songs, and newspaper ads in lessons. They did role-playing and practice teaching, received instruction in operating tape recorders and film projectors, and learned from Guy Carawan how to lead freedom song sessions in their classes. They were encouraged to improvise: if a blackboard wasn't available, writing on paper dry-cleaning bags hung on a broomstick worked well enough. More broadly, discussions of Black history coupled with an overview of the current movement augmented the training and, as Mrs. Clark liked to say, linked literacy to liberation.

That winter of 1961, Fayette County, Tennessee, sent a twelve-person delegation for teacher training, but few had more than basic literacy skills themselves. The new teacher candidates, who had voted for the first time only a few months before, came in knowing nothing about how their government worked but left as "freedom fighters" determined to open a citizenship school at home. In the first six months of 1961, Highlander would train eighty-eight teachers who returned to forty communities across the South, organizing citizenship classes for over 1,500 adults. By spring, Fayette County had opened twelve citizenship schools with 141 residents enrolled. Armed with basic literacy skills, enhanced self-confidence, political awareness, and freshly issued registration cards, these citizens, each in their own way, joined the movement.

Mrs. Clark had dashed around visiting all the citizenship classes in session that fall and early winter, paying special attention to the new classes in Savannah,

Huntsville, and west Tennessee. She traveled by bus, sitting up front, in the fifth row. The porters carried her six heavy bags aboard, filled with materials and books and film reels, and out of habit placed them at the back of the bus, where they assumed she would sit. That's not where she sat. The driver would often bark at her to move to the back, but she simply refused, telling him she knew the law—segregation on interstate transit was illegal—she knew her rights, and she could sit anywhere she chose. She was "testing the buses," as she put it. The drivers would grumble but give up—it wasn't worth their time to mess with an old lady—and Clark sat, satisfied she had made her point. Very soon hundreds of young people would join her in testing the buses as Freedom Riders.

A librarian noticed Mrs. Clark's distress on the staircase and brought her to the hospital. It was, as feared, another heart attack, four years after her first cardiac trouble at Highlander. It wasn't a major attack with severe heart damage, the doctors assured her, but it was a cry of distress from her body. The doctors insisted she stay in the hospital to rest for at least two weeks.

Septima had indeed been under strain. Besides the workload and the travel, there was her mounting agitation over the fate of Highlander and the citizenship schools. Highlander was stranded in excruciating limbo while waiting to learn its legal fate, and she was, she felt, being kept in the dark. In the latest terms being discussed with SCLC, she was to train citizenship schoolteachers recruited by Rev. King's organization at Monteagle, with SCLC picking up the cost of her salary. While the SCLC announced ambitious plans to send 240 potential teachers to twenty-one training workshops in the next year, providing instructors for citizenship schools serving over twenty thousand Black adults in the South, the financial and logistical terms of the arrangement remained murky. It was all unsettling to her.

The doctors recommended that Septima take a medical leave from Highlander to restore her strength, and Myles was concerned that the citizenship schools were too much for her to handle any longer. At Septima's suggestion, Horton asked Bernice to join the Highlander staff to share the load of the citizenship program, even if no one seemed to know exactly where the program was headed.

Horton seemed to be darting from one crisis to the next. Highlander was in desperate financial shape, as the legal fight with Tennessee drained its coffers and foundations grew anxious about committing money to such an endangered enterprise. Rallying to help, Highlander's friends were hosting fundraising parties around the country. Guy Carawan organized a benefit concert at Carnegie Hall in New York City with Pete Seeger as the headliner and Rev. Fred Shuttlesworth as a rousing master of ceremonies. The February 21, 1961, concert showcased Highlander's place at the center of the civil rights movement, with performances by SNCC leaders James Bevel, Bernard Lafayette, and their schoolmates from American Baptist Theological Seminary singing as the Nashville Quartet. Teenager Jamila Jones appeared with her friends in the Montgomery Gospel Trio. "Overcome," which had already blossomed from the Highlander theme song into the anthem of the civil rights movement, made its Carnegie Hall debut at this concert, with Carawan and Seeger leading the audience on guitar and banjo.

Donations were coming in, but not enough to erase all the red ink on Highlander's ledger. Negotiations with the SCLC dragged on. Negative press reaction to the Highlander-SCLC's citizenship school partnership further rattled Horton. He probably wasn't surprised by the vitriol expressed by Highlander's usual antagonists, like the *Chattanooga News–Free Press*, which blasted the alliance "to train Negro leaders to agitate for all kinds of forced racial integration." More infuriating was an article in the *New York Times*, quoting anonymous "observers" who believed the affiliation "raised serious questions of prestige" for SCLC, as "Highlander's controversial status" would scare away "Southern whites of liberal of moderate persuasion" from supporting Dr. King's conference.

The big lie—roundly and repeatedly disproven—that Highlander was communist because it practiced and promoted integration would not die. As the movement strengthened, the lie intensified and spread. Soon giant billboards began popping up along highways and roads across the South. The signs displayed an enormous photograph depicting rows of people sitting on chairs in a crowded room. The image was bland and boring—a static tableau of people sitting—but its message was meant to shock.

The audience in the photo was integrated, white and Black people sitting next to one another—forbidden behavior in the Jim Crow South, sure to catch the eyeballs of passing motorists. But it was the text superimposed on the photo that carried its explosive theme: a thick, dark arrow pointed to a Black man, neatly dressed in short-sleeved shirt and tie, sitting in the front row, listening intently. Emblazoned on the arrow was one word: KING. A banner caption, stretched across the top of the billboard, read: "Martin Luther King at Communist Training School."

The photo was Ed Friend's creation, taken at Highlander's twenty-fifth-anniversary symposium almost four years before and made famous in the Georgia Education Commission's propaganda brochure. There were close to a million copies of that brochure in circulation by now, and the billboards were meant to further undermine Dr. King's reputation by publicly questioning his patriotism.

The billboards were funded by the recently formed, ultra-right-wing John Birch Society, with support from local White Citizens' Councils. Portraying King's "subversive" links to Highlander, the billboards were intended to scare off popular support, funding, and recruitment for both the SCLC and Highlander, and they endangered their joint citizenship education project.

--- ◆ ---

While Clark recuperated in Charleston in early 1961, Horton was rearranging the pieces of the citizenship program puzzle. He had secured a large grant from the Field Foundation to fund teacher training for the SCLC-affiliated citizenship schools but since SCLC did not have federal tax-exempt status, the foundation could not give the grant monies directly to SCLC. It was agreed that Highlander would administer the grant on behalf of SCLC. Horton offered the job of administering the grant and coordinating the program to a young Black minister he had only recently met. Rev. Andrew Young, a twenty-eight-year-old Congregationalist minister, impressed Horton when he attended a Highlander "New Alliances in the South" workshop in early winter. Young, raised in New Orleans, was working for the National Council of Churches in New York City but was eager to return home to the South to find a role in the movement.

Young had also heard the rumors about Highlander's "communist" reputation, so before deciding to accept Horton's offer, he asked a friend to do some investigating. "I don't want to give in to this McCarthy-type of red-baiting," Young explained to his friend. "But neither do I want to have people hounding me about Highlander Folk School for the next fifty years." Assured there was nothing substantive to the allegations, Young accepted Horton's invitation to join the staff as director of leadership training.

Horton believed Young could bring vitality and fresh thinking to the mountain—he was smart, engaging, energetic—and would especially appeal to the SNCC college students, whom Horton viewed as emerging leaders of the movement. Mrs. Clark was a good teacher and fine person, but she was old enough to be the SNCC students' grandmother; Horton himself was older than their parents.

With spring blooming on the mountain, Horton began feeling somewhat optimistic again, despite all Highlander's troubles. He was preparing for the future by bringing Andy Young on staff and protecting the citizenship schools with elaborate arrangements. He had also decided to remarry, bringing Aimee Isgrig, a Chicago educator and civil rights advocate almost twenty years his junior, to Monteagle as his wife. Horton's upbeat mood was also based on his confidence Highlander would be rescued by the US Supreme Court when the school's eventual appeal of Tennessee's rulings came before the justices. He and Highlander would not only be vindicated, but the case could also produce a landmark decision by striking down Tennessee's segregation statute. All the misery will have been worth it.

In the first week of April 1961, the Tennessee Supreme Court announced its decision—upholding, as expected, Highlander's lower court convictions for selling alcohol and running the school for personal profit. What was not anticipated, however, was that the Tennessee court declined to consider Highlander's conviction for violating Tennessee's segregation statutes; that element of the case was dropped. Upholding the two other convictions was enough to strip the school of its charter, the justices explained, so there was no need to "pass upon the constitutional question as to the mixing of white and colored in the same school." This was a highly strategic move on the part of the Tennessee high court, devastating for Highlander. With the segregation aspect removed, there was no longer any constitutional legal question involved, making a US Supreme Court review unlikely. Tennessee had blocked Horton's path to vindication.

Highlander was now in "real trouble" Horton admitted, but he was not giving up. The school's legal team came up with a new approach, petitioning the US Supreme Court to review the Tennessee convictions as violations of Highlander's Fourteenth Amendment rights; the school was being prosecuted for its interracial character, they argued. The American Civil Liberties Union supported Highlander's petition, and NAACP's Thurgood Marshall offered to be an adviser on the case, but without a federal constitutional issue to latch on to, Highlander's appeal had a very slim chance of being considered by the high court.

So long as the appeal was pending, however, the legal clock was stopped, stalling the harsh penalties Tennessee had in store for Highlander: not only the annulment of its charter, but the forfeiture of all its property to the state. Like a man faced with a terminal illness, Horton rushed to put Highlander's affairs in order.

The Field Foundation determined it could no longer continue funding Highlander-affiliated projects, anticipating that the school would soon lose its tax exemption along with its charter, so the recent grant for the SCLC-Highlander citizenship school project could not proceed as planned. Highlander could no longer administer the grant funds, and the foundation insisted the teacher training could not be held on Highlander's premises. Everything was falling apart. Myles would have to scramble to salvage the citizenship schools, and in the frantic search for a rescue plan, he left Septima and Bernice stranded, and exasperated, on the sidelines.

The women were not in Monteagle for most of the winter and spring while they supervised the citizenship schools in session and Clark recovered from her heart attack. The distance added to their feelings of alienation, as they received precious little information about the fate of the citizenship program or their place within it. Convinced that neither Highlander nor SCLC cared enough about the citizenship program to save it, in late May 1961 Clark and Robinson both took the eight-hour examination for acceptance into the Kennedy administration's new Peace Corps. They wanted to take their literacy and citizenship teaching experience to Africa, where Black people in the new democracies might benefit from their skills.

While Clark and Robinson fumed, Horton was plotting to save the citizenship program, though he kept the two women most invested in the project totally out of the process. He was brainstorming with a small committee of men—Andrew Young, James Wood of the SCLC, and Maxwell Hahn, the director of the Field Foundation—to devise a solution. Rev. Young offered an early demonstration of his diplomatic skills by using his ministerial connections to the United Church of Christ to convince its American Missionary Association, United Board of Homeland Ministries to step in as a kind of citizenship school silent partner. The American Missionary Association was enthusiastic about getting involved in the modern civil rights movement, as its own origins lay in the abolition movement, and later as the sponsor of hundreds of schools for emancipated Black students, from elementary grades to Fisk and Howard Universities. An affiliation with citizenship education fit perfectly into its historic profile. The Board of Homeland Ministries would serve as a pass-through agency for the Field Foundation grant and make available one of its own properties as a teacher training facility. It was a complicated but clever scheme, with many moving parts. Two of those "parts" were Septima Clark and Bernice Robinson.

In early June, Clark and Robinson were notified of the new concept: what the committee of men had decided for them, without them. The citizenship program was to split into two pieces: Clark would leave Highlander and move to Atlanta to work for SCLC, leading citizenship teacher training. Robinson was to remain in Monteagle, running Highlander's own citizenship training program for other organizations outside the SCLC umbrella. (This assumed Highlander was somehow able to survive.) Young would also move to Atlanta to become director of SCLC's renamed Citizen Education Project, becoming Clark's boss. Horton was proud of the carefully constructed package. Clark and Robinson were irate.

"We refuse to be swapped around like horses," the women protested bitterly in a letter to Horton. "We don't think anyone can plan *for* us, but *with* us."

They did not want to be separated—"We have decided that we will work together while training, regardless of who pays who"—they insisted. Most of all they resented being treated like property, bartered and moved without consultation or consent. Septima was furious, but even more, she was hurt. She felt Myles, whom she considered a colleague and friend, was not being honest or respectful. "I've never seen that side of you," she told him, with a mixture of disappointment and sorrow.

Horton was taken aback by the women's reactions and annoyed when they voiced their complaints directly to SCLC and the Field Foundation. Exhausted and exasperated, he became defensive: "I am sorry that you felt it necessary to take the planning out of my hands," he replied to Clark. "Despite the fact that I can understand why Negroes sometimes become impatient with those of us who are unable to move as fast as they think we should."

"Septima sometimes assumes that she is a victim of white prejudice and chicanery, even though everything possible is being done by all of us," Horton wrote to Hahn of the Field Foundation, belittling Clark's complaints.

During the summer, both Clark and Robinson were offered places in the Peace Corps, with the opportunity to teach in the newly independent nation of Ghana. It was very appealing. "Our work with the grassroots is a great part of me. There is nothing I enjoy more than working with these people," Clark explained to Horton, whether those Black people were in America or Africa. "The remaining workable years of my life will be promoting citizenship programs somewhere somehow. I'll work wherever I'm needed and wanted."

Horton knew the citizenship program couldn't afford to lose Clark and Robinson. Starting from scratch without their experience and expertise would set the program back just when it needed to jump forward. He tried to assure them there would be plenty of opportunity to work together, many points of contact and room for collaboration. In truth, both women understood that the citizenship program could be saved only by securing a new home, and that the SCLC was the best option. Their objections were based on principle: Black women should not be treated this way. "I have been tossed around like a poor relative while a decision was being made," Septima told the Warings.

In the end, Robinson did not want to leave the citizenship schools, they were too important to her: she agreed to take the position at Highlander. Clark, too, was dissuaded from joining the Peace Corps: "I yielded to the pleadings of many of Highlander's contributors," she explained to the Warings. "They did not want the program to die."

She agreed to move to Atlanta, not Africa. "I felt that the South needed me most."

CHAPTER TWENTY-SIX

Freedom Rides

S eptima Clark squeezed into the passenger seat of a two-toned green Buick sedan and set out on the road trip. It was mid-summer '61, she had just arrived at the SCLC a few weeks before, and now she was joining her two new Citizen Education Program (CEP) colleagues—Andrew Young and Dorothy Cotton—on a two-week recruitment tour through the Deep South. They were on the hunt for "the natural Black leaders of the South" who had "PhD minds, but third-grade educations" to train as citizenship schoolteachers and local movement leaders.

The goal of the trip was to introduce the citizenship program to new communities and to introduce the CEP staff to local activists, a first step in establishing a relationship of trust. The long and hot, exhilarating but exhausting expedition was also an intense bonding experience for the three CEP staffers, who were just learning to work together.

Before arriving in Atlanta, Clark had met Cotton only once before, when the young organizer was sent by Dr. King to attend a Highlander workshop in early 1961. Cotton had helped launch the desegregation movement in Petersburg, Virginia, with her pastor and mentor, Rev. Wyatt Tee Walker. Walker was now the executive director of SCLC, replacing Ella Baker (who'd left SCLC to work for SNCC), and he had brought Cotton with him to Atlanta. With a graduate degree in education, Cotton was especially interested in Highlander's citizenship schools and eager to meet Mrs. Clark. Dorothy found Septima welcoming and gracious—they enjoyed tea together alone before the Highlander workshop began and found they shared a similar belief in the power of education.

Cotton augmented her commitment to the cause with infectious enthusiasm. She effortlessly captured the attention of any room, often by breaking into song. She was, as Andy Young described her, "pecan-brown with dancing eyes, full of energy, devotion, and talent as a speaker and singer." She would bring all those gifts to the citizenship program. While Dorothy had married in college, she and her husband had grown apart—he did not share her activist inclinations—so they had separated. The movement had become her life, and this road trip marked the beginning of an exciting new role.

Andy Young, boyishly handsome and charming, was already a family man, with a wife and three daughters. He was a novice to movement work, with no teaching experience apart from leading Bible study. Still, he was an ordained minister, and most importantly, he was a man, so it seemed only natural to the SCLC leadership to appoint Young director of the CEP program, placing him in charge of two women with far more experience and paying him a significantly larger salary.

When the trio rolled into the Deep South cities and towns in Cotton's green car, people often mistook the CEP delegation for a traveling family—mother, son, and daughter. The misconception was amusing, but in some ways it wasn't far off the mark. Clark (sixty-three) was older than both Young (twenty-eight) and Cotton (thirty-one) combined; she had been working for Black freedom long before they were born. Clark—just six months after her heart attack—took the rigors of the trip in cheerful stride. Her junior colleagues treated her with deference and respect, knowing they had a lot to learn—about the citizenship schools, the movement, and about life—from Mrs. Clark.

They took off from McIntosh County, Georgia, about forty miles south-west of Savannah, where the five-day teacher training workshops were to be held each month. Housed in the former Dorchester Academy, an American Missionary Association school for freed slaves, the building needed some repairs, but it seemed like an ideal locale for training a new generation of Black citizen educators and activists.

From Dorchester, they motored through central Georgia, then south into Alabama and Louisiana, stopping in some of the larger towns, making contact with community leaders to learn who was active in the movement. If they had no contacts, they would walk into a Black-owned barber shop, beauty parlor, gas station, or funeral home, knowing independent businesspeople were often involved in movement activities. From Louisiana they followed the Mississippi River north to Natchez and Jackson, where they met with the energetic NAACP Mississippi field secretary, Medgar Evers. On to the historic all-Black city of Mound Bayou, then to Cleveland, where they consulted with movement leader Amzie Moore about his voter registration efforts, and to Clarksdale, where they were introduced to local activists Aaron Henry and Vera Mae Pigee. They drove across the Delta to Greenwood, east to Tuscaloosa, then Birmingham, where Rev. Fred Shuttlesworth welcomed them. These local leaders became early champions of the citizenship schools, recognizing the program's potential not only to boost voting power, but to also stimulate civil rights activity in their areas. Almost every place on this road trip itinerary eventually became a famous site of struggle—the hub of intense voter registration operations and desegregation direct action—with citizenship schoolteachers and their students deeply involved.

While the three CEP envoys were roving around the Deep South, hundreds of Freedom Riders were continuing to board buses and crowd jail cells in some of the same cities they passed through. The rides had begun in early May, with a group of thirteen white and Black volunteers, including John Lewis, taking seats on Greyhound and Trailways buses to challenge persistent segregation on interstate buses and in bus terminal facilities. Federal law prohibited such segregation—the Supreme Court had ruled it unconstitutional back in 1946—but the southern states simply ignored the court order, the federal government didn't bother enforcing it, and the bus companies went along. A recent Supreme Court decision, *Boynton v. Virginia*, in December 1960, reaffirmed the previous ban on segregation and extended it to the restrooms, waiting rooms, water fountains, and dining facilities at bus terminals. The Freedom Riders hit the road to test whether the southern states were complying with the law of the land.

Lewis and his Black and white comrades set off from Washington, DC, on May 4, 1961, on a planned 1,500-mile journey to New Orleans. They sat together on the buses, used the "whites only" bathrooms and food counters. At night they spoke at local colleges and churches about their mission and slept in the homes of host families. In the first days, they faced only mild resistance—though Lewis was beaten in a bus terminal in South Carolina—but when they reached Alabama, trouble was waiting.

On Sunday, May 14, just outside the city of Anniston, the Freedom Riders' buses were attacked by the Ku Klux Klan, which had coordinated the assault in advance with local authorities. The police agreed to allow the Klan free rein to assail the Freedom Riders for a set amount of time; law enforcement would be conveniently absent, with a promise of no arrests when they eventually did arrive. A hundred Klansmen and supporters armed with clubs, pipes, bricks, and bombs set upon the Greyhound bus carrying the riders. They slashed the tires, smashed windows, threw a firebomb inside, then blocked the doors to prevent the passengers from escaping as smoke and flames filled the interior. When the riders did manage to burst through an escape door—just before the bus's fuel tank exploded—they fell into the hands of the Klan mob, which clubbed and stoned them.

An hour later, when a Trailways bus bearing more Freedom passengers pulled into the Anniston station, there was a different Klan group waiting. They pummeled the passengers before the bus pulled away to drive to Birmingham, with terrorizing Klansmen still on board. In the Birmingham bus terminal, still another white horde awaited, armed with baseball bats and bicycle chains. The city's police commissioner, Eugene "Bull" Connor, made sure there were no police on duty to restrain the ensuing bloody riot. There were, however, plenty of news reporters and photographers to capture the scene and broadcast it around the nation and the world, embarrassing the Kennedy administration.

The violence convinced James Farmer of the Congress of Racial Equality, who had organized the Freedom Ride, to cancel the remainder of the trip. Diane Nash and the Nashville Student Movement leaders denounced the cancellation, calling it a capitulation to white hate, and mobilized a fresh crew of riders from Nashville to continue the mission. When this group reached Birmingham, still another mob—hundreds of screaming white men and women armed with ax handles, tire irons, and even gardening tools—ambushed the riders in the terminal, knocking many unconscious, and assaulting the journalists covering the story as well. Another white mob attacked the riders when they reached Montgomery.

The Freedom Riders were escorted out of Alabama by a military convoy. As soon as they stepped off the bus in Jackson, Mississippi, they were arrested and sent to jail, then transferred to the state's notoriously brutal Parchman Penitentiary, where they were beaten and tortured. They kept up their spirits through the forty-day ordeal by singing, day and night, the freedom songs they had first learned from Guy Carawan, supplemented by new songs they composed in their cells. The singing especially annoyed the prison guards, who bellowed for them to stop and physically punished them when they refused.

Soon the original Parchman prisoners, including John Lewis, James Bevel, and a student from Howard University, Stokely Carmichael, were joined by more than three hundred Freedom Riders, who had boarded buses bound for Jackson, determined to get arrested and flood the jails.

The Freedom Rides marked another shift in the movement, "an upsurge in our aggressiveness," as Lewis described it. The riders had turned media attention to the South's savage suppression of Black civil rights. They had gained public sympathy and provoked the White House to intervene, pushing Attorney General Robert Kennedy to demand that the Interstate Commerce Commission enforce the existing desegregation rules.

The riders had jolted the Kennedy administration into a rude awakening: it couldn't just ignore the South's defiance of federal law, yet it was still uncertain how much political capital to expend forcing compliance. President Kennedy's advisers felt that the type of confrontations exemplified by the sit-ins and Freedom Rides were too provocative, too dangerous, and ought to be curbed. They thought that Black activists' energy should be channeled into something more productive. The administration's best and brightest minds searched for an alternative.

———◆———

In the summer and fall of 1961, buses on a different movement mission began rolling onto the campus of the Dorchester Cooperative Community Center in southeastern Georgia, carrying fresh groups of citizenship schoolteacher trainees. Once every month, buses would pull up to Dorchester's white-columned brick building, delivering the next class to begin training. They slept in men's and women's dorm rooms fitted like barracks, with rows of bunk beds and communal bathrooms. Air-conditioning consisted of handheld cardboard "church fans" on popsicle sticks. Everyone ate their meals together, but unlike at Highlander, there wasn't integrated seating, because there were rarely any white people there.

Each group got acquainted by singing their first set of spirituals and freedom songs, led by Cotton's vibrant soprano, and shared their personal stories in a session of prayer and testimony. They delved into a daily schedule of instruction, discussion, and practice on subjects ranging from history and civics to politics to pedagogy. They learned Mrs. Clark's method of teaching reading and writing and the logistics of operating a citizenship school, as well as organizing techniques. When they boarded the buses to return home, the newly minted teachers were expected to sell the idea of citizenship education to their neighbors, begin recruiting for their classes, and promote voter registration— and movement activities—in their communities.

Each month, Clark, Cotton, and Young made the six-hundred-mile round trip from Atlanta to the Dorchester training center. Cotton lived in an apartment in Atlanta, Young had just bought a house for his family, and Clark was boarding in a room near the SCLC offices. She stayed there on those weekends she wasn't teaching at Dorchester or visiting her sister and granddaughter Yvonne home in Charleston. Monday mornings she would take off again to a town somewhere in the South, usually one where a Dorchester graduate was teaching a citizenship school, or where a SCLC affiliate branch had requested help in mobilizing.

Mrs. Clark recruited for Dorchester, as she had for Highlander, by burrowing herself into Black communities. She sat in church pews, beauty parlor and barber shop chairs, living room sofas and diner stools, listening to what people were talking about, worried about, were desperate to change. She would ask local ministers, teachers, and community elders to recommend those "natural leaders" who might be interested in becoming citizenship schoolteachers. She would convince these potential leaders to come to Dorchester for training, sweetening the invitation with the promise of paying their travel and board expenses, plus a $30 monthly stipend for teaching, made possible by the Field Foundation grant. When they arrived, Clark and Cotton taught these men and women how to become citizen-educators but also gave them an education in leadership, instilling in them an understanding of the freedom movement and a grounding in nonviolent resistance.

"I teach them to teach others how to use the rights and privileges the boycotters, picketers, and sit-inners have obtained for them," Clark explained to the Warings. "The Community has to be brought up to the level of the action of the students. We have to plan strategy moves and actually take them by the hands. They must use the lunch counters, station facilities, etc. They must learn to not give their seat to a white person on the bus."

It was an especially propitious moment for this type of movement education, Clark believed, as the Freedom Rides had struck a new spark of interest within the Black community. Once again, she credited young people with leading the way. "I think that the Freedom Riders have forced many whites to reevaluate their stereotyped ideas about Negroes and their desires," she told the Warings. "Most of all it creates the tension without which progress is impossible."

The Kennedy administration did not agree with Mrs. Clark's belief in the benefits of racial tension, nor did they share her admiration for the positive effects of the sit-ins and Freedom Rides. The world was watching, and the horrifying images of racial conflict undercut the president's foreign policy initiatives in Africa and Asia. His standing as leader of the "free world" might be put into question if the Black citizens of his own country were treated like this. Avoiding the root causes of the conflict, the White House's goal was to sublimate those tensions.

Even as the Freedom Rides were rumbling across the South, the Kennedy administration was developing a plan to harness the momentum of the civil rights movement, redirecting it from protest and confrontation to the quieter work of voter registration. Knowing the southern bloc in Congress would never approve funds for promoting Black voting, the administration had entered secret discussions with liberal-leaning private foundations to sponsor the idea. The Taconic, Marshall Field, New World, and Stern Family foundations agreed to contribute substantial amounts toward the creation of a Voter Education Project (VEP), a nongovernmental agency administered by the Southern Regional Council. The VEP invited civil rights organizations—NAACP, SCLC, Urban League, CORE, and SNCC—to apply for grants to support their own voter registration work. Many of the perennially cash-strapped rights groups viewed the VEP as a welcome new source of funds and eagerly signed on. The leaders of SNCC were not so sure.

The debate within SNCC over whether to join the VEP came close to tearing the fledgling organization apart. Everyone in the movement understood that the motivations of the Kennedy administration in promoting VEP were hardly idealistic but realpolitik: tamping down the fires of racial confrontation would make the administration's life easier. In addition, those new Black voters created by VEP could mean more Black ballots marked for Kennedy in his reelection bid in 1964. The other rights organizations found the promise of steady support for their registration campaigns an acceptable bargain. Most members of SNCC did not.

It wasn't just a question of money—SNCC had little and could use the infusion of cash. Participation in VEP presented an existential question to the young activists: What was SNCC's purpose? What was its role in the movement? SNCC was built on the foundation of nonviolent, direct-action campaigns powered by young people demanding their rights. Its brand of disciplined, creative protest had achieved remarkable results in a short time; SNCC was just two years old. Deflecting its edgy energy into sedate voter registration seemed like a betrayal of its own identity, many SNCC leaders believed, a hijacking of its mission. Yet others in SNCC saw the virtue, even the need for, of taking up voter registration work if they were serious about making long-term change in American society.

Ella Baker summoned SNCC leadership to Highlander in August 1961 to thrash out this dilemma. The debates in the library were loud and emotional as each side argued its case. "Voting versus marching, registering versus 'riding,'" was the essence of the choice, as John Lewis saw it. He, along with SNCC founders Diane Nash, James Bevel, Marion Barry, and Bernard Lafayette, pleaded for the organization to stay true to its roots, dedicated to the successful protest strategies that had won respect and, more importantly, results. Others argued that voting rights were the bedrock of all other rights in a democracy, the path to Black political power, more valuable than sitting with whites at a lunch counter or on a bus. The schism seemed irreconcilable and a split inevitable.

Mrs. Baker listened closely, as she always did, careful not to steer the discussions or even calm tempers. She let everyone have their say. Then she proposed a solution: Why not accommodate both strategic approaches within SNCC? There could be a wing that concentrated on direct-action campaigns and another focused on voter registration work. There was no need to divide, and possibly weaken, the organization. Diane Nash became head of the direct-action section, and a student from Charlotte named Charlie Jones led the voting department. The SNCC veterans left Monteagle Mountain exhausted but optimistic, ready to move forward.

CHAPTER TWENTY-SEVEN

Born Again

I n late summer 1961, Myles Horton pulled the emergency rip cord. Soon after Ella Baker and the SNCC leaders departed Monteagle, he activated the escape hatch mechanism he'd been building for most of the past year. The first gears of the plan were already engaged. Months before, one of Highlander's generous benefactors had purchased and donated a seventy-five-acre plot of land northeast of Knoxville as a refuge if Highlander was forced to leave Monteagle. Horton filed legal papers incorporating a new entity, the Highlander Research and Education Center, with himself and several members of the Folk School board as its executives. The time had come for the next step.

This was Horton's revenge upon Tennessee, his proof that Highlander was not a single physical place but an ineffable idea. The freshly formed Highlander Research and Education Center applied to the Tennessee secretary of state for a charter establishing a new general welfare institution, to be located in Knox-ville. The structure and purpose of this entity were identical to that of the Folk School, including an explicit intention to operate as an integrated facility. It was just a change of name and place.

Technically, there were no red flags to impede a routine approval by the state; politically, there were land mines. Horton was prepared for them. When Tennessee made noises about denying approval of the new charter, Myles knew he had the law on his side. A brand-new corporation was legally "just a new-born babe," he maintained, entering the world with no history and no baggage. There was no legal reason to deny a charter, Horton told the Tennessee bureaucrats, and if the state tried, for obviously political reasons, the Justice Department's civil rights division had promised to intervene. A charter for the new Highlander Center was in Horton's hands by the end of August. Highlander prepared to move.

In the first week of October, the US Supreme Court declined to hear Highlander's appeal of its charter revocation. The legal fight was over. The

Tennessee courts appointed a receiver to oversee the liquidation of all Highlander's land, buildings, and equipment, with all proceeds going to the state. While the state could unjustly seize Highlander's physical assets in Monteagle, Horton insisted, no one could "confiscate the ideas" the Highlander staff would carry with them to Knoxville.

A short caravan of cars drove down Monteagle Mountain, packed with boxes and records, the paper history of Highlander's life. The convoy turned northeast toward Knoxville, with Myles Horton and his wife Aimee driving one car, Bernice Robinson and other staffers in another, Guy Carawan and his bride Candie Anderson joining the procession.

There was no money to build on the rolling farmland that had been purchased for Highlander's escape, so Horton rented a dilapidated old mansion in Knoxville. There were no grounds to speak of, no beautiful vistas of the mountains, but the house had enough room for the staff to live upstairs, with classrooms and an office below, and limited dorm space for workshop participants. It was in a rather run-down city area, the pleasantries of a rural retreat were gone, but it would enable a fresh start.

Horton's plan was to continue as a place for activists to meet and strategize. He wanted to continue leadership training for independent organizations, outside the SCLC, that requested help. Bernice Robinson would be sent into the field to collaborate with Hosea Williams in Savannah, Esau Jenkins in the Lowcountry, Amzie Moore and Bob Moses in Mississippi. Highlander would forge an increasingly deep relationship with SNCC, where Horton served as the group's education consultant. Guy and Candie would provide the singing and cultural aspects of the Highlander programs.

Meanwhile, Esau Jenkins was also hatching another of his grand plans. While continuing the islands' citizenship schools, he wanted to expand the "second step" political education program for newly enfranchised Black voters, supplemented by a South-wide training internship for movement activists and community leaders. Anchoring these projects would be a brand-new Progressive Club community center on Johns Island, with meeting space, a dormitory for visitors, and a basketball court for the island's young people. It was going to cost money, but he was going to ask Horton for help. Esau did not dream small.

Guy and Candie's plan was to continue working with Highlander, both in Knoxville and in the field. Guy was also in demand at the teacher training sessions at Dorchester, where Mrs. Cotton enjoyed singing with "the skinny white boy" who sang the old songs with such soul. He was still singing at SNCC meetings and direct-action locations, but he was seriously rethinking his place in the burgeoning movement. There were many young Black activists with powerful voices, well trained in their churches, who could sing with more intensity, and lead with more authenticity, than he could. He had played an important part in creating this "singing movement," teaching and spreading the rich legacy of Black music recast as freedom songs. He wasn't going to retire, just shift his focus. He would continue singing where he was invited, but he added another tool to supplement his guitar and banjo—a tape recorder. He would begin working more as a journalist or historian of the movement than a performer. The activists themselves didn't have time or energy to write down what they were doing in the heat of their battles for justice, no chance to step back to capture a scene or emotion. But Carawan could.

As a wedding gift, Candie had bought Guy a state-of-the-art Ampex reel-to-reel tape recorder. He had some training in field recording and turned to his friend Alan Lomax for advice. He had already produced one LP record about the Nashville sit-ins, presenting the songs and narration of the student leaders in a studio re-creation of their extraordinary campaign. Carawan had sent the tapes to Moses Asch at Folkways Records in New York City, who was impressed by the first-person vibrancy of the aural report. Asch not only released *The Story of the Nashville Sit-Ins* on the Folkways label but also told Carawan to send more dispatches from the movement battlefields. Guy and Candie Carawan began traveling to movement hot spots across the South as sympathetic supporters and chroniclers, bearing witnesses to the struggle and lending an ear to the sounds of history being made.

———— ◆ ————

A cold winter rain and stiff wind could not dampen the enthusiasm of the thousand or so people who trudged up the muddy roads of Monteagle Mountain on December 16, 1961, to attend the auction of Highlander's possessions. It was the first of Tennessee's liquidation sales of the folk school's property, and the scene was described as some mixture of "a picnic, a circus, and the dissection of a corpse." The campus had been ransacked and looted in the weeks since the buildings had been shuttered by the state, but there was still plenty of furniture, linen, farm, and kitchen supplies up for bidding. The auctioneer even sold the cans of beans in the pantry. Monteagle women's clubs operated concession booths on the grounds, selling food and warm drinks. A few of Highlander's local friends and board trustees attended the sordid event and offered to pay upward of $3,000 for the school's five-thousand-volume library, but the auctioneer sold it to a used-book dealer for $425 instead.

The buildings and 175 acres of real estate would be sold later, including Myles Horton's own house, and that of his mother, who also lived on the campus. Neither received any proceeds from the sale of their privately owned property. A lawyer who had been one of Highlander's trial prosecutors was the successful bidder on the library building, which he turned into a private club. The main house was not on the block: it had already been burned down by arsonists.

CHAPTER TWENTY-EIGHT

Ready from Within

W e are getting calls from everywhere to help," Mrs. Clark had reported to the Warings in late 1961, dashing off a letter upon her return from another Citizen Education Program recruitment trip through Florida, Louisiana, and Alabama. In a few days she was off again to visit three towns in Mississippi. "This is a great action program."

Action was the answer. Taking action to reclaim equal rights was a matter of will, Clark believed, and it was the mission of the CEP to nurture that will in both individuals and Black communities. It was her job to make ordinary people "ready from within" for the struggle, giving them knowledge and the confidence to act.

In many ways, Mrs. Clark's role in the CEP was a continuation of the one she had molded for herself at Highlander, but greatly expanded and with even more travel required. More parachuting into unfamiliar towns, more beds in kind strangers' homes, more prospecting for community leaders in the rough.

One week each month, Clark was in residence at Dorchester, and during the other three she was on the road, combining recruiting with visits to the citizenship classes opened by her newly trained teachers. Mrs. Clark's family in Charleston was not happy about her traveling to these dangerous places in the Deep South. Chilling reports of beatings and even murder of voter registration workers were becoming more frequent. Septima mostly shrugged off her family's concerns, but it was true that the Mississippi Sovereignty Commission, the Magnolia State's internal segregation police force, would soon open a file with her name on it, supplementing her FBI file mentions.

Clark wrote her letters to the Warings on SCLC letterhead now. Working within a religious organization was comfortable for her as a churchgoing woman. She was, however, bothered by the SCLC ministers' dismissive attitude toward women's role in the movement. This annoyed Dorothy Cotton, too, as it had Ella Baker, but Clark hoped that once she and Cotton were allowed to prove their worth, their counsel would be taken more seriously. Clark did miss the beauty of Monteagle Mountain and living and working in Highlander's intentional, integrated society, which had given her such hope as a vision of the future. She worked almost exclusively with Black people now. But she was working with and for her people, at the very epicenter of the movement, and this was, despite the pain of the transition, where she believed she was meant to be.

Andy Young mapped out a strategic plan: The CEP staff would target the 188 counties in the southern states where Blacks constituted a majority of the population but a tiny fraction of registered voters. In many cases, zero voters. These were the places where Black votes could have the most profound effect, an opportunity to topple white political power and really change things. But these were also the places where Black people were poorest, most isolated, most oppressed, most frightened. These were the hardest places to crack but that held the most potential.

It would be the great challenge of the citizenship schools to break this cycle. In the next few years, the CEP would methodically follow Young's map, establishing hundreds of citizenship schools in the Mississippi Delta, the Black belt of Alabama, the east coasts of North and South Carolina, regions of Georgia and Florida, and the Tidewater section of Virginia. In addition, the CEP staff would respond to Black communities, rural and urban, requesting SCLC help in preparing their residents for action. In Albany, Birmingham, Greenwood, Jackson, Selma, and in dozens of cities, towns, and hamlets in between, the CEP staff would be there to get the people ready.

———◆———

"I'm Gonna Do What the Spirit Say Do," Dorothy Cotton sang, before she spoke a word. Cotton always opened gatherings with a song, to set the tone and draw people together, and this spiritual was her favorite. It was an ideal way to welcome each new group of volunteer teachers arriving at Dorchester. She would just start singing and soon have everyone joining in, clapping and ready for the week of living and learning together.

Cotton, Young, and Clark began by asking participants to introduce themselves, sharing with the group not only where they came from but also what brought them to the class. "Then the people would speak," Cotton recalled. "They would unburden themselves, talk about what they had lost, about what they wanted, about how they had come to be there." Extraordinary testimonials were shared, aching stories of resolve, courage, and faith in the face of oppression and humiliation.

Some who had come to Dorchester were already race men or women, with years of service to community betterment organizations and the NAACP. Some had never desired, or dared, to be involved in racial or political matters. Most had never been able to vote. Some were well educated, businesspeople and professionals, while others were just off the plantations, barely literate. Many had never traveled so far away from home. The common thread was that the men and women sitting in the high-ceilinged assembly room at Dorchester had decided that they could no longer accept the restricted lives imposed upon them by white society. And they were ready to do something about it.

One trainee from Georgia reported that the white woman who employed her had recently asked: "What's wrong with the Negroes? They're not acting like niggers anymore."

"They've grown up and awakened," the aspiring citizenship teacher informed her employer. "They want some of the pleasant things you've had." Citizenship classes in her town could hasten that sort of awakening, and that was why she had come to Dorchester.

Another woman said she had argued with her son about his involvement in demonstrations, trying to convince him to stay away from what she called "the mess in the street." He asked her if she thought the way she was treated as a second-class citizen was right, if she minded the indignities Black Americans were made to endure. Her son's questions shook her. "And the cobwebs commenced a' movin' from my brain," she told her classmates at Dorchester. She wanted to learn how to shake the cobwebs from her neighbors' brains, too.

Some who came to Dorchester quietly admitted they were nervous about attending the training sessions. The volunteers understood that teaching these citizenship classes would likely place them, and their families, in danger. "I wasn't that brave," Pearlie Ealey, a twenty-one-year-old from rural Tattnall County, Georgia, admitted, "because I remember Emmett Till." But once the teacher training began, "it took some of the fear out of me." When Ealey began teaching her two citizenship classes back home, she was warned by friends that the Klan might cause trouble. She refused to be intimidated and felt a change within herself. "More of the fear left. And courage kind of took its place."

Dorothy Cotton wrote CITIZEN in big letters on the blackboard in the week's first lessons on "practical civics." The chalk letters served the dual purpose of teaching the spelling of the word and prompting a wide-ranging discussion on the meaning of citizenship and democracy, especially what it meant to Black citizens long denied participation in their own government.

"We'd ask them about the government in their hometown," Mrs. Clark recalled. "They knew very little about it. They didn't know anything about the mayor," or town council, or sheriff. "We had to give them a plan of how these people were elected, how [those] who had registered to vote could put these people in office, and of how they were the ones who were over you." Studying this flow chart of governmental power helped students understand the structures of racism bearing down upon them and gave them a map of entry points into the process, where pressure could be applied to force change.

"OK, folks, today we're going to talk about the C-O-N-S-T-I-T-U-T-I-O-N," Cotton would next write on the board, sparking another deep conversation about the rights guaranteed to every citizen under the US Constitution, but so often denied southern Black citizens.

"Before we started talking about the Constitution we would sing together, we would invoke the spirit," Mrs. Cotton later explained in her memoirs. "We would sing about anything we felt. We would sing about the abuses we suffered, like not being allowed to vote."

The class would talk about the history of the Constitution and the amendments that secured their freedom and rights: the Thirteenth Amendment that freed their forebears from chattel slavery; the Fourteenth that gave them the right to due process under the law (which few of them had ever enjoyed) and their rights as full citizens; the Fifteenth giving Black men (but not women) the vote. Special emphasis was given to the First Amendment, guaranteeing their right to peacefully assemble and to protest, no matter what the local police chief said. "They learned that maybe the Constitution hadn't meant them when it was written," Cotton said proudly, "but by God, they were going to appropriate it for themselves."

The Dorchester trainees received lessons in Black history and literature, a legacy of achievement and pride most had never been told about before. They explored the background and goals of the current civil rights movement, including the philosophy and techniques of Gandhi's nonviolent protest. For the ministers in attendance, Andy Young oriented the citizenship schools and the movement within the context of Christian theology with his talk on "Ballots and the Bible."

Mrs. Clark trained them to create and teach the citizenship schools in their area, from recruiting students to escorting them to the courthouse to register. "We were trying to make teachers out of these people," she explained, many "who could barely read and write." But with a lifetime of experience and wisdom, and a desire to right their nation's wrongs, "they could teach."

The Dorchester workshops were "intellectual and emotional at the same time," as Cotton described them, featuring prayer, personal testimony, and spiritual uplift. "We encouraged people to express themselves, their emotions as well as their ideas."

The intensity of the trainees' week at Dorchester was leavened by field trips to historic sites, and in mild weather, the Black beaches at Hilton Head, where some of the students enjoyed their first glimpse of the ocean. They filled soda bottles with sand as proof of the experience, to show the folks back home. They played volleyball, danced to the music of a record player. And everyone sang.

"We would sing songs of sorrow and songs of hope," Cotton recalled, old gospel songs and new freedom songs. Every night, they closed with an emotional group singing of "We Shall Overcome."

One night, Mrs. Vera Mae Pigee, a trainee from Mississippi, called out a new lyric of the song, as it was being sung in her town of Clarksdale. Mrs. Pigee was a longtime NAACP activist who had already been arrested for leading desegregation protests at a Greyhound bus station. Under her leadership, Clarksdale was becoming known as a regional movement center; things were happening. "We changed the words," Pigee told her classmates at Dorchester. "We don't sing We Shall Overcome Someday. We sing it: We Shall Overcome TODAY."

"The people who left Dorchester went home to teach and to work in voter registration drives," Mrs. Clark explained. "They started their little citizenship classes, discussing the issues and problems in their own towns."

"They went home," Clark said with pride. "And they didn't take it anymore."

———◆———

The movement was also being carried in the knapsacks of young SNCC field organizers fanning out into the countryside in the fall of 1961. Having resolved to operate on a double track—one steering nonviolent protest campaigns, the other piloting voter registration—SNCC joined the Voter Education Project and shared in its funding resources. Even before the VEP began dispensing money, SNCC field secretaries were already heading into some of the regions on Andy Young's map, aiming to spark movement interest and promote action. They slipped into the most dangerous areas, embedding themselves in communities in Georgia, Alabama, and Mississippi. They were, as one reporter described them, "nonviolent guerrilla fighters" operating deep behind enemy lines.

When Charles Sherrod, twenty-two, and Cordell Reagon, eighteen, arrived in the small city of Albany, Georgia, in September 1961 to attempt a voter registration drive, they knew that although Black citizens comprised 40 percent of the city population, very few voted. White power was firmly entrenched and violently enforced. The pair slept on bare floors or in abandoned cars, mingling with local Black high school and Albany State College students, drinking soda and shooting hoops with them. All the while they talked about the goals of the movement and the need for young people to press for change.

Albany's Black adults were wary of the SNCC guys who had materialized in their midst, but Sherrod and Reagon's earnest approach slowly won their trust. Soon the pair were training Albany's teenagers in nonviolent protest techniques and running registration clinics for adults. When the students began sit-ins challenging segregation of the town's bus stations and hundreds of students were jailed, the community rallied to support them—and join them—launching the "Albany Movement."

The citywide demonstrations and mass arrests that rocked Albany for the next months were an extraordinary outpouring of frustration channeled into action and powered by song. At the Albany Movement's first mass meeting in November, four hundred people, young and old, stood together to learn to sing "We Shall Overcome" for the first time. Bernice Johnson, a nineteen-year-old student at Albany State who had been expelled for participating in the demonstrations, joined the chorus: "When I opened my mouth and began to sing, there was a force and power within myself I had never heard before. Somehow this music . . . released a kind of power and required a level of concentrated energy I did not know I had."

Miss Johnson was a talented, exuberant singer who would subsequently use her voice to fortify the Albany Movement, organize for SNCC, and then spread the message of the movement to the nation as one of the touring Freedom Singers. "Songs were the bed of everything," Johnson said of the community solidarity forged by singing in the Albany Movement, "and I'd never seen or felt songs do that before."

Guy Carawan also came to Albany and was dazzled by the passionate force of the a capella singing he heard in the mass meetings, admiring the natural skill of song leaders like Bernice Johnson. He put down his guitar and took up his tape recorder to produce, with his friend Alan Lomax, *Freedom in the Air*, a documentary album of the songs, words, and protests of the Albany Movement, donating all proceeds to SNCC. In the next years, Guy and Bernice Johnson (soon to sing with, and marry, SNCC organizer Cordell Reagon) would work together to bring the freedom songs to national attention.

The singing may have been great, but the goals of the Albany campaign were too broad: the immediate desegregation not just of transit facilities but of all public spaces. There were no discrete victories to sustain momentum. At one point, over seven hundred people were in jail, but city government and business leaders refused to negotiate in good faith.

Stuck in a stalemate, Albany's local Black leaders called for the person they hoped could command media attention and exert pressure: Dr. Martin Luther King Jr. After months of working in the trenches, the young SNCC field organizers resented the call for King to rescue the campaign. The minister came to the city in December but failed to win any concessions and was forced to make an embarrassing retreat, deflating the energy of the Albany campaign.

In the wake of King's departure, Andy Young and Dorothy Cotton went to Albany in early 1962 to pick up the pieces. They decided that the galvanized but frustrated Albany community could benefit from "on the job" citizenship training, so they began offering workshops in one of the local churches. They also convinced some of the people SNCC had organized, including the expelled Albany State students, to come to Dorchester for a week of more intense training. The young contingent received special lessons in Black history, emphasizing the writings of W. E. B. Du Bois, to place their protest into historical and political context. They learned about the political structure of their state and city, how the political parties worked. They also learned how to set up citizenship schools and employ proven voter registration techniques.

At Dorchester, the CEP staff were impressed with the Albany students' sincerity and courage and blown away by their singing. On their first night at the center, Bernice Johnson and some of her fellow students began to sing the songs that inspired and sustained the Albany Movement. "They created a style of singing that was unique and beautiful and captivating," Dorothy Cotton recalled.

The Albany students returned home to open several citizenship schools in the city, supplementing SNCC's voter registration efforts. When Revs. King and Abernathy returned to Albany in early summer 1962 to revive the movement, they brought the CEP staff with them, although King was soon forced by a federal court injunction to leave the city again.

Mrs. Clark stayed in Albany for another two weeks, reenergizing the city's citizenship schools and boosting the voter registration drive. The Democratic primary for governor was approaching in September 1962, posing a choice between staunch segregationist Marvin Griffin (whose Education Commission had persecuted Highlander) and a young, more moderate candidate, Carl Sanders, who promised to obey federal law on school integration. Black votes could make a difference.

"I stood at the courthouse door, for eight or ten days, from morning until late afternoon," Mrs. Clark related, "telling the Black people as they came up, 'Go ahead and register.'"

White officials tried to trick the hopeful registrants into believing that the coming election was a "white primary" in which they were not entitled to vote. Clark urged them to stay, assuring them of their voting rights; white primaries had been outlawed in Georgia years ago.

The people of Albany did register, thousands of new names placed on the rolls. The registration drive spread to neighboring counties, with rallies and preparation clinics held in local churches. In late summer, three of these churches were bombed, then burned to the ground by arsonists. The perpetrators were not pursued. On primary election day, thousands of newly registered Black voters in Albany and surrounding towns defied threats of violence to cast their ballots. The Black vote helped the moderate Sanders win in the Albany area, contributing to his statewide victory over Griffin. The new voters also gave Black businessman Thomas Chatmon enough support in his bid for a seat on the city commission to force a runoff election. Chatmon didn't win the seat, but the close results rattled Albany's white officials in a way the protest demonstrations had not. The following spring, the city commission began repealing racial segregation ordinances. In practice, full desegregation would require years of sustained agitation by the city's Black citizens, but the legal change was a start.

At the time, the Albany Movement was viewed as a chaotic failure. But the city's Black citizens did not believe their campaign had failed, even if it did not achieve all its goals. "What did we win? We won self-respect," A. C. Searles, the editor of a local Black newspaper, declared. "It changed all my attitudes. This movement made me demand a semblance of first-class citizenship."

"If things are going to change, you will have to change them," Dorothy Cotton, Septima Clark, and Andrew Young preached in their citizenship training classes. "We must be the change."

CHAPTER TWENTY-NINE

Tremor in the Iceberg

M ississippi was known as "the iceberg" among civil rights workers: hostile, impenetrable, the most dangerous territory. In the summer of 1962, Bernice Robinson was summoned there.

Mrs. Robinson was now directing citizenship education and field work for Highlander at the new Knoxville location. Highlander's site and staff were diminished, its budget pinched. Nevertheless, Robinson quickly established citizenship classes in Knoxville, and another in nearby Oak Ridge. She continued her projects with beauticians, many of whom were teaching citizenship classes while also funding and staffing the Tent City health clinic in Fayette County, where people who had tried to register were still living as refugees. And she was frequently invited by Septima Clark and Dorothy Cotton to help train new citizenship teachers at Dorchester.

Robinson and Horton were also collaborating with Jenkins on his ambitious plans to make Johns Island a center for movement political training. With Highlander's help he had secured enough funding to begin construction on a shiny new Progressive Club building on the island, providing a home for his South-wide Voter Education Internship program and a community center for island residents. Esau was often invited to share his organizing expertise at the teacher training and leadership workshops Bernice directed for Highlander, as well as those Septima and Dorothy held for SCLC. Jenkins deftly moved across organizational boundaries and rivalries, managing to keep his balance while serving on the Highlander, and soon the SCLC, boards of directors.

Meanwhile, Horton was concentrating on rebuilding Highlander. He needed to raise operating funds by expanding the school's project portfolio and was anxious to reestablish Highlander's stature as a catalyst for the movement. He strengthened his ties to SNCC, whose philosophy of grassroots development was more in sync with his own than SCLC's reliance on top-down authority. SNCC felt comfortable with Horton and Highlander, too, as the young organization had already used the Monteagle campus numerous times as a safe space for debating its future, guided by Myles's tough questions. In the early summer of 1962, Horton arranged for SNCC field organizers to gather in Knoxville for training in voter education and registration drive tactics, led by Bernice Robinson. Among those attending from Mississippi was a bookish, intense young man named Robert Parris Moses, who had been toiling in Delta towns for more than a year. Moses bore the scars from beatings, jailings, and shootings to prove it.

Raised in a Harlem public housing project, Bob Moses held a graduate degree in philosophy from Harvard and was working as a high school math teacher when, inspired by the student sit-ins, he left to join the movement. Encouraged by Ella Baker, Moses joined SNCC and made his way south to answer the call from local leader Amzie Moore for help with voter registration. Moses arrived on Moore's doorstep in Cleveland, Mississippi, and at Amzie's kitchen table the two men sketched a plan for a statewide voter registration drive. Amzie Moore was a respected and aggressive NAACP organizer who held no illusions about the dangers his work entailed: he never slept in his own bed at home, always under it, to dodge the bullets of night riders shooting into his house. Moore drove Moses around the state, introducing the soft-spoken northerner to local Black activists who could aid the campaign.

Moses first planted himself in McComb, in the southwest corner of the state, and began knocking on doors, urging Black citizens to take the enormous risk of trying to register to vote, something most had never considered. He set up prep clinics to help them fill out the registration forms and study the arcane constitutional questions they would be asked on the test. The clinics were like stripped-down versions of Mrs. Clark's classes, without the literacy and full citizenship training. This meant the clinics couldn't help those who were illiterate, limiting the registration campaign's reach. As a teacher, Moses was aware of the need for a more comprehensive educational component, but he didn't have the capacity for it yet.

Moses accompanied small groups of registration hopefuls to the county courthouse; only a few succeeded in registering, but even that modest success aroused the ire of whites in the area. Moses was arrested numerous times, run off the road, and beaten over the head, requiring stitches to close the wounds. In one shocking incident, one of Moses's registration campaign volunteers, Herbert Lee, a farmer and father of nine, was shot in the head in broad daylight by an incensed white state legislator. The murderer was promptly acquitted. The Black community in McComb erupted in protests. Hundreds were arrested, and Moses was jailed again. He smuggled out a note from his cell to his colleagues outside:

"This is Mississippi, the middle of the iceberg," he scribbled. But he was not discouraged. He could hear one of his SNCC cellmates singing in a clear tenor—"Michael Row Your Boat Ashore"—the same spiritual Mrs. Clark had sung in her cell near Monteagle two years before.

"Christian brothers don't be slow," Moses transcribed the lyrics he heard. "Alleluia. Mississippi's next to go, Alleluia."

"This is a tremor in the middle of the iceberg," Moses wrote from his cell. That tremor would continue to shake Mississippi as Moses and his comrades carried the registration campaign to other parts of the state, engaging local people to join them.

In early June 1962 Moses traveled with other SNCC field workers to the Highlander training workshop in Knoxville, where Bernice Robinson offered a crash course in registration and voter education techniques. She impressed upon them the value of creating classes for functional illiterates in their areas to broaden the registration base and bring more rural people into the movement. She brought in Esau Jenkins from Johns Island and Hosea Williams from Savannah to talk about the practical politics of registration work and the difficulties they should expect to face. This was the type of grounding the field staff needed, as many had plunged into the project with enthusiasm but no experience. Robinson's ability to connect with the young SNCC workers and smoothly convey the concepts they needed to know impressed Moses enough that he asked her to come to Mississippi to evaluate the registration projects in progress. She set off, alone, for Mississippi.

Her first stop was Jackson, where she conducted a workshop for field organizers, similar to the one she had led at Highlander. Bob Moses was in charge of SNCC's voter campaign in Mississippi, partnering with CORE, NAACP, and SCLC to work under the umbrella of the Council of Federated Organizations (COFO). Robinson trained staff from all the COFO partners.

From Jackson, Robinson drove to Cleveland, home of Amzie Moore, which she used as a base to recruit participants for a workshop on political education at the Mt. Beulah Christian Center. She was pleased to see that her cousin Seppie had already trained teachers and established citizenship schools in Cleveland,

Clarksdale, and rural Ruleville, providing a solid foundation for the registration push about to begin.

At the Mt. Beulah workshop, Robinson and a roster of attorneys and law students conducted classes on voting law and government structure, instructing the field organizers on using maps and census reports to plan registration drives. Then it was on to Greenwood, Greenville, Clarksdale, and Vicksburg, where Robinson observed the work of the SNCC field staff who had attended her Highlander workshop in Knoxville, helping them with their projects. She found enthusiasm in the Black communities she visited, but she also saw fear. She had recruited eight people in Greenwood to attend her workshop at Mt. Beulah, but "fear prevented six of them from attending," Robinson reported. Others were interested in attending, "but fear of reprisals and intimidations inhibited them."

"This fear is real, not imaginary," Robinson emphasized. "In Ruleville, Negroes must be off the street by 12 p.m. curfew, or be arrested and held in jail until a fine is paid," she reported. "In Greenwood, a Negro woman went to register, but the registrar told her to leave her name and address, and she would be called and told when to come back. However, a white couple living near her came to her house the next morning and told her that they would burn her house if she went back to register."

When the white community got wind of plans for Robinson's workshop at Mt. Beulah Christian Center, the local sheriff and White Citizens' Council members hauled the director of the center into a four-hour interrogation, demanding the names of everyone participating in the program. "They showed him pictures of Myles Horton," Robinson recounted, "telling him that Myles was Director of 'that Communist Highlander Center' and that he shouldn't be connected with it."

"The night we opened the workshop, I was told to 'soft-pedal' my connections with Highlander," Bernice reported, and there were threats to blow up the meeting place. Mississippi Sovereignty Commission investigators were watching the meeting, recording the license plate numbers of the attendees, marking them for future harassment on the roads. The commission opened a file on Mrs. Robinson, too.

The fear was real, and Robinson could feel it. But there were Black Mississippians, many of them women, who refused to give in to the fear. Some of them had already dared to travel to Dorchester to train with Septima Clark and Dorothy Cotton, opening citizenship schools in their towns. More would soon make that trip, taking another step in the political awakening of their communities.

———————◆———————

Mrs. Vera Mae Pigee did not need any awakening; she had been a Mississippi NAACP activist for years in Clarksdale, working alongside state chairman Aaron Henry and field secretary Medgar Evers. When the CEP trio visited Clarksdale on their first road trip, Andy Young noticed that while Henry was a respected and vigorous leader, Mrs. Pigee "really ran the operations."

Like Rosa Parks, Vera Mae Pigee shepherded Mississippi's young people into the movement as director of the state's NAACP Youth Councils and led an active youth chapter in Clarksdale. Her hair salon was a social center and political clubhouse for Clarksdale's Black women. "I think freedom and talk freedom with my customers," Mrs. Pigee said proudly.

She had first attended a Highlander workshop at Monteagle in 1960 with her daughter, Mary Jane, a college student studying music, who loved the singing spirit of the place. The Pigee women came up with a slyly subversive idea: invite Guy Carawan to sing with Mary Jane in the first interracial concert ever held in Clarksdale, a benefit for the Youth Council in January 1961. Guy and Candie came to Clarksdale, staying with the Pigees, and Guy shared the stage with Mary Jane, accompanying their duets on his banjo. This was too much for the Clarksdale sheriff, and when the Carawans tried to drive out of town to return home, they were pulled over for speeding, threatened, and hauled into the police station. Undaunted, the Carawans returned to Clarksdale the following year for an encore performance with Mary Jane.

Mrs. Pigee signed on as one of the CEP's first teacher recruits, closing her beauty shop for a week in November 1961 to travel to Dorchester for training. Barely two weeks after returning from Dorchester, she and another CEP teacher walked into the "whites only" waiting room of the Clarksdale Greyhound station to buy a ticket for Mary Jane to travel home from college for Christmas. Pigee drank from the white water fountain, used the white restroom, and set into motion a series of community acts of defiance that eventually forced the desegregation of the station.

This was the kind of fearless, resourceful spirit Pigee brought to her citizenship classes, which met in her beauty parlor after-hours, with the shop's curtains drawn. She welcomed both women and men into her female sanctum, leading them in studying the hard words on the literacy test and the parts of the Mississippi constitution they would have to know to register. She also engaged them in discussions about their rights, about the need to stand up to reclaim them, the power of their vote. During the day, while she styled her customers' hair, she would try to convince them to register, quiz them on the required questions, prepare them to make the trip to the courthouse. She enrolled her citizenship students, along with her customers, and Youth Council teenagers in her small army of movement foot soldiers.

She led them with the spirit of a righteous warrior: when night riders' bullets ripped into her home in the summer of 1963—barely missing the bed where she and her husband were sleeping, the bullets lodged in the family's piano—she resumed her movement work the next day.

———— ✦ ————

When Bob Moses entered Amite County, west of McComb, to organize for registration in July 1961, one of the first people he met was fifty-five-year-old NAACP chapter president Eldridge Willie Steptoe. Steptoe, who held secret NAACP meetings at his farmhouse to escape the wrath of local law enforcement and the Klan, greeted Moses with the words: "I've been waiting for you."

Steptoe had been trying to register to vote since the early 1950s but was repeatedly rejected by the local registrars. Moses convinced Steptoe to go to Dorchester to train to teach citizenship classes, and Andy Young noticed that the wiry, sharp-witted farmer "really absorbed" the concept of the program "like a dry sponge." Steptoe returned to Amite County to begin organizing classes, held on his farm. He gave his students practice in writing and spelling, tutored them on the strange words they would encounter on the literacy test—"miscegenation," "prevarication," "fornication"—and prepared them to interpret passages of the state constitution. When they were ready to take the test, he loaded his students into a horse-drawn wagon and drove them to town, the county seat of Liberty.

In front of the courthouse, he was stopped by a sheriff: "What do you want, boy," the sheriff demanded. "I came to redish," Steptoe answered, using the local pronunciation for "register." The sheriff pointed his gun at Steptoe and asked again: "What did you say, boy?" Steptoe repeated his intention. The sheriff cocked his gun and asked once more. Steptoe stood his ground: "If I lives, I aims to redish." Steptoe's determination was remarkable, knowing his good friend Herbert Lee had recently been murdered on account of his registration work. Steptoe and his citizenship students tried and failed to register that day, but they would be back.

Though few Black citizens of the Delta who dared to take the registration test were placed on the rolls, the white community noticed the surge in attempts, the mass meetings, the public marches to the courthouses. There were jailings, beatings, bombings, and shootings. In early 1962, in a callous move to collectively punish the Black communities where registration action had begun, white officials of several Delta counties blocked access to federal food and fuel subsidies, the canned and dried staples that rural Black families depended upon through the winter, when there was no work in the fields. Destitute families suffered hunger and cold, but the cruelty of this maneuver sparked an outpouring of northern sympathy and help. Comedian Dick Gregory chartered airplanes to bring food and clothing donations to the region, and truckloads of food arrived from the North, though in some instances, when the trucks reached the Mississippi line, the drivers were arrested and the trucks' contents destroyed. To the immense frustration of civil rights workers, there was little effective response by the federal government to these brazen episodes of retribution.

Hattiesburg businesswoman Victoria Jackson Gray vented her own frustration by becoming a citizenship teacher. She had graduated from college, taught school, and owned her own successful cosmetics sales business, yet she had tried to register six times and was refused by the white registrar at every attempt. She had had enough, and in the summer of 1963 Gray volunteered to go to the Dorchester center for teacher training. Smart, organized, and energetic, Gray impressed Clark and Cotton and soon she was not only teaching but also supervising all the CEP classes in the Hattiesburg region.

Mrs. Gray was able to both recruit students and proselytize for registration while going door-to-door selling her Beauty Queen cosmetics line. As an independent businesswoman, she carried her sample case holding creams, lotions, and lipsticks, along with registration and citizenship class materials, into Black homes with little fear of losing her job or clientele. Her increasing responsibilities in the CEP, as a teacher and paid supervisor, and her deepening involvement in other aspects of the movement, distracted her from the business, but she found great satisfaction in her new political work. Her husband, however, was fired from job after job when his employers learned that his wife was an activist, and the dangers of her work seeped into her home. She had to get accustomed to her "phone ringing at two o'clock in the morning and you're told what's going to happen to you," she explained. "Get these ugly letters in the mail. Some people used to be your friends and associates, they kind of distance themselves." This was the price for asserting her rights as an American.

That price was small compared to the tribulations of Mrs. Gray's fellow Mississippi CEP teacher Fannie Lou Hamer. Hamer was a forty-six-year-old plantation worker in Sunflower County who had first joined her family in the cotton fields when she was just six years old (she was the youngest of twenty children) and had little formal schooling. Yet she loved to read and could figure well, and she was able to work her way up to a clerical position as timekeeper and payroll assistant on the Marlow plantation, where she and her husband and two adopted daughters lived in a sharecropper's cabin.

Bob Moses and James Bevel were holding meetings in the area in the late summer of 1962, trying to stir some movement excitement among the plantation sharecroppers. Hamer walked into one of those meetings in a Ruleville church and heard Rev. Bevel, a mesmerizing speaker, give an impassioned sermon on God's challenge to Black men and women to reclaim their rights, especially the right to vote. Bevel was working for SCLC now as voter registration field organizer in Mississippi, employing his oratorical and singing gifts to fire up his audiences. His words and fervor stirred Mrs. Hamer. "I never heard that Black people could be able to vote," she marveled. When the call went up for volunteers to travel to the county seat to register to vote, she found herself raising her hand high.

On the last day of October 1962, Mrs. Hamer and seventeen other registration hopefuls boarded a bus for the trip to the Indianola courthouse. None of them succeeded in registering that day, though Hamer attempted to pass the literacy test. On the way out of town their bus was stopped and the driver arrested; his bus was "too yellow," the police alleged. The passengers were left, stranded and frightened, on the side of the road for hours. Mrs. Hamer kept up her neighbors' spirits by leading them in gospel songs, including her favorite, "This Little Light of Mine." When the driver was finally released and the group reached Ruleville, Hamer discovered that word of her registration attempt had already reached her employer—the court registrar had called him. The plantation owner stormed into the Hamer shack and confronted Fannie Lou, giving her an ultimatum: withdraw her registration application or lose her job and be thrown out of the crude dwelling she and her husband, "Pap," had lived in for eighteen years.

"I didn't go down there to register for you," she told her boss and landlord, "I went down there to register for myself." She packed her bag and left that night. Pap stayed with the children to finish the harvest season. Fannie Lou stayed with friends in town for a few days, then moved in with relatives in the next county. Believing Hamer was still staying with the friends in Ruleville, Klan nightriders pumped sixteen bullets into the room where she had been sleeping. But Mrs. Hamer wasn't there. She had gone to join the movement.

Mrs. Hamer became a staff field worker for SNCC, circulating through the plantations of Sunflower County, convincing other sharecroppers to dare to register. Soon she signed up to become a citizenship schoolteacher, traveling to Dorchester for training, where Dorothy Cotton and Septima Clark were taken by her energy, grit, and big, soulful voice. Mrs. Hamer led the Dorchester class in singing "This Little Light of Mine," and it became part of the citizenship school repertoire. Back in Ruleville, Mrs. Hamer opened her first citizenship class in a church basement.

"See, that's how we developed a momentum," Bevel would explain. "So when you start talking about all those folks in Mississippi, that's how you train local leadership. Take them off to the Citizenship Schools, they start organizing their own communities."

With creativity and courage, Fannie Lou Hamer did organize her community, shining her light into a dark and demoralized corner of the Delta. Soon, together with her fellow Mississippi citizenship teachers and SNCC activists, she would shake the foundations of the iceberg.

CHAPTER THIRTY

Project C

A s the epicenter of the movement shifted to Birmingham, Alabama, in the spring of 1963, Mrs. Clark and the CEP staff were pulled there to prepare the city's Black citizens for a massive, and risky, campaign. The secret code word was Project C. The C stood for confrontation.

This confrontation in Alabama's largest city was perilous but necessary, Dr. King and the SCLC leadership believed. Something dramatic, even drastic, needed to be done to rattle the Kennedy White House enough to get the administration behind a comprehensive federal civil rights law, one with teeth. Nine years after the *Brown* decision, school desegregation had made little real progress in the South. State massive resistance stood fast against constitutional law, with no apparent consequences. In some places, entire school systems shut down rather than integrate. Black voting power was still being stymied. Even with the citizenship schools helping overcome literacy test barriers and voter registration drives encouraging thousands of Black citizens to make the dangerous trip to the courthouse, most applicants were still turned away by intransigent white registrars. Those who did manage to register faced economic ruin or bloody retaliation from their white neighbors, whose actions went unpunished.

The movement's demonstrations and boycotts, sit-ins, and Freedom Rides had achieved some success in abolishing select segregation and discrimination practices in certain cities, but most southern areas remained solidly under Jim Crow, and White Citizens' Council, rule. At the same time, thousands of Black organizers and peaceful demonstrators had been arrested, beaten, tortured in jail, murdered. Pleas for federal government protection and prosecution went, with rare exceptions, unheeded, as the Kennedy administration remained unwilling to alienate segregationist southern senators whose votes were needed to pass the White House's signature economic and Cold War measures. Justice Department efforts were spotty and ineffective.

The only thing that seemed to stir the Kennedy White House into action on civil rights was bloody mayhem at home resulting in embarrassment on the world stage. The virulent white riots on the University of Mississippi campus the previous fall, sparked by Black military veteran James Meredith's attempt to enroll, had caused two deaths, the wounding of hundreds of unarmed federal marshals, and an international furor before the White House finally intervened. If violent confrontation was what it took to grab the attention of the national press, shake the conscience of the American people, and force action from the White House, then that's what Project C would deliver in the streets of Birmingham.

The project was meticulously planned, beginning with an SCLC strategy retreat held at the Dorchester Center in January 1963. The careful plotting took into account the bitter lessons learned in Albany, where confusion and missteps forced SCLC's embarrassing retreat. Project C must be massive, strategic, and disciplined. Thousands must be willing to peacefully demonstrate and go to jail. And they must be prepared. Birmingham's Rev. Shuttlesworth laid the groundwork, and the SCLC sent Rev. James Lawson to the city to teach nonviolent philosophy and tactics to those willing to sign pledges to commit to the protests, knowing they would face the brutal machinations of the city's commissioner of public safety, Theophilus Eugene "Bull" Connor.

Citizen education was another crucial element in preparing the city's Black community for the campaign, so contingents of neighborhood leaders were sent to Dorchester for training. The CEP staff was also dispatched to Birmingham to run citizenship workshops, helping residents understand their constitutional rights, why it was necessary to demand those rights by protesting and then secure them with the power of the vote. It was citizenship school on the field of battle.

Project C kicked off on April 3 with a manifesto listing demands and a coordinated campaign of mass meetings, marches on city hall, lunch counter and library sit-ins, voter registration demonstrations, and an Easter boycott of Birmingham's downtown stores. During the first week of the campaign, hundreds of citizens participated in the direct actions and were met by police batons and dogs; scores were arrested. The city tried to clamp down on the protests with a court injunction, which campaign leaders refused to obey, leading to the arrest of King and Abernathy (Shuttlesworth was already in jail) on Good Friday, April 12.

While held in solitary confinement, King scribbled a passionate moral justification of Black protest and a stinging rebuke of white liberal gradualism on scraps of paper smuggled out of his cell. King's twenty-page statement was ignored by the press at the time and was not published until more than a month later, but his *Letter from a Birmingham Jail* would become one of the most famous testimonials of the movement.

The direct-action protests continued, but by late April Project C was faltering. The price of bail bond had been raised to $2,500 for each arrested protester, the campaign's bail funds were tapped out, and volunteers willing to stay in jail indefinitely hard to find. The campaign was also not winning sympathetic coverage in the northern press.

Dr. King called in James Bevel and his wife Diane Nash, both masters of direct action, to help. Bevel came up with a new and controversial strategy: use Birmingham's schoolchildren to protest—and go to jail. Dr. King initially opposed the idea but, facing the collapse of his major initiative, reluctantly allowed Rev. Bevel to organize the "children's crusade."

Bevel recruited youngsters from Birmingham's high schools, and even elementary schools, as young as nine or ten years old—often without their parents' permission—to join the protests. In the basement of the Sixteenth Street Baptist Church, the meeting center of the campaign, Dorothy Cotton and Septima Clark used their teaching skills to train the children in how to behave: how to meet billy clubs, tear gas, attack dogs, fire hoses—without lashing back. How to sing freedom songs to ease fear. The children were instructed to wear raincoats to protect their skin against the fire hoses, tuck toothbrushes into their pockets for their time in jail.

Through it all, they must remain nonviolent. "Do you think you can take the slaps?" Mrs. Clark would ask the students. "Because they will slap your face or they will knock you down. Do you think you can take it?" She knew that nonviolence was not an instinctual response; it must be learned and practiced. "If you can, and turn around and move on, or go to jail, all well and good," she would tell them gently but firmly. "If you can't, don't go down. Stay in this room with me."

Mrs. Clark called upon all her teaching talents, maternal empathy, and movement toughness to impart these lessons to the children. She also summoned her faith, to trust that putting children in harm's way was wise and necessary, that God would protect them. She did not know if some might be killed in this battle for their future.

On May 3, 1963, the Black children of Birmingham began marching and demonstrating, were chased and bitten by police dogs, blasted off their feet by water cannon. Almost two thousand of them were dragged off to jail. All of it was captured by news cameras and reporters from around the world, who began paying attention to the city when the children appeared on the streets.

The scenes of police attacks on Birmingham's children reportedly sickened President Kennedy in the White House. The president sent the Justice Department's Burke Marshall to Birmingham to broker a settlement, pressuring the city's white power structure to enter negotiations, with Andy Young leading the talks for SCLC. An agreement was eventually reached, meeting most of the campaign demands. The hundreds of jailed children were released (though NAACP lawyer Constance Baker Motley had to fight in federal court to overturn their expulsion from school, Birmingham's cruel attempt to punish the students for their participation in the protests), and over the next months "whites only" restrictions were gradually dismantled in Birmingham.

———◆———

Project C was a pivotal movement victory, not just because a major southern city was forced, by peaceful mass protest, to change its official racist policies, but because the courage and discipline of the Black citizens of Birmingham gave other southern communities confidence to demand their own rights. During the summer of 1963, in the first ten weeks following Birmingham's uprising, a reported 758 direct-action protests swept through 186 cities, with almost fifteen thousand people arrested for demanding equality.

Among those arrested were Esau Jenkins, a leader of Charleston's response to Birmingham: a direct-action push to desegregate the city's business district. The campaign included weeks of mass meetings in the city's Black churches, marches and rallies on the downtown streets, and attempts to enter segregated business establishments. Jenkins was arrested for "trespassing" as he and several of his NAACP colleagues entered a hotel lobby with the intention of eating in the hotel restaurant.

In Savannah, Hosea Williams was thrown behind bars for more than two months after leading weeks of huge nighttime protest marches and boycotts of downtown stores, which paralyzed the city in the summer of 1963. The protests and boycott were so painful to merchants that they pressed the city to negotiate a remarkable desegregation agreement. While under activists' pressure

Savannah had already moved to desegregate many public facilities, now the city rescinded all municipal segregation ordinances and opened hotels, movie theaters, and swimming pools to Black clientele. Dr. King praised Savannah as "the most integrated city south of the Mason-Dixon line."

Quite a few of these summer 1963 protests were led by local leaders, like Jenkins and Williams, who were affiliated with Highlander. Many of the protests were marshalled by citizenship teachers mentored by Septima Clark, Bernice Robinson, and Dorothy Cotton, and citizenship school alumni helped power these campaigns in the streets.

In its first two and a half years of operation at the Dorchester center, the CEP had trained more than a thousand citizenship teachers from eleven southern states. These teachers returned home to open six hundred classes, enrolling more than ten thousand adult students, resulting in the voter registration of twenty-eight thousand people in their communities. Many more students who tried but were denied registration still carried the lessons and political awareness of their class experience. "They walked, talked, and acted like new people," as one Georgia citizenship schoolteacher described the effect of the class on her students, "with determination and more courage to face the future."

"It was just a quiet building base of community by community across the South," Dorothy Cotton would explain. "People were going back [from Dorchester] saying they're not gonna take segregation and discrimination anymore. And they'd go back and just act differently, which meant very often sitting in, demonstrating, registering and voting, running for public office. It meant just a whole new way of life and functioning."

The entire citizenship education ecosystem was expanding and deepening, fed by a variety of streams. Clark, Cotton, and Young still embarked on leadership recruitment expeditions in search of "natural leaders." Their efforts were supplemented by Robinson and Horton, who were training SNCC field organizers in Highlander educational methods, and as these field workers spread into new territories, they directed promising local leaders to Dorchester for training. The registration initiatives sponsored by the Voter Education Project also supplied teacher candidates, and Dorchester alumni did their own recruiting, recommending others in their community for training. Once they returned home, these citizenship teachers needed support and supervision as they opened their classes, but Clark could not cover all the ground herself, while Cotton and Young were spending more time on SCLC direct-action campaigns.

Clark was skeptical of the SCLC's new emphasis on flashy demonstrations over the slow and prosaic work of educating Black citizens to understand their rights. Television cameras were not interested in poor people tracing the letters of the alphabet with pencils, though that act could be more transformative than any march. As the SCLC plotted more campaigns, Clark expressed her displeasure directly to Dr. King. "Direct action is so glamorous and packed with emotion that most young people prefer demonstrations over genuine education," she wrote in a memo to King. When the demonstrations ended, and the excitement ebbed, the awakened communities needed knowledge to organize and advocate for themselves.

She was encouraged that Andy Young acknowledged CEP's growth by bringing on new field staff: Bernice Robinson switched over from Highlander to join Clark as a CEP roving field supervisor, and Annell Ponder, a highly qualified young woman with both teaching experience and a graduate degree in social work also joined the team.

Tall and poised, enthusiastic and empathetic, the thirty-year-old Ponder was first dispatched to the Savannah area in November 1962, where Hosea Williams had been conducting his multipronged campaign to desegregate public facilities and register voters. Williams sent dozens of people to Dorchester for training, opening new citizenship classes at a fast pace, and promoting interest in voting by running for local office himself. He relied on graduates of the citizenship classes to turn out for demonstrations and build his base of voters.

When Mississippi began to heat up in early spring 1963, Ponder was called to Greenwood, where the murder of another voting rights worker sparked an intense and coordinated registration campaign, supplemented by citizenship classes and leadership training. Ponder worked with Bob Moses and his young COFO activists to support the Delta residents who refused to be intimidated by increasingly violent reprisals, especially those brave enough to volunteer as citizenship teachers. In early June 1963, Ponder selected a few of these teachers, including Fannie Lou Hamer, to attend an advanced training workshop on voter registration and community development held at Jenkins's new Progressive Club community center on Johns Island.

Clark, Jenkins, and Ponder led the workshop, and after five days of study, discussion, and singing, Ponder and her Mississippi delegation headed back to Greenwood on an overnight Trailways bus. About thirty miles from their destination, in the town of Winona, the bus pulled into a rest stop, where the group attempted to use a restroom and lunch counter marked "whites only." Police and highway patrolmen soon surrounded them and ordered them to leave. When Ponder insisted that, under federal law, they were entitled to use the facilities, the police chief barked, "Ain't no damn law! Get up and get out of here." As they were taught in the workshop, they took down the license plate numbers on the police cars to report the incident. The CEP workers were immediately arrested, pushed into patrol cars, and taken to the county jail. No charges were lodged against them; they were not allowed to telephone family or lawyers.

During the following days and nights, the members of the Mississippi delegation were savagely beaten. Uniformed police and highway patrolmen hit the three women and one man with fists, blackjacks, and belts until they were swollen, bruised, and bloody. While one of the prisoners was being tortured, the others were forced to listen to the screams. Mrs. Hamer was singled out for special punishment, including rape, when the police chief learned she had tried to register Black voters in Ruleville. The chief ordered two Black prisoners to beat Hamer, compounding the pain with insult. When the prisoners, hitting Hamer with all their might, exhausted themselves, the highway patrolmen took over. Hamer was finally dragged back to her cell, bruises covering her head and body, her legs black and stiff from internal bleeding. Miss. Ponder's eyes were bloodshot and swollen shut, her lip busted open. Mrs. Hamer, lying on a cot in severe pain, led her fellow prisoners in singing hymns and freedom songs through the night.

No one knew where the CEP group was, only that they had not returned home. Ponder was supposed to join Robinson in leading a workshop in Greenwood, but she had not shown up. Alarmed, a contingent of SNCC workers in Greenwood set off to find the CEP teachers, following a hint they might be in Winona. There they were met by police and a posse of White Citizens' Council and Klan toughs, who beat SNCC organizer Lawrence Guyot till he was almost unconscious, then dragged him to the Winona jail on the charge of attempted murder.

An emergency call went out from SNCC: the prisoners in Winona were in grave danger. Dr. King asked Andy Young to rescue them. Young enlisted James Bevel and asked Dorothy Cotton if they could borrow her car to drive from Atlanta to Winona. She said yes, but only if she could go with them on the mission. Young refused: "Just give us the keys," he snapped.

"Those are women in jail in Winona," Cotton shot back. "If Mrs. Hamer is brave enough to challenge Mississippi, I'm brave enough to help her get out of jail."

Cotton took the wheel of her car and started the engine. Young and Bevel jumped in. Young negotiated the release, and four days after they had been arrested, the battered prisoners limped out of the Winona jail. Annell Ponder, through swollen lips, whispered just one word as she left the jail, a soft but defiant declaration: "Freedom!"

CHAPTER THIRTY-ONE

A Living Petition

While Annell Ponder, Fannie Lou Hamer, and the other CEP teachers were being beaten in the Winona jail in June 1963, Alabama governor George Wallace was "standing in the schoolhouse door" guarding the entrance of the University of Alabama with his body against entry by two Black students. Playing for the cameras, Wallace bombastically taunted President Kennedy and railed against the federal court order that the students be admitted.

In the White House, John F. Kennedy was getting tired of the pompous theatrics, and open contempt, of southern governors. He was also worried that the post-Birmingham demonstrations rocking the South might spiral out of control. The president abruptly decided to announce—that night, on national television—that he was going to introduce into Congress his long-promised civil rights legislation. His advisers were aghast: there was no bill drafted, there was no speech written. The president requested that the nation's TV networks give him fifteen minutes of airtime at eight o'clock on June 11, 1963. A speech was hastily written, and Kennedy ended up ad-libbing the finale of his address, but the message was clear and strong:

"We preach freedom around the world, and we mean it. But are we to say to the world and much more importantly to each other—that this is the land of the free, except for the Negroes, that we have no second-class citizens, except Negroes.... Now the time has come for this nation to fulfill its promise.... We face a moral crisis as a country and a people. A great change is at hand, and our task, our obligation, is to make that revolution, that change, peaceful and constructive for all."

Dr. King immediately wrote a note congratulating President Kennedy: "It was one of the most eloquent, profound, and unequivocal pleas for Justice and the Freedom of all men ever made by any President."

That same night, barely four hours after Kennedy's speech, thirty-seven-year-old Medgar Evers, the NAACP's Mississippi field secretary and the most prominent civil rights worker in the state, was shot dead in the driveway of his home in Jackson by a Klansman hiding in a honeysuckle bush.

———— ♦ ————

Bernice Robinson dropped her coffeepot and lost the grip on her cup when news of Evers' murder came over the radio early the next morning. She was supposed to meet with Evers that very afternoon in Greenwood, a strategy meeting to discuss details of the voter registration workshop for COFO field workers she was to direct that week. Annell Ponder was scheduled to be at the meeting too, but she was just being released from the Winona jail.

Robinson's Greenwood workshop went on, though she, Bob Moses, and everyone else attending were badly shaken. "Amid all the chaos," Robinson reported, "we were able to get in three full days of discussion on problems common to all the communities—fear, lack of local leadership, lack of organization, police brutality." Despite the grief and fear of that terrible week in June, those working inside the Mississippi iceberg left the workshop "even more determined" to get Black citizens registered, Robinson noted, "and to overcome the many barriers facing the Negro today."

The civil rights bill promised by President Kennedy, the legislation that might lift some of those barriers, was still being drafted in the White House. Not surprisingly, most southern congressmen and senators vowed to defeat any such legislation. When the Senate Commerce Committee opened hearings on the administration's bill in mid-July 1963, a parade of southern state officials trekked to Washington to denounce it.

Among those testifying were Mississippi governor Ross Barnett, Alabama governor George Wallace, and Arkansas attorney general Bruce Bennett. During their testimonies, all three railed against the bill as part of a communist conspiracy to weaken America, maintaining that the civil rights movement, and its leaders, were directly controlled by communists. They warned that Congress would be abetting the communist takeover if it passed President Kennedy's legislation. Asked by northern senators to provide some proof of this assertion, each of the segregation champions reached into their briefcases and pulled out the same documentary evidence: the Georgia Education Commission's 1957 brochure, "MLK at Communist Training School," featuring Ed Friend's photograph of the minister at Highlander. The big lie was on exhibit in the chambers of the

US Senate. The brochure also took on new life in the pages of southern newspapers, reprinted to bring pressure on Congress to kill the bill.

As Highlander popped up in congressional testimony and news reports, the FBI began a secret intelligence-gathering operation to find the names and records of all Highlander staff, trustees, and supporters, all students and discussion leaders who had attended the center's workshops and meetings. This amounted to a roll call of movement leaders and activists, and each name would be checked and added to the FBI files. The agency's bureau in Knoxville was instructed by headquarters to make sure this scrutiny "did not become public knowledge."

Efforts to defeat the bill were aided by a sophisticated lobbying campaign in Washington operated by the newly formed, patriotic-sounding Coordinated Council for Fundamental American Freedoms, whose sole purpose was to derail the bill. The committee was spearheaded and sponsored by the Mississippi State Sovereignty Commission, in collaboration with other southern state segregation agencies, and with secret funding from a wealthy New Yorker named Wickliffe Preston Draper. The reclusive, Harvard-educated heir to a textile fortune, grandson of a Confederate general, Draper displayed a particular fondness for white supremacist causes. He had also established a foundation dedicated to promoting eugenics and Nazi racial hierarchies. Alarmed by the prospect of federally mandated racial mixing, Draper funneled almost a quarter of a million dollars to the Coordinating Committee for its fight against the civil rights bill.

Also working to defeat the legislation was the Citizens Councils of America, Inc., which used its popular radio broadcast, Citizens' Council Radio Forum, to blast the legislation as the Kennedy administration's appeasement to communism. Not to be outdone, Governor Wallace demanded that his state endow itself with not just one but a pair of official segregation agencies (a Legislative Commission to Preserve the Peace and a Sovereignty Commission) to bolster the southern offensive against the bill in Washington and cripple the civil rights movement at home.

Movement leaders plotted their own lobbying strategy and recognized that to counter the segregationists' influence on the Hill, they needed to demonstrate to Congress, in a dramatic way, popular support for the bill. Plans for a March on Washington for Jobs and Freedom took shape rapidly, if not exactly smoothly, over the summer, organized by movement veterans

A. Philip Randolph and Bayard Rustin. After some reluctance, all the major rights organizations agreed to participate and mobilize Black communities across the country to attend, with progressive labor unions joining the effort. Black publications gave the event prominent space, leaflets were handed out on street corners, signs placed in store windows, and pickup trucks carrying loudspeakers drove through Black neighborhoods: "Freedom Now Movement hear me," the trucks blared. "We are requesting all citizens to move into Washington—to go by plane, by car, bus, any way you can get there—walk if necessary."

Citizenship schoolteachers and students helped mobilize their communities, and many took seats in the chartered buses headed north to Washington. Even those who couldn't make the trip promoted the march in their neighborhoods, raised money for transportation, made signs and sandwiches for the travelers. This gathering was to be "more than just a demonstration," organizers announced: "The Washington March is a living petition—in the flesh—of the scores of thousands of citizens of both races who will be present."

"It will be orderly, but not subservient," the organizers promised. "It will be proud, but not arrogant. It will be nonviolent, but not timid. It will be outspoken, but not raucous."

More than a quarter of a million people converged on Washington on August 28, 1963. They first gathered at the Washington Monument to hear Odetta and Peter, Paul, and Mary sing freedom songs, then marched to the Lincoln Memorial, softly chanting "We Shall Overcome" along the way. On the steps below Lincoln's feet, speakers representing the major movement organizations, plus religious leaders and union officials, gave speeches. John Lewis, representing SNCC, was forced to edit his most incendiary criticisms of the administration and Congress, statements considered too antagonistic, possibly jeopardizing legislative support for the bill. Lewis still managed to point out the weaknesses of the pending bill—especially its lack of strong protections for voting rights and peaceable assembly—and delivered a passionate rebuke to those who asked Black citizens to patiently "wait" for their freedom.

Septima Clark was at the march, together with many of the movement's key women leaders, some who had been in the struggle for decades, many who were serving on the front lines, risking their lives. But these women were not allowed to give an address at the march nor were they permitted to participate in any substantive way. They couldn't even march with the men. They were relegated to a parallel march on a different avenue leading to the Lincoln Memorial.

Movement philosopher and attorney Pauli Murray complained about this marginalization of women's contributions while the march was still in the planning stages, as did several others. March organizers replied with their version of a solution: a token "Tribute to Women" inserted awkwardly into the program, in which the names of half a dozen women leaders would be read aloud. The women could stand, smile, and wave.

Mrs. Clark was not among those honored. Neither was Ella Baker. Or NAACP veterans Ruby Hurley or Modjeska Simkins. Rosa Parks was acknowledged, but she was frustrated by the way women, the backbone of the movement, were being relegated to second-class status at the march. "The march was a great occasion," as she would later describe it, "but women were not allowed to play much of a role."

"Those of us who did not sing," Mrs. Parks noted dryly, referring to the only women prominently featured on the program, the great performers Marian Anderson and Mahalia Jackson, "didn't get to say anything." Rosa was particularly annoyed by the way she and her friend Septima "were being treated like hostesses" at the event, expected to be gracious and silent.

"Nowadays, women wouldn't stand for being kept so much in the background," Parks would later reflect, "but back then, women's rights hadn't become a popular cause yet."

These women, who had shouldered much of the burden of the struggle for years, were not included in the delegation of movement leaders who, following the march, met with President Kennedy in the White House to discuss the civil rights bill. The next morning, the women held their own meeting at a Washington hotel, venting their frustrations about the sexist attitudes displayed not only at the march, but by the movement in general.

None of this came as a surprise to Mrs. Clark. Ella Baker had warned her about the SCLC male ministers' dismissive attitude toward women. In the two years Clark had served on the SCLC staff at a high level, she had noticed that she and Dorothy Cotton were rarely allowed to bring up issues at executive council meetings; Dorothy fumed when the men expected her to serve them coffee. The women's reports were always scheduled at the end of meetings and hastily run through. "[Martin] was not aware of his tendency to ignore [Septima's] substantive comments or undervalue her work," Andy Young recalled. "Martin was oblivious to the existence of any issues on his staff regarding gender equity."

"Those men didn't have any faith in women, none whatsoever," Clark maintained. She was simultaneously annoyed and amused by Ralph Abernathy's habitual questioning of her presence on the executive council. "Why is Mrs. Clark on this council?" Abernathy would ask with a note of disgust. Each time, Abernathy had to be reminded of Clark's crucial role in the CEP and the CEP's value to the SCLC. "It was hard for him to see a woman on that executive body," Clark explained. "As a man, he didn't feel as if women had really enough intelligence to do a thing like what I was doing."

Nevertheless, the Washington march was a huge success: massive, peaceful, dignified. Congress was forced to pay attention, as popular response to the march increased pressure to act on the civil rights bill moving slowly through a maze of committees on the Hill. March attendees went home even more determined to keep up their part in the fight.

But barely two weeks after they had returned home from the Washington march, on a Sunday morning in mid-September 1963, they were stunned and stricken by the news bulletin out of Birmingham. The Sixteenth Street Baptist Church, the hub and heart of the Birmingham protest campaign, where demonstrators took courage in prayer and strength in freedom songs, had been bombed, ripped apart by sticks of dynamite placed by Klan bombers. Four little girls, ready for Sunday school in their frilly church dresses and Mary Jane shoes, lay dead in the rubble.

This was too much. This loss was unfathomable, this sacrifice too great. These girls were every Black family's daughters. The movement stood paralyzed by grief, confused by questions. "Where in the world do we go from here?" Dorothy Cotton and many of her colleagues in the movement wondered in the days following the bombing, even as Dr. King presided at the girls' funerals. "But we would go on. The violence would not stop us. It did not stop us."

It did not stop Black Mississippians from conducting their "Freedom Vote." In an impressive feat of civic imagination, the COFO initiative constructed an entire election apparatus from scratch, giving Black citizens the chance to learn how the electoral process worked (at least how it was supposed to work) and demonstrate to them the important role they could play in making decisions about their own governance.

The project put into practice many of the lessons taught in the citizenship classes, so it was no wonder CEP teachers and students formed the core of the huge organizing effort. All through the summer, CEP-affiliated men and women, led by Fannie Lou Hamer, Victoria Gray, Aaron Henry, Vera Mae Pigee, and Amzie Moore, joined Bob Moses's COFO staff and volunteers in canvassing, leafleting, and persuading their neighbors to participate. They stood up to speak about the Freedom Vote in their churches and clubs, conducted practice in filling out ballots, tacked notices on trees.

The civil rights bill was still languishing in Congress in early November 1963 when more than eighty-three thousand Black Mississippians cast their ballots in the Freedom Vote. They walked to the informal polling places in their communities, the churches and schools, beauty and barber shops, funeral homes, grocery stores, and gas stations where ballot boxes were placed. For those frightened to be seen voting in these places, mail-in ballots were provided. Black citizens of Mississippi marked their ballots for their own NAACP state president, Aaron Henry, for governor.

It was, of course, make believe. Their votes didn't count in the official Mississippi gubernatorial election—from which they were essentially barred—but it mattered in a more profound way. They had learned to vote. They had practiced first-class citizenship. And they had dispelled the myth that Black people in Mississippi didn't care about voting. Now all the Freedom Voters needed was President Kennedy's civil rights bill to allow them to vote for real.

But by late November President Kennedy was dead, his civil rights bill was stalled in Congress, and a new president, a southerner, was sitting in the White House.

That new president, Lyndon Baines Johnson of Texas, surprised the nation with his first speech to Congress on November 27, 1963, declaring that the civil rights bill was his top legislative priority. While the nation was still stunned and grieving Kennedy's assassination, Johnson positioned the bill's passage as a fitting memorial to the slain president, ratcheting up pressure on Congress to honor the fallen chief. Movement activists were not at all sure Johnson was sincere in his promise to champion the bill. Whether Johnson meant to roll up his sleeves to push the bill through—or would be content to just let it die on Capitol Hill—remained to be seen.

While civil rights leaders waited for proof of the president's sincerity, in early December Septima Clark made her way to the federal courthouse in Oxford, Mississippi, to attend the trial of the policemen who had brutalized Fannie Lou Hamer and Annell Ponder in the Winona jail. Ella Baker joined her in the gallery. After days of wrenching testimony, the jury of twelve white men deliberated, and within an hour returned with a unanimous verdict: not guilty.

Sitting in the courtroom, a strange feeling came over Mrs. Clark as the lies of white men triumphed over the sworn testimony of Black women. Though she wanted to practice Rev. King's ethos of meeting hate with love, she was unable to do so in that Oxford courtroom. Instead, she felt herself wishing that the courtroom chandelier would drop down on the white policemen's heads and kill them. Right there. Justice. "My mind wasn't non-violent," she admitted.

Soon Fannie Lou Hamer and Annell Ponder, their wounds still raw, were walking the corridors of Congress, testifying in hearings and lobbying for the civil rights bill. They forced legislators to look into their battered faces to see how Black citizens suffered if they dared to exercise their constitutional rights.

———◆———

Congress returned from winter recess in early 1964 having received an earful from constituents back home about the civil rights bill. Under pressure, more House members announced support for the bill, providing leverage to bring it out of committee to the floor of the House. During nine days of debate in January, more than a hundred hostile amendments were proposed to water down the bill or saddle it with "poison pill" provisions, including adding "sex" to the language prohibiting "employment discrimination based on race, color, religion, and national origin." House members took the "sex amendment" as a joke—it was introduced by a Virginia segregationist—but when it received the support of a dozen women representatives, this unlikely bid for women's equality gained passage. What began as a comical poison pill would become the legal foundation for protecting the rights of women and gay people into the twenty-first century.

In the first week of February, the House finally passed its version of the civil rights bill—stronger than the original Kennedy version, weaker than House liberals had hoped—by a two-to-one margin. It arrived at the Senate, where the bill's floor managers, after much wrangling and some fancy footwork, managed to maneuver it out of reach of Mississippi senator James Eastland's Judiciary Committee, well-known as "the graveyard" of civil rights legislation. In the previous decade, Eastland had buried 120 civil rights measures there. Jumping over Eastland's committee, the bill landed directly on the Senate floor for debate.

"We shall now begin to fight the war," pledged Senator Richard Russell of Georgia, and on March 30, 1964, the longest filibuster in American history began.

CHAPTER THIRTY-TWO

Practicing Democracy

The Senate girded for this legislative war. Each side appointed commanders and captains, huddled in strategy meetings, hovered over tallies. Proponents of the bill assembled a bipartisan battalion of whips, captains, and floor managers. Opponents relied on their favorite defense weapon, the filibuster. They divided into three platoons, each with six senators, responsible for speechifying in the well of the Senate for hours at a stretch. While one team of talkers pontificated on their shift, the others rested, then took up the filibuster baton, relay race–style. The only day off was Sunday.

The Southern bloc in the Senate dug in for the long haul. Senator Russell used a map and a chart to introduce his own amendment to the bill, creating a federal "Racial Relocation Commission" to apportion the nation's Black population evenly among all the states. His facetious scheme would relocate Black citizens from the South into the North and West, forcing those distant do-gooders attempting to foist integration and social equality on the South to "practice what they preach."

As the filibuster droned on through the spring of 1964, both supporters and opponents of the bill worked to influence senators. The Coordinated Council for Fundamental American Freedoms, the lobbying arm of the Mississippi Sovereignty Commission, took the lead in opposing the bill. It invited representatives of the national Realtors, manufacturers, and retail associations to its Capitol Hill headquarters for drinks and briefings on the dangers the bill held for business interests forced to comply with its nondiscriminatory requirements. The council launched a major offensive to influence public opinion in the North, buying full-page advertisements in major newspapers and mailing a million letters and pamphlets with menacing titles like "The Federal Eye Looking Down Your Throat" to residents of northern states whose senators supported the bill.

Through the spring, as the Senate filibuster rolled on, Mississippi civil rights activists began planning their most ambitious project yet, Freedom Summer. The centerpiece of the project was the creation of fifty "freedom schools" and community centers across the state, introducing poor Black Mississippians, especially young people, to Black history, literature, and politics—subjects forbidden in the state's segregated school system. The goal was to instill a sense of pride and hope in both adults and youngsters, while openly discussing the rights being denied them under Jim Crow.

The freedom schools were modeled on Septima Clark's citizenship schools, and she was invited to New York City for a curriculum-planning meeting organized by Bob Moses and Myles Horton, who was an educational consultant to SNCC. Mrs. Clark chaired the freedom schools' remedial education committee, designing an adaptation of her adult literacy lessons to help prepare Mississippians to register to vote.

SNCC's plan was to import over a thousand white college students from the North and West into Mississippi to organize, canvass, and teach. The wisdom—or folly—of recruiting middle-class white students from the nation's elite universities to work with the rural poor, in the most violent southern state, split the SNCC leadership. It revived all the tensions over white participation in a Black freedom movement that had roiled SNCC at its formative meetings at Highlander four years earlier. But the argument that white students would bring national attention to conditions in the state, and perhaps help sway Congress to pass the civil rights bill, ultimately prevailed.

While white men in Washington maneuvered, bickered, and bargained over the civil rights bill through the spring of 1964, eager white college students prepared to enter Mississippi, employing teaching methods and educational philosophies passed to them by Septima Clark and Myles Horton.

———— ♦ ————

The Senate filibuster was in its second month when Guy and Candie Carawan brought together more than fifty southern song leaders from seven states for a "Sing for Freedom" workshop in Atlanta, sponsored by Highlander, SNCC, and the SCLC. Myles Horton, Dorothy Cotton, and Andy Young understood the importance of song in the movement, how it served as both a balm and a weapon for nonviolent warriors, and they were at the workshop to lead discussions and lend their voices.

Attendees learned the latest movement song repertoire and ways to use music to energize and sustain community action. They swapped songs from different movement cities and made up new, impromptu verses in evening jams. Activists from Birmingham, Albany, Selma, Nashville, and Americus sang the new songs popularized in their campaigns. The Freedom Singers gave their interpretations of the movement playlist, singers from the Sea Islands exposed young activists to the roots of the songs they were singing, and CEP teacher Mrs. Holloway and her citizenship students from Wagner, South Carolina, performed a favorite freedom song from their class.

At the end of the workshop, everyone took home a pocket-size "We Shall Overcome" songbook—easy to carry into the field, into the mass meetings, and into the jails—the places the movement song leaders were headed.

———————◆———————

While Senator James Eastland was taking his turns as a filibusterer trying to protect his state from the civil rights bill, the Mississippi Sovereignty Commission was working to protect the state from the Freedom Summer "invasion." The commission dispatched its investigators to meet personally with the sheriffs of every county in the state, acquainting them with state laws that might be useful in dealing with civil rights agitators, including some brand-new laws hurriedly passed by the state legislature. The commission also held conferences with city and county officials to coordinate efforts to handle the influx of unwanted visitors. Local sheriffs beefed up their staffs, deputized citizen posses—filled with Klan members—and invested in stockpiles of weapons. In Jackson, Mayor Allen Thompson outfitted a truck with armor, search lights, sirens, and mounted machine guns to protect his city.

The commission also employed a network of Black informants, and in addition to several ministers paid to report on the movement activities of their parishioners, it placed a spy in the COFO headquarters office in Jackson. Posing as an eager volunteer for the cause, the informer boasted of how well he "blended in" while making regular reports to the commission. As plans for Freedom Summer progressed, the informer removed and photocopied files containing details about some of the students accepted into the summer project, including their names, colleges, and hometowns, as well as their identification photos. This information was forwarded to the commission and shared with law enforcement partners around the state.

———— ✦ ————

Breaking a Senate filibuster required a two-thirds majority—sixty-seven senators—to approve a motion for cloture, the parliamentary procedure for ending debate. As summer neared, the bill's managers knew they didn't have the votes. Even some senators who supported the bill were loath to interfere with the sacred Senate tradition of the filibuster. The only way to reach the magic number for cloture depended on the support of minority whip Everett Dirksen, who could bring along some of his Republican colleagues. Dirksen had his price, which was softening some of the enforcement provisions in the employment sections of the bill to appease business interests. Intense negotiations with Dirksen went on for weeks. Finally, Dirksen agreed to support a cloture vote and carry a few Republican senators with him.

On June 10, the seventy-fourth day of the Senate filibuster, Senator Harry Byrd of Virginia gave its last gasp in an all-night, fourteen-hour speech on the floor. An hour later, the Senate clerk called the roll on the motion to invoke cloture. The galleries were packed with anxious civil rights supporters. CBS newsman Roger Mudd stood on the steps of the Capitol broadcasting a live play-by-play of the vote, the aye or nay of each senator relayed to him from inside the chamber.

———— ✦ ————

The Senate roll call was proceeding in Washington as the first few hundred Freedom Summer volunteers began arriving for a week of orientation and training on the campus of Western College for Women in Oxford, Ohio. Here they received a crash course in teaching math and Black history, conducting canvassing and voter registration prep, and responding nonviolently to the harassment they were sure to face. Their families had been required to post a $500 bond for bail if they were arrested. They did role-playing and freedom song singing and lived in the dorms with experienced Black COFO field workers, who found some of their new white colleagues smug and dangerously naive. Movement notables from Bob Moses to Bayard Rustin, James Lawson to Ella Baker briefed the young volunteers. Myles Horton was there to lead some of the discussion groups, and if the style of the orientation week bore a strong resemblance to a Highlander workshop, that was no coincidence. Black informants for the Mississippi Sovereignty Commission were also at the orientation, taking note of the organizers and participants.

———— ◆ ————

The Senate vote on cloture was going to be tight; every member was needed on the floor. The vote tally displayed on newsman Roger Mudd's scoreboard perched on the Capitol steps bounced up and down as the roll call marched through the alphabet. When the name of Senator Clair Engle of California was called, there was no response. A long pause. Engle was suffering from a malignant brain tumor and could not speak, but he had insisted on being carried into the chamber to vote. He slowly raised a shaky hand to his face and pointed, three times, to his eye. He was voting aye for cloture.

The motion for cloture passed by a margin of four votes. The Senate had never defeated a filibuster against a civil rights bill before. The bill was immediately taken up by the full Senate, and the proceedings dragged on for another nine days. Finally, on June 19—a date celebrated in southern Black communities as Juneteenth, marking the anniversary of the late arrival of news of the Emancipation Proclamation to the slaves of Texas—the Senate passed the Civil Rights Act of 1964 by a vote of seventy-three to twenty-seven.

The Civil Rights Act abolished segregation in all public spaces, mandating that hotels, restaurants, theaters, sports arenas, gas stations, and retail stores provide equal service and facilities to all. It also ordered the desegregation of public parks, playgrounds, swimming pools, and libraries and authorized federal intervention to desegregate schools. The act prohibited discrimination by employers or labor unions based upon race, religion, national origin, or sex and created a federal employment opportunity commission to investigate complaints.

While the act went a long way toward abolishing official segregation, it did little to protect or promote voting rights; stronger provisions had been stripped out of earlier versions of the bill to speed its passage. What remained was a hodgepodge of odd compromises. The act did not outlaw literacy tests but set a sixth-grade education as the standard for being "presumed literate" in federal elections. This would not help the millions of rural Black citizens who had not been able to attain six years of schooling—they would still be subject to the capricious exams. And the act didn't do much to curb the power of racist registrars, it required them only to "apply uniform qualification procedures" to white and Black applicants, a stipulation that could easily be fudged. It gave no federal protection to voters or voting rights workers.

The day after the Senate vote, the first cohort of Freedom Summer volunteers finished their orientation and departed Ohio to take up their assignments in Mississippi. Andrew Goodman, a twenty-year-old white student from New York, drove to his posting in Meridian, a county seat about a hundred miles east of Jackson, in a car with two more experienced field workers he had met at orientation: white social worker Michael Schwerner from New York and Black CORE volunteer and native Mississippian, James Chaney. After reaching Meridian, the three men set off to investigate the recent burning of a Black church. The church's congregation had agreed to host a freedom school. The Klan learned of this, ambushed and beat several of the church's lay leaders, and torched the church.

On the way back to Meridian from their inspection, the Freedom Summer workers' car was stopped by police outside the town of Philadelphia for speeding, a common harassment ploy. They were arrested, held in the city jail for hours, then released into the night. They were never seen again.

Bob Moses was standing with Myles Horton at the orientation in Ohio on June 22 when they received word of the missing volunteers. Moses was stunned but not surprised. John Lewis flew to Meridian to help in the search parties. President Johnson ordered the FBI to investigate, but Director Hoover resisted. Senator James Eastland insisted the disappearance of the workers was just a communist-inspired publicity stunt. National press and television reporters flocked to Mississippi to follow the story of the missing white volunteers.

The civil rights workers were still missing—though the charred remains of their station wagon had been found in a swamp—when President Johnson used seventy-two ceremonial pens to sign the Civil Rights Act into law on July 2. Witnessing the historic moment in the East Room of the White House were the leaders of the major civil rights organizations, joined by a special guest, Rosa Parks. In his televised remarks at the signing, Johnson spoke of the challenge ahead: "My fellow citizens, we have come now to a time of testing. We must not fail. Let us close the springs of racial poison."

As the president spoke, thousands of Black citizens of Mississippi, most of the SNCC field staff, and almost a thousand, mostly white, volunteers from the North were plunging into Freedom Summer. Working side by side, they opened forty-four freedom schools across the state, where more than twenty-five hundred youngsters came to learn basic subjects, but more radically, to expand their knowledge of the world. The volunteers staffed freedom houses and community centers for recreation, freedom singing, and political discussions. They set up libraries of donated books—history, philosophy, poetry—opening a world of knowledge and art otherwise beyond the reach of the state's Black students.

A hundred volunteer doctors, nurses, and psychologists staffed temporary health clinics, bringing treatment to the rural poor. A hundred and fifty lawyers and law students came into the state to represent those arrested. Three hundred ministers, priests, and rabbis lent their spiritual support and manual labor to the project. The Freedom Summer staffs taught literacy and citizenship classes to adults, using Septima Clark's system, and went door-to-door for voter registration. Annell Ponder was a statewide supervisor for the project, and dozens of Mississippi women and men Mrs. Clark had trained as CEP teachers, who had returned home to assume roles as community leaders, were also deeply involved. Everyone was taking enormous risks.

Indeed, Freedom Summer was a season of terror in Mississippi. Incensed by the passage of the Civil Rights Act, the "invasion" of outsiders, and the arousal of Black political activity, white Mississippians lashed out in revenge. Over the course of the summer, there were more than a thousand arrests of freedom volunteers and local residents on spurious charges. Eighty reported beatings and kidnappings. Thirty bombings of private homes, freedom schools, and movement offices, and thirty-five church burnings. Thirty-five shootings and six deaths, including the murders of the three rights workers in Neshoba County, whose remains were finally discovered buried in an earthen dam, bullet holes in their bodies.

Yet Freedom Summer was also a joyous shout of hope amid despair and terror. And it set the scene for an exuberant performance of democratic ideals: shut out of the regular electoral process, Black Mississippians created their own, even establishing an independent political party. During the course of Freedom Summer, over sixty thousand citizens enrolled as members of the Mississippi Freedom Democratic Party and were invited to help choose delegates to the 1964 Democratic presidential convention. Working with SNCC and a team of legal advisers, they held precinct and district caucuses—sometimes conducted in cotton fields or under trees—and gathered 2,500 people in Jackson for a MFDP state convention, where sixty-eight delegates and alternates were chosen, including CEP teachers Fannie Lou Hamer, Victoria Gray, Willie Steptoe, and Hartman Turnbow. In late August, just as the last of the Freedom Summer volunteers were leaving, the delegates piled into buses and headed to Atlantic City to challenge the legitimacy of the state Democratic Party and rock the foundations of Mississippi's political white hegemony at the national level.

The MFDP crashed the Democratic Party national convention, upsetting the party establishment and infuriating President Johnson, who used bare-knuckle pressure tactics to quash the MFDP insurgency. (No matter that the official, all-white Mississippi delegation had already announced they were supporting the Republican nominee for president.) Fannie Lou Hamer's testimony before the convention's credentials committee, raw and emotional, was broadcast to a national audience and replayed on the nightly news. She told of the punishments she had endured for trying to register to vote in Indianola, the beatings she suffered in the Winona jail for her voting rights activism, and the violent methods used to deny Black Mississippians their right to participate in American democracy.

"If the Freedom Party is not seated now, I question America," she declared into the microphone.

The Freedom Democrats were offered an insulting compromise—two nonvoting seats on the convention floor in exchange for dropping their challenge—which they refused, and left Atlantic City frustrated and angry.

"We had made our way to the very center of the system. We had played by the rules," as SNCC's John Lewis, who'd accompanied the delegates, described the sense of betrayal he shared. "Done everything we were supposed to do . . . had arrived at the doorstep and found the door slammed in our face."

For many SNCC activists, the abandonment by their white political allies at the convention, coming on the heels of the unchecked violence they had endured during Freedom Summer, disillusioned and embittered them. Still, the television audiences who viewed Fannie Lou Hamer's impassioned testimony flooded the White House and Congress with thousands of telegrams and phone calls demanding stronger protections for Black voting rights. Whether those pleas would be heeded depended upon the fall elections.

CHAPTER THIRTY-THREE

Lay Our Bodies on the Line

D ear Citizenship Teacher," began the letter sent out by CEP headquarters staff in the fall of 1964. "We are urging all Citizenship School folk to spend every possible moment between now and Election Day getting people out to vote. Whether you continue your class or not, please work as hard as you can to beat Goldwater in November. Urge all of your class members and neighbors to see that everyone in town votes. We must defeat Goldwater!"

The Republican senator from Arizona, Barry Goldwater, had voted against the Civil Rights Act in the Senate, advocated states' rights, and showed little interest in appealing to Black voters. If Goldwater prevailed, decades of civil rights gains could be lost, even the new Civil Rights Act might wither for lack of enforcement, and further progress would be doomed. President Lyndon Johnson, despite his machinations in Atlantic City, was at least sympathetic, had pushed hard for the Civil Rights Act, and was promising to do more, if reelected. If movement leaders delivered the Black vote to him, they might have leverage to convince him to strengthen voting rights.

Dr. King abandoned his nonpartisan policy to campaign for Johnson across the country. The SCLC staff, including citizenship school students who were just learning how their government worked, were recruited into the effort. As the election neared, Mrs. Clark was in a small church in rural South Carolina helping ready citizenship school graduates to vote for the first time. They had managed to pass the literacy test and register, but there was still some trepidation about voting. To motivate them, she applied a little dose of guilt to her stern lecture: if they did not show up to vote on election day, "it would be a slap in the face to all that had been suffered and done before," she reported. She was pleased that every one of the citizenship graduates "voted, and voted for Johnson."

Lyndon Johnson won the election in an historic landslide, collecting 96 percent of the national Black vote. Thanks to voter education and registration campaigns, the number of registered Black voters nationwide had more than doubled since the 1960 presidential election (from an estimated five million vot-ers to about twelve million), and Black turnout on election day was astounding. In the northern and western states, 72 percent of eligible Black voters went to the polls, and even in the southern states, where registration was so restricted and voting still a dangerous affair, 44 percent of eligible Black citizens cast ballots, 95 percent of them for Johnson. Civil rights leaders pointed to the electoral map math: if Black citizens were free to register and vote in the southern states, they could offset white voter defections.

Johnson's victory was a relief for the civil rights community, but the fall of 1964 was an uneasy time for the movement. Even with the hard-won Civil Rights Act beginning to forcibly change the South's segregation practices, unrelenting violence still targeted Black citizens trying to reclaim their voting rights, and relief was nowhere in sight. Civil rights leaders feared another round of urban unrest was brewing in northern cities, driven by poverty and despair. As the war in Vietnam expanded, thousands of young Black men were being drafted into the military to fight for their country, defending democracy in Southeast Asia while they were denied democracy, decent jobs, and equality at home. The SCLC was struggling to gain traction for another major campaign. Rev. King was being hounded by the FBI, which was surveilling and blackmailing him, threatening to undermine his reputation, his movement, and his marriage. Meanwhile, Malcolm X and the Nation of Islam were having success convincing frustrated young Blacks to reject integration and nonviolence. King was being called an Uncle Tom.

SNCC was falling apart, riven by internal dissension and group despair. A corrosive cynicism had seeped into the organization since the summer violence in Mississippi, the defeat in Atlantic City, and the slow progress elsewhere in the South. SNCC leaders were questioning the purpose of their organization and doubting the value of working with white allies. Many young SNCC activists had lost patience and, worse, hope.

At this anxious moment in late 1964, Rev. Dr. Martin Luther King Jr. was notified that he had won the Nobel Peace Prize. Septima Clark was invited to join Dr. King's entourage accompanying him to Oslo, paying her own way. It was her first, and only, trip abroad, an extravagance she could hardly afford, but she justified it simply: "When a Southern Black man could win a Nobel Peace Prize," she reasoned, she was going to be there to witness it.

Clark traveled with King to London, then to the prize ceremonies in

Oslo and Stockholm. Amid the ornate trappings and pageantry, what was most remarkable to Mrs. Clark was the outpouring of excitement from ordinary, very white, Norwegians welcoming the young Black minister, serenading him with "We Shall Overcome" on the street. What was important to her was that the world was honoring not just a man but a nonviolent freedom movement, her movement. Mrs. Clark kept every program, every itinerary, every news clipping from the trip as mementos.

Septima's only disappointment was that she could not share the excitement of the journey with the Warings. She did not write long letters with detailed accounts of the trip to them. She did not visit them when she landed in New York on her return from Europe. The friendship had frayed.

Elizabeth Waring had taken offense to a passage in Clark's 1962 memoir, *Echo in My Soul*, which described the 1950 speech she had given to the Charleston YWCA as "vitriolic." Considering that in that speech, Mrs. Waring had denounced the city's white elites as sick and degenerate, vitriolic seemed an apt adjective, but Elizabeth was furious, rejecting Septima's explanations.

Septima knew by now that Elizabeth was a high-strung woman who seemed to enjoy being angry about things and disappointed in people. Septima had learned to take these outbursts in stride. When Elizabeth lambasted civil rights leaders for not moving quickly or aggressively enough or criticized Septima's own work in citizen education as too passive and gradualist, Septima had to explain to her white friend, living comfortably on Fifth Avenue, the realities of poor southern Black people struggling under unremitting violence and oppression.

"To be unmercifully truthful, I don't really feel that Mrs. Waring had that much knowledge of the life of the Blacks," Clark would later recall. Elizabeth stopped answering Septima's letters and phone calls. When Septima tried to visit in New York, Elizabeth turned her away. The friendship had been perhaps the most important one of Septima's life, and it pained her to lose it.

"My dear, dear friends," she wrote to them in the fall of 1964, a final attempt to heal the breach. "Though we're miles apart and I'm still a traveling salesman, the friendship exists." It would always exist in her mind and heart. She closed with a plaintive wish: "Do hope that both of you are happy."

———◆———

On his return from Oslo, Dr. King pushed President Johnson on his promise to take up voting rights legislation once reelection was secured. Yes, he was going to do it—eventually—Johnson told King, but it wasn't possible to get voting rights through the Congress for another year or more. The president couldn't afford to further alienate the powerful southern legislators whose votes he needed to pass his Great Society initiatives—Medicare and Medicaid, funds for education and social welfare, job programs—all of which could help Black Americans in a direct way, Johnson reminded King. Voting rights were equally important, the minister insisted. Not now, the president repeated. It wasn't politically possible now.

Dr. King left Washington empty-handed and disappointed. He had been honest with the president: Black people couldn't wait for the perfect political moment. If the president wouldn't bring voting rights to Congress, the movement would demand the vote in the streets. On January 2, 1965, King announced the next SCLC campaign: demanding the vote in the streets of Selma, Alabama.

"We at SCLC feel that now we have to push harder than ever to break the police state in Alabama," Septima Clark wrote to the Warings in her last letter to them. "We will have to take up the torch and lay our bodies on the line once more. We have to do more demonstrations."

Within days of King's announcement, Mrs. Cotton and Mrs. Clark were dispatched to Selma, the seat of Dallas County, to prepare the Black community for the campaign by setting up citizenship schools. They made the rounds of churches and civic meetings, recruiting teachers and neighborhood leaders, getting them to Dorchester for training. They had the advantage of an existing citizenship school base and strong support from local leaders like Marie Foster and Amelia Boynton, who were both CEP teachers and founders of the Dallas County Voters League, the movement arm in Selma. Mrs. Boynton and her entire family were longtime activists. The 1960 Supreme Court decision *Boynton v. Virginia*, which outlawed segregation in interstate transportation facilities and sparked the Freedom Rides, was brought by Amelia's son, a law student who had been arrested for trespassing in a whites-only bus depot café.

Mrs. Boynton and her husband had led the local the NAACP branch, and when it was banned in Alabama in 1956, she helped establish the Voters League. In recent years she'd partnered with waves of SNCC organizers, who had tried to make a dent but left in frustration. Boynton led desegregation demonstrations, ran voter registration drives, and conducted citizenship schools. In the spring of 1964, she challenged a white incumbent congressman in the Democratic primary, with the campaign slogan "a voteless people is a hopeless people." She knew her chances were slim, as less than 3 percent of Black citizens were registered to vote in Dallas County. Statewide, although African Americans comprised half of the Alabama population, only 1 percent were registered to vote. It wasn't for lack of trying. When Boynton led 350 people to the courthouse to register in October 1963, they were beaten and fired from their jobs.

Marie Foster had tried, and failed, eight times to register. A single mother who went back to high school and junior college to become a dental hygienist, Foster was determined to crack open the voting barriers in her city. She trained with Clark and Cotton to become a citizenship schoolteacher and went home to organize a class, but fear was so pervasive she could recruit only a single student, a seventy-year-old man who wanted to learn to write his name. Slowly, more students were drawn to her literacy classes, where they also received a solid dose of civics and movement education. The bravest graduates enrolled in the Voters League, knowing that voting was still just aspirational in Selma.

The CEP had already bolstered citizenship efforts in the area with a Selma Literacy Project during the Freedom Summer of '64, sending Clark-trained northern volunteers to conduct classes. In July, days after the signing of the Civil Rights Act, John Lewis arrived to work with Boynton and Foster on a registration march to the Dallas County courthouse, which ended with Lewis and fifty hopeful voters, including citizenship class graduates, arrested. The incident also prompted a local judge to impose an outrageous injunction, forbidding the discussion of racial issues by any gathering of three or more people, effectively shutting down movement work. Amelia Boynton and Marie Foster traveled to Atlanta to beg Dr. King and the SCLC for help.

———— ◆ ————

Beginning in early January 1965, the campaign in Selma was cold and brutal. Hundreds of citizens repeatedly marched from the redbrick Brown Chapel AME Church to the Dallas County courthouse, willing to stand for hours in the winter rains to register to vote, knowing they might lose their jobs and jeopardize their family's security. They were burned with electric cattle prods, clubbed on the courthouse steps, and beaten bloody by county police and deputized posses commanded by the hot-tempered county sheriff, Jim Clark. Within weeks, more than three thousand people had been jailed in Selma and adjacent towns. Selma's citizens kept up their courage in nightly mass meetings, where a rotating roster of movement luminaries sang, prayed, and exhorted them to keep up the fight. All the campaign leaders and organizers were jailed at some point—King, Abernathy, Bevel, Lewis—but it was the arrests and abuse of local women leaders like Amelia Boynton and Marie Foster, and schoolchildren chased and beaten by Sheriff Clark in a sadistic rage, that caught the attention of the news media and provoked outrage around the country and abroad.

Septima Clark, Dorothy Cotton, and Annell Ponder traveled back and forth from Selma, where they held makeshift citizenship classes to prepare the Black community for voter registration, and Dorchester, where they trained the city's emerging leaders. Clark and Cotton lived in a spare bedroom in Amelia Boynton's house while in Selma, with Andy Young bunking in another room.

As the weeks went by, the campaign took a toll on the community. Families were hurting. Parents were in jail, injured, or thrown out of work for their involvement in the registration drive. Children were skipping school to join the protests. Hardly anyone succeeded in getting registered. But while registering was the goal of the campaign, the essential point was to dramatize to the world—especially to Congress and the White House—the difficulty and suffering Black citizens were forced to endure for even trying to register in Selma.

So it was especially striking to see more than a hundred of Selma's public schoolteachers—who had always shied away from movement involvement, knowing they could be fired—march to the courthouse on January 22 to demand to register. Many carried toothbrushes in their pockets, the practical symbol of their determination to go to jail. They were cheered by their students along the way, threatened by their superintendent at the courthouse door, and pushed back down the courthouse steps by police clubs jabbed into their bellies. They rose to their feet and marched up the steps again.

The campaign pushed into mid-February: more attempts to register, more arrests and beatings, hundreds in jail. Registration demonstrations at courthouses in the surrounding county seats drew a violent response. In Marion, a young Vietnam veteran trying to protect his mother from a state trooper was shot. Eight days later he died. Anger and grief gripped the Black community, and some called for revenge. James Bevel proposed instead a nonviolent expression of rage: a march from Selma to the capital in Montgomery to confront Governor Wallace.

On Sunday, March 7, Hosea Williams, representing SCLC (Dr. King was not in town), and John Lewis, not representing SNCC (which had not officially endorsed the march), set off on the first leg of this march to Montgomery, leading a procession of six hundred people across the Edmund Pettus Bridge.

CHAPTER THIRTY-FOUR

Ain't Nobody Gonna Turn Us 'Round

The marchers came over the crest of the Edmund Pettus Bridge, a span over the Alabama River named for a Confederate officer, US senator, and Klan Grand Wizard. On the far side of the bridge, they saw a barricade of flashing police car lights, a mass of two hundred state troopers and sheriff's deputies, and a contingent of deputized civilians, some on horseback, carrying leather bullwhips. Governor Wallace had given orders banning the march, authorizing state and local police to take any steps necessary to halt it.

The marchers continued on the down slope of the bridge, the first rows reaching the end of the ramp. The commander of the state troopers barked through a bullhorn ordering John Lewis and Hosea Williams, at the front of the crowd, to turn back. Lewis and Williams responded by kneeling and bowing their heads in prayer. While they were on their knees, the commander ordered: "Troopers advance!"

A line of troopers slammed into the first rows of marchers, swinging clubs and whips, then pushed deeper into the crowd, bashing heads and ripping flesh. The hundreds on the bridge were trapped, suspended over the river, with no defense against the onslaught. The staccato thuds of wood against bone and the zing of whips mixed with screams and cries for help. Horses charged into the panicked crowd, hoofs trampling bodies, riders swinging ropes and rubber tubes wrapped in barbed wire. Tear gas enveloped the fleeing marchers, choking and burning them. Those who made it onto land were chased and beaten by the troopers and posses, augmented by mobs of white vigilantes wielding ax handles and yelling rebel cheers.

Citizenship teachers Amelia Boynton and Marie Foster, marching in the first rows, were both clubbed. Foster's knees were whacked, and she was knocked to the ground. Boynton was hit in the head, stumbled, then was brought down by a series of additional blows. A trooper stood over her body, beating her and firing tear gas straight into her face, bellowing: "Get up, nigger! Get up and run." Lewis' skull was fractured, and he sustained a concussion. Blood was everywhere. At least a hundred more marchers were injured in the melee, dozens requiring hospitalization. Even more were sickened by the tear gas.

The vicious frenzy did not end on the bridge. Horses chased escaping marchers through the streets of the adjacent Black section of Selma, galloping up the steps of the Brown Chapel to whip those seeking refuge in the church. Police barged into other churches, hurling men they found there through the stained-glass windows. Officers threw tear-gas bombs into Black homes to drive the residents into the street, where they were attacked.

As night fell, survivors of the terror gathered in the Brown Chapel to tend to injuries and comfort one another. Amelia Boynton lay semiconscious. Marie Foster had to be carried in, her knees swollen and bruised. For those in the church, the wounds were physical but also psychic. There was a sense of defeat and, worse, humiliation. They had been beaten and whipped like animals. Like slaves. At one point, the crying and moaning turned into slow, dirgelike humming. The humming took on a tune, and the tune began to be sung: "Ain't gonna let nobody turn me 'round, Turn me 'round, Turn me 'round . . . " The song took on new verses: "Ain't gonna let George Wallace turn me 'round. Ain't gonna let no state trooper turn me 'round. Ain't gonna let no horses turn me 'round. Ain't gonna let no tear gas turn me 'round . . . "

The singing spread through the church, getting louder and stronger, accompanied by clapping. Crying and clapping. Singing the freedom song together gave the Black citizens of Selma courage, restored their strength and spirit.

By the time the singing began in the church in Selma, film footage and photos of the police rampage on the Pettus bridge were being broadcast on every television network, going to press on the front page of every national newspaper. Several networks interrupted their programming for a special report from Selma. Reporters, who themselves had been attacked, gave graphic first-hand accounts, in the fashion of war correspondents. The public reaction was immediate and intense. For ordinary Americans, far from the southern racial battlegrounds, the pictures from Selma were a turning point. The White House and congressional offices were flooded by requests from angry constituents demanding the federal government do something to protect Black voting rights.

By the next morning, protesters surrounded federal buildings and courthouses in cities around the country—New York, Boston, Philadelphia, Chicago, San Francisco, and a sit-in occupied the Department of Justice building in

Washington. Demonstrators threw their bodies down on Pennsylvania Avenue, in front of the White House, and picketers began a day and night vigil of singing and praying around the president's residence. Ten thousand people, led by Michigan governor George Romney and Mrs. Rosa Parks, marched through downtown Detroit. Demonstrators snarled traffic in Manhattan's midtown and Chicago's Loop as the protests spread to more than eighty cities. "The mournful, determined tones of 'We Shall Overcome' rang out from Miami to Seattle," the *New York Times* reported.

The national outpouring of outrage over the events in Selma, which came to be known as Bloody Sunday, both forced President Johnson's hand and gave him an opening to compel Congress to act on voting rights. He summoned his attorney general and aides and told them to prepare a voting rights bill immediately.

Dr. King also recognized the political potential of the sudden shift in public awareness and vowed to resume the march. He issued a plea for clergy of all faiths to join him in standing up to fear and hate in Selma. With less than two days' notice, almost five hundred ministers, priests, rabbis, nuns, and lay religious leaders streamed into the city, with hundreds more civil rights supporters making their way to Alabama. The Black community of Selma welcomed the visitors into their churches and homes, where people slept on sofas, pews, floors, under tables, and even in bathtubs.

As people poured into Selma, the White House pressured Dr. King to cancel the march. The scenes from Selma had tarnished American's image abroad. In heated negotiations President Johnson promised voting rights relief if King would abandon the march, and he implied his support for legislation depended on the decision to cancel. The pressure intensified when an Alabama federal district judge issued an injunction against the march, greatly complicating the decision for King.

Dr. King secretly accepted a compromise: he would lead the march over the bridge but then turn around, postponing the full march until the injunction could be lifted. Shoulder to shoulder with faith leaders from around the nation, and with two thousand marchers behind him—who were not aware of the compromise—King walked partway over the bridge, knelt in prayer, rose to join in an emotional singing of "We Shall Overcome" and then did a U-turn, leading the procession back over the bridge to Browns Chapel. There was confusion and anger in the church as King tried to explain his decision to the disappointed marchers. They would march again, he promised, though he had made a bargain under duress with a white southern president and could not know for certain whether the deal would be honored.

Less than a week later, President Johnson made good on his promise, standing before a joint session of Congress in a televised address to the nation. "I speak tonight for the dignity of man and destiny of Democracy," Johnson began, calling the events in Selma a turning point in the nation's history, comparable to Lexington and Concord.

For the next forty minutes, Johnson offered a passionate history lesson in the ways some states continued to deny the right to vote to Black citizens, paying special attention to the literacy tests. Looking straight at his former southern congressional colleagues, he intoned: "The command of the Constitution is plain. . . . It is wrong—deadly wrong—to deny any of your fellow Americans the right to vote."

The president announced his solution: He was sending to Congress a bill "designed to eliminate illegal barriers to the right to vote," striking down restrictions in all elections—federal and state and local—that were used to deny Black citizens their suffrage.

"What happened in Selma is part of a far larger movement," Johnson emphasized. "It is the effort of American Negroes to secure for themselves the full blessings of American life. Their cause must be our cause, too. Because it's not just Negroes, but really it's all of us, who must overcome the crippling legacy of bigotry and injustice." Johnson paused, then spoke slowly and deliberately:

"And we shall overcome."

Dr. King was watching President Johnson's speech on a television set in the living room of Selma dentist and movement stalwart Sullivan Jackson, brother of Marie Foster. Crowded into the room were other King aides and a wounded John Lewis. Tens of millions of Americans were also watching the broadcast. The group in Selma was shocked when they heard the words of their anthem uttered by the president. "Can you believe he said that?" King's aides shrieked at the screen. Lewis glanced over to King and saw him wipe tears from his cheek. Lewis himself was deeply moved, but many of his SNCC comrades were not impressed, lamenting that Johnson, whom they did not trust, had "spoiled a good song."

Johnson sent his voting rights bill to Congress on March 17, little more than a day after his speech. The federal judge's injunction against the march to Montgomery was also lifted. March organizers had five days to prepare for a massive demonstration with complicated logistics. Thousands of people would be walking fifty miles over five days; they needed places to camp, food to eat, lights, toilets, emergency medical supplies. They also needed some assurance of safety, which the Alabama government refused to provide. President Johnson signed an executive order nationalizing the Alabama National Guard and called up two thousand US Army troops and a thousand military police to escort the marchers.

From her home in Detroit, Rosa Parks watched the news images from Selma with despair. When Dr. King called to invite her to participate in the march to Montgomery, she felt she must go. She didn't have the money to make the trip, but she appealed to the United Auto Workers union, which provided funding for her fare. She flew from Detroit to Atlanta, then took a bus to the city she had been forced to leave eight years before.

Guy and Candie Carawan received a call from SNCC executive director James Foreman, who asked them to help lead singing on the march. Guy packed his guitar, they left their toddler son with a babysitter, and they made their way to Selma. In Knoxville, Myles Horton also heeded the call to march and left Highlander for Alabama.

At around noon on Sunday, March 21, more than three thousand marchers, led by Dr. King, left Brown Chapel AME Church, singing "We Shall Overcome" and carrying American flags, walked safely over the Pettus bridge. They continued onto Route 80, the Jefferson Davis highway, guarded by US soldiers and military jeeps. The first leg of the march was a seven-mile hike to the first campsite on land loaned by a Black farmer. Guy and Candie were among the marchers, helping keep the spirited singing going for hours. Army helicopters buzzed overhead to scout the route. Demolition experts swept ahead, defusing the packages of dynamite they found planted on the route.

The next two days of the march would travel through Lowndes County, where the highway narrowed from four to two lanes, and by court order, only three hundred people were allowed to march through this section of the road. The rest, including the Carawans, returned by bus or special train to Selma. Those three hundred chosen to continue—250 were the Black citizens of Selma and surrounding counties who had sacrificed so much in this campaign—bedded down in sleeping bags under two giant open tents (one for men, one for women) as the temperature fell below freezing and a coating of ice covered the campsite. Trucks ferried food to the camp from the church basements of Selma, where church women cooked all day and night to feed the marchers.

The marchers trudged through cold rain and ankle-deep mud, fought wind, fatigue, and foot blisters, ate cold meals, and fought off fire ants at their campground. But they kept walking and singing. Marie Foster walked the entire way, fifty-four miles, in pain from her bruised and swollen knees. As the marchers passed the shacks of Black tenant farmers along the road, residents came out of their houses, waving and crying.

On the fourth day, the highway widened, and the core group was joined by thousands of supporters from all around the country. By evening they reached the outskirts of Montgomery, where they were sheltered on the grounds of the City of St. Jude, a Catholic hospital and social services agency serving the Black community. That night, an estimated twenty thousand people watched a four-hour Stars for Freedom concert, organized by Harry Belafonte, including musicians (from Tony Bennett and Lena Horne to Nina Simone and Leonard Bernstein), comedians (Dick Gregory, Mike Nichols, and Elaine May), actors (Ossie Davis and Ruby Dee), and literary star James Baldwin. They spoke and performed from a makeshift stage supported by coffin boxes loaned by a local Black funeral parlor.

Septima Clark climbed onto a chartered bus to escort her Alabama citizenship students from Dorchester to Montgomery. They joined the marchers assembled at the staging area at St. Jude for the final six-mile walk to the capitol building downtown. Myles Horton also joined this "easy part" of the march that morning, taking what he called the "lazy" option of walking only the last segment. Mrs. Parks was also marching on this final leg.

As Parks and the marchers headed toward the city, they passed large billboards facing the road, erected by the local White Citizens' Council. She immediately recognized them. Looming above was the photo of Parks, King, and Horton sitting together at Highlander in 1957, under the headline "Martin Luther King at Communist Training School."

Parks linked arms with her old Montgomery comrade Ralph Abernathy to walk the final blocks alongside Ralph Bunche and Martin and Coretta King.

They were heading into the downtown district when from the upper-story windows of an office building leaflets came tumbling down on the heads of the marchers, falling like huge flakes of snow on the sidewalk. The flyers were miniature versions of the billboards they had passed on the road: "Martin Luther King at Communist Training School." FBI agents monitoring the march reported the paper barrage to Director Hoover at headquarters.

When they reached the Alabama state capitol building, Guy Carawan was already there, with Belafonte, Joan Baez, Peter, Paul, and Mary, and other musicians warming up the crowd with freedom songs. There was a tremendous spirit of joy and pride as an estimated twenty-five thousand people spread to overflow the capitol plaza and surrounding streets. The Alabama department of public safety's subversive unit was recording everything.

The official program of speeches began, with remarks from a who's who of the national movement, with special honors for the Alabama activists, including Amelia Boynton. Ralph Abernathy, acting as master of ceremonies, brought Rosa Parks to the podium, introducing her as "the first lady of the movement" to wild applause.

Mrs. Parks came up to the microphone, nervous, her voice soft. She spoke of growing up in Alabama, living in fear of the Klan. Then she switched to the leaflets that had been dropped on the marchers and the billboard standing on the highway, as she denounced the "propaganda" attempting to label Dr. King as communist. She affirmed her own ties to Highlander and attested that it was the place she had learned that "there are decent people of every color."

The climax of the ceremonies was Dr. King delivering a ringing tribute to the perseverance of Black Americans in their quest for freedom and equal rights:

"I know some of you are asking today, 'How long will it take?' I come to say to you this afternoon, however difficult the moment, however frustrating the hour, it will not be long, 'cause truth pressed to the earth will rise again," he exclaimed. "How long? Not long. Because no lie can live forever. How long? Not long. Because the arc of the moral universe is long, but it bends toward justice."

Three days later, during questioning from reporters on television's *Meet the Press*, Dr. King was asked about the billboards plastered along the march route and around Alabama, claiming he had attended a communist training school. After one of the most pivotal and dramatic months in the history of the civil rights movement, King was forced to spend time again refuting the lie.

Meanwhile, in Montgomery, the Alabama Legislative Commission to

Preserve the Peace and the Alabama Sovereignty Commission made plans to use the surveillance recordings they had made of the march and rally at the capitol to produce a documentary. They hired a production company to create the film, whose purpose was "to document Communist infiltration, direction, and control of the march." It was titled *We Shall Overcome*. The goal of the film was to erode congressional and popular support for the voting rights bill.

CHAPTER THIRTY-FIVE

Signatures

With the nation still reeling from the images of hopeful Black voters beaten bloody in Selma, the voting rights bill entered Congress on March 17, 1965, with bipartisan support, including sixty-six cosponsors in the Senate. The president's voting rights bill was surprisingly strong; it "had teeth," as John Lewis described it. The legislation eliminated literacy and character tests as qualifications for registration. There were strong enforcement provisions in the bill, targeting states and counties with a history of suppressing Black suffrage: defined as jurisdictions where less than half the eligible voting population was registered, or had voted, in the 1964 presidential election.

The bill empowered the US attorney general to appoint federal examiners to assume responsibility for qualifying voters in these places, overriding intransigent local registrars, and it provided for assignment of poll observers to assure the security of Black ballots on election day. To curtail any new schemes blocking the path to the polls, these states and counties were also required to submit any changes made in voting procedures to the US Justice Department for review, a procedure called "preclearance."

The legal bedrock of the new voting bill was enforcement of the Fifteenth Amendment, which in 1870 had ensured a citizen's right to vote "shall not be abridged or denied" on account of race or color. The most radical, and contentious, aspect of the bill was that it brought voting regulations and oversight under the purview of the nation's executive branch, removing authority from the states, which, under the Constitution, control voting requirements and procedures in their jurisdictions. This set the stage for another explosive states' rights battle played out in the halls of Congress.

"Let me make myself clear," announced Mississippi senator James Eastland, chairman of the senate Judiciary Committee, who had proudly smothered every civil rights measure sent to his committee. "I am opposed to every word and every line in it." Senator Herman Talmadge of Georgia called the bill "grossly unjust and vindictive in nature," and Louisiana senator Allen Ellender promised "to talk against it as long as God gives me breath."

———◆———

Congress was still wrestling over the bill in early May when Clark, Robinson, and Ponder carried their pencils and stencils to Selma. The city was still shell-shocked from the violence and upheaval of the winter and spring, and many residents were wary of any further agitation. At least 150 Selma and Dallas County citizens who had attempted to register, or joined demonstrations during the recent campaigns, had been fired from their jobs. They had marched proudly to Montgomery, but then had to return home with no US Army to protect them and Sheriff Jim Clark still in charge. They didn't want any more trouble.

Under pressure from the Justice Department, one of the small concessions the Dallas County registrar made to calm protests was to create a registration wait list. Black citizens could sign their names in an "appearance" book and would be given a number, then called to appear for registration sometime later. It required being able to write one's name, in cursive, in the appearance book. Many Black voters could not do that. The handwriting clinics Mrs. Clark came to establish would prime the registration pump for the time when the voting rights bill became law. On that glorious day the gates to registration promised to swing open—no more tests, and federal registrars would be in charge—and those signatures in the appearance book could be traded for official registration certificates.

Yet when Clark and Robinson tried to work through the churches, as was the SCLC method, and enlist local ministers to support the project, they got the cold shoulder. "They didn't want us to teach the people how to write their names," Clark complained. Too many churches had been bombed for hosting movement activities, and the ministers claimed they couldn't take a chance. Clark also suspected that some ministers did not want the white bankers and merchants in town to suspect they were involved in teaching Blacks to write their names in preparation for voting. After a few weeks, even Bernice Robinson had lost patience, as had the other CEP staffers. "They couldn't take the foolishness from those preachers and they left," Clark reported. "I stayed on . . . and trained others to help me do the work."

Mrs. Clark bypassed the nervous ministers and went straight to the people.

The sixty-seven-year-old grandmother walked around the Black neighbor-hoods of the city day and night recruiting. She'd persuade one man, then ask him to bring some friends. The friends brought their friends. Clark took them all to lunch, and while they were eating, she talked to them about registering and voting, what it could mean to them. She held a meeting, gauged interest, and was convinced that people would attend handwriting class if she could find teachers.

Word finally got around to some of Selma's Black schoolteachers, who were on summer break. Clark assured them that the SCLC had money to pay them for their efforts—$1.25 an hour—and she could train them in her name-writing techniques, the ones she and Bernice had perfected in the first citizenship schools.

Annell Ponder came over from Atlanta to help Clark, and Amelia Boynton, Marie Foster, and the Dallas County Voters League intervened to convince some ministers, known to be sympathetic to the movement, to allow the classes to meet in their buildings. Soon fifty Selma schoolteachers and other local women were teaching handwriting classes in church basements and their own kitch-ens. There were two-hour classes in the morning, afternoon, and evening, five days a week. "It didn't take us but twenty minutes to teach a woman to write her name" with the muscle-memory tracing method used in the citizenship schools, Clark boasted.

Still, Mrs. Clark advised her teachers to conceal the purpose of the hand-writing clinics. Preparing to register and vote was still considered a risky act for many in Selma. Septima suggested the classes should be promoted as a self-improvement project, a way to learn how to sign checks, write letters, apply for jobs, and other practical everyday tasks. Handbills distributed around town advertising the clinics did not mention voter registration at all.

Clark and Ponder managed to slip in a good dose of citizenship education into the handwriting clinics. Ponder organized the handwriting tutors into a "CEP club" to work with the Dallas County Voters League on registration drives, and those who were heading to the courthouse to sign their names were urged to join the Voters League.

———◆———

Senate advocates of the voting rights bill made their first move the day it arrived in the chamber on March 17. They maneuvered to break the stranglehold Senator

Eastland traditionally exerted on civil rights legislation, setting a time limit on the Judiciary Committee's deliberations. The committee had just fifteen days to report out the bill to the full Senate.

The full Senate was still debating the bill toward the end of May. There were hot points of contention even among supporters of the legislation. Arguments over whether the bill should include an outright ban of the poll tax threatened to tear the coalition of supporters apart. The recently ratified Twenty-Fourth Amendment had banned poll taxes for federal elections, but some states were still requiring payments to vote in state and local elections. Civil rights advocates called for abolition of the poll taxes. The Johnson administration favored doing away with them, too, but wasn't sure Congress had constitutional authority to do so. Republicans were wary of any infringement on states' power to levy taxes.

In another corner were the southern senators hoping to cripple or kill the bill. They realized they didn't have sufficient manpower to sustain a lengthy, exhausting, speechifying filibuster as they had often done in the past. Instead, they launched a different kind of delaying tactic.

For weeks, the Senate chamber was consumed by a deluge of amendments attempting to neuter the bill. The southern senators introduced amendments all day, every day, forcing the body to debate and vote on every single one. How long this would go on, no one knew. There were something like seventy amendments in the hopper for consideration. Three attempts to end debate had already failed. Grim jokes about continuing the debate through Christmas circulated on the floor. The White House was getting anxious.

By the last week of May, Senate leadership had finally tired of the amendment-overload tricks of the southern bloc, and on May 25 they mustered enough votes to invoke cloture on debate. The next day, May 26, the Senate version of the voting rights act, without a ban on the poll tax, was passed by a solid vote of seventy-seven to nineteen. But it was still stuck in the House.

———— ✦ ————

Mrs. Clark would remain in Selma for three months, but no Black family dare let her stay in their house, "because the whites knew me so well, they would have harassed anyone I stayed with." She had to rent a room in a motel. She and Annell Ponder were overseeing dozens of classes, yet until the voting rights bill could get through Congress and become law—and the literacy tests were abolished—the handwriting clinic graduates Clark sent to the Dallas County courthouse to sign their names had no guarantee they would ever be allowed to register. To Clark's dismay, fifty or more Selma teachers and other women involved in the handwriting clinics were fired from their jobs for participating. Some would eventually regain their employment; others never did. In the meantime, Clark had to appeal to Dr. King to send money to buy groceries for those who had been fired.

———— ◆ ————

In early June the House was still working on its version of the voting rights bill. The House Judiciary committee, chaired by civil rights champion Emanuel Celler of New York, had managed to strengthen the bill, most notably with a complete ban on the poll tax, which had been compromised in the Senate, and added protection for civil rights workers. Celler called upon freshman John Conyers of Michigan, the first Black representative to serve on the Judiciary Committee, to testify in support of fortifying—and swiftly approving— the bill. Conyers obliged: "Unless we pass a voting rights bill this year which will quickly and finally secure the vote to all Americans regardless of race," Conyers told his colleagues, "I fear the increased feelings of discontent may reach epidemic proportions." In Conyers's district office in Detroit, his newly hired staff member, Mrs. Rosa Parks, was happily setting up her desk and keeping track of the bill's progress.

But some House members were focused on delaying, not speeding, the bill. As usual, segregationist Howard Smith of Virginia threatened to hold the bill captive in his Rules Committee, but his bluster didn't work this time. While Smith denounced the voting rights bill as a "vendetta" against the southern states—"dripping venom . . . from every paragraph and sentence"—he got the message that his colleagues were not going to tolerate his hostage-taking routine. Facing the prospect of a discharge petition, Smith dawdled for a couple of weeks, held a string of hearings, but then finally, under pressure, released the bill to the full House in early July.

———— ◆ ————

While deliberations over voting rights dragged on in Washington, Esau Jenkins was on the ground, sweating through his white button-down shirt, knocking on doors in the summer heat to find more Black citizens to register. The Charleston County registration office was open for only two days in July, with limited hours, so it was a frantic rush to get people enrolled and almost impossible for working people to make it to the courthouse. The narrow window was a purposeful ploy to make registration inconvenient and cumbersome; he had been complaining about this for years. Now he was threatening to begin picketing the courthouse, pressing for extended evening and Saturday registration hours.

It had been nearly a decade since Esau, Septima, and Bernice had opened the first citizenship class on Johns Island. Now tens of thousands of Black people had passed through the citizenship schools, become first-class citizens and the backbone of the movement all over the South. There were still an estimated two million unregistered Black voters in the southern states. Jenkins had managed to get sixty-six registered in his county during the two-day July registration window. Another eighteen had failed the literacy test. He would sign them up for citizenship classes and prepare them for next time. But this process was too slow. Where was the voting rights bill?

———— ♦ ————

In the second week of July, as the House continued debating the bill, southern congressmen took turns insisting that there were no voting problems for Black citizens in their states. Legislative relief was totally unnecessary. Representative Hale Boggs of Louisiana sat in the chamber, listening to his colleagues' soliloquies. Boggs was a rising star in the Democratic Party, elected House majority whip. He was no integrationist: he had signed the Southern Manifesto after the *Brown* decision, voted against the civil rights bills of '57, '60, and '64. But he had quietly decided to support the voting rights bill. There was something essential about the right to vote he couldn't deny or rationalize away. He was also getting an earful about it at home from his wife, Lindy, and college-age daughter, Cokie, who thought he should take a more public stand in support of the bill. No, he insisted, he wasn't going to stand up and give a speech about the bill, he just intended to say aye when the House clerk called his name.

Late in the evening of another long session of House debate on July 9, 1965, Boggs was listening to one of his Louisiana colleagues make a final assault on the bill, claiming that Black people could vote freely in his home state, that there was no restriction or intimidation. This was a lie, and something snapped in Representative Boggs. He stood to speak.

"I wish I could stand here as a man who loves his state . . . and say there has not been discrimination," Boggs began, and all eyes were upon him.

"Unfortunately, it is not so." In his district, he told his colleagues, there were three thousand eligible Black voters, but less than one hundred were registered. "Can we say there has been no discrimination? Can we honestly say that from our hearts?"

The chamber hushed as Boggs concluded. "I shall support this bill, because I believe the fundamental right to vote must be a part of this great experiment in human progress under freedom, which America is." Boggs returned to his seat as his colleagues gave him a standing ovation. That night, the House voted 333 to 85 to pass the voting rights bill. Among those voting aye were twenty-one southern Democrats.

Lyndon Johnson was not as pleased as he might have been. The House and Senate versions of the voting rights bill were different. The inclusion of a poll tax ban in the House version but not the Senate's meant the bill would need to be reconciled by a conference committee drawn from both chambers. This meant another delay, contentious negotiations that might cripple the bill or place it in limbo. Even if the bill emerged, it would require a return trip to both chambers for approval, risking another chance for detainment in committee or even another filibuster. The opponents were playing for time. Congress would need to be pushed.

President Johnson's mood grew dark as the House-Senate conference committee working on the voting rights bill deadlocked. It was the end of July, and there had been no progress on the sticking issue of the poll tax: the Senate wanted a softer approach, while the House conferees insisted on an outright ban. Neither side would budge and attempts to broker a deal were rebuffed. Congress was itchy to go home. The voting rights bill could die on the conference table.

Exasperated, the president turned to his attorney general to come up with a solution—fast. Attorney General Nicholas Katzenbach devised a legal workaround that might satisfy all factions. In exchange for House liberals removing their poll tax ban amendment from the bill, Katzenbach would substitute legal language declaring that Congress recognized that state and county poll taxes abridged the right to vote, and upon the bill's passage the DOJ would immediately bring suit to stop those states still charging poll taxes. Taking this path through the courts might be slower, but it was a safer way to secure the same result, Katzenbach argued. For this idea to work, the attorney general needed the immediate help of one man: Rev. Dr. King.

With the assistance of the FBI, whose close surveillance tracked King's every move, Katzenbach found King at a hotel in Cleveland. The attorney general explained the possibility of the bill dying in the conference room if not resuscitated soon. If King could issue a statement endorsing the Katzenbach compromise, reassuring liberal House members that he approved of the plan, they might feel more comfortable backing down and accepting it.

Over the phone, King and Katzenbach negotiated the wording of the minister's statement deep into the night. In the morning, the attorney general carried King's endorsement to the conferees: "While I would have preferred that the bill eliminate the poll tax . . . once and for all," King agreed to say, "I am confident that the poll tax provision of the bill—with vigorous action by the Attorney General—will operate finally to bury this iniquitous device."

King's approval was enough to swing the liberal House members on the conference committee toward agreement. Sent back to Congress for approval, the bill was not subjected to any further parliamentary tricks or ideological grandstanding. Even the southern bloc knew the fight was over. By August 4, both chambers had passed the Voting Rights Act of 1965.

President Johnson rushed to sign the act into law just two days after passage. In a nationally televised ceremony held in the Capitol Rotunda, the president proclaimed: "Today is a triumph for freedom as huge as any victory that has ever been won on any battlefield." Surrounding the president's desk at the official signing were the leaders of the major civil rights organizations, including Martin Luther King Jr. representing SCLC and John Lewis of SNCC. Rosa Parks was also there, and they all received a ceremonial signing pen from the president. Lewis would later display his pen on the wall of his living room.

———————— ◆ ————————

Septima Clark was still working in Selma the day the Voting Rights Act was signed, and the moment was sweet. During the summer her handwriting clinics had trained seven thousand Black citizens in Selma and Dallas County to sign their names on the registration appearance book, and each had been given a number. Now they could, and did, trade that number for a registration card.

The "federal men," as Mrs. Clark called the examiners sent by the Justice Department, arrived in Selma just three days after the signing of the Voting Rights Act. Dallas County, with its woeful history of suppression, was one of the first to be assigned federal examiners empowered to register voters. The examiners were volunteer civil servants—Agriculture Department staff, post office employees—who underwent three days of special training before being dispatched to the counties where Black registration was especially low and warranted intervention.

On the first morning, three hundred eager Black citizens lined up early outside Selma's federal building, where the examiners set up an office on the third floor. Many in the line were graduates of citizenship classes or handwriting clinics. The line up the three flights of stairs was long, the wait hot and slow, but there were no threats, no police clubs, just a polite welcome. To the surprise and delight of the Black registrants, they were addressed as "sir" and "madam" when they reached the examiner's office. There was no literacy test, no abstruse questions, just a simple form asking for their name, address, years of residency, and other basic information. If they could not read or write, the examiners offered to read the questions to them and write down their answers. That was it. Then they stood, raised their right hand, and swore that the answers were true and they would abide by the laws of Alabama. One hundred and seven Dallas County Black citizens became registered voters on that first day; more were in line at closing time and were invited to return the next morning.

Unlike the county registration office, which was open only one or two days a month with short hours, this federal site would be open every business day, nine to five, until everyone who wanted to register was accommodated. Mrs. Clark packed up her pencils and teaching materials and returned to Atlanta, satisfied with the auspicious beginning.

On the first day an astounding 1,144 new names were placed on the voting rolls of the initial nine southern state counties placed under federal supervision. By the end of the first week, that number rose to seven thousand new registrants. Esau Jenkins reported that 1,207 Black citizens of Charleston County had registered to vote in just three days. By the end of August, just three weeks after the signing of the Voting Rights Act, at least sixty thousand new Black registrants had been enrolled by federal examiners in four of the southern states targeted for intervention—Alabama, Georgia, Louisiana, and Mississippi.

This is not to say all ran smoothly. To minimize friction with southerners in Congress, the Justice Department did not take an aggressive enforcement stance and declined to send registration examiners to many of the counties where intervention was sorely needed. The DOJ tried to persuade districts to comply voluntarily, and some did, but others remained obstinate. Soon it became obvious that more examiners would need to be dispatched to more places, and the Justice Department only reluctantly intervened. Physical and economic reprisals against Black voters who registered persisted, yet the Justice Department's prosecution of this harassment, now a federal crime, was spotty.

Still, the gates were opening. Thousands of Mrs. Clark's citizenship school graduates across the South, who had been prepared by the classes but then turned away or rejected by the registrars—and punished for trying—could now, with pride and dignity, register to vote. They need not be frightened to take hold of the first-class citizenship she had promised to them.

CHAPTER THIRTY-SIX

Eyes on the Prize, Hold On

S ome might have thought Septima Clark's work was done. The Voting Rights Act had abolished the registration literacy tests, eliminating the need for the basic reading and writing lessons at the heart of the citizenship classes. The act also made it a federal crime to deprive any person of their right to vote—with a penalty of up to five years in prison and a steep fine—so Black citizens should begin feeling safer registering and going to the polls. The Civil Rights Act of 1964 outlawed racial discrimination practices.

It might be time for Mrs. Clark to go home to Henrietta Street, as the movement had achieved several of its major goals. Indeed, many white Americans believed the civil rights crusade had, with enactment of the pair of federal civil rights laws, accomplished all it needed to do, should declare victory, and retreat into history. Mrs. Clark disagreed.

The citizenship classes had always been about more than simply voting and literacy. It was training for the mind and spirit, learning a new way of thinking, feeling empowered and self-reliant. It was about learning to question, analyze, and take action. Moving from what is, as Myles Horton liked to say, to what ought to be. It was about building confident, competent, and engaged Black citizens who took responsibility for their communities and demanded a voice in their government. That kind of education was still vital and needed, perhaps more than ever.

While the SCLC praised the CEP as "our most vital and positive program" at the 1965 annual meeting and highlighted Clark's handwriting clinics in Dallas County as the program's major contribution of the year, Andrew Young, now SCLC's executive director, knew that the Voting Rights Act had shifted priorities within the organization. "It made people think it [CEP] was no longer necessary," Young observed. It would be up to Clark and Cotton to prove that their education program was still relevant.

Mrs. Clark knew her work was not done, and she was determined to continue. The Black people of the South, her people, needed to learn how to make good use of their vote, how to improve their communities, and benefit by their citizenship. She was sixty-seven years old, her hair completely gray, her eyes weakening. She needed orthopedic shoes, had trouble with her teeth, was bothered by allergies. She had a history of heart attacks. Her work was physically taxing: so much travel, irregular meals, uncomfortable beds. In her travels on behalf of the movement she had been in a train wreck, a bus crash, and an airplane accident. She had been arrested, tear-gassed, and dynamited. She'd faced down the Klan and knelt in prayer before a sheriff's armored tank. As long as she was needed and could stay steady on her feet, she would keep working.

There was still strong demand for citizenship schools and leadership development, so Clark continued training teachers at Dorchester—including some of her most promising Selma handwriting clinic instructors—and traveling through the southern states, visiting classes and assessing the needs of different communities. Bernice Robinson and Annell Ponder made their rounds in the field, supervising CEP teachers and helping organize voters' leagues and community improvement clubs. Robinson continued working with Esau Jenkins on his leadership training initiatives in the Lowcountry. Ponder maintained her contact with Victoria Gray, Fannie Lou Hamer, and the Mississippi Free Democratic Party, where more candidates prepared to run for office, an agricultural labor union was forming, and community cooperatives were in the works.

Back at the SCLC offices in Atlanta, Clark and Cotton refined the citizenship class curriculum to incorporate lessons about the civil rights and voting rights laws, adding information on the new federal health, education, and jobs programs of President Johnson's Great Society and War on Poverty. Citizenship teachers were encouraged to discuss these programs with their students and instruct them in how to access these benefits to which they, as citizens, were entitled.

Clark and Cotton also gradually retooled the CEP curricula to mesh with SCLC's new focus on economic inequality, housing, and employment opportunity—the next frontier for the movement. The explosion of frustration and rage in the Watts neighborhood of Los Angeles, which erupted just days after the Voting Rights Act went into effect, was stark evidence that the movement needed to broaden its geographic focus and policy vision, beyond the South and beyond voting, into economic discrimination. As Ella Baker had said in Mississippi the year before: "Even if segregation is gone, we will still need to be free; we will still have to see that everyone has a job. Even if we can all vote, but if people are still hungry, we will not be free."

Citizenship schoolteachers and supervisors around the South began to utilize their administrative experience to bring those anti-poverty programs into their communities. CEP teachers became paid program managers for Head Start preschools, day care centers, health clinics, and employment training bureaus. Esau Jenkins worked to get a Head Start program on Johns Island and was later appointed to the Office of Economic Opportunity regional advisory committee. CEP teacher Viola McFerren brought the first Head Start preschools to Fayette County, Tennessee. Ethel Grimball, the first teacher on Wadmalaw Island, and Victoria Gray in Mississippi became Head Start directors in their regions.

Their former students formed the nuclei of voters' leagues, which, thanks to increased Black registration and voting power, were gaining greater political leverage. They were also instrumental in forming local citizens' clubs, whose petitions for improved roads, street lighting, water, sewage, and electricity were suddenly given more attention in city halls.

———— ♦ ————

In the spring of 1966, Clark and Cotton were back in Alabama, preparing Black communities to use their hard-won registration cards to vote in the state's Democratic Party primary elections. The 1966 elections would be the first test of Black voter participation since the enactment of the Voting Rights Act. Residents were both nervous and excited, especially in counties where Black candidates, including several CEP teachers, were running for office. Still, a hundred years of violent suppression were hard to erase in the minds of many going to the polls for the first time.

Mrs. Clark was in Wilcox County, a poor, rural area southwest of Selma, where no Black Americans were registered to vote in 1964, as a history of brutal white suppression kept the population frightened. Now, since the Voting Rights Act, there were 3,600 registered, half of all eligible Black citizens in the county. Mrs. Clark spent a week in the county seat of Camden encouraging people to vote but reported that "many Negroes panicked on election day." She understood their anxiety. "It was hard for them to come off a plantation and be sworn in by the plantation boss who was a poll watcher." Who would protect them from his reprisals when they returned home to their shack on the plantation? The federal men couldn't be everywhere. Clark noticed that even the poll watchers, integrated for the first time—one white, one Black, sitting next to each other at a table—were nervous. "Their hands shook as they tried to check the rolls," she recalled.

Clark was almost amused to watch the discomfort of a white farmer who voiced his disgust at being forced to stand in line at the voting booth with Blacks, but she was grateful there was no violence. "A great force was at the polls," she wrote to a friend, "because we had no bloodshed."

For all the excitement, the Alabama primary was a disappointment. Lurleen Wallace, wife of Governor George, won in a landslide. Twenty-four Black candidates in Alabama did well enough to qualify for the primary's runoff contest later in May, but only a few managed to win nomination. In response to the Selma demonstrations, the Montgomery march, and the Voting Rights Act, a concerted campaign to register a million new white Alabama voters succeeded in diluting the strength of the Black vote. And some Black voters, so new to the political process, could not conceive of anyone but a white man holding office; it was too strange a concept. They just thought that was "the way it's supposed to be," Clark observed sadly. To the disappointment of Alabama movement activists, the Black vote did not rally to support Black candidates.

Despite these disappointments, one sweet victory of this election cycle was the decisive role Black voters in Selma and Dallas County played in defeating Sheriff Jim Clark's bid for reelection. They swung their support to his moderate white challenger, who promised to treat them fairly and appoint Black deputies. The vote sent shock waves through Alabama: the Black voters of Dallas County ousted the man who'd beaten them on the Pettus Bridge.

Clark and Cotton traveled on to Sunflower County, Mississippi, in early May 1966, where Victoria Gray was conducting a political education workshop, bringing together MFDP delegates and CEP teachers and students in advance of that state's primary election. A number of CEP teachers were on the ballot, including Holmes County farmer Ralthus Hayes, running for Congress. Two CEP teachers in Greenwood had already mounted campaigns for mayor and the city commission, and Fannie Lou Hamer was planning a run for the state legislature in the next cycle.

Clark brought with her the hard lessons of the Alabama primary, where registration had soared yet support for Black candidates was weak. Threats of eviction and job loss still frightened Black voters from confronting the white power structure. Clark and Cotton suggested the Freedom Democrats begin workshops to introduce their candidates to the public, organize street captains, poll workers, and observers to counteract white intimidation. Outside the church where the workshop was being held, the Sunflower police chief and two deputies circled around in a squad car, a machine gun conspicuously displayed on the front seat.

The white political establishment had found there were other ways, besides direct intimidation, to stymie Black aspirants to elected office. In the fall of 1965, SNCC national communications director Julian Bond was elected to the Georgia state legislature as a representative from Atlanta. The all-white legislature refused to seat him, ostensibly on account of his opposition to the Vietnam War and the draft. Bond's views were deemed unpatriotic and a violation of his oath of office, so the legislature wouldn't allow him to take the oath. Bond took the legislature to court, but the Alabama federal circuit court ruled his ejection was not a violation of his freedom of speech. In 1966, the US Supreme Court overruled this decision, determining Bond had been unlawfully denied his seat in the legislature.

In the fall of 1966, Bond would be running again for the seat he had been forced to vacate—and he would win again—and would serve in the Georgia legislature, as a delegate and senator, for the next two decades. But the machinations used to dilute or deny Black electoral power—refusing to seat duly elected officials, the creation of gerrymandered and at-large districts that diffused the Black vote and made electing Black candidates more difficult—would persist.

———— ✦ ————

Esau Jenkins wore many political hats but held no official elected office. Still, the Black residents of Charleston County and the Sea Islands looked to him as their representative, their advocate, and leader. As Jenkins made his rounds in the summer of 1966, attending meetings, organizing projects, his presence was announced by his white and green Volkswagen minibus chugging up the road, the vehicle with his personal motto painted on the back panel: "Love is Progress, Hate is Expensive."

Jenkins would be the first to acknowledge that progress was also expensive but worth the cost. He was working hard to bring federal dollars from the government's anti-poverty programs into his region to help his neighbors. He had already established a Head Start program and was applying for funds for a day care center. Flexing the power of his political organizations, he had pressured the city to hire the first Black bus drivers and garbage truck drivers, the kind of steady public service jobs his community needed. And at long last his Citizens' Committee of Charleston County was about to open a credit union, with the goal of freeing Black residents from the discrimination, exorbitant rates, and even retribution they faced from white-owned banks. A credit union could help stimulate homeownership and business development, and the area's citizenship schoolteachers and students were among the first to join. Keeping money within the Black community and expanding job opportunities had always been a priority for Jenkins, beginning with the humble cooperative grocery store in the front of the old Progressive Club building, where the first citizenship class met behind its shelves. Now Bernice Robinson served as an officer of the Community Owned Federal Credit Union.

Jenkins was also organizing intense voter registration drives while expanding his second-step programs to train Black southerners to participate in the political process, whether as voters, campaign managers, or candidates for office. Before the primary and general elections, his Citizens' Committee of Charleston held candidate forums and studied the background and platforms of those running for office, so voters could make informed choices. He also ran a series of voter preparation workshops for illiterates. These people had not attended citizenship school classes, but now that the registration literacy test had been abolished, they could vote. Recognizing that those lacking literacy skills could distinguish numbers more easily than letters, the workshops taught them how to identify the candidates they wanted to vote for by the number of the box with the candidate's name printed on the ballot. They practiced pulling the lever corresponding to the numbered box on a model voting machine.

Another semester of his South-wide Voter Education Internship would soon begin, bringing a new cadre of community organizers from around the South to his Sea Island Center on Johns Island. He took pleasure in knowing the center had also become a place for the island's young people to gather, play basketball, roller-skate, and dance to a record player.

Jenkins served on so many boards and committees, it was hard to keep count: the Progressive Club, his church, the Citizens' Committee and its various offshoots, the Credit Union, the Charleston NAACP, the Highlander Center, the national SCLC board, as well as the SCLC staff as a field secretary for South Carolina. He had recently returned from Washington, DC, where he represented South Carolina at the White House Conference on Civil Rights. Dr. King had published a tribute to him and visited his home on the island. He was featured in a *National Geographic* article.

Jenkins was beloved—the Moses of his People, as Septima Clark called him—but also envied, and he certainly had rivals, detractors, even enemies in the region. Yet even his challengers gave him begrudging respect. They watched him drive his van to his many appointments and projects, his meetings and workshops and protests, spreading his stubborn mantra of love and progress by word—as painted on his van—and by deed.

———————◆———————

Myles Horton was still partnering with Jenkins on the Highlander-sponsored South-wide Voter Education Project at the Sea Island Center as well as other initiatives.

Horton also maintained his ties to SNCC, as the Highlander Center in Knoxville hosted their staff meetings, retreats, and even a poetry workshop. But with the departure of Bob Moses and his emphasis on education and the internal divisions riling the organization, Horton's role as an adviser was ending. John Lewis would soon be rejected by the organization he had helped found, replaced by a new leader, Stokely Carmichael, and a new policy of Black-only membership and participation. The organization took a new motto: Black Power.

Horton pivoted Highlander's attention back to its roots, helping poor whites in Appalachia. He increasingly saw the effects of poverty as the root cause of societal problems for Blacks, whites, Hispanics, and Native Americans and believed Highlander could contribute more by working with its own poor white neighbors. Horton steered Highlander to look inward into its home territory and also outward to liberation struggles in South America and Africa.

Even if Highlander was no longer so deeply involved in racial matters, its enemies didn't seem to notice or care. Threatening phone calls arrived day and night, and the Klan paraded outside Highlander's home in Knoxville. (Horton hosted a festive garden party on the lawn to watch the Klan spectacle, which embarrassed the hooded marchers.) In the fall of 1966, two firebombs crashed through the center's windows. The "King at Communist Training School" billboards were still posted on roads around the South, and there were also postcards circulating with the same image. One candidate for office in the South Carolina legislature campaigned on a promise to investigate the voter registration activities of Esau Jenkins's Progressive Club, claiming Highlander was using the project to spread communism. The Tennessee legislature was seriously contemplating another investigation of Highlander as a subversive organization, with the intent of closing it down. Again.

Like Horton, Guy Carawan felt the sudden chill of being a white man in the Black freedom movement. He continued arranging music festivals of traditional Black music, working closely with Bernice Johnson Reagon of the Freedom Singers, and he brought the Moving Star Hall Singers to the Newport Folk Festival and the Smithsonian Folklife Festival in Washington, DC. But Guy and Candie left the South, at least temporarily, to spend two years in New York City producing books and record albums on the history of the movement through its songs and the singers and storytellers of Moving Star Hall.

Song had nourished and sustained the movement, but after the Selma-to-Montgomery march, there was less singing and more arguing, especially among the young activists of SNCC. It saddened Carawan, but he understood. "A lot of these same people who, a few years earlier, had made up these songs and done a lot of singing, along with strategy and tactics and the real moving, decided—We're too bitter to sing anymore."

CHAPTER THIRTY-SEVEN

Sister Help to Trim the Sail

I n the fall of 1966, Septima Clark joined another movement, one she had belonged to in spirit all her life. Long before it was called "women's liberation," she had been a single mother, sole breadwinner, and an independent working woman for years. She had been raised in a household where her mother was the boss, made the family decisions, and stood her own ground when white men tried to intimidate her.

Now in her late sixties, Mrs. Clark chafed under the expectations that women were to be seen but not heard, be decorative but not decisive, content to do the work and remain in the background. Yet she would admit that when she first became politically active with the NAACP, she let men do the talking. She held her tongue, kept her thoughts to herself. She, too, had to learn to speak up, and she spent the rest of her career trying to coax Black women out from the shadow of their men.

She knew the civil rights movement was sustained by women: in the mass meetings, the phone trees and kitchen brigades, on the picket lines and marches. She already knew what historians would later recognize: in the modern civil rights struggle, men led, but women organized.

Rarely did women receive the credit they deserved. Not just Ella Baker and Rosa Parks, Diane Nash and Dorothy Height, Ruby Hurley and Dorothy Cotton, who worked with the national organizations. But all the state and local leaders who executed policies and created campaigns, who mobilized the grass roots. The church women, the club women, the sharecroppers, the maids, teachers, and housewives who risked all to organize a boycott against segregated stores in their city, a petition drive to desegregate the schools, who joined a voter registration line at the courthouse or taught a citizenship class. They were the true commanders who remained on the ground, guiding their communities, long after the out-of-town movement leaders had left. Women were the foundation of the movement, and it had been Clark's mission to expand and solidify that foundation by training thousands of local women, encouraging them to find their voice. "I think the civil rights movement would never have taken off if some women hadn't started to speak up," she would say later.

A decade before, in those first meetings on Johns Island, she had seen Esau Jenkins, a man she loved and admired, simply dismiss the comments or suggestions of any woman who had the temerity to speak up. In the intimate space of the women's dorm rooms at Highlander or Dorchester, Clark had heard women—many away from their homes and families for the first time—talk candidly among themselves about how they concealed their thoughts from their menfolk. It wasn't much better in the high sanctum of the SCLC's executive council, where she and Dorothy Cotton were rarely able to express their opinions, and those comments were often ignored or dismissed with laughter by the male ministers, even Dr. King.

In the fall of '66, Mrs. Cotton was finally promoted to become director of the CEP, after three men had held the position. Septima was glad; Dorothy deserved the post. She was devoted to the work of CEP and had been doing much of the administration anyway. Cotton was already in King's inner circle of advisers and shared a special relationship with him—a closer relationship than Mrs. Clark possibly realized. That it had taken so long for the men of the SCLC to place an experienced woman at the head of one of its departments was not surprising. It fit Ella Baker's description of the SCLC from years before, Clark felt, and was indicative of the entire movement's dim view of women with brains.

Clark eagerly accepted Virginia Durr's invitation to join her in Washington at a national conference of the recently formed National Organization of Women (NOW) in the fall of 1966. Durr arranged for Clark to stay in a luxurious suite in "a swell hotel"—very unlike her usual travel accommodations—and to give an address before the conference on "The Need of Women Challenging Male Dominance." Septima didn't get to enjoy the comforts of her suite very much, she was so busy in meetings and discussion groups, reporting on the conditions Black women were living under in the South. Clark found the experience satisfying, surrounded by mostly white, northern feminists eager to learn about the trials of Black southern women. She would not burn her bra but would eagerly return for NOW meetings as she embraced this other struggle for equality.

The CEP program was now led by women, but Mrs. Cotton took the reins at a difficult time. The most recent Field Foundation grant was coming to an end, and Field officials warned that its support of the program would decline and, in the near future, end. Additional funding sources needed to be cobbled together and a new vision for the program articulated.

Cotton and Clark worked up a series of grant proposals, moving the CEP into a second phase. They presented plans to enhance the CEP's basic literacy training with lessons in politics and community organizing, consumer education, social service support opportunities, health care, and family planning. Voter registration was still important, but not primary, as the doors to registration had sprung open. CEP teachers would concentrate on breaking the next barrier restricting the progress of Black communities: poverty.

As the SCLC broadened its scope into economic justice, launching a Poor People's Campaign and Operation Breadbasket, it moved into Chicago to organize the city's Black ghettos around housing and job demands. The CEP followed with an ambitious scheme of classes emphasizing literacy for job training. Many Black southerners who had migrated to the North for greater opportunity were held back by the inferior education they had received in their home states. The CEP classes offered remedial reading, writing, arithmetic, and communication skills directly related to obtaining jobs. In the citizenship school tradition, the instructors of these classes were local people who could relate to the students and serve as role models. The CEP's education template was simple and adaptable, and the classes were popular, though the SCLC's foray into Chicago was less successful and rather short-lived. The targeted strategies that had worked in the South, whose culture and politics the leaders of SCLC instinctively understood, did not translate well in the colder climes of northern cities. And Dr. King's call for a deeper economic restructuring, a more fundamental war on poverty, was more disturbing to the comfort of northern liberals than battling Jim Crow in the distant South had been.

———————◆———————

At this point, the new leaders of the Student Nonviolent Coordinating Committee had jettisoned the concept of nonviolence. They had seen too much violence and not enough justice. Those who still held to the old credo of a pacifistic, integrated, "beloved community" were forced out of SNCC: John Lewis went back to college; Bernard Lafayette joined SCLC as a program director; Bevel was already on the SCLC staff; Julian Bond was in the Georgia legislature. Robert Moses, traumatized by his experiences and disappointments in the movement, changed his name to Parris (his middle name), moved to Canada to escape the Vietnam draft, and would soon relocate to Africa.

Stokely Carmichael, born in Trinidad and raised in New York City, became the head of SNCC, replacing the old leadership with his own followers, the fellows Mrs. Clark called the "Black Power Boys." Carmichael was making speeches and appearing on TV preaching Black Power, denouncing nonviolence, challenging Dr. King as weak.

Septima could understand why many of the young people of SNCC were angry and distrustful of white people, after being beaten and tortured in prison, watching their friends and comrades murdered or maimed. They had never raised a hand in their own defense, just went limp and were carted off to jail, singing freedom songs. They had accomplished a great deal but now were disillusioned—and bitter—that reliance on voting and changing laws had not immediately brought about the fundamental changes they had imagined. The South wasn't suddenly transformed.

That's not how change works, Mrs. Clark tried to explain to Carmichael when she invited him to dinner in Atlanta to talk. Clark admired Carmichael in many ways: he was an imaginative and fearless, if impulsive, organizer, but she thought he was arrogant and often failed to think things through. "Can't you find something else to tell these young men to do other than to have them going around with their fists clenched saying Black Power and intimidating black people up and down Auburn Avenue?" Clark asked him. "Don't you think you could train them to something better than take sticks and knock out the windows of these merchants?" Carmichael just laughed.

Mrs. Clark did agree with Carmichael on one policy issue, as did Dr. King: the war in Vietnam. She deplored the way tens of thousands of young Black men were being drafted out of high school to fight in Vietnam while they faced discrimination and limited opportunities at home. Too many of the Black boys conscripted "came home in a box like cold meat," she lamented, having given their lives for their country, a country that still did not respect Black men. Clark began working with the American Friends Service Committee in antiwar activities.

Septima was at the Riverside Church in New York with Dr. King in April 1967 when he made his speech denouncing the war. She was proud of his stance. Soon the money for anti-poverty programs would dry up, diverted to fund the war. Eventually northern liberals would stop sending checks to SCLC in favor of supporting antiwar protests. In the meantime, Dr. King lost the support of many white friends for his early opposition to the war. He was criticized in the northern press, and many of his civil rights colleagues vehemently disagreed with his decision to publicly speak out against the war. They thought it was detrimental to the movement.

In late July 1967, Dr. King brought his message of poverty and war to Charleston, at the invitation of Esau Jenkins and the Citizens' Committee of Charleston. Jenkins planned the event as the climax of the Highlander-sponsored Voter Education Internship summer session and the kickoff for a massive voter registration drive. King entered a nervous city that resembled a territory under martial law. In the previous two weeks both Detroit and Newark had exploded in flames and armed conflict—forty dead in Detroit, twenty-six in Newark—with more disturbances still raging in several other cities.

Charleston officials were not pleased the minister was coming to their city. The KKK held a rally on the night before his arrival. Federal, state, and local law enforcement officers were mobilized to keep the peace. The city was on edge. Mrs. Clark, however, was delighted. Dr. King was going to have tea at her house, use it as a quiet place to relax in the afternoon before his speech. It was a great honor to have him come to her humble home. Clark's granddaughter Yvonne, a teenager now, willingly lent Dr. King her bedroom to rest and dress before his speech. The scent of his aftershave lingered for days. Police cars blocked Clark's street while King was there, and armed officers patrolled the area. The neighbors shut their windows and pulled the curtains.

Esau and Septima sat on the stage with the reverend, and about three thousand people crowded into the municipal hall. Dr. King spoke passionately for almost an hour without notes. He mentioned the war in Vietnam in all his speeches these days, but today he knew he also had to address the urban uprisings. "As I look at our brothers and sisters engaging in violence in our cities, I must continue to say—however much they refuse to listen to me—that this isn't the way. From a moral point of view, it isn't the way. From a practical point of view, it isn't the way.

"A riot does more harm to Negroes than to anyone else. So I'm not gonna give you a motto or preach a philosophy of burn baby burn. I'm gonna say build baby build. Organize baby organize."

King urged everyone to use the power of their vote to place people in office who would help the cause of civil rights and equality. But he did not sugarcoat the realities of the situation: "Don't get complacent. We made some strides. We made some progress here and there, and it hasn't been enough. It hasn't been fast enough. We still have a long, long, way to go."

The applause was vigorous, but the atmosphere in the auditorium remained tense. At one point a loud noise, described as a "bang," startled the audience and frightened those sitting on the stage behind King. It sounded like a gunshot. Only King did not flinch.

It had been almost twenty years since Clark was on the stage of the Coming Street YWCA with another controversial speaker, Elizabeth Waring. It had marked the beginning of her friendship with the Warings. Just a few months after Dr. King's visit to Charleston, on January 11, 1968, Judge Julius Waties Waring died in New York. He made his last journey to Charleston to be buried in the family plot in Magnolia Cemetery. Elizabeth was not well enough to make the trip, and Mrs. Clark remembered that only about a dozen white people were present. The judge's nephew, *News and Courier* editor Thomas Waring, declined to attend. But more than two hundred Black people turned out to honor the man they called "Our Judge." A memorial service was conducted by the Charleston NAACP in a church near the cemetery, followed by a long, silent cortege of Black mourners, including Septima, accompanying their judge to his final resting place. The judge's daughter planted a magnolia sapling near his grave. Vandals uprooted the tree. Elizabeth Waring died later the same year, and she was buried next to the judge. "There weren't but nine of us there," Mrs. Clark said sadly.

By early 1968 SNCC had, for the most part, disintegrated. The SCLC was faltering. Fundraising was much harder, and public support was withering. A white backlash to Black advancements, and the urban disturbances, was rising. The war in Vietnam was consuming the nation's resources and attention. Dr. King's opposition to the war had split the movement. The minister was under tremendous strain, his health was suffering, his mood was depressed and volatile. The SCLC staff were squabbling among themselves.

Mrs. Clark was alarmed. She had already written King a series of motherly, or perhaps teacherly, letters urging him to slow down and take better care of himself. "If we are to keep a world renowned leader healthy, wholesome, and efficient, some of the burdens must be shared," she had written to him in the summer of 1967. "You are certainly more valuable healthy than sick, and God help us all if you become exhausted to the point of a non-active person. May God help you to help yourself."

In the late winter of 1968, she wrote to him again. She was distressed by the constant demands by movement activists that King lead every march and demonstration in cities north and south. Not only was it a strain on King, and on the SCLC, but it was also bad for the health of the movement, since it stunted the development of a broader leadership base. The citizenship schools, from their beginning at Highlander, were all about leadership cultivation and training. Giving ordinary people the strength and confidence to lead, learning by doing. So it pained her that the SCLC did not practice this basic tenet of leadership development. "When I heard the men asking Dr. King to lead marches in various places, I'd say to them: You're there. You're going to ask the leader to come everywhere? Can't you do the leading in these places?"

She wrote a letter to King "asking him not to lead all the marches himself, but instead to develop leaders who could lead their own marches," she would later explain. King read the letter aloud at an executive staff meeting, and everyone laughed. "It just tickled them; they just laughed." No one supported her; no one spoke up.

In March 1968, when Rev. James Lawson asked King to come to Memphis to lead a march of striking sanitation workers, Clark urged him not to go. "I just felt that he had disciples in Memphis . . . and those people could go and lead a march. He didn't have to lead them all." She spoke to King about it and wrote another letter to him. She received no reply.

CHAPTER THIRTY-EIGHT

Going Home

S eptima Clark was home in Charleston when she got the call. It was the evening of Thursday April 4, 1968. Dr. King had been in Memphis, preparing
to lead another march of the sanitation workers. As he stood on the balcony of
the Lorraine Motel, he was killed by a single shot from a high-powered rifle.
Mrs. Clark did not cry, not then.

She was too busy to grieve. Her phone rang incessantly that night. Calls and
condolences from friends and colleagues. A young white minister working near
Charleston called, he was anxious about the safety of his family. "They were
afraid they would be hurt as Black people expressed their anger," she explained.
"They were nervous, very much so." She took the minister, his wife, and their
two young children into her home. They slept on the floor of her living room.
One of her Poinsette cousins came to her door, too. The house was full. "We
spent the night, that whole night, talking and working here."

Through the night, Clark was on the phone arranging memorial services
on Johns and the other nearby islands. It was important for the Black communities there to come together to mourn, to let God console them, to cry in one
another's arms. She wanted to make sure they had a place and time to do that.
Across the nation, Black communities expressed their shock and anger in the
streets. There were violent disturbances in 110 cities that night and during the
days that followed.

Bernice Robinson was in the field supervising CEP classes when she
heard the news of King's assassination. Distraught, she jumped into her car
and drove straight to Atlanta to mourn with the SCLC staff. She hoped to
attend a memorial service in Columbia, South Carolina, on her way home,
but the city was placed under curfew and the service was canceled.

In Hattiesburg, Mississippi, CEP supervisor Victoria Gray directed her
community's grief into nonviolent action, organizing a three-day work stoppage
and a weeklong bus and school boycott to protest slow progress in promised

improvements. She wanted to use the tragedy to mourn but also mobilize. That's what Dr. King would have wanted.

Reached by Charleston newspaper reporters that night, Esau Jenkins expressed not only his sorrow but also his fears of what the assassination meant for the future of the movement. King's death would encourage the young militants, the Black Power types, Jenkins fretted. "Now they're going to ask what good has it done for a man to preach nonviolence for eleven years. We just don't have a selling point to persuade the militants now."

Dorothy Cotton had been in Memphis with Dr. King. She flew back to Atlanta just a few hours before the shooting, and was at home, taking a nap, when her doorbell rang. She rushed to the King family house on Sunset Avenue, the street illuminated by the flashing lights of police cars and filled with grief-stricken people. "As I took in this scene, reality sank in," Cotton recalled. "I screamed and screamed as I drove around to locate a parking spot."

Andy Young was in Memphis, standing in the courtyard below the motel balcony when the shot tore through King's neck. In a stunned trance, Young began making necessary arrangements.

The next morning, Mrs. Clark went over to the islands to make further preparations for the church memorial services on Sunday. Afterward, she went to Atlanta for the funeral. She was still too shocked to cry. It wasn't until she returned home after the funeral that the tears began to flow. "When I returned to Charleston and clerks in the store and people on the street asked me about the death and funeral, I could not speak for weeping."

Ralph Abernathy, suddenly elevated to the presidency of the SCLC, vowed that the Poor People's march to Washington that King had planned would go on, now as a memorial to the fallen leader. The SCLC staff, many of whom had expressed strong doubts about the march and had trouble recruiting participants, poured themselves into preparations to distract themselves from grief.

The march was philosophically bold but logistically shaky. Caravans of buses, trains, trucks—and a mule train of wagons—embarked from eight starting points across the country, converging on the capital, where Resurrection City, a tent camp (housing, at one point, seven thousand people), was constructed on the National Mall. The goal was to make the poor visible to Congress and the nation, with demands for a living wage and health care for the most vulnerable Americans. Citizenship teachers across the South participated.

Septima Clark and Bernice Robinson were assigned to coordinate logistics for the caravan's passage through South Carolina. They recruited participants, raised funds, and arranged for transport, food, and supplies. Robinson joined the procession as it passed through the city but then returned to her CEP work.

Myles Horton was excited about the Poor People's campaign. He had met with King to discuss it just days before the assassination and had come away optimistic. Horton believed he'd "glimpsed the future" of a coalition of impoverished people of all races and places bonding together to demand government support for decent lives. The synergy could be powerful. Highlander erected a tent at the Resurrection City campsite, holding workshops and discussions, and Horton posed for a photo of himself napping on the grass, the Capitol dome in the background. Guy Carawan was also at the encampment, performing and leading songs at the Soul Center cultural tent.

But Resurrection City was, for the most part, a disaster. It was difficult to keep everyone housed, fed, and occupied; hygiene, morale, and discipline suffered. Spring rains turned the encampment into a muddy, squalid field. Congress paid no attention to the campers, and the White House ignored them. The goals had been lofty but vague, and the point of it all dissolved. By June, police forcibly cleared the site.

SCLC was broke. The staff was demoralized, without strong leadership or direction. Later in the summer, as the SCLC teetered, Andy Young came up with a radical plan to revive morale and institutional purpose. Instead of relying so heavily upon direct-action confrontations, the good-versus-evil morality dramas that stirred the national conscience, the SCLC needed to return to its grass roots, focusing on the "hard detailed job of organizing and building local power units that can sustain themselves," Young wrote to the SCLC board and staff. These "power units" would take the form of community education centers, based upon what Young considered the most substantial program of the SCLC—the citizenship schools.

Young pointed to the thousands of community leaders trained as CEP teachers who could anchor citizen education centers in counties across the southland, providing literacy and job skills tutoring, consumer education, health and family planning classes. The permanent centers could also serve as incubators for economic development initiatives, a clearinghouse for federal program enrollment, and a meeting place to plan political action. The work of the centers would be based on the philosophy of the citizenship schools, allowing local communities to define their own problems and needs but equipping the staff with the tools and information required to guide the process. Young presented his ambitious plan to the SCLC board, but it was never realized.

———————◆———————

Though Black registration in the southern states surged—from 2.6 million registered voters in 1966 to 3.1 million in 1968—the 1968 presidential election set the movement back to a significant degree. George Wallace inflamed the campaign with his white-grievance rhetoric, and Richard Nixon ran on a platform of racial fear. Hubert Humphrey, a true civil rights champion, received the great majority of Black votes but was soundly defeated, sandbagged by the Vietnam War and party divisions. The election of Nixon in November 1968 ushered in an administration hostile to civil rights enforcement, curtailing the activities of the DOJ's civil rights division. The Nixon White House also dismantled the Office of Economic Opportunity, which had funded important community development projects, while a more conservative Congress took hostile aim at specific programs benefiting Black neighborhoods. In petty revenge for her Mississippi Free Democratic Party campaign to unseat him a few years before, Senator John Stennis launched a fraud investigation of Victoria Gray's Head Start program in Hattiesburg.

Yet there were hopeful signs sprinkled across the election map, emerging from the grass roots. The number of Black elected officials in the southern states had quadrupled since enactment of the Voting Rights Act, from fewer than one hundred at all levels of government in 1965 to 385 by the end of 1968; by 1972, the number southern Black office holders would swell to 873.

That year, Shirley Chisholm of New York became the first Black woman to win a seat in Congress. And across the South, hundreds of Black candidates, including CEP graduates and teachers, ran for state, county, and municipal offices. Twelve Black candidates were elected to the Georgia state legislature; nineteen won contests for justice of the peace in Alabama. The first Black man elected to the Mississippi state legislature in a century took his seat, another was elected a county supervisor, and fifteen Black candidates became election commissioners across the state. Five Black candidates won election to city councils in Arkansas. Many of these campaigns were aided by the political organization classes offered by Bernice Robinson, Esau Jenkins, and Victoria Gray in addition to comprehensive Black candidate workshops run by the

SCLC, the Voter Education Project, and Highlander. These efforts taught first-time candidates and neophyte voters how to work within the political system.

The CEP staff also began spreading the gospel of economic independence to Black communities. In their visits to CEP classes in the field, Clark and Robinson encouraged the formation of credit unions and economic cooperatives as engines of community self-sufficiency and growth. Jenkins had championed these concepts for years, and they were now taking off. In the fall of 1967, former CEP teacher Fannie Lou Hamer organized the Freedom Farms Cooperative in Sunflower County, Mississippi. With support from donors she purchased forty acres—later expanded to almost seven hundred acres—of prime Delta farmland and a began a "pig bank" to provide food to about 1,500 poor families. The coop wasn't just a humanitarian effort, it was political as well, defending Black Mississippians' hard-won voting rights, still jeopardized by economic retaliations: "Where a couple of years ago white people were shooting at Negroes trying to register," Mrs. Hamer explained, "now they say, 'go ahead and register—then you'll starve.'"

In Alabama, a farm machinery co-op was spearheaded by CEP grads. In isolated Gee's Bend, which hosted several citizenship classes, Black women formed a co-op to market their extraordinary quilts, created from used overalls and other old clothing fabrics. Another Alabama CEP teacher prepared fifty local residents for the federal post office examination, taking advantage of the equal opportunity provisions of the 1964 Civil Rights Act. In Augusta, Georgia, a mother and daughter pair of CEP teachers opened the Southland Sewing Center, which recruited volunteer instructors to train students in marketable sewing skills. Local families donated sewing machines and irons, a textile mill donated cloth, and the hats, aprons, and children's clothes made by the sewing center were sold to the community at "pay what you can" prices.

Cotton and Clark continued monthly training sessions, now sometimes held at the Penn Community Center in Frogmore, South Carolina, but attendance in the citizenship school classes was dropping. In 1969 funding for the CEP hit a crisis stage, as the Field Foundation reduced its funding and placed a requirement for matching funds as a condition of support. Cotton had to scramble to meet payroll, aided in part by a surprise check from Governor Nelson Rockefeller of New York (a devoted benefactor to the movement), which helped the CEP limp into 1970. Still, in late 1969, sixty-one citizenship teachers were actively holding classes in eight states, and in mid-1970, seventy teachers were operating classes in six states. The last teacher training session at Dorchester, where Clark and Cotton prepared thirty-two people from four states to lead their communities, closed in the spring of 1970. The Citizen Education Project came to a quiet end.

Most of the senior staff began leaving the SCLC that year. Andy Young quit his post as SCLC executive vice president to run for Congress in Georgia's fifth district around Atlanta. He won the Democratic primary but lost the general election. Bernice Robinson, having completed a training course in community development management at the University of Wisconsin, left the CEP in early 1970 to become a supervisor for the South Carolina Commission for Farm Workers, working with Volunteers in Service to America (VISTA) recruits. She remained active in Esau Jenkins's projects, serving on the board of the Community Owned Federal Credit Union, the Citizens' Committee, and the Charleston Political Action League.

Dorothy Cotton stayed on at the SCLC a while longer, then left to become director of the Head Start program in Birmingham and surrounding Jefferson County, Alabama. She subsequently joined the staff of Atlanta's first Black mayor, Maynard Jackson.

Myles Horton also retired as executive director of Highlander in 1970, stepping away from the center's day-to-day administration but remaining deeply involved in policy and programming. Soon he would move with the center to a site in New Market, about twenty-five miles outside Knoxville, where a new Highlander campus was being built on a hilltop, with a view of the mountains.

In the spring of 1970, Septima Clark also decided it was time to leave. The SCLC gave her a testimonial banquet at the now-desegregated Francis Marion Hotel in Charleston. "The air has finally gotten to the place that we can breathe it together," she told the guests who feted her with tributes and presented her with the SCLC's Martin Luther King Jr. Award, inscribed: "To Septima Poinsette Clark for Great Service to Humanity."

Fifteen years after she had begun working with Esau Jenkins on his idea for a literacy school, Mrs. Clark was going home. The citizenship school program she had built had formally trained roughly twenty-five hundred citizenship teachers in the nine years the program was under the auspices of the SCLC, in addition to the several hundred teachers Clark and Robinson had trained at Highlander. The CEP teachers had organized nine hundred citizenship schools in eleven southern states, conducting over seven thousand classes, enrolling almost twenty-seven thousand people. When combined with the early Highlander-sponsored classes, that number swells to more than forty thousand adult students. Those citizenship teachers and students not only became registered voters themselves, but they also influenced their family, friends, and neighbors to take the risk of registering. By conservative estimates, the citizenship schools directly influenced the enrollment of hundreds of thousands of new voters.

More fundamentally, the program changed lives. Besides acquiring literacy skills—and gaining self-confidence—impoverished and powerless adult students emerged from the citizenship classes with a new sense of identity and political awareness. They were armed with an appreciation of their history, knowledge of their rights, and an understanding of how to demand and utilize those rights. They conveyed that sense of empowerment to their communities.

"These are the people who became your catalysts, who became your inspiration," as Mississippi CEP supervisor Victoria Gray observed, "who were willing to go out on that line, who were willing to go to jail."

The teachers and graduates of the citizenship schools powered the movement. According to Septima Clark, Andy Young described the citizenship schools as "the base on which the whole civil rights movement was built." Those alumni then began leading their communities, running for office, feeling their strength.

"If you look at the Black elected officials and the people who are political leaders across the South now," Young observed a decade after the last CEP class closed, "it's full of people who had their first involvement in civil rights in the citizenship training program."

Before she left the SCLC, Clark made a prescient list of the structural barriers that American Blacks still faced: "Political systems which have code words like 'bussing' and 'welfare' and 'no quota systems' and 'crime in the streets' to signal their fear of Black people," she wrote. "Economic systems which reject so many of the basic human needs of the poor and the weak in favor of the wealthy. Health care systems which provide neither health nor care for the powerless. Legal and penal systems which persistently place large overwhelming numbers behind bars and which place whites in almost all seats of authority."

The struggle was not over.

CHAPTER THIRTY-NINE

Good Chaos

M rs. Clark returned to Charleston in June 1970, but having just celebrated her seventy-second birthday, retirement was not on her agenda. "I only retired from a payroll," she joked to a friend. She had so many meetings and appointments. "I won't change."

She resumed her community work, joined new boards, and took up new causes. She had a busy schedule of lectures and conferences around the country, speaking about education, civil rights, women's rights, and she ran workshops on the Vietnam War for the American Friends Service Committee. She visited colleges to speak to students, continued her association with the National Organization of Women, and became involved with the Black Women's Community Development Foundation, which supported women's groups undertaking political action and leadership training. Along with Ella Baker and Fannie Lou Hamer, Clark participated in the foundation's Black feminist symposium in Chicago in January 1972, which brought together women of different generations and outlooks to discuss goals and strategies for the future.

Closer to home, Clark continued her commitment to health care issues, advocating for community health centers, day care centers for working mothers, and improved facilities for the elderly. She advised Black women employees of Charleston's Medical College Hospital engaged in a bitter four-month strike. When a young girl was killed by a car at a busy Charleston intersection, Clark organized a circle of women to donate a dollar a month to employ crossing guards. She mentored promising young Black high school students, wrote letters to colleges on their behalf, and secured scholarships for them. She worked with her sorority on public health and charitable endeavors.

Septima continued to partner with Esau on political education and mobilization projects and became active in the Charleston Political Action League, which vetted and endorsed Black candidates for office. In the fall of 1969 Esau himself was appointed by Charleston County legislators to fill an empty seat on the Board of Trustees of the District 9 School Board, the local board governing Johns Island schools. It was only a temporary appointment, filling the term of a white man who'd died in office, but Jenkins used his position to advocate for Black students and teachers and help implement federal court orders to finally desegregate Charleston County schools—fifteen years after the *Brown* decision.

A Black man had already won election to the Charleston City Council—there would be six Black council members by 1975—and in the fall of 1970 Jenkins and Clark helped elect local civil rights leader Herbert Fielding to the South Carolina legislature, one of the first three Black representatives to take seats in the statehouse since Reconstruction.

In the next election cycle, Clark signed on as campaign treasurer for a Black woman running for Congress in a South Carolina district near Charleston. Septima knew Victoria DeLee as a fearless movement activist whose home had been riddled with bullets—then burned to the ground—as revenge for her efforts to desegregate her county's public schools. DeLee's campaign literature borrowed a phrase from Shirley Chisholm's slogan, touting DeLee as "Unbossed, Unbought, and Unsold." As expected, DeLee lost the election, but her campaign generated excitement.

In the 1972 elections, both Bernice Robinson and Andrew Young decided to practice what they had preached in the citizenship training sessions: Black citizens must participate in government and take responsibility by running for office. Young again campaigned for Congress, this time winning the seat for Georgia's fifth district, and Robinson made a bid for the South Carolina House of Representatives. She campaigned in the evenings and on weekends, after her regular workdays, shaking hands and discussing issues. She held a "grand crab crack" fundraiser to build interest and a modest campaign war chest. Mrs. Robinson faced skepticism, and opposition, from some local Black politicians but was not deterred. When she was defeated in the Democratic primary, she ran a petition campaign for a spot on the general election ballot. Even though she didn't come close to winning election, she made history as the first Black woman to run for the South Carolina legislature.

———— ◆ ————

In late October 1972, Esau Jenkins was driving back from a meeting at Highlander. One of his young organizing interns was at the wheel. It was dark, maybe slippery. There was a crash; Esau was injured and taken to the hospital. He seemed to be recovering well, keeping up with election news from his hospital bed. But then an aneurysm burst, and he was gone.

Mrs. Clark was in California, where she had spent several weeks as a scholar in residence at a state university. The news was a shock. As she hurriedly packed to leave, she dashed off a postcard to Rosa Parks in Detroit to let her know: "Esau passed on Monday. Am going home for the funeral."

More than a thousand people attended Jenkins's funeral services. Septima was there, together with Bernice. Myles, Guy, and Candie came from Highlander. On the night before the funeral, a celebration of Jenkins's civic life was held at a large church in Charleston: the mayor of the city spoke, as well as elected officials from the county and state. US senator Ernest "Fritz" Hollings attended. Rev. Abernathy of the SCLC gave the eulogy. Bernice Robinson also spoke, representing the officers of the Citizens' Committee of Charleston. Jenkins had changed the political landscape of the South Carolina Lowcountry.

The following day, family, friends, and his beloved islanders sang Jenkins's favorite hymn—"A Charge to Keep I Have"—at the funeral service in his own Wesley United Methodist Church on Johns Island. "I believe Esau would not want this to be a funeral service but a graduation day for him," the officiating minister said. "I know if he could say a word . . . he would talk about Voter Registration. He would talk about the C.O. Federal Credit Union and how it has helped the people. On the eve of this election he would be talking about voting." Esau Jenkins's motto, "Love is Progress. Hate is Expensive," was printed on the funeral program. He was laid to rest in the church cemetery, in the fertile soil of his home island.

———— ✦ ————

In the 1974 electoral cycle both Bernice Robinson and Septima Clark paid homage to their dear friend Esau by doing what he would have wanted them to do. Bernice campaigned again for election to the state legislature. And Septima, who had recently celebrated her seventy-sixth birthday, announced her candidacy for a seat on the Charleston County Consolidated School Board, the same school board that had fired her almost two decades before, when she refused to renounce her membership in the NAACP.

She campaigned with homemade, hand-lettered signs ("for Quality Education Vote CLARK!!!") emphasizing her teaching experience. On election day that November, near the second anniversary of Esau Jenkins's death,

Mrs. Septima P. Clark was elected to represent the city of Charleston on the county school board, becoming the first woman, and only the second Black person, ever to take a seat on the board.

Mrs. Clark became a moral force within the school board, and her fellow board members looked to her as a calming and clarifying influence in their sometimes contentious deliberations. As always, she was soft-spoken but also outspoken, asking hard questions and not accepting flimsy answers.

On the school board, she advocated for better teacher salaries and working conditions. Surrounded by businessmen on the board eager to trim budgets, she emphasized the importance of including music and art—and Black history—in the curriculum, as well as a subject close to her heart—citizenship education. Students needed to be taught "how change comes about," Clark insisted, "to develop their own thinking and not accept unjust things but . . . change them."

In 1978, just past her eightieth birthday, Clark ran for reelection to the Charleston County school board and won another four-year term.

That same year, Clark was awarded an honorary doctorate of humane letters degree from the College of Charleston, whose campus was situated just blocks from the house where she was born. In the nineteenth century, one of the college's trustees, Joel Poinsette, had owned her enslaved father.

"I cannot describe how I felt when they notified me of my nomination to this honor," Clark told a reporter. "It was like being Cinderella . . . just after she puts on her glass slipper. After all, this is the same college the campus of which I have passed so often, not being allowed to enter it as either a student or a teacher."

Until 1967, the college had been whites-only. One of its most distinguished alumni was Judge Julius Waties Waring. Clark was the first Black person awarded an honorary degree by the College of Charleston. At the award ceremony, Dr. Septima Poinsette Clark wore her academic robes with pride and panache.

By the time she retired from the school board in 1982, at the age of eighty-four, Septima had achieved the acceptance and recognition from her native city and state she had been seeking for so long. South Carolina gave her the Order of the Palmetto, the state's highest civilian award. She attended the dedications of a Charleston day care center and a portion of a major downtown expressway, both named in her honor. Clark also succeeded in pressing the state legislature to reinstate at least some her pension, which she had lost when she was forced from her teaching position in 1956. The governor admitted that she and other South Carolina teachers had been "unjustly" fired for their affiliation with the NAACP.

In the wider world, the woman once considered radical and dangerous was lauded as the Mother (or sometimes the Grandmother or Queen Mother) of the Movement. She accumulated award plaques to fill many walls, including the Living Legacy Award from President Jimmy Carter, bestowed upon her at the White House.

"I just tried to create a little chaos," Septima Clark would say, explaining her role in the struggle. "Chaos is a good thing. God created the whole world out of it. Change is what comes of it."

S eptima Clark (1898–1987) After her service on the Charleston school board, Mrs. Clark continued her community work. In declining health, she moved with her sister Lorene to the Sea Islands Health Care Center on Johns Island, a facility established by Esau Jenkins, the Citizens' Club, and island graduates of the citizenship schools. She died there on December 15, 1987. Lorene Poinsette died four weeks later. Today, Mrs. Clark is honored in national and regional museum exhibits, in paintings, plays, and murals, and on the South Carolina state coin issued by the US Mint.

The **Esau Jenkins (1910–1972)** Scholarship Fund, which Septima Clark and Bernice Robinson established in his memory, sent Black students from the Sea Islands and Charleston to colleges around the nation. A bridge linking Johns and Wadmalaw islands is named for him, and Esau Jenkins Village, an affordable-housing development, broke ground in 2024. Jenkins' Volkswagen minibus, with his motto "Love is Progress, Hate is Expensive" painted on the back panel, was restored by volunteers and exhibited on the National Mall in Washington, DC, in 2016. The Jenkins family donated the back panel to the Smithsonian National Museum of African American History and Culture, where it is on display in the museum's permanent collection.

Following her two campaigns for a seat in the South Carolina legislature, **Bernice Robinson (1914–1994)** remained active in political affairs in Charleston, AME church women's organizations, and civil rights movement legacy projects. Robinson earned her living as a VISTA supervisor and frequently lectured about the importance of adult literacy and citizenship education. She remained close to her cousin Seppie.

Myles Horton (1905–1990) lived and worked on the Highlander campus in New Market, Tennessee, for another twenty years after stepping down as director. He traveled widely, visiting liberation movements abroad, while also focusing his attention on the social and economic problems of rural Appalachia.

Myles was buried next to his wife, Zilphia, in the Summerfield cemetery on Monteagle Mountain.

Guy Carawan (1927–2015) served as Highlander's music director until his retirement in the late 1980s. He and Candie continued to perform, write books, record, and produce albums documenting the music of the civil rights movement, the Sea Islands, and Appalachia. At this writing, Candie continues to live in the log cabin they built on the Highlander campus in New Market.

The Highlander Education and Research Center is in its ninety-third year of operation in Tennessee, continuing to train organizers and activists working for social, economic, and environmental justice in the South. Highlander's mission still makes it the target of attacks: In March 2019 the campus was firebombed, destroying an administration building; white supremacist symbols were found painted at the scene. Undeterred, just a few weeks later, Highlander broke ground for its newest building, the Septima P. Clark Education Center.

The version of **"We Shall Overcome"** revised by Zilphia Horton, Pete Seeger, Frank Hamilton, and Guy Carawan was copyrighted in 1960 to protect the song from commercial exploitation, while still encouraging its free use as a liberation anthem. Royalties from commercial use of the song were administered by the Highlander Center's We Shall Overcome Fund, which used the proceeds to support grants to innovative artistic and cultural projects in communities around the South. The song is now in the public domain.

After retiring from the SCLC, **Dorothy Cotton (1930–2018)** held positions as an administrator for Head Start programs, served in the administration of Atlanta mayor, Maynard Jackson, and in 1982 became Director of Student Activities at Cornell University. The Dorothy Cotton Institute, established in 2008 in Ithaca, New York, continues her work in community building and leadership training. The Dorothy Cotton Jubilee Singers carry on her passion for performing Black spirituals and hymns.

Andrew Young (1932–) was elected to three terms in Congress representing the district around Atlanta. He left Congress in 1977 when he was appointed US ambassador to the United Nations by President Jimmy Carter. Young was elected mayor of Atlanta in 1981 and reelected in 1985. Young continues his work through the Andrew J. Young Foundation based in Atlanta.

Rosa Parks (1913–2005) worked in the Detroit district office of Congressman John Conyers from 1965 until she retired in 1988. She continued to lend her active support to a range of social justice causes. Parks was accorded many honors, including the Presidential Medal of Freedom, the Congressional Gold Medal, and over twenty honorary degrees from universities around the world. Several states celebrate Mrs. Parks's birthday (February 4) or the date she refused to give up her seat (December 1) as state holidays.

Ella Baker (1903–1986) left the southern movement in 1967 to return to her home in Harlem but remained an activist, involved in social justice and women's rights campaigns. Among the progressive initiatives which have been named in her honor are a community center for at-risk youth in Boston; a cooperative housing project in Washington, DC; a school in New York City; and the Ella Baker Teacher Training Institute of the Children's Defense Fund, which prepares teachers for the CDF's national Freedom Schools program.

Fannie Lou Hamer (1917–1977) continued her fierce advocacy for voting rights and equality in her native Sunflower County, Mississippi. The Freedom Farms Cooperative she established there provided poor sharecroppers with not only sustenance, but also financial education classes, vocational training, childcare, and housing opportunities. In 1972 Mrs. Hamer was elected a Mississippi delegate to the Democratic National Convention; she was also a founder of the National Women's Political Caucus.

Vera Mae Pigee (1924-2007) moved from Mississippi to Detroit in the 1970s, continuing her work for the NAACP and earning her bachelors degree in sociology, as well as an honorary doctorate for her civil rights leadership.

Robert (Bob) Moses (1935–2021) became a Vietnam War draft resister, moving to Canada and then Tanzania, where he taught mathematics. Returning to the United States in 1976, Moses developed the "Algebra Project," teaching math skills to minority middle and high school students. Moses considered math literacy essential to achieving full citizenship and equal opportunity in the modern world. He based the Algebra Project on the philosophy of the citizenship schools and freedom schools, using it as a community-building project. The credo of the Algebra Project—"Math literacy is the key to 21st century citizenship"—echoes Septima Clark's philosophy of "Literacy Means Liberation."

John Lewis (1940–2020) left SNCC to complete his college education at Fisk University, then continued his work for voting rights as director of the Voter Education Project. He served on the Atlanta City Council for five years, and in 1986 was elected to Congress, representing Georgia's fifth district for seventeen consecutive terms. He was a champion of civil and voting rights protections, and extolled as "the conscience of the Congress."

The **Mississippi State Sovereignty Commission** continued to be funded by the state until June 1973; it was finally abolished in 1977 and its records sealed for fifty years. The American Civil Liberties Union spent two decades fighting to open the files to the public, and in 1998, by court order, the records were unsealed. Revealed in the files was the extent of the Commission's illegal surveillance and investigation methods—information on more than eighty-seven thousand citizens was kept on record—as well as its complicity in the murder of the three Freedom Summer workers in Neshoba County in 1964. Today the files are available online.

Judge J. W. Waring (1880–1968) In 2015 the federal courthouse in Charleston was renamed the J. Waties Waring Judicial Center in his honor.

ACKNOWLEDGMENTS

W hile writing this note of thanks, I took an hour to cast my early vote in the 2024 general election. Accompanying me into the polling place—in my mind and heart—was Septima Clark.

I've spent the past six years thinking about Mrs. Clark every day. It has been my honor to write this book about her extraordinary life's work battling injustice through education, invigorating our nation's democracy by training "first class" citizens to have the confidence and skills to reclaim their voting rights.

Mrs. Clark, and her original collaborators in the Citizenship School project—Esau Jenkins, Bernice Robinson, Myles Horton—have remained unheralded American heroes for too long. With pencils as their weapons against Jim Crow, they helped to construct the twentieth century civil rights movement from the ground up. They, and the tens of thousands of volunteers who participated, as teachers and students, in the more than nine hundred citizenship schools established in the southern states, faced intimidation, economic retribution, and violence for their commitment to the ideal of government by and for the people, and equality under the law. They met that danger with faith, creativity, and resolve. *Spell Freedom* is my tribute to their courage, and my effort to lift up their names and celebrate their legacies.

Sadly, sixty years after the Voting Rights Act was enacted, voting rights are once again endangered, especially for minority citizens. I hope this book gives inspiration to those now on the front lines of defending our most sacred democratic right, and to those organizing their communities to use the power of the vote.

Authors need community to accomplish their task. A writer might sit at her desk for years, toiling in solitude (breaking the silence with occasional unprintable mutterings), but she is not really alone: surrounding her, supporting her, is a constellation of communities, each providing their own kind of sustenance.

Beyond the corners of my little desk in Baltimore I know there is a dedicated community of publishing professionals who've committed their time

ACKNOWLEDGMENTS

and talents to bring *Spell Freedom* into the world. My publishers at Atria/One Signal have been steadfast in their support and generous in their attention. I am grateful to Julia Cheiffetz for her early enthusiasm and eagerness to publish this story. My editors, Alessandra Bastagli and Abby Mohr, applied their formidable red pen skills to these pages, shaping and sharpening the text; associate editor Rola Harb has kept the ball rolling. Publicity director Joanna Pinsker and my marketing team of Dayna Johnson and Aleaha Renee are working their magic to ensure *Spell Freedom* finds its readers. Senior production editor Jason Chappell and production manager Vanessa Silverio have deftly piloted the manuscript through all of its stages, and designer Davina Mock-Maniscalco has given the book a refined appearance. My copyeditor Daniel Seidel and proofreaders Karen Tongish and Kimberly Monroe-Hill have kindly saved me from grammatic embarrassment.

My partner in this and all bookish adventures is my savvy and spirited literary agent, Dorian Karchmar at William Morris Endeavor. Dorian brings her creativity, passion, and navigational skills to all of her projects, most especially this one, and it is a joy to have her by my side. I trust her guidance, cherish her friendship, and admire her discerning ear for the music of a well-tuned sentence. My thanks also to Dorian's able assistant Sophia Bark for keeping us on track.

Another community I want to salute are the scholars who preceded me in investigating Septima Clark and the citizenship schools. For lighting my path, I want to thank: Katherine Mellon Charron for her excellent biography of Clark, and the innovative digital mapping project of Clark's life she produced using materials from the Avery Research Center in Charleston; and David P. Levine, Jerome Franson, Sandra B. Oldendorf, and Deanna M Gillespie for their groundbreaking dissertations on the citizenship schools. Gillespie's book, drawn from her thesis, exploring Black women's political culture and the citizenship schools, was very valuable, as was Francoise N. Hamlin's book about the movement in Clarksdale, Mississippi, and Kim Ruehl's recent biography of Zilphia Horton. The writings of Keisha Blaine on Fannie Lou Hamer, Jeanne Theoharis on Rosa Parks, and Martha Jones on Black women voting activists were illuminating. The scholarship of Tomiko Brown Nagin, Linda T. Wynn, and Nico Slate was very helpful, as were studies by Rhea Estelle Lathan and Alexandra Bethlenfalvy.

The depth and richness of this story is to be found in several archival collections, and I am grateful for the help of many dedicated archivists and librarians. Susan Williams, archivist at the Highlander Education and Research Center, is the institution's faithful memory bank, and she has been a terrific resource for me. At the Moorland-Spingarn Research Center at Howard University, Sonja Woods persevered through the pandemic lockdown, when the archive was shut, to locate and copy Septima Clark's revelatory correspondence with Judge and Elizabeth Waring and speed it to my desk; those letters provide the spine of this story, and I cannot thank her enough. At the Avery Research Center at the College of Charleston, Georgette Mayo, Erica Veal, and Aaisha Haykal have been of immense help, both during my research visit and in answering long distance queries. At the Tennessee State Library and Archives in Nashville, the always-helpful Lindsay Hager found the many boxes I needed, and at the Nashville Public Library, Laura Scott managed to secure the photographs I required even though the library was closed for repairs—superwoman!

At the Wisconsin Historical Society archives Lee Grady and his staff have been eager to share their knowledge of the Highlander collection housed there, and Lisa Marine was of great assistance in obtaining photographs. Thanks to Ross Cooper at the Special Collections Research Center at Appalachian State University; Mathew Turi at the Wilson Library at University of North Carolina, Chapel Hill; and Benjamin Stone at Stanford University Libraries for their help. Shout-out to Malcolm Hale at the South Carolina History Room at Charleston County Public Library for digging up documents to answer some very obscure questions. My thanks also to Norma Berry at Johns Hopkins University for enabling my library research, and Randy Morgan for designing a stunning book website. Very special thanks to Karen Berman who allowed me to use her aunt Ida Berman's beautiful photographs of Highlander and the first citizenship schools.

My archival research was enriched by interviews with people who bring a personal connection to this history. Septima Clark's grandchildren, Yvonne Clark-Rhines and Neri Clark offered their eyewitness accounts and family insights, and I am grateful for their unique contributions. Candie Carawan welcomed me into her home on the Highlander campus, and subsequently spent hours on the telephone with me, in addition to sharing the Carawans' unpublished memoir of the movement. Robin Bates and Phoebe Bates in Sewanee shared dinner, documents, and valuable memories of Highlander, and Mary Barrett Brewer offered details of her father's legal defense of the school. Angelina Butler, Roger Phenix, Harry Boyte, and Bruce Hartford shared their experiences in the civil rights movement, and Sally Hare contributed delicious details of growing up in segregated Charleston.

Several historians of the mid-twentieth century civil rights movement have offered perspective and provided encouragement for this project in lively conversations and correspondence. Taylor Branch has been extraordinarily generous in sharing his insights and his research notes with me, including his interview of Septima Clark. From the beginning of this project Jonathan Eig has been wonderfully supportive and helpful. Conversations with Marjorie Spruill, Diane McWhorter, Patricia Sullivan, Alida Black, Elizabeth Griffith, and Judge Richard and Belinda Gergel were very important contributions to my understanding.

While digital research has become indispensible, I still find it important to do the field work of visiting the places I'm writing about. Making this possible in Charleston was the hospitality of Arlene Shawinsky and Peter Rosenthal, including Arlene's excellent tour of Johns and Wadmalaw islands to see the sites of this story, and Marjorie Spuill provided an exhilarating tour of Charleston in her convertible. In Knoxville, Wanda and John Sobieski provided not only a home base but also valuable connections to Highlander sources. In Nashville, my friends Jeanie Nelson and Will Martin and Margaret Behm and Harlan Dodson took me into their homes and gave me my Tennessee bearings. Jeanie was also my guide to Monteagle and Sewanee, navigating through the mountains in the pouring rain. My New York City family, Babette Krolik and Harry Greenwald, always have a pillow waiting for me.

Writing a book can be a lonely business, and I rely on the love, support—and indulgence—of friends and family to see me through. Enormous thanks to my friends, near and far, who, over the stretch of years, gingerly ask "How's the book going?" and forgive my long silences, declined invitations, and monomaniacal behavior. As ever, my love to Sam Babbitt for being my devoted reader and cheering squad.

It is to my family—my husband and children—that I owe my tenderest expression of gratitude. In the interim between my last book and this one our family has grown, with marriages and births, affording me enormous joy—and happy distraction. My son Teddy and his wife, Becky, welcomed baby Lily, and my daughter Abby and her husband, Alejandro, have enlivened our world with their children, Alessandra and Gavriel. A new generation of future readers—and voters! My brother David has taught us all how to live bravely.

Making this book—and all else in my life—possible and meaningful is my husband, Julian. *Spell Freedom* is dedicated to him. *Ad Astra.*

NOTES

Prologue

1 *Emancipation Proclamation*: Mary McLoud Bethune in *Atlanta Daily World*, June 25, 1954, p. 4; William M. Boyd, "The Second Emancipation," *Phylon (1940–1956)* 16, no. 1 (1955): pp. 77–86. "1 Equality in Our Time: An Editorial," *Los Angeles Sentinel*, May 20, 1954, p. A1; Chicago *Defender*, July 24, 1954, p. 6.

1 *"southern way of life"*: a euphemism for racial segregation used by apologists of the region's Jim Crow discriminatory policies.

1 *"Black Monday"*: Representative John Bell Williams of Mississippi called the day of the US Supreme Court's *Brown* decision in May 1954 "Black Monday" in a speech on the House floor. The term was subsequently popularized by the White Citizens' Councils and other opponents of desegregation.

4 *they could join secretly*: Bernice Robinson interview with Sue Thrasher and Eliot Wigginton, November 1980, published in Eliot Wigginton, ed., *Refuse to Stand Silently By: An Oral History of Grass Roots Social Activism in America 1921–1964* (New York: Doubleday, 1992), p. 245.

4 *"tea and pee together"*: Septima Clark quoting Myles Horton in Clark, *Ready from Within: Septima Clark and the Civil Rights Movement*, ed. Cynthia Stokes Brown (Trenton, NJ, Asmara, Eritrea: Africa World Press, 1990), p. 7.

4 *"Radical Hillbilly"*: see "Bill Moyers Journal; 725; The Adventures of a Radical Hillbilly," 1981-06-05, Public Affairs Television & Doctoroff Media Group, American Archive of Public Broadcasting (GBH and the Library of Congress), Boston, MA, and Washington, DC.

5 *Suddenly, the doors*: Myles Horton with Judith Kohl and Herbert Kohl, *The Long Haul: An Autobiography* (New York: Teachers College Press, 1998), p. 85.

Chapter 1: Monteagle Mountain

7 *a Charleston friend*: the friend was Anna D. Kelly, executive secretary of the Coming Street YWCA in Charleston. Septima Poinsette Clark, with LeGette Blythe, *Echo in My Soul* (New York: E. P. Dutton & Co., 1962), pp. 119–20.

8 *a full scholarship*: Clark, *Echo*, p. 120; Septima P. Clark (henceforth SPC) to Myles Horton, June 21, 1954, Mss. 265, Box 9, Highlander Research and Education Center records (henceforth HREC/Wis), Wisconsin Historical Society, Madison.

9 *improve their lives*: Horton biographical details in Horton, *Long Haul*; Frank Adams with Myles Horton, *Unearthing Seeds of Fire: The Idea of Highlander* (Winston-Salem: J. F. Blair, Publisher, 1975); John M. Glen, *Highlander: No Ordinary School* (Knoxville:

University of Tennessee Press, 1996); Dale Jacobs, ed., *The Myles Horton Reader: Education for Social Change* (Knoxville: University of Tennessee Press, 2003).

9 *race relations*: "Report of Special Highlander Executive Council Meeting," April 27–28, 1953, Box 5, Folder 9, Highlander Folk School Manuscript Collection 1932–1966, Tennessee State Library and Archives (henceforth HFS/TSLA), Nashville.

10 *"school for problems"*: SPC interview with Eugene Walker, July 30, 1976, Interview G-0017, Southern Oral History Program Collection, University of North Carolina, Chapel Hill. "Building in the Democracy Mountains: The Legacy of the Highlander Center," interview of Myles Horton by Danny Collum, in April 1986 issue of *Sojourners*. Reprinted in Jacobs, *Horton Reader*, p. 43.

10 *Ruby Cornwell*: Clark's friendship with Mrs. Cornwell is documented in Clark's correspondence with Judge Julius Waties Waring and his wife, Elizabeth Waring, found in Julius Waties Waring Papers, Moorland-Spingarn Research Center, Howard University (henceforth Waring/M-S). Cornwell's correspondence with the Warings can be found in the Ruby Pendergrass Cornwell Papers, AMN 1039, Avery Research Center for African American History and Culture (henceforth Avery), College of Charleston.

12 *simply astonishing*: SPC describes the incident in a letter to the Warings, July 11, 1954, Waring/M-S; Clark, *Ready from Within*, p. 30.

12 *began dictating*: Horton usually dictated his business letters. HREC/Wis, Part 2, Audio, 807/Al2; examples of Horton's letters to supporters, spring 1954, in Box 110-12, f312, Waring/M-S; also see Glen, *No Ordinary*, p. 179; Thomas Bledsoe, *Or We'll All Hang Separately: The Highlander Idea* (Boston: Beacon Press, 1969), p. 83.000

13 *Clark carried*: SPC to Elizabeth Waring, July 11, 1954, Waring/M-S.

13 *Without Judge Waring*: SPC's relationship with the Warings discussed at length in Clark, *Echo*; Katherine Mellen Charron, *Freedom's Teacher: The Life of Septima Clark* (Chapel Hill: University of North Carolina Press, 2009); and SPC correspondence with the Warings in Waring/M-S.

13 *want to learn*: Clark, *Ready*, p. 30.

13 *Clark's ambitions*: these are discussed in Clark's 1953 and 1954 letters to the Warings in Box 110-9, f 224-226, Waring/M-S, and in summer–fall 1954 letters to Myles Horton in Box 9, HREC/Wis.

14 *role of Black teachers*: some topics discussed in this workshop are mentioned in "Annotation Summary of the HFS Audio Collection, 1953–1963," HFS/TSLA.

16 *Zilphia Horton*: biographical details in Kim Ruehl, *A Singing Army: Zilphia Horton and the Highlander Folk School* (Austin: University of Texas Press, 2023); Vicki K. Carter, "The Singing Heart of Highlander Folk School," *New Horizons in Adult Education and Human Resources Development* 8, no. 2 (Spring 1994); Chelsea Hodge, "The Coal Operator's Daughter: Zilphia Horton, Folk Music, and Labor Activism," *Arkansas Historical Quarterly* 76, no. 4 (Winter 2017): pp. 291–307; Zilphia Horton Folk Music Collection, TSLA. The history of "Overcome" from Pete Seeger and Bob Reiser, *Everybody Says Freedom: A History of the Civil Rights Movement in Songs and Pictures* (New York: W. W. Norton, 2009), p. 8; the song's origins with striking women, in Ruehl, *Singing Army*, pp. 147–59; Seeger in Wigginton, *Refuse to Stand Silently By*, pp. 275–78; Guy Carawan and Candi Carawan, *Sing for Freedom* (Montgomery: New South Books, 2007), pp. 8–9.

16 *"register and vote"*: Horton quoted in "End Tenn. Workshop for Better Schools," *Chicago Defender*, July 24, 1954.

Chapter 2: Henrietta Street

17 *"so new, so different"*: SPC to Warings, July 11, 1954, Waring/M-S.

17 *"their second child"*: biographical details in Clark, *Echo*; Clark, *Ready*; Charron, *Freedom's Teacher*; Clark interview by Jacqueline Hall, July 25, 1976, Interview G-0016, Southern Oral History Program Collection (#4007), University of North Carolina, Chapel Hill; Clark interview by Eugene Walker, July 30, 1976, Interview G-0017, Southern Oral History Program Collection, (#4007), UNC; Eliot Wigginton, *Refuse to Stand Silently By*, pp. 3–21; Clark interview by Robert Penn Warren, March 18, 1964, in his series "Who Speaks for the Negro?" Vanderbilt University Library, https://whospeaks.library.vanderbilt.edu/interview/septima-poinsette-clark.

19 *"never a servant"*: Clark interview by Hall, p. 10.

20 *set off*: description of her journey in Clark, *Echo*, pp. 32–36.

21 *Johns, like most*: historical details from Carawan and Carawan, *Ain't You Got a Right to the Tree of Life? The People of Johns Island—Their Faces, Their Words, and Their Songs* (Athens: University of Georgia Press, 1989); "Survey Report, James Island and Johns Island, Historical and Architectural Inventory," Preservation Consultants, Inc., South Carolina Department of Archives and History, 1989.

21 *Septima's lodging*: Clark, *Ready*, pp. 108–9.

21 *Promise Land School*: Clark, *Ready*, p. 104; Clark, *Echo*, pp. 37–38.

21 *no desks*: Clark, *Ready*, pp. 105–6; Charron, *Teacher*, pp. 65–69; Clark, *Echo*, pp. 38–40.

22 *to the parents*: Clark, *Ready*, p. 110.

22 *She was embraced*: Charron, *Teacher*, pp. 73–74; Clark, *Echo*, p. 54.

22 *"quite a struggle"*: Clark, *Ready*, p. 108.

22 *her Diet*: Clark, *Ready*, p. 109.

22 *hot potato*: Clark, *Ready*, p. 105.

22 *Victoria visited*: Charron, *Teacher*, p. 66.

23 *"anyone to see"*: Clark interview by Hall, p. 32.

23 *launched a campaign*: Charron, *Teacher*, pp. 89–95.

23 *petition drive*: Clark, *Echo*, p. 61; Charron, *Teacher*, pp. 91–93.

23 *first Black teachers*: Charron, *Teacher*, p. 95.

23 *brush with resistance*: Charron, *Teacher*, p. 92.

24 *"bursting down"*: Charron, *Teacher*, p. 98.

24 *Neri Clark*: for Septima's courtship with Neri see Clark, *Echo*, pp. 62–67; Clark, *Ready*, p. 111; Charron, *Teacher*, pp. 101–4.

24 *voodoo*: Clark, *Ready*, p. 111.

25 *"over my dead body"*: Clark, *Ready*, p. 112.

25 *Septima was despondent*: Clark, *Echo*, pp. 67–68; Charron, *Teacher*, pp. 107–8.

26 *held secrets*: Clark, *Ready*, p. 113.

26 *becoming a Methodist missionary*: Clark, *Echo*, p. 70.

26 *"a lot of sorrow"*: Clark, *Ready*, p. 114.

27 *a fourteen-year-old boy*: Clark, *Ready*, p. 42.

27 *switch from cotton*: Jenkins in Carawan, *Tree of Life*, p. 144.
27 *had a social life*: for SPC's time in Columbia, see Charron, *Teacher*, pp. 116–38.
27 *sleepless nights*: Charron, *Teacher*, p. 161.
27 *war work*: Charron, *Teacher*, pp. 159–61.
28 *first "radical act"*: Clark, *Echo*, p. 82. For the teacher salary campaign see Clark, *Echo*, pp. 82–83; and Clark, *Ready*, p. 117.
28 *her mother's stroke*: Clark, *Ready*, p. 118.
28 *learned to drive*: Clark, *Ready*, p. 42.
29 *plunged into her agenda*: SPC to Warings, July 11, 22, August 3, 1954, in Waring/M-S; SPC to Horton, July 22, 1954, Box 9, HREC/Wis.
29 *"just stole the chance"*: Ibid.
29 *"They like the ideas"*: Ibid.
29 *convince him*: Clark, *Ready*, p. 43. Clark describes her recruitment of Jenkins, HFS Audio Collection, UN Workshop, August 6, 1954, HFS/TSLA.

Chapter 3: Esau's Bus

31 *great plan*: Esau Jenkins biographical details in Esau Jenkins Papers, Avery; Carawan and Carawan, *Tree of Life*; HREC/Wis, Boxes 33 and 24; Highlander Folk School Audio Collection, HFS/TSLA; Charron, *Teacher*, pp. 223–25; Wigginton, *Refuse to Stand Silently By*; Jenkins entry in South Carolina Encyclopedia, https://www.scencyclopedia.org/sce/entries/jenkins-esau/; Esau Jenkins interview transcript, May 1968, Ralph J. Bunche Collection, Moorland-Spingarn Resarch Center, Howard University.
33 *Moving Star Hall*: Guy and Candie Carawan, *Tree of Life*, pp. 64–93; Guy Carawan, "Singing and Shouting in Moving Star Hall," *Black Music Research Journal* 15, no. 1 (Spring 1995): pp. 17–28; National Registry of Historic Places Nomination Form, National Park Service, US Department of the Interior, 1982.
35 *"be able to vote"*: Alice Wine in Carawan, *Tree of Life*, p. 149; Wigginton, *Refuse to Stand*, p. 248; Frank Adams, *Unearthing Seeds of Fire*, pp. 112–14. Clark's account of Wine in *Echo*, p. 136 and *Ready*, p. 46.
35 *"I cannot"*: Carawan, *Tree of Life*, p. 149.
35 *"hard words"*: Ibid.
36 *strong attachment*: Clark signed her July and August 1954 letters to Horton and the HFS staff "Love to All" in Box 9, HREC/Wis.
36 *vivid, Gullah-flavored*: Annotation of HFS Audio Collection, UN Workshop, August 2 and 6, 1954, HFS/TSLA.
36 *"not for sale"*: Carawan, *Tree of Life*, p. 150.
37 *in flux*: Adams, *Seeds of Fire*, pp. 110–11; Carl Tjerandsen, *Education for Citizenship: A Foundation's Experience* (Chicago: Emil Schwarzhaupt Foundation, 1980), Chapter 4. Full text at: https://comm-org.wisc.edu/papers2003/tjerandsen/Chapter4.html. Stephen Preskill, *Education in Black and White: Myles Horton and the Highlander Center's Vision for Social Justice* (Oakland: University of California Press, 2021), pp. 175–76.
37 *"rugged strength"*: SPC to Myles Horton, July 22, 1954, Box 9, HREC/Wis.
37 *"finding your way"*: Clark in Wigginton, *Refuse*, p. 240.

37 *"not get killed"*: Jenkins in Carawan, *Tree of Life*, p. 152; Tjerandsen, *Education*, p. 16; Nan Woodruff, *Esau Jenkins: A Retrospective View of the Man and His Times*, Avery, cited in David P. Levine, "Citizenship Schools" (PhD diss., University of Wisconsin, 1999).

Chapter 4: The Judge

38 *rowboat*: Richard Kluger, *Simple Justice: The History of Brown v. Board of Education and Black America's Struggle for Equality* (New York: Vintage/Random House, 2004), p. 14.

39 *"got no money"*: Kluger, *Simple Justice*, p. 4; Claudia Smith Brinson, *Stories of Struggle: The Clash over Civil Rights in South Carolina* (Columbia: University of South Carolina Press, 2020) p. 38.

39 *law mandated*: strict racial segregation of schools was written into the 1895 South Carolina state constitution. Brinson, *Stories of Struggle*, p. 33.

39 *for every dollar*: in the 1949–50 school year, Clarendon County spent $179 for each white student in its schools, $43 for each Black student. Kluger, *Simple Justice*, p. 7.

39 *Equal Everything*: Kluger, *Simple Justice*, p. 18.

39 *"educational advantages"*: Brinson, *Stories*, p. 49.

40 *before Christmas*: Kluger, *Simple Justice*, pp. 23–25; Brinson, *Stories*, pp. 50–53.

40 *lift a finger*: Richard Gergel, *Unexampled Courage: The Blinding of Sgt. Isaac Woodard and the Awakening of President Harry S. Truman and Judge J. Waties Waring* (New York: Farrar, Straus and Giroux, 2019), p. 227.

41 *"Is this the price"*: Kluger, *Simple Justice*, p. 24. See also "Things That Happened Since 1949" in the Joseph A. DeLaine Papers, South Caroliniana Library, University of South Carolina, Columbia, South Carolina, https://digital.library.sc.edu/collections/joseph-a-de-laine-papers-ca-1918-2000.

41 *help DeLaine*: SPC to Warings, March 10, 1952; July 2, 1952; October 13, 1953, June 21, 1954; October 31, 1955, all in Box 110-9, Waring/M-S.

41 *to his chambers*: Gergel, *Unexampled Courage*, p. 218.

41 *Waring was*: biographical details in Gergel, *Unexampled Courage*; Tinsely E. Yarbrough, *A Passion for Justice: J. Waties Waring and Civil Rights* (Oxford: Oxford University Press, 1987); Kluger, *Simple Justice*, pp. 295–301; David W. Southern, "Beyond Jim Crow Liberalism," *Journal of Negro History* 66, no. 3 (Fall 1981): pp. 209–27.

42 *helped gather evidence*: Clark, *Echo*, pp. 80–83.

42 *"just another"*: Gergel, *Unexampled*, p. 105.

42 *"legal head whipping"*: Yarbrough, *Passion*, p. 43.

42 *"was so fair"*: Ibid.

43 *"baptism of fire"*: Gergel, *Unexampled*, p. 132; Yarbrough, *Passion*, p. 53; the Woodard crime and trial are detailed in full in Gergel, *Unexampled*.

43 *handed down another*: Waring's decisions in these cases are discussed in Kluger, *Simple Justice*, pp. 297–301; Gergel, *Unexampled*, pp. 178–99.

44 *Editorials in the city's*: Gergel, *Unexampled*, pp. 184 and 192.

44 *Petitions called for*: attacks and impeachment detailed in Gergel, *Unexampled*, pp. 192–96; 208–12; Yarborough, *Passion*, pp. 90–94; 143–48; 149–71.

44 *interesting to invite*: SPC relates this incident in Clark, *Echo*, pp. 95–100. Clark, *Ready*, pp. 24–26; Yarborough, *Passion*, pp. 127–40; Charron, *Teacher*, pp. 193–98.

44 *Klan trying to plunge*: Clark, *Echo*, p. 99; Clark, *Ready*, p. 26.

45 *"selfish and savage"*: Yarborough, *Passion*, pp. 130–31.

45 *paralyzed with fear*: Clark, *Echo*, p. 100; SPC-Walker interview, p. 29.

45 *receiver off the hook*: Clark, *Echo*, p. 100.

45 *appear on television's*: *Meet the Press* program, NBC television network, February 11, 1950; Yarborough, *Passion*, pp. 135–40.

45 *invited to dine*: Clark, *Echo*, p. 102.

46 *She was self-conscious*: SPC to Warings, June 14, 1959, Box 110-9, Waring/M-S; Clark, *Echo*, p. 27.

46 *Lonesomest Man*: *Collier's Magazine*, April 29, 1950.

46 *"That's a dangerous thing"*: Clark, *Ready*, pp. 27–28.

46 *an accusing finger*: Clark, *Echo*, pp. 105–6; Clark, *Ready*, pp. 28–29.

47 *"don't want to hear"*: Gergel, *Unexampled*, p. 218.

47 *"this is the case"*: Ibid. Gergel references this exchange from the oral history interview of Alexander Rivera, Duke University Libraries, June 2, 1995, pp. 47–48. Rivera, a photojournalist and friend of Marshall, was in the federal courthouse when Marshall left Judge Waring's chambers and recounted his meeting with Waring.

48 *"where you want to be"*: Gergel, *Unexampled*, p. 218.

48 *the "good" dolls*: Gergel, *Unexampled*, pp. 225–27; Kluger, *Simple*, pp. 315–21.

48 *first in line*: Kluger, *Simple*, pp. 346–47.

48 *report every detail*: Charron, *Teacher*, p. 211.

49 *"a bodyguard"*: Diary of Elizabeth Avery Waring, June 19, 1951, entry, Waring/M-S.

49 *if he were killed*: Ibid.

49 *"segregation in education"*: Gergel, *Unexampled*, p. 239.

49 *"it must go"*: Ibid.

49 *Waring reviewed drafts*: Gergel, *Unexampled*, p. 243; Yarbrough, *Passion*, p. 223.

50 *"keep my fingers"*: SPC to Warings, June 17, 1953, Waring/M-S.

Chapter 5: Red Roadshow and Black Monday

51 *"They're treating me"*: "Witness Ejected at Hearing," *New York Times*, March 21, 1954, p. 1.

51 *"We know about you"*: Preskill, *Education in Black and White*, p. 138. See also letter from Horton to Judge Waring, April 17, 1954, Box 110-12, Waring/M-S.

51 *"Red Roadshow"*: Dorothy Zellner, "Red Roadshow: Eastland in New Orleans, 1954," *Louisiana History: The Journal of the Louisiana Historical Association* 33, no. 1 (Winter 1992): pp. 31–60.

52 *colleagues*: the others were James Dombrowski, a white Methodist minister and social justice activist who was staff director of Highlander for a decade; Aubrey Williams, who'd served in the Roosevelt New Deal administration and returned to Alabama to fight for liberal causes; and Virginia Durr. All were also board members of the Southern Conference Educational Fund, whose mission was to work for racial equality.

52 *defiantly mute*: Virginia Durr's performance on the stand is recounted in Glen, *No Ordinary*, pp. 176–79 and Adams, *Seeds of Fire*, pp. 194–200. Alfred Maund, "Battle of New Orleans: Eastland Meets His Match," *The Nation*, April 3, 1954, pp. 282–83. Photo of Durr powdering her nose in *Newsweek*, March 29, 1954, p. 26.

53 *"Take him out"*: Adams, *Seeds*, p. 199; Horton interview by Jack Rabin, November 16, 1974, Jack Rabin Collection on Alabama Civil Rights and Southern Activists, Special Collections, Pennsylvania State University Library; Zellner, "Red Roadshow."

53 *hometown paper*: *Charleston News and Courier*, March 21, 1954.

53 *newspaper coverage*: "Ejected Witness Denies He Is a Red," *New York Times*, March 23, 1954, p. 12; "Justice Black Kin Accused of Pro-Red Acts," *Chicago Tribune*, March 20, 1954, p. 12.

53 *making a little game*: Horton interview by Rabin.

53 *strain on Zilphia*: Ruehl, *Singing Army*, p. 211.

54 *promised to protect*: Horton interview by Rabin.

54 *"want to congratulate you"*: Bledsoe, *Or We'll All Hang Separately*, p. 83.

54 *need all the help*: Horton to Bob Ran, March 22, 1954, Box 110-12, Waring/M-S.

54 *"When the word"*: Warren's reading copy with handwritten insertion, Manuscript Division, Library of Congress, www.loc.gov/exhibits/brown-brown.html#obj83 including quotation from Earl Warren.

55 *clearly echoing*: Yarbrough, *Passion*, pp. xiii–ix, 224.

55 *stopped the presses*: "Extra, Extra," *Chicago Defender*, May 22, 1954, p. 1; "Defender Ready for Decision," *Chicago Defender* (National Edition), May 29, 1954, p. 2.

55 *"atom bomb"*: *Chicago Defender*, May 29, 1954, p. 11.

55 *"I rejoice"*: Bethune recounting her May 17 radio comments in a column for the *Atlanta Daily World*, June 25, 1959, p. 4.

55 *"not abide"*: *New York Times*, May 18, 1954, p. 1.

55 *"most serious blow"*: *New York Times*, May 18, 1954, p. 20.

55 *"never will be"*: AP dispatch in (Tucson) *Arizona Daily Star*, May 18, 1954, p. 1.

55 *"Black Monday"*: John Bell Williams entry in Mississippi History Now, Mississippi Department of Archives and History, https://www.mshistorynow.mdah.ms.gov /issue/john-bell-williams-fifty-fifth-governor-of-mississippi-1968-1972.

55 *"thought of Waties"*: Gergel, *Unexampled*, p. 247, citing Poppie Cannon's *Gentle Knight*, a memoir of her husband, Walter White; Yarbrough, *Passion*, pp. x–xi.

56 *"really happy"*: Harry and Eliza Briggs filmed interview for *Eyes on the Prize* documentary series, 1985, Corporation for Public Broadcasting, https://americanarchive.org /catalog/cpb-aacip-151-wo8w951k14.

Chapter 6: Radical Hillbilly

57 *in a dream*: Myles Horton biographical details from Horton, *Long Haul*; Jacobs, *Myles Horton Reader*; Glen, *Highlander: No Ordinary School*; Adams, *Seeds of Fire*. Interviews: Bill Moyers Journal, 725 and 726, "Adventures of a Radical Hillbilly," 1981, op. cit.

58 *"I can't sleep"*: Horton, *Long Haul*, p. 55.

59 *"too poor"*: Jacobs, *Horton Reader*, p. 12.

59 *spasm of fear*: Ruehl, *A Singing Army*, p. 211, citing Horton undated essay "Family" in Box 1, Myles Horton Papers, Wisconsin Historical Society, Madison.

59 *called her daughter*: Jacobs, *Horton Reader*, p. 39.

NOTES

Chapter 7: Prepare

60 *"Where do YOU"*: handbill for NAACP school rally, with Septima Clark annotation, sent to Myles Horton, September 1954, Box 9, HREC/Wis.

60 *one of the speakers*: Clark wrote on the handbill: "I will give the summary of our desegregation workshop here." Ibid.

61 *"I'm busy"*: SPC to Warings, August 31, 1954, Waring/M-S.

61 *white citizens*: Neil R. McMillen, *The Citizens' Council: Organized Resistance to the Second Reconstruction* (Champaign: University of Illinois Press, 1994); John Bartlow Martin, "The Deep South Says Never," *Saturday Evening Post* (five-part series), June 15–July 13, 1957.

61 *plan every detail*: SPC to Warings, August 31, 1954, Waring/M-S; Yarbrough, *Passion*, pp. 227–28; program for Waring Testimonial, November 6, 1954, in Septima P. Clark Papers, Avery; "Friends Honor Judge in Charleston," *Carolina Times* (Durham, NC), November 20, 1954, p. 1; photographs in Maude Veal Jenkins Collection on J. W. Waring, Amistad Research Center, Tulane University, New Orleans, LA, and in Waring/M-S.

61 *"Seems like some"*: Yarbrough, *Passion*, p. 228.

62 *"overjoyed at the love"*: Yarbrough, *Passion*, p. 227.

62 *"freedom loving friends"*: SPC to Warings, October 1, 1954, and November 16, 1954, Waring/M-S.

62 *on the ballot*: "Voters Have Decisions to Make," *Charleston News and Courier*, October 31, 1954, pp. 1 and 8; *Charleston Evening Post*, November 1, 1954, p. 1; interview of William Saunders by Tom Dent, https://digitallibrary.tulane.edu/islandora/object/tulane:54127.

62 *"Man, Esau"*: Carawan, *Tree of Life*, p. 152.

62 *of the 200*: Tjeredsen, *Education*, p. 17; Carawan, *Tree of Life*, p. 152; Clark, *Ready*, p. 45.

62 *welcomed Zilphia*: Jenkins to Zilphia Horton, October 28, 1954, Box 67, HREC/Wis.

63 *Zilphia met*: Zilphia Horton report on trip to Johns Island, ibid.

63 *sympathetic bond*: Zilphia Horton to Esau Jenkins, November 18, 1954, ibid.

63 *kept his finger*: Zilphia Horton report on Jenkins and Johns Island, op. cit.

63 *smoothed the way*: "Report of Myles' Trip to the Sea Islands," January 1955, Box 67, HREC/Wis.

64 *Sea Island world*: Tjerdsen, *Education*, p. 18.

64 *first of many*: Horton and the Highlander staff's early work with Clark and Jenkins on Johns Island is documented in correspondence and reports found in Box 67, "Sea Islands," HREC/Wis, including "Summary of Community Leadership Training Activities Involving Esau Jenkins, Johns Island, S. C. Through March 1955."

Chapter 8: Deliberate Speed

65 *only intensified tensions*: Kluger, *Simple Justice*, pp. 719–20.

65 *court should impose*: Kluger, *Simple Justice*, pp. 723–39.

65 *unsure of how to proceed*: Kluger, *Simple Justice*, pp. 739–49. On President Eisenhower, pp. 667–68 and pp. 729–30; Charles Ogletree, *All Deliberate Speed: Reflections on the First Half Century of Brown v. Board of Education* (New York: W. W. Norton, 2004), p. 3 and pp. 125–27.

66 *segregated civic and charity*: Clark discusses this frequently in letters to the Warings, for example, September 21, 1951, Waring/M-S.

66 *come to the realization*: Clark's reports on her work on Johns Island with Jenkins are detailed in a series of letters to Myles Horton in 1955 and 1956 found in Box 9, HREC /Wis. Horton's visits to the island and consultations with Clark and Jenkins are detailed in a series of reports and memos found in Box 67, HREC/Wis.

66 *made ten trips*: Clark to Highlander, Report of Recruiting, September 3, 1955, Box 9, HREC/Wis.

67 *fifty new voters*: Summary of Leadership Activities, Esau Jenkins, p. 4; Index to Developments on Johns Island, July 22, 1955, in Box 67, HREC/Wis.

67 *called Brown II*: Kluger, *Simple*, pp. 747–49.

68 "SLOW": Thurgood Marshall quoted in Ogeltree, *All Deliberate Speed*, p. 10.

68 *financial ruin*: essay on Elmore by Professor Bobby J. Donaldson, https://www .100daysinappalachia.com/2020/03/how-one-man-fought-south-carolina -democrats-to-end-whites-only-primaries-and-why-that-matters-now/.

69 *"Now that the Supreme Court"*: SPC to Warings, June 1, 1955, Waring/M-S.

Chapter 9: The Woman from Montgomery

70 *She was mum*: Rosa Parks's first visit to Highlander detailed in: Rosa Parks, *My Story* (New York: Puffin Books, 1992), pp. 102–7; Jeanne Theoharis, *The Rebellious Life of Mrs. Rosa Parks* (Boston: Beacon Press, 2013), pp. 35–42; Clark, *Ready*, pp. 31–34; Douglas Brinkley, *Rosa Parks* (New York and London: Viking Books, 2000); Charron, *Teacher*, pp. 234–35.

71 *sewing for her family*: Theoharis, *Rebellious*, pp. 35–36.

71 *She and her husband*: Parks biographical information in Parks, *My Story*; Theoharis, *Rebellious*; Brinkley, *Rosa Parks*; Wigginton, *Refuse*.

72 *"rather tense"*: Theoharis, *Rebellious*, p. 17, citing 1981 interview of Parks for the documentary *You Got to Move*, Lucy Massie Phenix Collection, State Historical Society of Wisconsin.

72 *getting on the bus*: Theoharis, *Rebellious*, p. 37.

72 *somewhat withdrawn*: Ibid.

72 *brought food*: this incident described by SPC in Wigginton, *Refuse*, p. 240.

73 *the smell*: Parks, *My Story*, p. 105.

73 *"washed away"*: Clark, *Ready*, p. 17. Quoting Parks in comments at a fundraising dinner for Highlander in Berkeley, California, December 1979.

73 *"First, the food"*: Parks in Wigginton, *Refuse*, p. 231.

73 *"found myself laughing"*: Theoharis, *Rebellious*, p. 38.

74 *"ease the shock"*: Parks handwritten notes of Highlander July–August 1955 School Desegregation workshop, Rosa Parks Papers, Walter P. Reuther Library, Wayne State University, Detroit, MI. Reproduced in Civil Rights Movement Archive, https: //www.crmvet.org/docs/5507park.htm.

74 *Claudette Colvin*: Theoharis, *Rebellious*, pp. 53–54 and 56–60.

74 *gently prod*: Clark, *Ready*, pp. 32–33.

75 *she was coaxed*: Theoharis, *Rebellious*, p. 39; Clark, *Ready*, p. 17.

75 *"I was forty-two years old"*: Parks, *My Story*, p. 106.

75 *"wouldn't stick"*: Clark, *Ready*, p. 3, Horton, *Long Haul*, pp. 148–49; Theoharis, *Rebellious*, p. 41.

75 *"first time"*: Wigginton, *Refuse*, p. 231.

75 *accompanied her*: Clark, *Ready*, p. 33.

75 *"Desegregation proves"*: Parks's handwritten notes, Parks Papers, Wayne State.

Chapter 10: We Shall

76 *"This is a thing"*: SPC to Warings, August 30, 1955, Waring/M-S.

76 *"like Trojans"*: SPC to Warings, August 15, 1955, Waring/M-S.

77 *"old ways of doing"*: Jenkins to Horton, April 28, 1955, Box 67, HREC/Wis. For the evolution of Jenkins's leadership, see Tjeredsen, *Citizenship*, pp. 18–22; also "Summary of Community Leadership Training Activities" and Myles Horton, "Report on trip to Johns Island," October 17–20, 1955, Box 67, HREC/Wis.

77 *actually a cousin*: Bernice Robinson biographical details from Wigginton, *Refuse*, pp. 171–90; Bernice V. Robinson Papers, AMN 1018, Avery; Clare Russell, "A beautician without teacher training: Bernice Robinson, citizenship schools and women in the Civil Rights Movement," *The Sixties: A Journal of History, Politics and Culture* 4, no. 1 (June 2011): pp. 31–50.

78 *"get too hot"*: Robinson in Wigginton, *Refuse*, p. 245.

78 *more surprised*: Robinson in Wigginton, *Refuse*, p. 247.

79 *"I need"*: Bernice Robinson quoting Jenkins in Charron, *Teacher*, p. 234. Reiterated by Jenkins in a 1960 interview for radio station KPFA, San Francisco, https://www.pacificaradioarchives.org/recording/pz0673535.

79 *"Let me see"*: Bernice Robinson in Wigginton, *Refuse*, p. 249.

80 *own funders*: Highlander's relationship with the Marshall Field Foundation is contained in the HFS administrative files, Box 49, Folder 8, HREC/Wis, and the Field Foundation Archives, Dolph Briscoe Center for American History, University of Texas at Austin. Relationship with the Emil Schwarzhaupt Foundation is chronicled in Tjerandsen, *Education*.

81 *Committee of 52*: See Brinson, *Stories of Struggle*, https://storiesofstruggle.com/white-citizens-councils.

81 *no legal right*: Ibid.

81 *"massive resistance"*: term originated by Senator Harry Byrd of Virginia for southern states' organized resistance to the *Brown* decision, in Equal Justice Initiative, https://segregationinamerica.eji.org/report/massive-resistance.html.

81 *In statehouses*: for resistance to *Brown*, see John Bartlow Martin, *The Deep South Says Never* (New York: Ballantine Books, 1957); Walter F. Murphy, "The South Counterattacks: The Anti-NAACP Laws," *Western Political Quarterly* 12, no. 2 (June 1959): pp. 371–90.

81 *Elloree*: details in "South Carolina's Plot to Starve Negroes" *Jet* viii, no. 24 (October 20, 1955): pp. 8–13; Candace Cunningham, "Hell Is Popping Here in South Carolina," *History and Education Quarterly* 61, no. 1 (February 2021).

82 *"elite, churchgoing"*: John W. White, "The White Citizens' Councils of Orangeburg County, South Carolina," in Orville V. Burton and Winfred B. Moore Jr., *Toward the*

Meeting of the Waters: Currents in the Civil Rights Movement of South Carolina during the Twentieth Century (Columbia: University of South Carolina Press, 2008), pp. 261–73.

82 *"uptown Ku Klux Klan"*: Historian John Dittmer credits journalist Hodding Carter II with coining the phrase: https://www.npr.org/2010/12/27/132364641/Mississippi -Citizens-Councils.

83 *lack of a "spine"*: SPC to Warings, October 31, 1955, Waring/M-S.

83 *brutally ravaged face*: *Jet*, September 15, 1955; *Chicago Defender* coverage began on September 10, 1955: "Nation Shocked, Vow Action in Lynching of Chicago Youth."

83 *not protesting the lynching*: SPC to Warings, October 31, 1955, Waring/M-S.

84 *the engine responsible*: Brinson, *Stories of Struggle*, "Prominent White Supremacists," op. cit.

84 *"Ugly Truth"*: written by Georgia attorney general Eugene Cook, Citizens' Council Collection, Archives and Special Collections, University of Mississippi Libraries.

84 *violent ways*: these attacks chronicled by Rev. DeLaine's daughter Ophelia, in Joseph A. DeLaine Papers, South Carolina Library, University of South Carolina, https://digital.library.sc.edu/collections/joseph-a-de-laine-papers-ca-1918 -2000/.

84 *"rather than let you"*: threat letter in FBI file HQ 44-3077, Joseph A. DeLaine Papers, op. cit.

85 *in retaliation*: Esau Jenkins to Myles Horton, September 29, 1955, Box 67, HREC /Wis. Discussed in Sandra B. Oldendorf, "Highlander Folk School and the South Carolina Sea Island Citizenship Schools: Implications for the Social Studies" (PhD diss., University of Kentucky, 1987), p. 76.

85 *Jenkins appealed*: Jenkins to Horton, September 29, 1955; Horton to Jenkins, October 13, 1955; Horton's "Notes on Johns Island, October 15, 1955," in Box 67, HREC/Wis. Also Clark to Horton, October 4, 1955, Box 9, HREC/Wis.

85 *"I want to be militant"*: SPC to Warings, November 15, 1955, Waring/M-S.

Chapter 11: Rosa's Bus
86 *"I could not"*: Theoharis, *Rebellious*, p. 64.

86 *"I had been pushed"*: Theoharis, *Rebellious*, p. 63, citing Parks interview published in Stewart Burns, ed., *Daybreak of Freedom: The Montgomery Bus Boycott* (Chapel Hill: University of North Carolina, 1987), p. 83.

87 *"Rosa? Rosa?"*: Clark, *Ready*, p. 34.

87 *"the quietest participant"*: Myles Horton and Rosa Parks interviewed by Studs Terkel, June 8, 1973, Studs Terkel Radio Archive, https://studsterkel.wfmt.com/programs /rosa-parks-and-myles-horton-discuss-highlander-folk-school-montgomery-bus -boycott-and.

87 *"When she came back"*: Virginia Durr to Myles and Zilphia Horton, January 30, 1956, in Patricia Sullivan, *Freedom Writer: Virginia Foster Durr Letters from the Civil Rights Era* (New York and London: Routledge, 2003), pp. 103–4.

87 *"Had you seen"*: SPC to Warings, May 3, 1956, Waring/M-S.

88 *Myles Horton wasn't shy*: "Mrs. Rosa Parks Reports on Montgomery Bus Protest," a

discussion with Myles Horton at Highlander, March 1956, https://www.crmvet.org > disc > 5603_parks_mbb.

88 *sprouted all over*: White Citizens' Council membership in Mississippi was probably closer to fifty-five thousand in 1956, according to David Halberstam, "The White Citizens Councils: Respectable Means for Unrespectable Ends," *Commentary*, October 1, 1956; "Citizen Councils" essay by John W. White in *South Carolina Encyclopedia*, https://www.scencyclopedia.org/sce/entries/citizens-councils/.

88 *The FBI counted*: FBI Director J. Edgar Hoover's report to President Eisenhower's Cabinet on "Racial Tension and Civil Rights," March 1, 1956, p. 15, Dwight D. Eisenhower Presidential Library, Papers as President, Cabinet, Series, Box 6, Cabinet Meeting of March 9, 1956, National Archives ID #12191321.

89 *an alliance*: Yasuhiro Katagiri, *Black Freedom, White Resistance, and Red Menace* (Baton Rouge: Louisiana State University Press, 2014), pp. 66–67; "Whose Constitution?" editorial, *New York Times*, December 31, 1955.

89 *fired up*: essay and photos in Brinson, *Stories of Struggle*, "SC Segregationist Rally," https://storiesofstruggle.com/white-citizens-councils; "Eastland Rally," *Montgomery Advertiser*, February 11, 1956.

89 *"do something"*: Katagiri, *Black Freedom*, p. 59.

89 *"origin of many of your problems"*: Katagiri, *Black Freedom*, p. 60.

90 *"Now I have"*: SPC to Warings, January 18, 1956, Waring/M-S; funeral notice in *Charleston Evening Post*, January 18, 1956, p. 2.

Chapter 12: Been in the Storm

91 *"Long years ago"*: "Am I My Brother's Keeper," in Carawan, *Tree of Life*, p. 141.

91 *Southern Manifesto*: *Congressional Record*, March 12, 1956, Eighty-Fourth Congress, Second Session, Vol. 102, part 4 (Washington, DC: Governmental Printing Office, 1956), pp. 4459–60.

92 *laid the groundwork*: Brent Aucoin, "The Southern Manifesto and Southern Opposition to Desegregation," *Arkansas Historical Quarterly* 55, no. 2 (1996): pp. 173–193; Anthony Badger, "The South Confronts the Court: The Southern Manifesto of 1956," *Journal of Policy History* 20, no. 1 (2008): pp. 126–42; John Kyle Day, *The Southern Manifesto: Massive Resistance and the Fight to Preserve Segregation* (Jackson: University Press of Mississippi, 2014).

92 *sang "Dixie"*: "Mississippi Votes for Interposition," *New York Times*, March 1, 1956, p. 67.

92 *took aim*: Walter F. Murphy, "The South Counterattacks: The Anti-NAACP Laws," *Western Political Quarterly* 12, no. 2 (June 1959): pp. 371–90; Katagiri, *Black Freedom*, pp. 20–21; "Southern States Try to Destroy NAACP," in Civil Rights Movement Archive, https://www.crmvet.org/tim/timhis56.htm.

92 *readied a bill*: "NAACP Limited by South Carolina," *New York Times*, March 18, 1956; Charron, *Teacher*, p. 243; Candace Cunningham, "'I Hope They Fire Me': Black Teachers in the Fight for Equal Education" (PhD diss., University of South Carolina, 2018), pp. 203–7.

92 *never a question*: SPC to Warings, March 28, 1956, and June 8, 1956, Waring/M-S.

92 *PTA conference*: *Charleston Evening Post*, December 7, 1955; Clark, *Echo*, p. 114; Charron, *Teacher*, p. 242.

93 *"saw your name"*: Clark, *Echo*, p. 115.

93 *"I just resolved"*: Ibid.

93 *provided no protection*: for a broader analysis, see Leslie T. Fenwick, *Jim Crow's Pink Slip: The Untold Story of Black Principal and Teacher Leadership* (Cambridge: Harvard Education Press, 2023).

93 *hundred thousand Black teachers*: Leslie T. Fenwick, "The Ugly Backlash to *Brown v. Board of Ed* That Nobody Talks About," *Politico Magazine*, May 17, 2022, https://www.politico.com/news/magazine/2022/05/17/brown-board-education-downside-00032799.

93 *sworn oath*: Cunningham, "Hell Is Popping," pp. 45–47; Murphy, *South Counterattacks*, pp. 380–81; "Timmerman Signs NAACP Employee Bill," *Charleston News and Courier*, March 18, 1956.

93 *"I just read"*: Myles Horton to Septima Clark, March 13, 1956, Box 9, HREC/Wis; Clark, *Ready*, p. 36.

93 *"We are members"*: Clark, *Ready*, p. 37. Clark, *Echo*, pp. 116–18; Charron, *Teacher*, pp. 243–44.

93 *She mailed*: Clark in Wigginton, *Refuse*, p. 242; Clark, *Ready*, pp. 37–38.

94 *"I don't know why"*: Clark, *Ready*, p. 37.

94 *"failures of my life"*: Ibid.

94 *the "segregation session"*: https://digital.library.sc.edu/exhibits/champions/volume-3-2/appendix; "Civil Rights Movement," essay by Orville V. Burton in *South Carolina Encyclopedia*, University of South Carolina, https://www.scencyclopedia.org/sce/entries/civil-rights-movement/.

94 *legislators moved to*: for details on southern state legislatures' actions against NAACP, see Murphy, "The South Counterattacks," pp. 373–88; "Southern States Try to Destroy NAACP," in Civil Rights Movement Archive, https://www.crmvet.org/tim/timhis56.htm#1956naacp; George Lewis, *Massive Resistance: The White Response to the Civil Rights Movement* (London: Bloomsbury Academic, 2006), pp. 92–95.

94 *Texas Rangers*: Doug J. Swanson, *Cult of Glory: The Bold and Brutal History of the Texas Rangers* (New York: Viking, 2020), p. 332.

95 *cost, and effort*: Lewis, *Massive*, p. 210.

95 *would not renounce*: Clark, *Echo*, pp. 115–17; Clark, *Ready*, p. 36; Clark to Warings, March 28, 1956, Waring/M-S.

95 *In Elloree*: Cunningham, "Hell Is Popping."

95 *"I anticipated"*: SPC to Warings, June 8, 1956, Waring/M-S.

95 *letter of dismissal*: Charron, *Teacher*, pp. 243–44.

95 *"Now for my household"*: SPC to Warings, May 3, 1956, Waring/M-S.

96 *"Why didn't you"*: Clark, *Echo*, p. 117.

96 *"They didn't feel"*: Clark, *Ready*, p. 37.

96 *"bowl of jelly"*: Clark, *Echo*, pp. 117–18.

96 *"You just let"*: Clark, *Ready*, p. 36.

96 *"My family"*: Charron, *Teacher*, p. 242; Clark, *Ready*, p. 37.

96 *"They were sore afraid"*: SPC to Warings, January 26, 1957, Waring/M-S; Clark, *Echo*, pp. 174–75; Clark, *Ready*, p. 39.

96   *"My mother had died"*: Clark, *Ready*, p. 36.

97   *having to consider*: SPC to Warings, May 3, 1956, Waring/M-S.

97   *would be appointed*: "Approves School Trustee Bill," *Charleston Evening Post*, March 21, 1956; SPC to Warings, March 22, 1956, Waring/M-S.

Chapter 13: Champions of Democracy

98   *Zilphia was alone*: a vivid account is in Ruehl, *Singing Army*, pp. 232–46.

98   *Myles was devastated*: Ruehl, *Singing Army*, p. 241, from undated essay by Myles, Box 1, Mss. 831, Myles Horton Papers, Wisconsin Historical Society; Adams, *Seeds of Fire*, pp. 80–81.

98   *Rosa seemed tired*: Theoharis, *Rebellious*, pp. 130–31.

98   *Durr was concerned*: Theoharis, *Rebellious*, pp. 136–38.

99   *offered Rosa a job*: Parks, *My Story*, p. 156. Rosa's mother, Leona McCauley, accompanied her to Highlander in December 1956. She told Rosa she didn't want to move to Monteagle "to be nowhere I don't see nothing but white folks."

99   *keep the family going*: Theoharis, *Rebellious*, p. 140.

99   *"the first lady"*: Horton, *Long Haul*, p. 190.

99   *been a supporter*: Mrs. Roosevelt's contributions and relationship to Highlander are detailed in Box 24, "Correspondence with Franklin and Eleanor Roosevelt 1936–64," in HREC/Wis; Eleanor Roosevelt's association with Highlander appears in many volumes of her FBI files, including Parts 4, 5, 9, 15, 17, 18, 27, 32, https://vault.fbi.gov /Eleanor%20Roosevelt.

99   *"Have you been called"*: Horton, *Long Haul*, p. 190.

99   *"If I'd known"*: Ibid.

99   *"Yes, he told me"*: Ibid.

99   *"My Day"*: "My Day," May 14, 1956, Eleanor Roosevelt Papers, Digital Edition, George Washington University, https://www2.gwu.edu/~erpapers/myday/display doc.cfm?_y=1956&_f=md003483.

100   *Clark took notice*: SPC to Warings, June 6, 1956, Waring/M-S.

100   *"a guide and some sort"*: Ibid.

100   *part of her "downfall"*: Clark interview by Jacqueline Hall, p. 73.

101   *"I'm so happy"*: Clark in Hall interview, p. 74. SPC's ambivalence about accepting the job is chronicled in Clark, *Echo*, pp. 167–73; SPC to Warings, June 22 and July 14, 1956, Waring/M-S.

101   *"don't want to leave"*: SPC to Warings, August 2, 1956, Waring/M-S.

101   *only Black staff*: Charron, *Teacher*, p. 246.

101   *willing to wait*: SPC to Warings, July 14, 1956, Waring/ M-S.

101   *couldn't sleep*: Clark, *Ready*, p. 39.

101   *topics had evolved*: Aimee Horton, *Highlander Folk School*, pp. 211–12.

102   *"Once you get"*: Transcript of UN Workshop, August 2–8, 1954, p. 156, HFS/TSLA, cited in Aimee Horton, *Highlander Folk School*, p. 217.

102   *own fight*: Clark in Wigginton, *Refuse*, p. 242; Clark, *Echo*, pp. 116–17; Hall interview, pp. 67–73; SPC to Warings, September 27, 1956, Waring/M-S.

102   *The brochure*: "Champions of Democracy," Highlander Folk School pamphlet, 1956, Box 12, Folder 2, HFS/TSLA.

102 *"Champions of Democracy"*: Ibid.

103 *"free feeling in my mind"*: Clark, *Ready*, p. 39.

103 run out of town: Clark, *Echo*, p. 169.

104 in North Carolina: SPC to Warings, October 15, 1956, Waring/M-S.

104 *"My dear, dear friends"*: SPC to Warings, January 2, 1957, Waring/M-S.

104 *"I can't bring"*: SPC to Warings, January 8, 1956, Waring/M-S.

104 televised conversation: "The New Negro," *The Open Mind*, PBS, February 10, 1957, in Gergel, *Courage*, p. 267.

104 *"The Rev. King"*: SPC to Warings, March 22, 1956, Waring/M-S.

105 *"masterful" presentation*: Clark to Mikki (HFS staff), October 22, 1956, Box 9, HREC /Wis; Clark in Wigginton, *Refuse*, p. 242; Hall interview, pp. 58–60.

105 the judges refused: Cunningham, "Hell Is Popping," pp. 50–56; Richard Reid, "Elloree 21: Teachers Changed Course of History," *Times and Democrat* (Orangeburg, SC), February 2, 2014.

105 the Elloree teachers: Cunningham, "Hell Is Popping," pp. 59–62.

105 *"can't lose my temper"*: SPC to Warings, October 15, 1956, Waring/M-S.

Chapter 14: The Grocery Store

106 had struck out: Clark, *Echo*, pp. 138–39; Clark, *Ready*, p. 47; also Jerome D. Franson, "Citizenship Education in the South Carolina Sea Islands" (PhD diss., Peabody College for Teachers, 1977), pp. 68–69.

106 need its own space: SPC to Mikii (Highlander staff), October 22, 1956, Box 9, HREC/Wis.

107 Within a week: Clark, *Echo*, p. 139; Franson, "Citizenship Education," pp. 69–70; Tjerandsen, *Citizenship*, pp. 25–26.

107 rehabbing the building: Charron, *Teacher*, pp. 248–49; Clark, *Echo*, p. 139.

107 *"we planned it"*: Clark, *Ready*, p. 47; Clark in Wigginton, *Refuse*, p. 243.

107 *"didn't have any windows"*: Clark, *Ready*, p. 47.

107 still not fully formulated: Charron, *Teacher*, p. 248.

108 the right teacher: Clark, *Echo*, p. 141; Horton, *Long Haul*, p. 101.

108 *"I never been"*: Robinson in Wigginton, *Refuse*, p. 249.

108 *"I told you"*: Robinson in Wigginton, *Refuse*, p. 249; Clark, *Echo*, p. 141; Robinson interview in "They Say I'm Your Teacher," produced by the Literacy Project from archival film from Lucy Massie Phenix's documentary about Highlander, *You Got to Move: Stories of Change in the South*, 1985.

108 *"That's exactly"*: Horton, *Long Haul*, p. 102.

108 *"We don't want"*: Robinson in Wigginton, *Refuse*, p. 249; Clark, *Echo*, p. 141.

109 *"a community worker"*: Ibid.

109 *"So there's nobody"*: Ibid.

109 she gave in: Robinson in Wigginton, *Refuse*, p. 249; and in "They Say," op. cit.

109 as a beautician: for analysis of beauticians' role as activists, see Tiffany M. Gill, *Beauty Shop Politics: African American Women's Activism in the Beauty Industry* (Champaign: University of Illinois Press, 2010); For Robinson's role in context, see Nico Slate, "Beauty and Power: Beauticians, the Highlander Folk School, and Women's Professional Networks in the Civil Rights Movement," *Journal of Social History* 55, no. 3 (2022): pp. 744–68; Clare Russell, "A Beautician without Teacher Training: Bernice

Robinson, Citizenship Schools and Women in the Civil Rights Movement," *The Sixties* 4, no. 1 (2011): pp. 31–50.

109 *"want to trust"*: Clark, *Ready*, p. 49.
109 *no stranger*: Ibid; Robinson in Wigginton, *Refuse*, p. 250.
109 *had any "friends"*: Tjerandsen, *Citizenship*, p. 28.
109 *gentle, oblique approach*: Robinson in Wigginton, *Refuse*, p. 250.
110 *It was a lawsuit*: Browder v. Gayle.
110 *creating an image*: Theoharis, *Rebellious*, p. 134.
110 *house was shattered*: Theoharis, *Rebellious*, p. 135.
110 *In Birmingham*: Taylor Branch, *Parting the Waters: America in the King Years 1954–63* (New York: Simon & Schuster, 1988), p. 198.

Chapter 15: Pencils

112 *was nervous*: Robinson in Wigginton, *Refuse*, p. 250.
112 *furniture meant for grown-ups*: Horton, *Long Haul*, p. 101.
113 *"They say"*: Robinson describes this first lesson in Wigginton, *Refuse*, pp. 250–51; "They Say," excerpt from Phenix documentary *You Got to Move*; letter to Carl Tjerandsen, fall 1974, Emil Schwarzhaupt Foundation Records, in Tjerandsen, *Citizenship*, p. 27.
114 *"teach me some things"*: Robinson in Wigginton, *Refuse*, p. 250.
114 *"sorta settled the folks"*: Robinson in Wigginton, *Refuse*, p. 251.
114 *burst of requests*: Ibid.
115 *formed an umbrella*: Branch, *Parting*, p. 199.
115 *crack of pencils snapping*: Horton, *Long Haul*, p. 103; Clark, *Ready*, p. 50.
115 *method suggested*: Clark, *Echo*, p. 148.
116 *grocery ads*: Robinson describes her methods and curriculum in Wigginton, *Refuse*, pp. 251–52; "Bernice Robinson's Involvement with Highlander School," memoir, B. Robinson Papers, Avery; "They Say" video; letter to Carl Tjerdansen quoted in Tjerdansen, *Citizenship*, p. 27.
117 *volunteered her time*: Robinson in Wigginton, *Refuse*, p. 250.
117 *"such anxious people"*: Robinson letter to Clark, January 20, 1957, quoted in Adams, *Seeds of Fire*, p. 117.
117 *"That's my name"*: Robinson in Wigginton, *Refuse*, pp. 252–53; "They Say."
117 *count on her fingers*: Robinson in Wigginton, *Refuse*, p. 251.
117 *listening in*: Myles Horton to Carl Tjerandsen, director of the Schwarzhaupt Foundation, February 16, 1957, Box 67, HREC/Wis.
118 *last session*: Clark, *Ready*, pp. 50–51.
118 *"not easily impressed"*: Horton to Carl Tjerandsen, February 16, 1957 p. 2, Box 67, HREC/Wisc.

Chapter 16: Anniversary

119 *felt a thrill*: SPC to Warings, May 20, 1957, Waring/M-S.
119 *spiritual and political*: "Prayer Pilgrimage for Freedom," May 17, 1957, Martin Luther King Jr. Research and Education Institute, Stanford University.
120 *"Give Us the Ballot"*: Martin Luther King Jr. Papers (Series I-IV), Martin Luther King Jr. Center for Nonviolent Social Change, Inc., Atlanta.

NOTES

120 *"King made it clear"*: SPC to Warings, May 20, 1957, Waring/M-S.

120 *a lonelier fight*: "Tax Exemption Revoked," Highlander Annual Report, October 1956–September 1957, p. 4, Race Relations Department of the United Church Board for Homeland Ministries records, Administrative Records, Highlander Folk School, Publications, Highlander reports, Amistad Research Center, Tulane University, New Orleans.

121 *friends to dig deep*: Aimee Isgrig Horton, *The Highlander Folk School: A History of Its Major Programs 1932–1961* (New York: Carlson Publishing, 1989), pp. 213–14.

121 *investigate and disrupt*: Woods, *Black Struggle*, pp. 85–97; Katagiri, *Black Freedom*, pp. 21–22.

121 *known at FBI headquarters*: FBI voluminous files on Highlander are recorded in nineteen parts, File 61-7511, at https://vault.fbi.gov/Highlander%20Folk%20School. A brief summary is available at Guide to the FBI Files on Highlander Folk School on Microfilm, Collection Number 5898 mf., Kheel Center for Labor-Management Documentation and Archives, Cornell University Library.

121 *carefully cross-referenced*: "Champions of Democracy," FBI Highlander Folk School files, Part 13. For an example of the FBI's cross-referencing, see FBI Files, Highlander, Part 12, Workshop brochure.

121 *Key Figures list*: FBI Memorandum, Director to DM Ladd, February 23, 1951, in Taylor Branch Papers, Subject Files, Highlander, Folders 645–46, University of North Carolina at Chapel Hill Library, Southern Historical Collection. Used with permission.

121 *credible evidence*: for example, see Memorandum, Director to SAC Knoxville, April 4 and 27, 1956, FBI Vault, HFS Part 12, pp. 9–13.

122 *"becoming a center"*: L. B. Nichols to Mr. Tolson, FBI Memorandum, August 30, 1957, FBI Vault, HFS Files, Part 12, p. 50.

122 *"You are instructed"*: FBI Memorandum, Director to SAC Knoxville, September 4, 1957, FBI Vault, HFS, Part 12, p. 51.

122 *no time to lie low*: Symposium and 25th Anniversary Celebration announcement, ARC_S001_B021_F001/6 Amistad Research Center, Tulane University, https://www-racerelations-amdigital-co-uk.proxy1.library.jhu.edu/.

122 *Hundreds of invitations*: "School Planning Seminar on South," *New York Times*, July 7, 1957.

123 *telephoned his friend*: Seeger Oral History interview by Joseph Mosnier, 2011, Civil Rights History Project, conducted by the Southern Oral History Program for Smithsonian Institution's National Museum of African American History and Culture and the Library of Congress, https://lccn.loc.gov/2015669138.

123 *also been dragged*: David Durant, Pete Seeger, and HUAC, sites.ecu.edu/cwis /2014/02/pete-seeger-and-huac/; Dahlia Lithwick, "When Pete Seeger Faced Down the House Un-American Activities Committee," *Slate*, January 28, 2014.

123 *August weekend*: "The South Looks Ahead," ARC_S001_B021_F016/21, https://www.racerelations.amdigital.co.uk. Seminar program at HFS/TSLA, https://teva.contentdm.oclc.org/digital/collection/highlander/id/1242.

123 *The fellow seemed earnest*: Ed Friend's Highlander Folk School photos and films in "Integrated in All Respects," Ed Friend Visual Materials Richard B. Russell Library for Politics Research and Studies, University of Georgia, Athens, Digital Library of Georgia, http://dlg.galileo.usg.edu/highlander/friended.html#series1.

124 *Friend kept busy*: Accounts of Ed Friend's infiltration of Highlander can be found in Howell Raines, *My Soul Is Rested: The Story of the Civil Rights Movement in the Deep South* (New York: Viking/Penguin, 1983), pp. 395–98; Bledsoe, *Hang*, pp. 86–89; Adams, *Seeds of Fire*, pp. 124–26; Glen, *No Ordinary*, pp. 181–82.

124 *"not paying for that"*: Horton quoted in Bledsoe, *Hang*, p. 89.

124 *give his talk*: "A Look to the Future," Address Delivered at Highlander Folk School's Twenty-Fifth Anniversary Meeting, September 2, 1957, MLK Institute, Stanford, https://kinginstitute.stanford.edu/king-papers/documents/look-future-address-delivered-highlander-folk-schools-twenty-fifth-anniversary.

125 *"song that haunts you"*: King quoted in David J. Garrow, *Bearing the Cross: Martin Luther King, Jr. and the Southern Christian Leadership Conference* (New York: William Morrow, 1986), p. 98. Another version, related by Pete Seeger, quotes King saying: "That song really sticks with you, doesn't it?" Seeger and Reiser, *Everybody Says Freedom*, p. 8.

Chapter 17: Communist Training School

126 *"little FBI"*: for the creation of the Georgia Commission, see Jeff Woods, *Black Struggle, Red Scare: Segregation and Anti-Communism in the South 1948–1968* (Baton Rouge: Louisiana State University Press, 2004), pp. 97–99; Katagiri, *Black Freedom*, pp. 94–96.

126 *"lavish" offices*: Trezzvant W. Anderson, "Called Most Vicious Dixie Group," *Pittsburgh Courier*, December 28, 1957.

126 *a state employee*: For Friend's background, see "Introduction to the Film," http://dlg.galileo.usg.edu/highlander/history.php.

127 *dispatched Ed Friend*: Katagiri, *Black Freedom*, pp. 108–17; Glen, *No Ordinary*, pp. 181–82; Adams, *Seeds of Fire*, pp. 122–26; see also Friend's testimony: "Investigation of Highlander Folk School, Grundy County TN Before the Joint Legislative Investigation Committee," March 4, 1959, Transcript beginning p. 427.

127 *Berry wasn't just*: Berry's wife was a secretary to a New York YMCA official who'd been invited but could not attend the anniversary event, sending the secretary in his stead. Berry was accompanying his wife.

127 *using him*: Horton in Raines, *My Soul*, p. 398.

127 *Little Rock*: see "Little Rock School Integration" and "Daisy Bates," entries at MLK Research and Education Institute, Stanford, https://kinginstitute.stanford.edu/little-rock-school-desegregation; "Little Rock Crisis," https://www.blackpast.org/african-american-history/little-rock-crisis-1957/2/; https://www.life.com/history/little-rock-nine-1957-photos/.

128 *"second Reconstruction"*: WSB-TV (Atlanta) news film of Governor Griffin, September 23, 1957, University of South Georgia, https://crdl.usg.edu/record/ugabma_wsbn_wsbn33584.

129 *presented Friend's findings*: Katagiri, *Black Freedom*, pp. 111–13.

129 *four-page broadsheet*: "Highlander Folk School: Communist Training School," Georgia Commission on Education, October 1957, http://dlg.galileo.usg.edu/highlander/efhf003.php.

NOTES

131 *printed, at taxpayer expense*: Katagiri, *Black Freedom*, p. 114.

131 *"put them in good hands"* : Katagiri, *Black Freedom*, pp. 114–15.

131 *a million copies*: Woods, *Black Struggle, Red Scare*, p. 107.

131 *issued a statement*: "For Immediate Release, October 5, 1957, Statement from Myles Horton, HFS, Monteagle, TN," NAACP Records, Folder 001516-013-0572, pp. 47–48, Library of Congress.

132 *sue Governor Griffin for defamation*: Glen, *No Ordinary*, p. 183.

132 *"The sharks"*: Horton letter to Roy Wilkins, November 7, 1957, NAACP Records, Folder 001516-013-0572, p. 46, Library of Congress. See also HFS Audio Collection 1953–1963, Horton outgoing correspondence tapes, October–December 1957, HFS/TSLA.

132 *"gestapo tactics"*: Ralph McGill, *Atlanta Constitution* editorial, October 31, 1957, cited in Katagiri, *Black Freedom*, p. 114.

132 *"I resent"*: Katagiri, *Black Freedom*, p. 117.

132 *deluged with inquiries*: see FBI Records, Highlander Folk School, Part 13, https://vault.fbi.gov/Highlander%20Folk%20School/Highlander%20Folk%20School%20Part%2013%20of%2019/.

132 *Hoover shot*: Director to SAC Knoxville, November 1, 1957, FBI Vault, HFS Part 13, p. 20.

132 *found none*: SAC Knoxville to Director, November 22, 1957, FBI Vault, HFS Part 13 p. 22.

133 *illustrious supporters*: "Leaders Defend School in South," *New York Times*, December 22, 1957, p. 43.

133 *added to her woes*: Theoharis, *Rebellious*, pp. 146–48.

133 *move away*: Theoharis, *Rebellious*, pp. 148–50.

133 *more indignant than frightened*: SPC to Warings, September 5, October 14, and November 14, 1957, Box 110-9, Waring/M-S.

134 *students of Clinton*: Rachel Louise Martin, A Most Tolerant Little Town: The Explosive Beginning of School Desegregation (New York: Simon & Schuster, 2023).

134 *"been really heartened"*: SPC to Warings, January 7, 1958, Waring/M-S.

134 *a mild heart attack*: Clark, *Ready*, p. 60.

Chapter 18: A Dangerous Place

135 *"I became so involved"*: Robinson in Wiggington, *Refuse*, p. 252.

136 *set up coaching squads*: "Transcription of a meeting at the home of Mrs. Septima P. Clark," February 17, 1959, Box 3, Folder 4, HFS/TSLA, cited in Deanna M. Gillespie, "'They Walk, Talk, and Act Like New People': Black Women and the Citizenship Education Program, 1957–1970" (PhD diss., Binghamton University, State University of New York, 2008), p. 68.

136 *"our intentions crystal clear"*: Martin Luther King Jr. Papers 1954–1968, Boston University, https://kinginstitute.stanford.edu/king-papers/documents/address-delivered-meeting-launching- sclc-crusade-citizenship-greater-bethel.

136 *Ella Baker*: For Baker's role, see Barbara Ransby, *Ella Baker and the Black Freedom Movement: A Radical Democratic Vision* (Chapel Hill: University of North Carolina,

2005), pp. 178–83. For NAACP opposition to the project, see Oral History interview with Ella Baker, September 4, 1974, by Eugene Walker (Interview G-0007), Southern Oral History Program Collection (#4007), https://docsouth.unc.edu/sohp/G-0007/excerpts/excerpt_8076.html.

136 *"Perhaps the greatest"*: Clark, *Echo*, p. 149.

137 *"I got it!"*: Robinson in Wigginton, *Refuse*, p. 253.

137 *on the voting rolls*: Tjerandsen, *Citizenship*, p. 29.

137 *"Everybody wanted to know"*: Robinson in Wigginton, *Refuse*, p. 253.

137 *exploratory trips*: Horton field reports, January 1958 and April 1958, Box 67, HREC/Wis.

138 *"speaking out"*: SPC to Warings, August 9, 1958, Box 110-9, Waring/M-S.

138 *were especially keen*: Glen, *No Ordinary*, pp. 164–65; Oldendorft, "Citizenship Schools," pp. 75–78; Charron, *Teacher*, pp. 254–58.

138 *"Kluxer associates"*: Horton to (Highlander Board Chair) George Mitchell, May 29, 1958, Box 21, HREC/Wis, in Glen, *No Ordinary*, p. 184.

139 *"Eleanor Clubs"*: South Carolina Encyclopedia; FBI files on "Eleanor Roosevelt Club of Negro Women," Memphis, Tennessee (File 100-1535), November 13, 1942, also "Eleanor Clubs," File 100-11347, January 25, 1943.

139 *"a confidential informant"*: FBI Memorandum, A. H. Belmont to L. V. Boardman, May 2, 1958, BUFILE 62-62735, Eleanor Roosevelt, cited in https://www.pbs.org/wgbh/americanexperience/media/filer_public/od/31/od318e47-9fef-409e-bbe7-6c8c4cebc1f7/eleanor_fbi_chattanooga.pdf.

139 *"Same informant"*: Ibid.

139 *bounty on*: Roosevelt historian Allida Black quoted in Sarah Booth Conroy, "In Eleanor Roosevelt's Orbit," *Washington Post*, March 11, 1996, p. D3.

139 *FBI warned*: Ibid. Also in Maureen Beasley, Holly Shulman, and Henry Beasley, eds., *The Eleanor Roosevelt Encyclopedia* (Westport: Greenwood Press, 2001), p. 238.

140 *"I was interested"*: Eleanor Roosevelt, "My Day, June 21, 1958," Eleanor Roosevelt Papers Digital Edition, 2017, https://www2.gwu.edu/~erpapers/myday/displaydoc.cfm?_y=1958&_f=md004151.

140 *"doing pioneer work"*: Mrs. Roosevelt's speech, June 17, 1958, Box 1, HFS/TSLA; account of the visit in Highlander Twenty-Sixth Annual Report, October 1957–September 1958, in Rosa Parks Papers, Library of Congress.

140 *"This school"*: Eleanor Roosevelt, "My Day, June 21, 1958," op. cit.

141 *"great ferment"*: SPC to Warings, August 9, 1958, Waring/M-S.

141 *"I see mobilization"*: SPC to Warings, August 1, 1958, Waring/M-S.

141 *"leaders in Little Rock"*: Ibid.

141 *new ways of confronting*: For descriptions of the seminars, see John Lewis (with Michael D'Orso), *Walking with the Wind: A Memoir of the Movement* (New York: Simon & Schuster, 1998), pp. 75–79.

142 *friend and adviser*: For brief biography, see essay on Lawson at SNCC Digital Gateway, https://snccdigital.org/people/james-lawson/, also at the MLK Research and Education Institute, Stanford University, https://kinginstitute.stanford.edu/lawson-james-m.

142 *urged Lawson*: Branch, *Parting*, pp. 204–5.

142 *aspiring Baptist ministers*: Lewis, *Walking*, p. 80.

142 *then a nineteen-year-old*: Lewis gives the best account of his youth in *Walking*, pp. 17–54.

142 *at the same table*: Lewis, *Walking*, p. 81.

143 *made a deep impression*: Lewis, *Walking*, pp. 81–82.

143 *"What I loved"*: Lewis, *Walking*, pp. 80–81.

143 *"schooled, sophisticated"*: Lewis, *Walking*, p. 81.

143 *"on fire"*: Lewis, *Walking*, p. 82.

Chapter 19: Our America

144 *Bruce Bennett*: Encyclopedia of Arkansas, https://encyclopediaofarkansas.net /entries/bruce-bennett-1154/; Little Rock Nine entry in Civil Rights Movement Archive https://www.crmvet.org/tim/timhis57.htm#1957lrsd.

144 *televised hearings*: Woods, *Black Struggle/Red Scare*, pp. 126–28; Katagiri, *Black Freedom*, pp. 141–44; Glen, *No Ordinary*, p. 185.

144 *"gladly come to Tennessee"*: "Shut Highlander Folk School, Advice of Arkansas Leader," *Chattanooga News–Free Press*, January 30, 1959; Katagiri, *Black Freedom*, p. 149; Bledsoe, *Hang*, p. 101; HFS/TSLA; Wilma Dykeman and James Stokely, "McCarthyism Under the Magnolias," *The Progressive* 23, no. 7 (July 1959): pp. 6–10.

144 *resolution authorizing*: Adams, *Seeds of Fire*, p. 128; Glen, *No Ordinary*, pp. 185–86; House Joint Resolution Number 26: A Resolution to Appoint an Investigating Committee to Investigate the Subversive Activities of Highlander Folk School, Grundy County, Tennessee, *House Journal*, January 26, 1959, p. 203.

144 *Bureau of Criminal Investigation*: "Highlander Probers Set Tracy City Trip," *Nashville Tennessean*, n.d., Clipping in Box 8, HFS/TSLA.

144 *"witch hunt"*: *Tennessean*'s editorial, January 29, 1959, reprinted in Bledsoe, *Hang*, pp. 101–2.

145 *festering sore*: *Chattanooga News–Free Press*, January 27, 1959.

145 *four locations*: Charron, *Teacher*, pp. 255–57; Clark, *Echo*, pp. 157–63; Glen, *No Ordinary*, pp. 164–65; Levine, "Citizenship Schools" dissertation, pp. 113–14; Tjerandsen, *Citizenship*, pp. 29–30; Deanna M. Gillespie, *The Citizenship Education Program and Black Women's Political Culture* (Gainesville: University Press of Florida, 2021), pp. 33–39.

145 *Ethel Jenkins Grimball*: Alexandra Bethlenfalvy, "Our Brother's Keepers: Ethel Grimball and the Wadmalaw Island Citizenship School" (MA thesis, Clemson University, 2016); Ethel J. Grimball interview by Tom Dent, https://digitallibrary.tulane.edu /islandora/object/tulane%3A53680.

146 *Alleen Brewer*: biographical details in https://www.edistopcusa.org/post/the-history -of-edisto-presbyterian-church-usa.

146 *Mary Lee Davis*: Gillespie, *CEP/Black Women*, p. 39; Clark, *Echo*, pp. 161–63.

146 *Marshall Field Foundation*: created in 1940 by Marshall Field III, grandson of the Chicago department store magnate. After Field III's death in 1960, the foundation split to pursue different philanthropic goals. The Chicago fund concentrated its giving on local projects. The New York foundation, led by Field III's wife, Ruth, funded projects addressing broad national social issues and became a major source of funding for the civil rights movement.

147 *"glorious gleam"*: Clark, *Echo*, p. 157.

147 *Reading Booklet*: in Box 2, Folder 14, HFS/TSLA.

147 *in secret session*: accounts of the legislative hearings in Glen, *No Ordinary*, pp. 187–92; Katagiri, *Black Freedom*, pp. 154–57; Adams, *Seeds of Fire*, pp. 127–31; Woods, *Black/Red*, pp. 128–29; Bledsoe, *Hang*, pp. 99–105; Ridley Wills II, "Highlander Folk School, Grundy County's Public Nuisance," *Tennessee Historical Quarterly* 66, no. 4 (Winter 2007): pp. 364, 366. Also in hearing transcripts: *Before the Joint Legislative Investigating Committee, State of Tennessee, in the Matter of: Investigation of the Highlander Folk School, Grundy County, Tennessee*, Closed Hearing, Tracy City, February 21, Public Hearing, Tracy City, February 26, and Public Hearing, Nashville, March 4, 5, 1959 (Nashville: Hix Brothers, 1959) in Investigative Committee Papers, Box 8, HFS/TSLA.

147 *"operated out of Moscow"*: Glen, *No Ordinary*, p. 188.

148 *stance was not popular*: The stance of the University of the South, Sewanee, professors is documented in the Highlander Folk School Collection and the Scott and Phoebe Bates Highlander Collection at University Archives and Special Collections, University of the South, Sewanee. Supplemented by the personal scrapbook collection of the Bates family and author conversations with Phoebe and Robin Bates, Sewanee, Tennessee, September 2021. See also Horton's February 9, 1959, "Letter to Sewanee Friends" thanking the faculty supporters, Box 8, Folder 6, HFS/TSLA.

148 *Vera McCampbell*: John Egerton, "The Trial of the Highlander Folk School," *Southern Exposure* 6, no. 1 (Spring 1978): pp. 82–89; Dan Wakefield, "The Siege at Highlander," *The Nation*, November 7, 1959, pp. 324–35; McCampbell discusses her firing in "Highlander Hearing at Altamont, Tennessee," September 16, 1959, Audio Disc 1a in Supplement Highlander Folk School Audio Collection, HFS/TSLA.

148 *"nothing immoral"*: *Nashville Tennessean*, February 27, 1959. Also in Adams, *Seeds of Fire*, p. 128; Glen, *No Ordinary*, p. 189.

148 *"Don't you know"*: Ibid.

149 *ridiculous, hearsay*: Glen, *No Ordinary*, 189–91.

149 *received their diplomas*: SPC Activity Report, Spring–Summer 1959, handwritten, Box 3, Folder 4, HFS/TSLA.

149 *"each man, get a man"*: Tjerandsen, *Citizenship*, p. 34.

149 *rip-roaring show*: descriptions of the hearing in *Nashville Tennessean*, March 5, 1959, pp. 1–2.

150 *"hot stuff"*: *Nashville Tennessean*, February 27, 1959, p. 8.

150 *the witness stand*: accounts of Horton's testimony in Horton, *Long Haul*, pp. 108–10; Glen, *No Ordinary*, pp. 190–91; Katagiri, *Black Freedom*, pp. 155–56; *Nashville Tennessean*, March 5, 1959, pp. 1–2; "Before the Joint Legislative Investigating Committee, Public Hearing, Nashville, March 4–5," op. cit.

150 *FBI refused to acknowledge*: clippings and correspondence in "Highlander Folk School," Part 19 of 19, FBI/The Vault.

150 *"'Black Monday' decision"*: Glen, *No Ordinary*, p. 190.

151 *"folk dance step"*: Photo and description in *Nashville Tennessean*, March 5, 1959, p. 2; also "Highlander Fling," *Nashville Banner*, March 5, 1959.

151 *"It was subversive"*: Edwin Friend's testimony in "Before the Joint Legislative Investi-

gating Committee," Public Hearing, Nashville, March 4, 1959, vol. 2, pp. 427–50, op. cit.; also *Nashville Tennessean*, March 5, 1959, p. 1.

151   *at a large blackboard*: photo and description in *Nashville Tennessean*, March 5, 1959, p. 2.

151   *"Run 'em out"*: Ibid.

152   *writing its report*: *Nashville Tennessean*, March 6, 1959, p. 1 and March 11, 1959, p. 1. The full report in Record Group 114, TSLA, https://sos-tn_files.tnsosfiles.com/forms /REPORT_OF_THE_SPECIAL_INVESTIGATING_COMMITTEE_ON_ HIGHLANDER_FOLK_SCHOOL_1959.pdf.

152   *his interest was piqued*: Reported in "Hearings Close on Folk School," Memphis Commercial Appeal, March 6, 1959, in HFS FBI file, Part 19 of 19, p. 20.

152   *had nothing to hide*: *Charleston News and Courier*, March 24, 1959, p. 1; "Myles Horton, Attractive Nuisance," *News and Courier*, March 25, 1952, p. 1.

152   *"fizzing bomb"*: "Spotting the Termites," editorial by Thomas Waring, *Charleston News and Courier*, March 28, 1959, p. 8a.

152   *"termites boring through"*: Ibid.

152   *snooping around*: Clark, *Ready*, p. 51.

153   *"make them better citizens"*: "Folk School Classes Here," *Charleston News and Courier*, March 11, 1959, pp. 1 and 9.

153   *Influence Felt*: *Charleston News and Courier*, March 12, 1959, p. 18a.

153   *"We do know"*: Ibid.

153   *were identified*: Clark was identified in *Charleston News and Courier* article on March 28, 1959; Robinson in March 11 article.

153   *"not a single white person"*: *Charleston News and Courier*, March 11, 1959, p. 1.

Chapter 20: We Are Not Afraid

154   *beam of light*: Robinson in Wigginton, *Refuse*, pp. 264–66.

155   *Yvonne would live*: Yvonne Clark author interview, January 21, 1922.

155   *ice cream cone*: Clark, *Ready*, p. 42.

155   *loud knocks*: Yvonne Clark, author interview, op. cit.

156   *"Where is Septima Clark?"*: Clark, *Echo*, p. 4. Accounts of the raid can be found in Clark, *Echo*, pp. 3–10; Clark, *Ready*, pp. 56–59; Charron, *Teacher*, pp. 268–70; Robinson in Wigginton, *Refuse*, pp. 264–66; Glen, *No Ordinary*, pp. 193–95; Bledsoe, *Hang*, pp. 107–13.

156   *"If they're violating"*: *Charleston News and Courier*, March 13, 1959, p. 1.

157   *"have you found"*: Clark, *Echo*, p. 4.

157   *"Never you mind"*: Ibid.

157   *"Look after Yvonne"*: Clark, *Echo*, pp. 4–5.

157   *"my grandmommie"*: Robinson in Wigginton, *Refuse*, p. 265.

157   *"Aren't you going to"*: Clark, *Echo*, p. 5.

157   *"What are my rights?"*: Clark, *Echo*, p. 7.

158   *Fourteen-year-old*: At this time in 1959, Jamila Jones was known by her birth name of Mary Ethel Dozier. Jamila Jones interview by Joseph Mosnier, April 2011, Civil Rights History Project Collection (AFC 2010/039), Archive of Folk Culture, American Folklife Center, Library of Congress, https://www.loc.gov/item/2015669108/.

158   *In the darkness*: Montgomery Improvement Association News, October 7, 1959, in Septima Clark office files, 1958–1968, Subseries 10.2, Southern Christian Leadership

Conference records, Manuscript Collection No. 1083, Stuart A. Rose Manuscript, Archives, and Rare Book Library, Emory University, Atlanta.

159 *"sing so loud"*: Jamila Jones interview, https://blogs.loc.gov/folklife/2014/02/tracing -the-long-journey-of-we-shall-overcome; also Mosnier interview; David Garrow, "We Shall Overcome and the Southern Black Freedom Struggle," https://www.david garrow.com/wp-content/uploads/2018/04/DJGWSOReport140417.pdf.

159 *"understood the power"*: Ibid.

159 *"should have been afraid"*: Clark, *Ready*, p. 57.

159 *"didn't feel too good"*: Ibid.

159 *"That's ridiculous"*: Clark, *Echo*, p. 8.

159 *"saw no such thing"*: Ibid.

160 *"get a good taste"*: Ibid.

160 *"test my blood"*: Ibid.

160 *jail cell by herself*: Clark, *Ready*, p. 58.

160 *heard her voice*: Carawan and Carawan, unpublished memoir, 1985, p. 23, courtesy Candie Carawan. Also author phone interview with Candie Carawan, December 2, 2021, and correspondence on the topic, July 30, 2023.

160 *learned from Harry Belafonte*: Clark, *Ready*, p. 58; Belafonte, p. 58. Belafonte sponsored several seasons of Highlander's youth camp for southern Black and white children, preparing them for integrated schools. He visited the camp and taught the song.

Chapter 21: Padlock

161 *under their mattress*: Clark, *Ready*, p. 58.

161 *as if nothing*: Ibid.

161 *splashed across*: *Chattanooga Free Press*, August 2 and 3, 1959.

161 *"I wasn't satisfied"*: *Nashville Tennessean*, August 2, 1959, pp. 1 and 6.

161 *dark shirtwaist dress*: Photo of Clark at the hearing, *Nashville Tennessean*, August 7, 1959, p. 1.

161 *"I have never before seen"*: Branstetter statement to the press, quoted in Charron, *Teacher*, p. 271.

162 *"let them scare me"*: Clark, *Ready*, p. 59.

162 *their alleged crimes*: "Highlander Aid Is Bound Over," *Nashville Tennessean*, August 7, 1959, p. 1.

162 *"public nuisance"*: "Tennessee Seeks to Close School," *New York Times*, August 13, 1959.

162 *Sloan's highly inventive*: Glen, *No Ordinary*, p. 195.

162 *"charges are proposterous"*: "Folk School Denies Charge of Liquor," *Afro-American* (Baltimore), August 29, 1959, p. 19.

162 *"threat to silence"*: "Aide at School Scores Closure Bid," *New York Times*, August 16, 1959.

162 *"padlock hearing"*: "Padlock Petition Hit," *Atlanta Daily World*, August 19, 1959, p. 2.

163 *"own fine character"*: All quotations from Charron, *Teacher*, p. 272.

163 *"The eyes not alone"*: Eleanor Roosevelt, "My Day," September 14, 1959, Eleanor Roosevelt Papers, Digital Edition, George Washington University, https://www2.gwu.edu /~erpapers/myday/displaydoc.

NOTES

163 *"carnival atmosphere"*: *Nashville Tennessean*, September 14, 1959, p. 6.

163 *"integrated whorehouse"*: A. F. Sloan quoted in Dan Wakefield, "Siege of Highlander," *The Nation*, November 7, 1959, p. 325.

163 *"Sex Parties"*: *Charleston News and Courier*, September 15, 1959.

163 *managed to discredit*: details on the padlock hearing in Glen, *No Ordinary*, pp. 196–99; Wakefield, "Siege"; John Edgerton, "The Trial of Highlander," *Southern Exposure* 6, no. 1 (Spring 1978): pp. 82–89; *Nashville Tennessean*, September 14, 15, 16, 17, 1959.

163 *broke the law*: *Nashville Tennessean*, September 17, 1959, p. 1; *Baltimore Sun*, September 17, 1959, p. 6.

164 *snap padlocks*: *Nashville Tennessean*, September 27, 1959, p. 10; photo of Horton at padlocking by Thorsten Horton, in Horton, *Long Haul*, p. 111.

164 *"can padlock a building"*: "Hold Workshop Despite Padlock," *Daily Defender* (Chicago), October 21, 1959; also Adams, *Seeds of Fire*, p. 133.

164 *sturdy new charge*: Glen, *No Ordinary*, pp. 199–200.

164 *previously denied*: "Mr. Sloan Does a Flip-Flop," *Nashville Tennessean* editorial, October 30, 1959; "New Charge," *Chicago Defender*, November 14, 1959, p. 22.

165 *on a northern tour*: Wakefield, "Siege"; Charron, *Teacher*, p. 273.

165 *Clark was indicted*: Glen, *No Ordinary*, p. 195.

165 *Baker came to Highlander*: Ella Baker to Committee on Administration, October 23, 1959, SCLC/Emory series 2, part 2; Gillespie, *CEP and Black Women*, p. 48.

165 *teacher John Scopes*: Glen, *No Ordinary*, p. 195.

166 *"'legal' in the heart"*: Wakefield, "Siege."

166 *violated its charter*: Accounts of the jury trial in Glen, *No Ordinary*, pp. 200–203; Adams, *Seeds of Fire*, pp. 134–40; Egerton, *Trial of Highlander*, op. cit.; Bledsoe, *Hang*, pp. 121–29; *Nashville Tennessean*, November 1, 3, 4, 5, 6, 7, 8, 1959.

166 *just forty-nine minutes*: "Tennessee Jury Rules on School," *New York Times*, November 7, 1959, p. 13.

166 *the guilty verdicts*: Adams, *Seeds of Fire*, p. 140–41; *Nashville Tennessean*, February 17, 1959.

166 *"Wind up your affairs"*: Adams, *Seeds of Fire*, p. 134.

Chapter 22: Sit at the Welcome Table

168 *turquoise Studebaker*: details from Candie Carawan, author interview, December 2, 2021; Guy's relationship with Septima also in Carawan interview by Frank Adams, Ashville, North Carolina, March 2002, L. Eury Appalachian Collection, Special Collections, Appalachian State University, Boone, North Carolina; Carawan draft memoir, 1985, pp. 8–11. Courtesy Candie Carawan.

168 *in the back seat*: Author interview with Candie Carawan.

169 *jacket and tie*: Ibid.

169 *"singing school idea"*: Clark to Highlander office, January 1960, Box 3, HFS/TSLA; Glen, *No Ordinary*, p. 165; HFS introduction of Carawan, July 1959, HFS/TSLA; Aimee Horton, *Highlander*, pp. 226–27; Carawan, "Report of Sea Islands Work" (1960–61), Box 8, HREC/Wis.

169 *Dafuskie Island*: Clark, *Echo*, pp. 163–66; SPC to Horton, January 27, 1959, Box 3, HFS/

TSLA; "Misc. Notes on Dafuskie Island," report of J. Gregory accompanying Septima Clark, January 1959, Box 38, HREC/Wis.

170 *ingenious approach*: Glen, *No Ordinary*, pp. 163–64; Levine, "Citizenship Schools" dissertation, p. 116.

170 *white magistrate judge*: Esau Jenkins interview in Carawan and Carawan, *Tree of Life*, pp. 154–55.

171 *mesmerized by the singing*: G. Carawan, "Singing and Shouting in Moving Star Hall," pp. 17–28.

171 *"most moving and democratic"*: Ibid.

171 *"a different echo"*: Carawan and Carawan, *Tree of Life*, p. ix; Carawan and Carawan, *Sing for Freedom*, pp. 99–100. Alice Wine is credited as lyricist of "Eyes on the Prize" song copyright, 1963.

172 *"If Greensboro can do it"*: Lewis interview, https://www.smithsonianmag.com/smith sonian-institution/lessons-worth-learning-moment-greensboro-four-sat-down -lunch-counter-180974087/.

172 *walking silently*: details of the Nashville sit-ins from Lewis, *Walking*, pp. 90–102; interview with John Lewis, conducted by Blackside, Inc. on May 14, 1979, for *Eyes on the Prize: America's Civil Rights Years*, Washington University Libraries, Film and Media Archive, Henry Hampton Collection; Linda T. Wynn, "The Dawning of a New Day: The Nashville Sit-ins, February 13–May 10, 1960," *Tennessee Historical Quarterly* 50 (1993): pp. 42–54; Branch, *Parting*, pp. 272–76; Carawan, "The Nashville Sit-In Story" liner notes, Folkway Records FH 5590, 1960; Seeger and Reiser, *Everybody Says Freedom*, pp. 26–34.

172 *"Oh my God"*: Lewis, *Walking*, p. 95.

173 *taken a new*: Civil Rights Movement Archive, 1960 Student Sit-Ins: https://www .crmvet.org/tim/timhis60.htm#1960background.

174 *making a mistake*: Lewis, *Walking*, p. 107.

174 *applauded the courage*: Branch, *Parting*, pp. 275–76.

174 *five times the number*: Glen, *No Ordinary*, p. 165.

174 *programs would proceed*: *Nashville Tennessean*, February 20, 1959, p. 2.

175 *"a new phase"*: Horton in "Class on Nashville sit-ins at Highlander Social Needs and Social Resources Workshop, March 18–20 1960," Box 5, HFS/TSLA.

175 *organizational savvy*: Ibid.

175 *"asking on the grapevine"*: Charron, *Teacher*, p. 290.

175 *On April 1*: "Sit in group opens Seminar," *Nashville Tennessean*, April 3, 1960, p. 6l; Carawan memoir, pp. 24–25; Branch, *Parting*, p. 290; Adams, *Seeds of Fire*, pp. 144–47.

176 *students wrestled*: Highlander Twenty-Eighth Annual Report, October 1959–September 1960, p. 2. See also "The New Generation Fights for Equality" college workshop report, April 1–3, 1959, Box 78, HREC/Wis; Aimee Horton, *Highlander*, pp. 241–45.

176 *"devil's advocate"*: Lafayette in Seeger and Reiser, *Everybody*, pp. 34–35.

176 *"I had never heard"*: Ibid.

177 *"capture our spirit"*: Lewis, *Walking*, p. 82.

177 *Candie Anderson*: Carawan memoir, p. 24.

177 *"If we were"*: Guy Carawan in Seeger, *Everybody*, p. 40.

177 *"a perfect song"*: Seeger, *Everybody*, p. 35.

177 *follow-up conference*: Ransby, *Ella Baker*, pp. 239–41.

178 *"No Fashions for Easter"*: Lewis, *Walking*, p. 105–6.

178 *three hundred students converged*: details of the Raleigh meeting in Ransby, *Ella Baker*, pp. 240–47; Lewis, *Walking*, pp. 107–8; Branch, *Parting*, pp. 291–92; Garrow, *Cross*, pp. 131–34.

178 *"More Than Hamburgers"*: Lewis, *Walking*, p. 108.

178 *bring his guitar*: Carawan memoir, p. 27.

178 *"When I saw Guy"*: Julian Bond in Carawan, *Sing for Freedom*, p. x.

178 *"Guy led the audience"*: Ibid.

179 *morning after*: Lewis, *Walking*, pp. 108–11.

179 *"We are not"*: Carawan memoir, p. 26; photograph of protesters singing "We Shall Overcome" after the Silent March, April 1960; Guy Carawan playing guitar, Nashville Banner Archives, Nashville Public Library, Special Collections.

179 *Fisk student Diane Nash*: *Nashville Tennessean*, April 20, 1960, p. 1; Lewis, *Walking*, p. 110.

179 *"Integrate Counters"*: *Nashville Tennessean*, April 20, p. 1.

179 *"Set Stage"*: *Charleston News and Courier*, October 6, 1960, p. 8.

Chapter 23: Wade in the Water

180 *"movement times"*: Horton, *Long Haul*, p. 114.

180 *"there are many doors"*: SPC to Ella Baker, July 11, 1960, Clark Papers, Avery.

181 *"startling and revealing"*: "New Alliances in the South" workshop, February 1961; "New Agenda for the White Southerner" workshop, May 1961; "Highlander's Role in the South," October 1961, in Highlander Twenty-Eighth Annual Report, 1960–61.

181 *the thorny issue*: "The New Agenda for the White Southerner in his New South," HFS publication, Box 7, Folder 16, HFS/TSLA; report of May 1961 workshop, Records of the Southern Christian Leadership Conference, Rose Library, Emory University, Part Programs, Highlander Folk School.

181 *dared to even try*: In the spring of 1940 NAACP organizer Elbert Williams of Haywood County was lynched after expressing interest in registering to vote. Richard LaVell Saunders, "Encouraged by a Little Progress: Voting Rights and the Contests over Social Place and Civil Society in Tennessee's Fayette and Haywood Counties, 1958–1964" (PhD diss., University of Memphis, 2012), p. 334, Memorializing Racial Terror: Elbert Williams, https://sites.lib.jmu.edu/lynchingmarkers/tn1940062.

182 *Civic and Welfare Leagues*: details in Linda T. Wynn, "Toward a Perfect Democracy: The Struggle of African Americans in Fayette County, Tennessee, to Fulfill the Unfulfilled Right of the Franchise," *Tennessee Historical Quarterly* 55, no. 3 (Fall 1996): pp. 202–23; "Cold War in Fayette County," *Ebony Magazine*, May 1960; "Tent City: Stories of Civil Rights in Fayette County, TN," Benjamin Hooks Institute for Social Change, University of Memphis, https://www.memphis.edu/tentcity/movement/index.php.

Chapter 24: Tent City

189 *"undeveloped potential"*: "Dr King Addresses Mass Rally," Jefferson County, Kentucky, SCLC Press Release, August 18, 1960, Manuscript Collection 1083, Part 3,

Series ix, Records of the Southern Christian Leadership Conference, Rose Manuscript, Archives, and Rare Book Library, Emory University, Atlanta (henceforth SCLC/Emory).

189 *With the collapse*: Branch, *Parting*, p. 264.

189 *support was split*: Branch, *Parting*, pp. 306–7.

189 *an October surprise*: Branch, Parting, pp. 358-370; Garrow, Bearing, pp. 144–149.

190 *"WE SAT-IN FOR YOU"*: Lewis, *Walking*, p. 116.

190 *"good overnight, and only one night"*: Jenkins quoted in Levine, "Citizenship Schools" dissertation, p. 120.

190 *kept a record*: William ("Bill") Saunders quoted in Charron, *Teacher*, p. 260.

191 *navigate the election ballot*: Clark, "New Developments in the Citizenship School Idea," memorandum, summer 1960, Box 38, Folder 2, HREC/Wis.

191 *North Charleston class*: Letter to Horton and Clark from Mrs. H. L. Leonard, Charleston Heights, South Carolina, November 16, 1960, Box 38, Folder 3, HREC/Wis.

191 *They convinced her*: SPC to Warings, October 24, 1960, Waring/M-S.

192 *the Black vote*: John F. Kennedy Presidential Library, https://www.jfklibrary.org/learn/about-jfk/jfk-in-history/civil-rights-movement. Kennedy helped win the release of King from jail in the last days of the campaign.

192 *grateful chief executive*: Ibid.

192 *nearly 100 percent*: voting statistics in Glen, *No Ordinary*, p. 166.

192 *the most stunning*: Branch, *Parting*, p. 382.

193 *Negotiations*: Report on Leadership Training Program, Highlander Folk School, November 23, 1960, Series 1, Box 138, Folder 8, SCLC/Emory.

193 *What impressed Wood*: Wood was Dr. King's administrative assistant and SCLC public relations director.

193 *balked at Horton's suggestion*: HFS, "Proposed Leadership Training Program," December 1960, Series 1, Box 136, Folder 10; "Memorandum on SCLC-Highlander Financial Arrangements," December 1, 1960, Series 1, Box 136, Folder 8, SCLC/Emory.

193 *new educational partnership*: MLK to SCLC affiliates, "Leadership Training Program and Citizenship Schools," n.d. (probably January 1961), Series 1, Box 136, Folder, 9, SCLC/Emory; "SCLC Starts Leadership Training Program," press release, February 14, 1961, Series 1, Box 136, Folder 10, SCLC/Emory.

194 *The evictions*: Jacque Hillman and Jimmy Hart, "Fayette, Haywood county blacks forced from their homes for trying to exercise right to vote," *Jackson Sun*, May 16, 2011; "Tent City, Tenn.," *Ebony Magazine*, March 1961, pp. 27–34; Robert Hamburger, *Our Portion of Hell: Fayette County Tennessee* (Oxford: University Press of Mississippi, 2022); Wynn, "Toward a Perfect," pp. 216–17; "Negroes Await Eviction Moves," *New York Times*, January 1, 1961; "Tent City: Home of the Brave," pamphlet, Industrial Union Department, AFL-CIO, 1961.

194 *Kefauver called*: Wynn, "Toward a Perfect," p. 217.

194 *"publicity stunt"*: "Negroes' Tent City Decried as Stunt," *New York Times*, December 29, 1960, p. 13.

194 *"They say"*: taped interview with Georgia May Turner by James Forman, Tent City, December 25, 1960, in Forman, *The Making of Black Revolutionaries* (Seattle: University of Washington Press, 1997), p. 126.

194 *Teamster Union truck drivers*: "Home of the Brave," op. cit.; also https://www
.memphis.edu/tentcity/movement/fayette-timeline-1960.php.

194 *grabbed the vote*: "Ballot-Box Heart of Freedom Village," *Afro-American* (Baltimore),
January 14, 1961, p. 9.

194 *weren't martyrs, but role models*: "Citizenship School Program: Fayette and Haywood
Counties, TN 1960–61," Box 38, Folder 8, HREC/Wis. The tent cities operated for
more than two years. In 1962, under legal pressure, white landowners in the counties
entered into a consent decree, prohibiting evictions used as punishment for voter registration. Evictions and punishments still continued, however.

Chapter 25: Literacy to Liberation

196 *climbing a flight*: Clark, *Ready*, p. 60.

196 *barely taken time*: SPC to Warings, January 11, 1961, Waring/M-S.

196 *brought more than fifty beauticians*: Nico Slate, "Beauty and Power: Beauticians, the
Highlander Folk School, and Women's Professional Networks in the Civil Rights
Movement," *Journal of Social History* 55, no. 3 (Spring 2022): pp. 744–45.

196 *responsibility of their profession*: Detailed accounts in Slate, "Beauty and Power," pp.
752–56; Charron, *Teacher*, pp. 279–80; Aimee Horton, *Highlander*, pp. 251–52; and
"Beauticians Meeting," February 26–27, 1961, in Box 38, HREC/Wis.

196 *boarded a bus to Montgomery*: Charron, *Teacher*, pp. 281–83; Glen, *No Ordinary*,
p. 168.

197 *The first cohorts*: Horton, *Highlander*, p. 234.

197 *In weeklong workshops*: on citizenship teacher training: Aimee Horton, *Highlander*,
pp. 230–34; Glen, *No Ordinary*, pp. 167–68; Tjerandsen, *Citizenship*, pp. 37–44;
Gillespie, *CEP and Black Women*, pp. 49–51. Clark reports in Box 38, HREC/Wis.

197 *linked literacy to liberation*: Clark, "Literacy and Liberation," *Freedomways*, First Quarter 1964.

197 *basic literacy skills themselves*: Charron, *Teacher*, pp. 278–89.

197 *came in knowing nothing*: Tjerandsen, *Citizenship*, p. 44; Tabulation of enrollment,
Citizenship Classes, October 1960–June 1961, Box 34, HREC/Wis.

197 *joined the movement*: Tjerandsen, *Citizenship*, p. 49.

198 *She traveled by bus*: Clark, *Ready*, p. 60.

198 *distress from her body*: Clark, *Ready*, pp. 60–61.

198 *the latest terms*: Glen, *No Ordinary*, p. 170.

198 *join the Highlander staff*: Gillespie, *CEP and Black Women*, p. 66.

199 *drained its coffers*: Glen, *No Ordinary*, p. 206; HFS reported over $7,500 in debt in fiscal
year 1961.

199 *benefit concert*: Carnegie Hall concert program, February 10, 1961, https://artsand
culture.google.com/story/the-civil-rights-movement-at-carnegie-hall-carnegie-hall
/LwUxBhNU52gZLg?hl.

199 *the vitriol expressed*: *Chattanooga News–Free Press*, February 23, 1961, Box 38, HREC/Wis.

199 *"More infuriating was"*: "2 Groups in South Training Negroes," *New York Times*, February 23, 1961, p. 28.

199 *giant billboards began popping*: Library of Congress photo, https://www.loc.gov/item
/98503183.

200 *funded by . . . John Birch society*: Woods, *Black/Red*, pp. 145–46; clipping from Citizens' Council publication, Citizens' Council Collection (1900), University of Mississippi, Oxford, https://egrove.olemiss.edu/citizens_clip/87.

200 *citizenship program puzzle*: Glen, *No Ordinary*, p. 170.

200 *only recently met*: Andrew Young, *An Easy Burden* (New York: HarperCollins, 1996), p. 130.

200 *heard the rumors*: Young, *Burden*, p. 132.

201 *especially appeal to SNCC*: Gillespie, *CEP and Black Women*, pp. 66–67.

201 *produce a landmark*: Edgerton, Trial of Highlander, https://www.facingsouth.org/trial-highlander-folk-school.

201 *for selling alcohol*: "Folk School Fails to Avert Closing," *New York Times*, April 6, 1961, p. 39; *Nashville Tennessean*, April 6, 1961, p. 1.

201 *there was no need*: Edgerton, Trial of Highlander, op. opt.; Glen, *No Ordinary*, p. 205.

201 *in "real trouble"*: Glen, *No Ordinary*, p. 205.

201 *legal team*: Highlander lawyers were white Nashville attorneys Cecil Branstetter and George Barrett, known for their work on behalf of civil rights activists.

201 *to be an adviser*: Glen, *No Ordinary*, p. 206.

202 *a slim chance*: Horton, *Long Haul*, p. 112.

202 *not proceed as planned*: Field Foundation: Gillespie, *CEP and Black Women*, pp. 67–68.

202 *stranded and exasperated*: Charron, *Teacher*, pp. 294–97; Glen, *No Ordinary*, p. 171.

202 *new Peace Corps*: Charron, *Teacher*, p. 295.

202 *his diplomatic skills*: Young, *Burden*, pp. 133–34.

203 *decided for them*: Charron, *Teacher*, p. 295; Horton to Clark, June 12, 1961, quoted in Clark and Robinson to Horton, June 19, 1961, Box 7, Folder 2, Clark Papers, Avery.

203 *"swapped like horses"*: Clark and Robinson to Horton, June 19, 1961, op. cit.

203 *"We have decided"*: Ibid.

203 *"I've never seen"*: Clark to Horton, June 29, 1961, Box 3, Clark Papers, Avery.

203 *"I am sorry you"*: Horton to Clark, June 21, 1961, Box 3, Clark Papers, Avery.

203 *"she is a victim"*: Horton to Maxwell Hahn, Field Foundation, June 19, 1961, Box 38, Folder 2, HREC/Wis.

204 *"Our work with the grassroots"*: Clark to Horton, July 3, 1961, Box 7, Clark Papers, Avery.

204 *"The remaining workable years"*: Ibid.

204 *tried to assure them*: Horton to Clark and Robinson, June 21, 1961, Series 3, Box 154, Folder 3, SCLC/Emory.

204 *"like a poor relative"*: Clark to Warings, August 15, 1961, Waring/M-S.

204 *"I yielded"*: Ibid.

204 *"the South needed me"*: Ibid.

Chapter 26: Freedom Rides

205 *"PhD minds"*: Young, *Burden*, p. 141.

205 *especially interested*: Dorothy Cotton, *If Your Back's Not Bent: The Role of the Citizenship Education Program in the Civil Rights Movement* (New York: Atria Books, 2012), pp. 98–99.

205 *"pecan-brown"*: Young, *Burden*, p. 141.

206 *larger salary*: Charron, *Teacher*, p. 305.

206 *often mistook*: Young, *Burden*, p. 141.

206 *They took off*: Young, *Burden*, pp. 141–42.

207 *rides had begun*: Lewis, *Walking*, pp. 130–39; Branch, *Parting*, pp. 412–24; for an expansive account, see Raymond Arsenault, *Freedom Riders: 1961 and the Struggle for Racial Justice* (Oxford: Oxford University Press, 2006).

207 *They sat together*: Lewis, *Walking*, pp. 140–43.

207 *coordinated the assault*: Lewis, *Walking*, p. 143; Branch, *Parting*, p. 420.

208 *armed with clubs*: Branch, *Parting*, pp. 417–20.

208 *The violence*: Lewis, *Walking*, pp. 144–47.

208 *reached Birmingham*: McWhorter, *Carry Me*, pp. 194–221; Lewis, *Walking*, pp. 146–58.

208 *Another white mob*: Lewis, *Walking*, pp. 154–58; Branch, *Parting*, pp. 444–50. A thousand Montgomery whites also besieged a mass meeting at Rev. Abernathy's church, restrained only by the tear gas and bayonets of federal marshals ordered by Attorney General Robert Kennedy. Branch, *Parting*, pp. 454–65; Lewis, *Walking*, pp. 158–62.

208 *Parchman Penitentiary*: Lewis, *Walking*, pp. 167–72.

209 *"an upsurge"*: Lewis, *Walking*, p. 176.

209 *provoked the White House*: On May 29, 1961, the Kennedy administration directed the Interstate Commerce Commission to desegregate all facilities under its jurisdiction; the order went into effect in November 1961. King Institute Stanford University, https://kinginstitute.stanford.edu/freedom-rides; Branch, *Parting*, pp. 278–79.

209 *channeled into something*: Branch, *Parting*, pp. 478–82.

209 *Dorchester Cooperative Community Center*: descriptions in Clark, *Ready*, pp. 62–64; Young, *Burden*, pp. 144–46; Cotton, *Back*, pp. 111–19.

209 *Each group*: Young, *Burden*, pp. 144–49; Clark, *Ready*, pp. 63–65; Cotton in Wigginton, *Refuse*, pp. 287–89.

210 *Monday mornings*: Clark, *Ready*, pp. 61–62; Charron, *Teacher*, p. 314.

210 *"I teach them"*: SPC to Warings, August 15, 1961.

210 *"forced many whites"*: SPC to Warings, August 28, 1961, Waring/M-S.

211 *developing a plan*: Branch, *Parting*, pp. 479–82; Evan Faulkenbury, *Poll Power: The Voter Education Project and the Movement for the Ballot in the American South* (Chapel Hill: University of North Carolina Press, 2019), pp. 29–31, 40–45. Steven F. Lawson, *Black Ballots* (Lanham: Lexington Books, 1999), pp. 261–64; Garrow, *Cross*, pp. 161–64.

211 *debate within SNCC*: Lewis, *Walking*, pp. 178–80; Ransby, *Ella Baker*, pp. 268–79; Branch, *Parting*, pp. 485–87.

212 *to thrash out*: Lewis, *Walking*, pp. 180–81; Ransby, *Ella Baker*, pp. 268–69; Branch, *Parting*, pp. 486–88; Clayborne Carson, *In Struggle: SNCC and the Black Awakening of the 1960s* (Cambridge: Harvard University Press, 1981), pp. 37–42.

Chapter 27: Born Again

213 *Months before*: Glen, *No Ordinary*, p. 207. The benefactor was Ethel Clyde, widow of a scion of the Clyde steamship company, who used her wealth to support a range of liberal causes.

213 *freshly formed*: Horton, *Long Haul*, pp. 110–12; Glen, *No Ordinary*, p. 207.

213 *"new-born babe"*: Jacobs, *Horton Reader*, p. 158.

214 *"confiscate the ideas"*: Horton quoted in *Chattanooga Times*, October 10, 1961, cited in Glen, *No Ordinary*, p. 207.

214 *caravan of cars*: description from Candie Carawan, author interview, December 2, 2021.

214 *no money*: Horton, "Confidential Memo to 300 Friends of Highlander," October 6, 1961.

214 *Horton's plan*: Highlander Twenty-Ninth Annual Report October 1960–September 1961; Aimee Horton, *Highlander*, pp. 233–35; Alden Morris described Highlander as a "movement half-way house" in *Origins*, pp. 139–57.

214 *grand plans*: Jenkins in Carawan, *Tree of Life*, pp. 156–59; Highlander Three-Year Report 1961–64.

214 *"skinny white boy"*: Cotton, *Back*, p. 105.

215 *rethinking his place*: Carawan memoir, p. 31; Carawans interview by Joseph Mosnier for the Civil Rights History Project, Smithsonian Institution and Library of Congress, 2011, p. 16; Carawans interview by Adams, transcript, Appalachian State, pp. 68–72.

215 *send more dispatches*: Carawan interview by Mosnier, Civil Rights History, pp. 16–17.

215 *"a picnic"*: description by Professor Scott Bates of University of the South, Sewanee, a Highlander Board member, in Edgerton, *Shades of Gray*, "Trial of Highlander," p. 72; Adams, *Seeds of Fire*, p. 141; Auction Notice, *Nashville Tennessean*, December 10, 1961, p. 157.

215 *The auctioneer*: Glen, *No Ordinary*, pp. 207–8; Edgerton, quoting Bates in Trial, pp. 71–72.

216 *offered to pay*: Glen, *No Ordinary*, p. 208.

216 *The buildings*: Egerton, *Trial*, p. 72; Adams, *Seeds of Fire*, p. 141.

216 *A lawyer*: Glen, *No Ordinary*, p. 208.

216 *burned down*: Adams, *Seeds of Fire*, p. 141.

Chapter 28: Ready from Within

217 *"We are getting"*: SPC to Warings, October 6, 1961, Waring/M-S.

217 *matter of will*: SPC to Warings, August 28, 1961, Waring/M-S.

217 *Mrs. Clark's family*: Yvonne Clark, Septima's granddaughter, described the family reaction, January 21, 2022, interview by author.

217 *open a file*: Septima Clark in Mississippi Sovereignty Commission files, Mississippi Department of Archives and History, https://da.mdah.ms.gov/sovcom/imagelisting .php. SPC appears in FBI files on Highlander Folk School and SCLC, https://vault.fbi .gov/search?SearchableText=Septima+Clark.

217 *annoyed Dorothy Cotton*: Cotton, *Back*, pp. 95–96 and 194. Andy Young on sexism at SCLC in *Burden*, p. 139.

217 *had Ella Baker*: Clark on Baker's discomfort at SCLC in Walker interview, p. 12; Hall interview, pp. 80–81. Dorothy Cotton discusses Baker's criticisms of SCLC in *Back*, pp. 94–96. Also see Levine, "Citizenship Schools" dissertation, pp. 219–22.

218 *miss the beauty*: Clark, *Echo*, p. 233.

218 *strategic plan*: Young, *Burden*, p. 143.

218 *sang, before she spoke*: Cotton profile in Seeger and Reiser, *Everybody*, p. 119; Cotton describes opening every session with song in *Back*, p. 126 and pp. 150–51.

218 *"the people would speak"*: Cotton in Seeger and Reiser, *Everybody*, p. 120; Cotton, *Back*, pp. 126–30; Young, *Burden*, p. 149.

219 *"What's wrong with"*: Clark reports this exchange to the Warings, August 28, 1961, Waring/M-S.

219 *cobwebs commenced*: Cotton in Wigginton, *Refuse*, p. 289.

219 *"wasn't that brave"*: Gillespie, *CEP and Black Women*, p. 63.

220 *wrote CITIZEN*: Clark, "Literacy and Liberation" essay, *Freedomways*; Cotton in Wigginton, *Refuse*, pp. 288–89; Cotton, *Back*, pp. 131–35.

220 *"We'd ask them"*: Clark, *Ready*, pp. 63–64.

220 *"Before we started"*: Cotton in Seeger and Reiser, *Everybody*, p. 120.

220 *"They learned that maybe"*: Cotton in Seeger and Reiser, *Everybody*, p. 121.

220 *received lessons in*: Young, *Burden*, pp. 146–48; Cotton, *Back*, pp. 131–35.

221 *"We were trying"*: Clark, *Ready*, p. 64.

221 *"intellectual and emotional"*: Cotton in Seeger and Reiser, *Everybody*, p. 120.

221 *field trips*: Young, *Burden*, pp. 148–49.

221 *filled soda bottles*: Clark interview by Walker, p. 16.

221 *"songs of sorrow"*: Cotton in Seeger and Reiser, *Everybody*, p. 120; Cotton, *Back*, p. 127.

221 *"We changed the words"*: Gillespie, *CEP and Black Women*, p. 97.

221 *"The people who left"*: Clark, *Ready*, p. 64.

221 *SNCC field organizers*: Lewis, *Walking*, p. 181.

222 *"nonviolent guerrilla fighters"*: Ibid.

222 *When Charles Sherrod*: for the beginnings of the Albany movement, see Lewis, *Walking*, p. 181, pp. 185–86; Branch, *Parting*, pp. 524–38; Seeger and Reiser, *Everybody*, pp. 71–73.

222 *"When I opened"*: Bernice Johnson (Reagon) quoted in https://snccdigital.org/events/albany-movement-formed/.

222 *"Songs were the bed"*: Reagon quoted in Seeger and Reiser, *Everybody*, p. 73; for more on the Albany "singing movement," see Seeger and Reiser, *Everybody*, pp. 53–67; Carawan and Carawan, *Sing for Freedom*, pp. 53–67.

223 *Carawan also came*: Carawan memoir, p. 36; also in Carawan interview by Adams, Appalachian State. Carawan, Lomax, and Gay, *Freedom in the Air: A Documentary on Albany, Georgia 1961–1962*, SNCC label.

223 *goals . . . too broad*: see Young, *Burden*, pp. 166–84; Branch, *Parting*, pp. 538–58; Carson, *In Struggle*, pp. 56–65; Lee Formwalt, "Albany Movement," New Georgia Encyclopedia, https://www.georgiaencyclopedia.org/articles/history-archaeology/albany-movement/.

223 *"on the job"*: Young, *Burden*, p. 171.

223 *come to Dorchester*: Young, *Burden*, pp. 171–73.

223 *"They created a style"*: Cotton, *Back*, p. 151.

224 *Democratic primary*: Young, *Burden*, pp. 180–81.

224 *"I stood at"*: Clark interview by Walker, p. 12.

224 *burned to the ground*: SCLC newsletter, September 1962, Civil Rights Movement Archive, https://www.crmvet.org/docs/sclc/6209_sclc_newsletter.pdf.

224 *Black vote helped*: Young, *Burden*, p. 181.

224 *Thomas Chatmon*: Civil Rights Movement Archive, https://www.crmvet.org/tim/timhis61.htm#1961albany.

224 *began repealing*: Ibid.

225 *"What did we win?"*: A. C. Searles, editor of the *Southwest Georgian*, quoted in Seeger and Reiser, *Everybody*, p. 81.

225 *"If things are going"*: Cotton, *Back*, p. 130.

Chapter 29: Tremor in the Iceberg

226 *Robinson quickly established*: Gillespie, *Citizen Education*, p. 76.

226 *projects with beauticians*: Nico Slate, "Beauty and Power," p. 757.

226 *shiny new Progressive Club*: Highlander Three-Year Report, 1961–64, p. 3.

227 *SNCC field organizers*: Highlander Three-Year Report, p. 2.

227 *Bob Moses*: biographical details from Branch, *Parting*, pp. 325–31; Carson, *In Struggle*, pp. 46–49; John Dittmer, *Local People: The Struggle for Civil Rights in Mississippi* (Urbana: University of Illinois Press, 1994), pp. 102–5.

227 *he never slept*: Myles Horton describes Moore's defensive sleeping habits in an interview by Jack Rabin, https://digital.libraries.psu.edu/digital/collection/rabin/id/2394/rec/1.

227 *planted himself in McComb*: Dittmer, *Local People*, pp. 103–8; Branch, *Parting*, pp. 492–500; Charles M. Payne, *I've Got the Light of Freedom: The Organizing Tradition and the Mississippi Freedom Struggle* (Berkeley: University of California Press, 1995), pp. 111–26.

227 *Herbert Lee*: on the killing of Lee, see Payne, *Got the Light*, pp. 121–23; Dittmer, *Local People*, pp. 109–10.

228 *"This is Mississippi"*: Moses quoted in Payne, *Got the Light*, p. 126 and Seeger and Reiser, *Everybody*, p. 162.

228 *a crash course*: Bernice Robinson, "Mississippi Voter-Education Report," July 19, 1962, Box 38, Folder 6, HREC/Wis; "Schedule for Voter Education Workshop June 4–9 1962," ibid.; audio recording of workshop, HREC/Wis, 515A/219-225; Payne, *Got the Light*, pp. 142–44.

228 *Her first stop*: all details from Robinson, "Mississippi Voter-Education Report," op. cit.

229 *"fear prevented"*: Mississippi Report, p. 2.

229 *"this fear is real"*: Mississippi Report, p. 4.

229 *"pictures of Myles Horton"*: Mississippi Report, p. 5.

229 *opened a file*: "Robinson, Bernice" in Mississippi Sovereignty Commission files, https://da.mdah.ms.gov/sovcom/imagelisting.php.

230 *Vera Mae Pigee*: see Francoise N. Hamlin, *Crossroads at Clarksdale: The Black Freedom Struggle in the Mississippi Delta after WWII* (Chapel Hill: University of North Carolina Press, 2012) and Dr. Vera Pigee, *The Struggle of Struggles* (Detroit: Harlo Press, 1991).

230 *"really ran the operations"*: Young, *Burden*, p. 142.

230 *"I think freedom"*: Pigee quoted in Hamlin, *Crossroads*, p. 73.

230 *first interracial concert*: Hamlin, *Crossroads*, pp. 80–81; Pigee, *Struggles*, pp. 31–32; Candie Carawan, author interview.

230 *Greyhound station*: Hamlin, *Crossroads*, pp. 73–74.

231 *in her beauty parlor*: Hamlin, *Crossroads*, pp. 65–69. Photo of Pigee's class meeting, p. 69.

231 *night riders' bullets*: Hamlin, *Crossroads*, p. 112.

231 *Eldridge Willie Steptoe*: biographical details from the SNCC Legacy Project, https://sncclegacyproject.org/in-memoriam-eugene-willie-steptoe/; Mississippi Encyclopedia essay by Professor Ted Ownby, https://mississippiencyclopedia.org/entries/ew-steptoe/; SNCC Digital Gateway, https://snccdigital.org/events/bob-moses-goes-to-mccomb/and https://snccdigital.org/people/e-w-steptoe/; Payne, *Got the Light*, pp. 113–14.

231 *"I've been waiting"*: https://snccdigital.org/people/e-w-steptoe/.

231 *"really absorbed"*: Young, *Burden*, pp. 153–54.

231 *horse-drawn wagon*: Ibid.

232 *"I came to redish"*: Ibid.

232 *callous move*: Payne, *Got the Light*, pp. 158–63; Dittmer, *Local People*, pp. 143–47.

232 *Victoria Jackson Gray*: Gillespie, *CEP and Black Women*, pp. 118–23; Dittmer, *Local People*, pp. 181–83; Charron, *Teacher*, pp. 326–27.

232 *door-to-door*: Gillespie, *CEP and Black Women*, p. 123.

233 *"phone ringing"*: Gillespie, *CEP and Black Women*, p. 122.

233 *the price was small*: Hamer biographical details in Charles Marsh, *God's Long Summer: Stories of Faith and Civil Rights* (Princeton: Princeton University Press, 1997), pp. 10–33. See also Kate Clifford Larsen, *Walk with Me: A Biography of Fannie Lou Hamer* (Oxford: Oxford University Press, 2021); Keisha N. Blain, *Until I Am Free: Fannie Lou Hamer's Enduring Message to America* (Boston: Beacon Press, 2021); Kay Mills, *This Little Light of Mine: The Life of Fannie Lou Hamer* (Lexington: University Press of Kentucky, 2007).

233 *"I never heard"*: Hamer interview, https://www.pbs.org/video/fannie-lou-hamer-stand-up-1ecoc6/.

233 *registration hopefuls*: Marsh, *Summer*, pp. 13–15.

233 *"too yellow"*: Marsh, *Summer*, p. 15.

234 *"I didn't go"*: Gillespie, *CEP and Black Women*, p. 100.

234 *join the movement*: Payne, *Light*, pp. 154–55.

234 *Dorchester for training*: Young, *Burden*, pp. 152–54; Cotton, *Back*, pp. 126–27; Clark, *Ready*, p. 63.

234 *"that's how"*: James Bevel interview by Aldon Morris in *Origins*, p. 239.

Chapter 30: Project C

235 *Alabama's largest city*: for origins and overview of the Birmingham campaign, see Civil Rights Movement Archive, https://www.crmvet.org/tim/timhis63.htm#1963bham. For full accounts, see Young, *Burden*, pp. 185–252; Branch, *Parting*, pp. 681–707; Garrow, *Cross*, pp. 225–65; Jonathan Eig, *King: A Life* (New York: Farrar, Straus and Giroux, 2023), pp. 284–304; Diane McWhorter, *Carry Me Home: The Climactic Battle of the Civil Rights Revolution* (New York: Simon & Schuster, 2001).

235 *shut down*: in 1959 the Prince Edward County, Virginia, school system shut its schools for five years, depriving Black children of education, while the county funded private "white academies" for white children. Civil Rights Movement Archive, "Massive Evasion," https://www.crmvet.org/tim/tim64c.htm#1964schoolint.

236 *University of Mississippi*: John F. Kennedy Presidential Library, "Integrating Ole' Miss," https://microsites.jfklibrary.org/olemiss/confrontation/.

236 *strategy retreat*: Young, *Burden*, pp. 188–92.

236 *on the field of battle*: Young, *Burden*, pp. 189, 192; Cotton, *Back*, pp. 208–10.

236 *kicked off*: Young, *Burden*, p. 203; Birmingham Campaign Timeline, https://www
.bhamwiki.com/w/Timeline_of_the_Civil_Rights_Movement_in_Birmingham
#Birmingham_Campaign_(April_3-May_10).

236 *scribbled a passionate*: Branch, *Parting*, pp. 737–40.

237 *"children's crusade"*: Cotton, *Back*, pp. 212–16; Young, *Burden*, pp. 236–41; Branch, *Parting*, pp. 756–81; Lewis, *Walking*, pp. 196–98.

237 *"Do you think"*: Clark, *Ready*, p. 7.

238 *"children of Birmingham"*: "500 are Arrested," *New York Times*, May 3, 1963, p. 1; "Dogs and Hoses Repulse Negroes at Birmingham," *New York Times*, May 4, 1963, p. 1.

238 *broker a settlement*: Young, *Burden*, p. 243–46; Eig, *King*, pp. 301–3.

238 *jailed children*: Tomiko Brown-Nagin, *Civil Rights Queen: Constance Baker Motley and the Struggle for Equality* (New York: Pantheon Books, 2022), pp. 189–99.

238 *first ten weeks*: Branch, *Parting*, p. 825.

238 *Charleston's response*: "14 Negroes Convicted of Trespassing," *Charleston Evening Post*, June 24, 1963, p. 11.

238 *thrown behind bars*: Gillespie, *CEP and Black Women*, pp. 89–90.

239 *"most integrated city"*: Raines, *My Soul*, p. 443.

239 *trained more than*: "SCLC Citizenship Education Program Statistical Report, July 1962–February 1964," Box 137, Folder 2, CEP Part 4, Series I/2/iii, SCLC/Emory.

239 *"They walked, talked"*: Gillespie, *CEP and Black Women*, p. 89, quoting Dorothy Boles, "Narrative from the West Gwinnett Citizenship School," 1963, CEP Part 4, Box 160, Folder 1, Series III/5, SCLC/Emory.

239 *"just a quiet building"*: Dorothy Cotton in Morris, *Origins*, p. 239.

240 *"so glamorous"*: SPC to MLK (n.d.; probably late 1963), Box 3, Folder 122, Clark Papers, Avery. Also quoted in Charron, *Teacher*, p. 319.

240 *Annell Ponder*: for biographical details, see SNCC Digital Gateway: https://sncc digital.org/people/annell-ponder/ *Washington Post*, October 26, 2018: https://www.washingtonpost.com/history/2018/10/26/decades-before-stacey-abrams -these-black-women-risked-their-lives-register-black-voters/.

240 *first dispatched*: Gillespie, *CEP and Black Women*, pp. 83–85.

240 *called to Greenwood*: Gillespie, *CEP and Black Women*, pp. 93–95, 118–20; Payne, *Light*, p. 166.

240 *worked with Bob Moses*: Ponder, "Citizen Education in the 'Heart of the Iceberg' essay," Fall 1963, Mss. 577, Box 16, Folder 5, Council of Federated Organizations (COFO) papers, Wisconsin Historical Society.

240 *town of Winona*: Affidavits of Fannie Lou Hamer and Annell Ponder, SNCC/COFO Freedom Information Service records, Micro 780, Reel 2, Segment 1, Wisconsin Historical Society. Additional accounts in Adams, *Seeds of Fire*, pp. 158–61; Young, *Burden*, pp. 253–58; Dittmer, *Local People*, pp. 170–173; Branch, *Parting*, pp. 819–21, 825.

241 *"Ain't no damn"*: Annell Ponder affidavit, p. 1, op. cit.

241 *"Just give us the keys"*: Young, *Burden*, pp. 254–55; Cotton, *Back*, pp. 216–18.

241 *"Those are women"*: Cotton, *Back*, p. 216.

242 *through swollen lips*: Ponder quoted in Adams, *Seeds of Fire*, p. 161.

Chapter 31: A Living Petition

243 *"standing in the schoolhouse"*: Branch, *Parting*, p. 821.

243 *pompous theatrics*: Branch, *Parting*, pp. 821–22.

243 *abruptly decided*: Branch, *Parting*, pp. 823–24.

243 *"We preach freedom"*: JF Kennedy, "Televised Address to the Nation on Civil Rights" June 11, 1963, transcript, John F. Kennedy Presidential Library, Boston, MA, https://www.jfklibrary.org/learn/about-jfk/historic-speeches/televised-address-to-the-nation-on-civil-rights.

243 *"most eloquent, profound"*: King to Kennedy, June 11, 1963, JFK Presidential papers, White House file, John F. Kennedy Presidential Library.

244 *dropped her coffee pot*: Robinson in Wigginton, *Refuse*, p. 298.

244 *"Amid all the chaos"*: Bernice Robinson activity report, June 15, 1963, Box 24, Folder 13, HREC/Wis.

244 *vowed to defeat*: Woods, *Black/Red*, p. 172.

244 *Among those testifying*: Woods, *Black/Red*, pp. 174–75; Katagiri, *Black Freedom*, pp. 222–26.

244 *same documentary evidence*: Ibid; and "Barnett Charges Kennedys Assist Red Racial Plot," *New York Times*, July 13, 1963, p. 1.

245 *secret intelligence-gathering*: FBI memo, Baumgardner to Sullivan, July 26, 1963, Part 14 of HFS FBI Files.

245 *newly formed, patriotic-sounding*: Katagiri, *Black Freedom*, pp. 226–30; "Coordinating Committee for Fundamental American Freedom" file, Burke Marshall Personal Papers, John F. Kennedy Presidential Library BMPP-028-002; "Vigorous Foe of Rights Bill," *Christian Science Monitor*, March 27, 1964.

245 *Wickcliffe Preston Draper*: Douglas Blackmon, "How the South's Fight to Uphold Segregation Was Funded," *Wall Street Journal*, June 11, 1999.

245 *Citizens' Council Radio Forum*: Mississippi State University Libraries, Special Collections, https://scholarsjunction.msstate.edu/mss-citizens-council-forum/.

246 *"Freedom Now Movement"*: https://www.naacpldf.org/march-on-washington/.

246 *"a living petition"*: "Civil Rights Leaders Urge a Proud and Orderly March," *New York Times*, August 25, 1963, p. 1; March on Washington for Jobs and Freedom program, August 28, 1963, NARA 5753043.

246 *forced to edit*: Lewis, *Walking*, pp. 216–31.

246 *any substantive way*: Theoharis, *Rebellious*, pp. 160–61.

247 *march with the men*: Theoharis, *Rebellious*, p. 161.

247 *Pauli Murray complained*: Theoharis, *Rebellious*, p. 160.

247 *"Tribute to Women"*: Theoharis, *Rebellious*, pp. 161–62.

247 *was acknowledged*: Theoharis, *Rebellious*, p. 162.

247 *she was frustrated*: Douglas Brinkley, *Rosa Parks* (New York: Viking/Penguin, 2000), p. 185.

247 *"much of a role"*: Parks, *My Story*, p. 165.

247 *"who did not sing"*: Parks, *My Story*, p. 166.

247 *"treated like hostesses"*: Brinkley, *Rosa*, p. 185.

247 *"Nowadays, women wouldn't stand"*: Parks, *My Story*, p. 166.

247 *held their own meeting*: https://kinginstitute.stanford.edu/freedom-black-women-speak-march-washington-jobs-and-freedom.

247 *Baker had warned her*: Clark interview by Walker, p. 12.
247 *serve them coffee*: Young, *Burden*, p. 139.
247 *"his tendency to ignore"*: Ibid.
248 *"any faith in women"*: Clark, *Ready*, p. 77.
248 *have really enough intelligence*: Clark interview by Walker, p. 11.
248 *"Where in the world"*: Cotton, *Back*, p. 223.
248 *their "Freedom Vote"*: Dittmer, *Local People*, pp. 200–206; Payne, *Light*, pp. 294–97.
249 *formed the core*: Gillespie, *CEP and Black Women*, pp. 123–26; "Delta Rights Movement Functions as Schoolhouse," *Jackson Free Press* (Mississippi), August 31, 1963.
249 *cast their ballots*: Dittmer, *Local People*, p. 205.
249 *first speech to Congress*: "Johnson Bids Congress Enact Civil Rights Bill with Speed," *New York Times*, November 28, 1963, p. 1.
250 *attend the trial*: Clark, Walker interview, p. 32; Taylor Branch, *Pillar of Fire* (New York: Touchstone, 1998), pp. 192–93.
250 *the courtroom chandelier*: Clark, Walker interview, p. 24.
250 *walking the corridors*: Young, *Burden*, p. 197.
250 *including adding "sex"*: Jo Freeman, "How 'Sex' Got into Title VII: Persistent Opportunism as a Maker of Public Policy," *Law and Inequality: A Journal of Theory and Practice* 9, no. 2 (March 1991): pp. 163–84.
251 *managed to maneuver*: Branch, *Pillar*, p. 267.
251 *"We shall now"*: Russell, *Congressional Record*, March 16, 1964, 5338–42. Quoted in Branch, *Pillar*, p. 267.

Chapter 32: Practicing Democracy

252 *each side appointed*: "Senate Rights Battalions Deploy," *Christian Science Monitor*, March 20, 1964, p. 9; "The Civil Rights Act of 1964: Long Struggle for Freedom," Library of Congress, https://www.loc.gov/exhibits/civil-rights-act/. Civil Rights Act in the Senate: https://www.senate.gov/artandhistory/history/civil_rights/civil_rights.htm.
252 *his facetious scheme*: "Relocate Negroes Evenly in States Russell Proposes," *New York Times*, March 17, 1964, p. 1.
252 *lead in opposing*: "Anti-Rights Bill Cry Linked to Racists," *Chicago Tribune*, March 15, 1964, p. C48; Yasuri Katagiri, *The Mississippi Sovereignty Commission* (Jackson: University Press of Mississippi, 2001), pp. 123–25 and 150–52; "Coordinating Committee" entry in Mississippi Encyclopedia, http://mississippiencyclopedia.org/entries/coordinating-committee-for-fundamentalamerican-freedoms/.
252 *"Looking Down Your Throat"*: "Anti-Rights Bill Lobby is Best-Financed Ever," *Washington Post*, March 22, 1964, p. A9; "Smear Campaign against Civil Rights Bill Condemned," *Afro-American*, March 21, 1964, p. 3.
253 *freedom schools were modeled*: Gillespie, *CEP and Black Women*, pp. 131–32.
253 *split the SNCC leadership*: Lewis, *Walking*, pp. 248–52; Dittmer, *Local People*, pp. 207–11; Ransby, *Baker*, pp. 324–25; Adams, *Seeds of Fire*, pp. 167–69.
253 *"Sing for Freedom"*: Carawan memoir, pp. 38–39; Guy and Candie Carawan, "Sing for Freedom" workshop album liner notes, Folkways Records (FK 5488).
254 *dispatched its investigators*: Katagiri, *Mississippi Sovereignty*, pp. 158–59.

254 *outfitted a truck*: Lewis, *Walking*, p. 254; Branch, *Pillar*, p. 239.

254 *Black informants*: Katagiri, *Mississippi Sovereignty*, pp. 159–60 and 162–63.

254 *whip Everett Dirksen*: CRA in the Senate, op. cit., Part 3; Branch, *Pillar*, p. 301; *Long Struggle*, Library of Congress. For a full account of the cloture negotiations and vote, see Todd S. Purdum, *An Idea Whose Time Has Come* (New York: Henry Holt & Co., 2014), pp. 286–312.

255 *last gasp*: Branch, *Pillar*, pp. 334–36.

255 *newsman Roger Mudd*: Purdum, *Idea*, p. 303.

255 *week of orientation*: Lewis, *Walking*, pp. 255–58; Dittmer, *Local People*, pp. 242–46; Branch, *Pillar*, pp. 351–54.

256 *taking note of*: Katagiri, *Mississippi Sovereignty*, pp. 162–63.

256 *Senator Clair Engle*: Civil Rights Bill in the Senate, Part 3, op. cit.; Branch, *Pillar*, p. 336.

256 *margin of four votes*: New York Times, June 20, 1964, p. 1.

257 *"apply uniform qualification"*: Civil Rights Act of 1964, PL 88-352, https://www.senate.gov.

257 *the three men*: Lewis, *Walking*, pp. 261–65; Dittmer, *Local People*, pp. 246–48.

257 *Bob Moses was standing*: Adam, *Seeds of Fire*, p. 172, from Adams interview of Horton.

257 *flew to Meridian*: Lewis, *Walking*, p. 264.

257 *publicity stunt*: Johnson conversation with Eastland, June 23, 1964, White House tape WH6406.14, Miller Center, University of Virginia, https://millercenter.org/the-presidency/educational-resources/mississippi-burning.

257 *seventy-two ceremonial pens*: New York Times, July 3, 1964, p. 1.

258 *plunging into Freedom Summer*: Bruce Hartford, "Mississippi Freedom Summer," Civil Rights Movement Archive, https://www.crmvet.org/tim/msfs64.pdf; Freedom Summer Digital Collection, Historical Society of Wisconsin, https://content.wisconsinhistory.org/digital/collection/; Dittmer, *Local People*, pp. 251–65.

258 *Mrs. Clark had trained*: Gillespie, *CEP and Black Women*, pp. 131–36; Victoria Gray Adams quoted in Levine, "Citizenship Schools" dissertation, p. 266.

258 *lashed out in revenge*: Lewis, *Walking*, p. 274; SNCC incident reports, Freedom Summer, https://sncclegacyproject.org/wats-reports/.

258 *created their own*: Ransby, *Baker*, pp. 330–35; Dittmer, *Local People*, pp. 279–83; Vicki Crawford, "African American Women in the Mississippi Freedom Democratic Party" in Collier-Thomas and Franklin, *Sisters in the Struggle*, Chapter 8; Mississippi Freedom Democratic Party records, Mss. 586, Wisconsin Historical Society; Victoria Gray Adams Papers, Special Collections M345, University of Southern Mississippi Library.

259 *crashed the . . . convention*: Lewis, *Walking*, pp. 283–90; Ransby, *Baker*, pp. 336–42; Blain, *Until I Am Free*, pp. 50–58; Branch, *Pillar*, pp. 456–76; "MFDP Challenge to the Democratic Convention," https://www.crmvet.org/info/mfdp_atlantic.pdf.

259 *"I question America"*: Testimony of Fannie Lou Hamer, National Democratic Convention, August 22, 1964, https://www.crmvet.org/docs/flh_ac.htm.

259 *"slammed in our face"*: Lewis, *Walking*, p. 291.

259 *embittered them*: Ibid.

Chapter 33: Lay Our Bodies on the Line

260 *"Dear Citizenship Teacher"*: Citizenship Education Program Staff to Teachers, October 12, 1964, Series III, Subseries 10.2, Box 546, Folder 3, SCLC/Emory.

260 *in a small church*: SPC to Warings, November 16, 1964, Waring/M-S.

261 *eligible Black voters*: Faulkenbury, *Poll Power*, p. 82; "Black Turnout in 1964 and Beyond," *New York Times*, October 17, 2014, https://www.nytimes.com/2014/10/17/upshot/black-turnout-in-1964-and-beyond.html.

261 *electoral map math*: Faulkenbury, *Poll Power*, p. 82; Gary May, *Bending Toward Justice: The Voting Rights Act and the Transformation of American Democracy* (New York: Basic Books, 2013), pp. 49–50.

261 *falling apart*: Lewis, *Walking*, pp. 291–93; Ransby, *Baker*, pp. 342–44; Carson, *Struggle*, pp. 133–54.

261 *"When a Southern Black man"*: Clark in Wigginton, *Refuse*, p. 314.

262 *kept every program*: souvenirs from the trip are in Clark's personal papers at Avery Research Center.

262 *when Elizabeth lambasted*: Charron, *Teacher*, pp. 287, 289; for example, see SPC to Warings, June 14, 1959.

262 *"unmercifully truthful"*: Clark interview by Jacqueline Hall.

262 *turned her away*: Tinsley, *Passion for Justice*, p. 238.

262 *"My dear, dear"*: SPC to Warings, November 16, 1964, Waring/M-S.

263 *do it—eventually*: Young, *Burden*, p. 326; May, *Bending*, p. 48.

263 *"have to push harder"*: SPC to Warings, November 16, 1964, Waring/M-S.

263 *dispatched to Selma*: Gillespie, *CEP and Black Women*, p. 146; Cotton, *Back*, p. 234.

263 *Amelia Boynton*: SNCC Digital Gateway, https://snccdigital.org/people/amelia-boynton/; Young, *Burden*, p. 338; *New York Times* obituary, August 26, 2015.

263 *challenged a white incumbent*: "Negro Woman Is a Candidate," *Washington Post*, March 11, 1964.

264 *courthouse to register*: Equal Justice Institute, https://calendar.eji.org/racial-injustice/oct/7#:~:text.

264 *Marie Foster*: "Marie Foster, Early Fighter for Voting Rights Dies," *New York Times*, September 12, 2003.

264 *outrageous injunction*: Branch, *Pillar*, p. 391.

264 *the campaign in Selma*: details from David J. Garrow, *Protest at Selma* (New Haven: Yale University Press, 1978); Charles F. Fager, *Selma 1965* (New York: Scribner, 1974); "Selma Voting Rights Campaign," Civil Rights Movement Archive, http://www.crmvet.org/images/imgselma.html; Young, *Burden*, pp. 342–53; Lewis, *Walking*, pp. 313–32.

265 *in a spare bedroom*: Young, *Burden*, p. 343.

265 *schoolteachers*: May, *Bending*, pp. 62–64; Young, *Burden*, p. 349.

265 *protect his mother*: Young, *Burden*, p. 353.

265 *expression of rage*: Young, *Burden*, pp. 353–54.

Chapter 34: Ain't Nobody Gonna Turn Us 'Round

267 *came over the crest*: Lewis, *Walking*, pp. 336–44; May, *Bending*, pp. 84–91; Taylor Branch, *At Canaan's Edge* (New York: Simon & Schuster, 2006), pp. 43–57; Garrow, *Protest*, pp. 73–77; Young, *Burden*, pp. 354–57.

267 *"Get up ... "*: May, *Bending*, p. 87; *New York Times*, March 8, 1965, p. 1.
268 *crying and moaning*: Sheyann Webb and Rachel West Nelson, *Selma, Lord, Selma* (Tuscaloosa: University of Alabama Press, 1980), report reprinted in "Bloody Sunday" Civil Rights Movement Archive, https://www.crmvet.org/tim/timhis65.htm #1965selmabloodysunday.
268 *film footage and photos*: Garrow, *Protest*, pp. 78–85; May, *Bending*, pp. 92.
268 *protesters surrounded*: May, *Bending*, pp. 93–95; Branch, *Canaan*, pp. 55–57.
269 *"The mournful"*: "Protests Spread Over the Nation," *New York Times*, March 15, 1965, p. 1.
269 *gave him an opening*: May, *Bending*, pp. 95–99; Garrow, *Protest*, pp. 81–82.
269 *issued an injunction*: Branch, *Canaan*, pp. 58–67; Young, *Burden*, pp. 357–59.
269 *In heated negotiations*: Branch, *Canaan*, pp. 65–73; May, *Bending*, pp. 99–101; Eig, *King*, pp. 428–30.
269 *then turn around*: Branch, *Canaan*, pp. 73–79; May, *Bending*, pp. 101–4; Young, *Burden*, pp. 359–61; Lewis, *Walking*, pp. 347–48.
270 *"destiny of Democracy"*: transcript of President Johnson's address in *New York Times*, March 16, 1965, p. 30.
270 *"Can you believe"*: Lewis, *Walking*, pp. 353–54.
270 *his voting rights bill*: *New York Times*, March 18, 1965, p. 1.
271 *complicated logistics*: Lewis, *Walking*, p. 356.
271 *executive order nationalizing*: Branch, *Canaan*, pp. 135–36; Fager, *Selma*, pp. 148–49.
271 *felt she must go*: Theoharis, *Rebellious*, p. 187; Brinkley, *Parks*, pp. 195–200.
271 *help lead singing*: Candie Carawan interview by author.
271 *Horton also heeded*: Jacobs, *Horton Reader*, p. 150.
271 *At around noon*: accounts of the march in Lewis, *Walking*, pp. 357–60; Fager, *Selma*, pp. 150–65; Young, *Burden*, pp. 363–67; Branch, *Canaan*, pp. 140–54 and 159–70.
272 *"easy part"*: Horton in Jacobs, *Horton Reader*, p. 150.
272 *passed large billboards*: Theoharis, *Rebellious*, p. 187; *Washington Post*, March 23, 1965, p. A1.
273 *came tumbling down*: Branch, *Canaan*, p. 162.
273 *FBI agents*: FBI memo, Selma to Director, March 25, 1965, FBI File No. 44-28544, cited in Branch, *Canaan*, p. 162.
273 *subversive unit*: "Speeches at the Alabama State Capitol at conclusion of the Selma-Montgomery March, March 25, 1965," Jack Rabin Collection on Civil Rights and Southern Activists, Penn State University Libraries, https://digital.libraries.psu.edu /digital/collection/rabin/id/.
273 *"first lady"*: Theoharis, *Rebellious*, p. 188.
273 *denounced the "propaganda"*: partial transcript of Parks's comments in "Speeches at the Alabama State Capitol," op. cit.
273 *"How long will it take"*: MLK's speech, King Institute/Stanford, https://kinginstitute .stanford.edu/our-god-marching.
273 Meet the Press: *Meet the Press*, March 28, 1965, NBC News, https://youtu.be/fAt sAwGreyE.
274 *surveillance recordings*: Katagiri, *Black/Red*, pp. 238–39.

NOTES

Chapter 35: Signatures

275 it "had teeth": Lewis, *Walking*, p. 361.

275 eliminated literacy . . . tests: *New York Times*, March 18, 1965, p. 1.

275 "Let me make": Eastman, Talmadge, and Ellender all quoted in May, *Bending*, p. 150. A detailed chronicle of congressional deliberations on the bill can be found in *Congressional Quarterly Almanac*, 1965, https://library.cqpress.com/cqalmanac/document.php?id=cqal65-1259651.

275 "appearance" book: Gillespie, *CEP and Black Women*, p. 149.

275 "They didn't want": Clark, *Ready*, p. 68.

276 "couldn't take the foolishness": Clark interview by Walker, p. 30.

276 straight to the people: Clark in Wigginton, *Refuse*, pp. 306–7.

277 Ponder came over: Ponder, "CEP Work in Selma, Alabama, May 10–25, 1965," Field Reports 1962–65, Box 155, Folder 26, Series III/4/ii, CEP/SCLC/Emory.

277 "twenty minutes to teach": Clark, *Ready*, p. 68.

277 did not mention voter registration: "Attention: Free Handwriting Clinics," Box 8, Folder 8, Clark Papers, Avery.

277 made their first move: *New York Times*, March 19, 1965, p. 1.

278 hot points of contention: the bill's passage through the Senate described in May, *Bending*, pp. 151–62.

278 debate through Christmas: May, *Bending*, p. 160.

278 "because the whites": Clark, *Ready*, p. 69.

279 were fired: Clark, *Ready*, p. 69.

279 "Unless we pass": Testimony of Congressman John Conyers, Michigan, before House Judiciary Committee, April 1, 1965, National Archives, https://www.archives.gov/legislative/features/voting-rights-1965/conyers.html?_ga=2.266567054.1475699095.1726858087-204747976.1723234065.

279 "dripping venom": Congressman Smith in *Congressional Record*, House, July 6, 1965, p. 15641-2.

279 knocking on doors: "66 Negroes Register as Voter Books Open," *Charleston News and Courier*, July 8, 1965, p. 1B.

280 Hale Boggs of Louisiana: May, *Bending*, pp. 164–65.

280 "I wish I could stand": Boggs quoted in *New York Times*, July 10, 1965, pp. 1, 9; May, *Bending*, p. 164.

281 Among those voting: *New York Times*, July 10, 1965, p. 1.

281 not as pleased: May, *Bending*, pp. 166–67.

282 Katzenbach found King: Branch, *Canaan*, pp. 269–70.

282 "While I would": Branch, *Canaan*, p. 270.

282 enough to swing: *New York Times*, July 30, 1965, p. 1.

282 "Today is a triumph": *New York Times*, August 7, 1965, p. 1.

282 display his pen: Lewis, *Walking*, p. 361.

282 clinics had trained: Clark, *Ready*, p. 68.

283 volunteer civil servants: Garrow, *Protest*, pp. 180–81; May, *Bending*, p. 172.

283 lined up early: May, *Bending*, pp. 172–75; *Southern Courier* 1, no. 5, p. 1, http://www.southerncourier.org/standard/Vol1_No05_1965_08_13.pdf.

362

283 *on the first day*: New York Times, August 11, 1965, p. 1; Garrow, *Protest*, pp. 181–82; Lawson, *Black Ballots*, pp. 329–30; May, *Bending*, p. 174.

284 *Esau Jenkins reported*: Charleston News and Courier, September 12, 1965, p. 23.

Chapter 36: Eyes on the Prize, Hold On

285 *"our most vital"*: "Summary of Ninth Annual Convention, August, 1965," quoted in Charron, *Teacher*, p. 332.

285 *"It made people think"*: Young quoted in Charron, *Teacher*, p. 332.

286 *Selma handwriting clinic instructors*: Gillespie, *CEP and Black Women*, p. 151.

286 *"Even if segregation"*: Baker speech at Hattiesburg Freedom Day, January 20, 1964, in Ransby, *Baker*, p. 319.

287 *became paid program managers*: Charron, *Teacher*, pp. 336–39.

287 *both nervous and excited*: "Alabama Negroes Key to Vote Today," New York Times, May 3, 1966, p. 1.

287 *"panicked on election day"*: SPC letter to Josephine Carson, May 20, 1965, Box 4, Folder 18, Clark Papers, Avery.

288 *"Their hands shook"*: Ibid.

288 *"A great force"*: Ibid.

288 *primary was a disappointment*: "Wife of Wallace Wins in Alabama," New York Times, May 4, 1966, p. 1.

288 *register a million*: May, *Bending*, p. 187.

288 *"supposed to be"*: Gillespie, *CEP and Black Women*, p. 160, from Victoria Gray, "Political Workshop in Sunflower," May 7, 1966, Victoria Gray Papers, University of Southern Mississippi, Hattiesburg.

288 *defeating Sheriff Jim Clark*: May, *Bending*, pp. 181–84, 188–91; Branch, *Canaan*, pp. 461–65.

288 *political education workshop*: Gillespie, *CEP and Black Women*, p. 160.

289 *in a squad car*: Ibid.

289 *Bond was elected*: "Georgia Legislature Refuses to Seat Julian Bond," SNCC Digital Gateway, https://snccdigital.org/events/georgia-legislature-refuses-to-seat-julian-bond/.

289 *"Love is Progress"*: Smithsonian National Museum of African American History and Culture, https://nmaahc.si.edu/object/nmaahc_2014.162.1.

289 *to help his neighbors*: Carawan and Carawan, *Tree of Life*, pp. 161, 168; Charleston Evening Post, July 15, 1966, p. 14; South Carolina Encyclopedia, https://www.scencyclopedia.org/sce/entries/jenkins-esau/.

289 *open a credit union*: Gillespie, *CEP and Black Women*, p. 168; "2nd Anniversary of C.O. Federal Credit Union, October 1968," draft program, Jenkins Papers, Avery; "500 Attend Meeting of Credit Union," Charleston News and Courier, January 27, 1969, p. 9.

290 *number of the box*: "Illiterate Voters Taught to Cast Ballot by Number," Charleston News and Courier, May 29, 1966.

290 *island's young people*: Carawan & Carawan, *Tree of Life*, pp. 156–57.

290 *White House Conference*: Charleston News and Courier, June 2, 1966, p. 46.

291 *published a tribute*: Martin Luther King Jr., *New York Amsterdam News*, May 10, 1962; Mrs. Clark mentions MLK's visit in Clark, *Ready*, p. 79.

291 National Geographic: *National Geographic* 139, no. 3, March 1971.

291 *Moses of his People*: Clark to Alice Spearman, March 29, 1961, Addendum Box 2, Part 1, HFS/TSLA.

291 *certainly had rivals*: Rev. G. C. Brown, "The Struggle Has Come With Esau," Carawan, *Tree of Life*, pp. 140–41.

291 *at the Sea Island*: Highlander Three-Year Report, 1961–64, pp. 3–4, Box 9, Folder 23, HFS/TSLA; Highlander Workshop News, November 1965, Box 84, Folder 7, HFS/TSLA.

291 *poetry workshop*: SNCC Poetry Workshop, May 27, 1965, Audio 515A/239, HREC/Wis.

291 *rejected by the organization*: Lewis, *Walking*, pp. 381–89.

291 *to look inward*: Horton, *Long Haul*, pp. 202–11; Adams, *Seeds of Fire*, pp. 181–89; Glen, *No Ordinary*, pp. 214–17.

291 *Klan paraded*: Horton, *Long Haul*, p. 173; Ku Klux Klan to Demonstrate at Highlander School, 1966, WBIR-TV Film and Video Collection (TAMIS-MIC 2007.001), Knox County Public Library.

291 *two firebombs crashed*: Glen, *No Ordinary*, p. 214.

291 *campaigned on a promise*: *Charleston News and Courier*, April 24, 1964, p. 11; Glen, *No Ordinary*, p. 214.

292 *felt the sudden chill*: Carawan memoir, pp. 41–46.

292 *"these same people"*: Guy Carawan quoted in Adams, *Seeds of Fire*, p. 157.

Chapter 37: Sister Help to Trim the Sail

293 *"men led, but"*: Charles Payne, "Men Led, but Women Organized: Movement Participation of Women in the Mississippi Delta," in Vicki L. Crawford, Jacqueline A. Rouse, and Barbara Woods, eds., *Women in the Civil Rights Movement: Trailblazers and Torchbearers* (Bloomington: Indiana University Press, 1993), pp. 1–12.

294 *"never have taken off"*: Clark, *Ready*, p. 83.

294 *simply dismiss the comments*: Clark, Hall interview, p. 88.

294 *was finally promoted*: Gillespie, *CEP and Black Women*, pp. 163–67.

294 *"swell hotel"*: Clark, *Ready*, p. 80.

294 *"Male Dominance"*: https://aaregistry.org/story/septima-p-clark-south-carolina-educator-and-civil-rights-activist/.

294 *coming to an end*: Gillespie, *CEP and Black Women*, p. 163.

295 *they presented plans*: Gillespie, *CEP and Black Women*, pp. 163–67.

295 *literacy for job training*: Young, *Burden*, p. 418; "Chicago Adult Education Project Report, 1967," Part 4, Series iii, Box 151:6, SCLC/Emory.

295 *traumatized by his experiences*: Lewis, *Walking*, pp. 366–67; Carson, *In Struggle*, pp. 156–57.

296 *"Black Power Boys"*: Clark, Walker interview, p. 37.

296 *angry and distrustful*: Clark, *Ready*, p. 75.

296 *"Can't you find"*: Clark, Walker interview, p. 37; Clark, *Ready*, p. 74.

296 *"box like cold meat"*: SPC to Josephine Carson (Rider), October 20, 1966, Box 4, Folder 18, Clark Papers, Avery.

297 *entered a nervous city*: details of MLK's visit to Charleston from *New York Times*, July 31, 1967; *Charleston News and Courier*, July 31, 1967; Charleston TV station WCSC, https://www.live5news.com/story/37266288/flashback-dr-king-visited-charleston-in-1962-july-1967/; Yvonne Clark interview by author, January 21, 1922.

298 *his last journey to Charleston*: Tinsley, *Passion for Justice*, p. 241.

298 *"but nine of us"*: Clark, *Ready*, p. 29.

298 *staff were squabbling*: Young, *Burden*, p. 433; Garrow, *Cross*, pp. 564–66.

298 *"If we are to keep"*: SPC to MLK, June 12, 1967, King Papers, King Institute, Stanford University, quoted in Garrow, *Cross*, p. 565.

299 *"When I heard"*: Clark, *Ready*, p. 77.

299 *"it just tickled them"*: Ibid.

299 *"I just felt that"*: Clark interview by Hall, p. 84.

Chapter 38: Going Home

300 *"They were afraid"*: Clark, *Ready*, p. 76.

300 *"We spent the night"*: Clark interview by Jean Claude Bouffard, 1982, transcript, University of South Carolina, https://digital.library.sc.edu/exhibits/champions/volume-1-2/part-1/septima-poinsette-clark-island-teacher/.

300 *arranging memorial services*: Clark, *Ready*, p. 76.

300 *drove straight to Atlanta*: Bernice Robinson, "Field Report for April-May-June, June 17, 1968," Box 560, Folder 7, Series 10/10.2, SCLC/Emory; Gillespie, *CEP and Black Women*, p. 177.

300 *her community's grief*: Gillespie, *CEP and Black Women*, p. 177.

301 *"Now they're going"*: *Charleston News and Courier*, April 5, 1968, p. 1.

301 *"took in this scene"*: Cotton, *Back*, pp. 264–65; also "Dorothy Cotton, Rights Champion . . . ," *New York Times* obituary, June 4, 2018.

301 *church memorial services*: Clark, *Ready*, p. 76.

301 *"When I returned"*: Clark, "The Movement I Remember," Clark Papers, Avery.

301 *memorial to the fallen leader*: Young, *Burden*, pp. 479–88.

301 *Caravans of buses*: caravan routes: https://nmaahc.si.edu/explore/stories/1968-poor-peoples-campaign-caravan-routes#.

301 *Resurrection City*: National Park Service, https://www.nps.gov/articles/resurrection-city.htm; "City of Hope," virtual exhibition, Smithsonian NMAAHC, https://static1.squarespace.com/static//SITES+City+of+Hope_Virtual+Exhibition.

302 *coordinate logistics*: Gillespie, *CEP and Black Women*, p. 178.

302 *"glimpsed the future"*: Horton, *Long Haul*, p. 118.

302 *posed for a photo*: Horton, *Long Haul*, p. 117.

302 *Soul Center cultural tent*: "City of Hope," exhibit, op. cit.

302 *"hard detailed job"*: Andrew Young to Ralph Abernathy, Board, and Executive Staff SCLC, August 13, 1969, SCLC records, Series iii/3.2, Box 177, Folder 20; also quoted in Gillespie, *CEP and Black Women*, p. 183.

303 *In petty revenge*: Gillespie, *CEP and Black Women*, p. 169.

303 *hopeful signs sprinkled*: Faulkenbury, *Poll Power*, pp. 106–7; John Lewis and Archie E. Allen, "Black Voter Registration Efforts in the South," *Notre Dame Law Review* 48 (1972).

303 *hundreds of Black candidates*: Faulkenbury, *Poll Power*, pp. 106–7.

303 *candidate workshops*: announcement of Black candidates workshop, June 1966, Highlander Center, cited in Tjerandsen, *Citizenship*, p. 61; Highlander Report (circa 1968) on Candidate Training, in Rosa Parks Papers, Library of Congress.

304 *Freedom Farms Cooperative*: Monica M. White, "A Pig and a Garden: Fannie Lou Hamer and Freedom Farms Cooperative," *Food and Foodways* 25, no. 1 (2017): pp. 20–39; SNCC Digital Gateway, https://snccdigital.org/events/fannie-lou-hamer -founds-freedom-farm-cooperative/.

304 *"white people were shooting"*: Hamer quoted in "Notes in the News: Going Hungry for Freedom," *The Progressive* 32, June 6, 1968. Cited in White, *Pig and Garden*, op. cit., p. 5.

304 *formed a co-op*: all examples from Gillespie, *CEP and Black Women*, p. 180.

304 *a surprise check*: Gillespie, *CEP and Black Women*, p. 181.

304 *actively holding classes*: Gillespie, *CEP and Black Women*, p. 184.

305 *lost the general election*: Young, *Burden*, pp. 507–11.

305 *become a supervisor*: Bernice V. Robinson résumé, Box 1, Folder 4, Robinson Papers, Avery.

305 *left to become*: Cotton, *Back*, pp. 276–78.

305 *"The air has finally"*: Clark, *Ready*, p. 120.

306 *"These are the people"*: Gray quoted in David Levine, "Learning for Liberation: The Citizenship Education Program and the Freedom Struggle," *American Educational History Journal* 38, no. 1 (2011): pp. 75–92.

306 *civil rights movement was built*: Young quoted by Clark in *Ready*, p. 70.

306 *"If you look"*: Young in Wigginton, *Refuse*, p. 282.

306 *made a prescient list*: Clark, undated document in SCLC//Emory files, quoted in Charron, *Teacher*, p. 353.

Chapter 39: Good Chaos

307 *"retired from a payroll"*: SPC to Josephine Clark, n.d. (after 1970), Box 4, Folder 18, Clark Papers, Avery.

307 *a busy schedule*: Charron, *Teacher*, pp. 346–49. Many of Clark's postretirement activities are mentioned in her personal correspondence contained in Clark Papers, Avery.

307 *Esau himself was appointed*: Gordon H. Garrett, Superintendent, Charleston County School District to Esau Jenkins, September 25, 1969, Box 1, Folder 12, Jenkins Papers, Avery.

308 *Herbert Fielding*: Clark knew Fielding from their service on the Charleston NAACP board. Fielding also was a longtime friend and political ally of Esau Jenkins.

308 *fearless movement activist*: Victoria DeLee campaign flyer, Clark Papers, Avery.

308 *Robinson made a bid*: "Bernice Robinson Announces Her Candidacy," Box 1, Folder 13; "You Have a Voice, So Make Your Choice," campaign advertisement for B. Robinson, 1972, Box 13, Folder 7, Robinson Papers, Avery; "Grand Crab Crack," campaign event, ibid.

308 *There was a crash*: Rev. James G. Blake witnessed Jenkins's death in the hospital: Blake interview by Thomas Dent, 1991, Box 147, Item 1, Amistad Research Center, Tulane University.

309 *"Esau passed"*: Postcard from Septima Clark to Rosa Parks, October 31, 1972, Clark Papers, Avery.

309 *a thousand people*: *Charleston News and Courier*, November 2, 1972, p. 18.

309 *Jenkins's civic life*: "Memorial Service for Mr. Esau Jenkins, Morris Brown AME Church, Charleston," November 1, 1972, Box 1, Folder 4, Jenkins Papers, Avery.

309 *"I believe Esau"*: Funeral Sermon by Rev. Willis Goodwin, Jenkins Papers, Avery.

309 *"Vote CLARK!!!"*: campaign sign in Clark Papers, Avery.

310 *looked to her*: Charron, *Teacher*, p. 347.

310 *"how change comes about"*: Clark in Wigginton, *Refuse*, p. 397.

310 *"like being Cinderella"*: "Belonging: College of Charleston Honors Septima Clark," https://discovering.cofc.edu/items/show/67.

310 *acceptance and recognition*: "Septima Poinsette Clark," biographical entry by South Carolina Encyclopedia, https://www.scencyclopedia.org/sce/entries/clark-septima -poinsette/.

INDEX

Elaine Weiss is an award-winning journalist, author, and public speaker. In addition to *Spell Freedom*, she is the author of *The Woman's Hour: The Great Fight to Win the Vote* and *Fruits of Victory: The Woman's Land Army of the Great War*. Elaine lives with her husband in Baltimore, Maryland. Find out more at ElaineWeiss.com.